# CD START INSTRUCTIONS

**1**   Place the CD-ROM in your CD-ROM drive.

**2**   Launch your Web browser*. See below if you do not have a Web browser.

**3**   From your Web browser, select Open File from the File menu. Select the CD-ROM (usually drive D for PCs and the desktop for Macs), then select the file called Welcome.htm.

\*   We have included the Microsoft Web browser Internet Explorer on this CD in case you do not have a browser or would like to upgrade or change your browser. Please review the CD-ROM appendix of this book for more information on this software, as well as other software on this CD.

## MINIMUM RECOMMENDED SYSTEM REQUIREMENTS

This CD-ROM is designed to work on both Macintosh and Windows operating systems.

### Macintosh System

- Computer: 680x

- Memory: 8MB of RAM

- Software: System 7.0 or higher

- Hardware: 2X CD-ROM drive

### Windows System

- Computer: 386 IBM PC-compatible

- Memory: 8MB of RAM

- Software: Windows 3.1, NT, or 95

- Hardware: 2X CD-ROM drive

# Investor's Web Guide

## Tools and Strategies for Building Your Portfolio

# Investor's Web Guide

## Tools and Strategies for Building Your Portfolio

### Douglas Gerlach

**LYCOS PRESS**

AN IMPRINT OF MACMILLAN COMPUTER PUBLISHING USA

EMERYVILLE, CALIFORNIA

| | |
|---|---|
| Publisher | Joe Wikert |
| Associate Publisher | Juliet Langley |
| Publishing Director | Cheryl Applewood |
| Acquisitions Editor | Renee Wilmeth |
| Development Editor | Nancy Warner |
| Copy Editor | Candy Crane |
| Production Editor | Ami Knox |
| Proofreader | Jeff Barash |
| Cover Design and Illustration | Bay Graphics |
| Book Design and Layout | Bruce Lundquist |
| Indexer | Richard Genova |
| Software Specialist | Sarah Ishida |

Lycos Press books are developed as a joint effort of Lycos and Que. They are published by Macmillan Computer Publishing USA, a Simon & Schuster Company.

Lycos ™ is a trademark of Carnegie Mellon University.

Lycos Press imprint books are produced on a Macintosh computer system with the following applications: FrameMaker®, Microsoft® Word, QuarkXPress®, Adobe Illustrator®, Adobe Photoshop®, Adobe Streamline™, MacLink® *Plus*, Aldus® FreeHand™, Collage Plus™.

Lycos Press, an imprint of
Macmillan Computer Publishing USA
5903 Christie Avenue
Emeryville, CA 94608
http://www.mcp.com/lycos

ISBN 0-78971-187-7

Manufactured in the United States of America
10 9 8 7 6 5 4 3 2 1

**Not so many years ago,** a coworker brought me a clipping from *The New York Times*. It was an article about investment clubs and how average investors were forming clubs, building portfolios, and beating the market. My colleague and I agreed that this seemed like a good idea, and we both immediately called the National Association of Investors Corporation (NAIC), the leading organization supporting the creation and operation of investment clubs, to request more information. We talked to friends, family members, and coworkers, and received enough interest to begin to make plans. Since none of our prospective club members had any real investing experience, I realized that it might be a good idea if I tried to learn a bit about investing myself before we got started.

That evening, I logged on to CompuServe, and searched for investing forums and resources on the service. I was quite surprised to find that NAIC had their own forum on CompuServe, and I quickly joined. Hours later, I had downloaded dozens of articles, programs, spreadsheets, and transcripts from the forum. There were numerous discussions under way on various topics, including using software to analyze stocks, how to form an investment club, and particular stocks. The forum was its own busy community of investors, including an investment club that only meets online in the NAIC Forum.

I eagerly read pages of files and printed out copies to share with my friends. I asked questions of other forum members about issues related to starting our own club. I used the resources that were offered to get started investing in stocks. More importantly, I realized the advantages that the online medium offered for investors, both in educating novices like myself and in providing access to investment data and research. The NAIC Forum on CompuServe became my primary online destination, and I actively participated in the forum's activities. Eventually I joined the Pioneer OnLine Investment Club, the world's first online investment club, and later became one of the forum sysops (a member of the staff, helping to lead discussions and supervise the forum's operations).

When the Internet began to grow in popularity, I started to explore Usenet newsgroups, discussion mailing lists, and Web sites, looking for other like-minded investors and the resources that could help us to become better investors. I was fortunate to find an e-mail discussion list for club and NAIC members. I joined and tried to share some of the knowledge that I had accumulated using the NAIC Forum over the years. I have long understood that teaching is a great way to learn.

I also evaluated the financial-related sites that were on the Web, trying to find those that might be helpful tools for online investors who shared my approach. At the time, a list of Internet resources for individual investors totaled just over one hundred sites, and my bookmark list of those resources became the basis for my Web site, Invest-O-Rama!

And, yes, we did start our own investment club in New York City, the Blue Chip Posse. Just like any club, we have had our ups and downs, but our portfolio continues to grow. I think it's safe to say that all of the Posse members have learned from the experience. We see the payoff of providing the means for our own continuing investment education to be far more important than high returns—though there's no doubt we're pleased with our above average returns compared to the market.

Today, there are thousands of financial sites on the Web, and hundreds more coming online each month. While this book includes more investing Web sites than any other book on the market, there are still thousands more to be explored.

**Among the people who helped** directly or indirectly with the creation of this book are Herb Barnett, Joe Craig, Bruce Wagner, Ellis Traub, Corry Dalmaso, Mary Ann Dash, Don Danko, Nancy Danko, the Directors of the NAIC Computer Group, the members of the Blue Chip Posse and Pioneer On-Line Investment Clubs, the volunteer sysops of the CompuServe NAIC Forum, the volunteer webops of the NAIC Web Site, and the many individual investors who are members of the CompuServe NAIC Forum and I-CLUB-LIST.

I would also like to acknowledge the leadership of the National Association of Investors Corporation, in particular, Thomas E. O'Hara and Kenneth S. Janke, Sr., and commend the outstanding progress they have made in educating millions of Americans about building secure financial futures by investing in common stock.

Finally, I am grateful to my wife Kathleen and son Weston, for exhibiting some of the best qualities of successful investors—namely, patience and keeping an eye on the long term—while their husband and father worked long days and late nights in writing this book. Hopefully, the return on *their* investment of faith will be sufficiently rewarding to compensate for the recent and temporary downturn in his parental and spousal duties.

**In the brief time** since the world has had point-and-click access to the multigraphic, multimedia World Wide Web, the number of people going online has exploded to 30 million at last count, all roaming about the tens of millions of places to visit in cyberspace.

As the Web makes its way into our everyday lives, the kinds of people logging on are changing. Today, there are as many Webmasters as novices, or newbies, and all are struggling to get the most from the vast wells of information scattered about the Web. Even well-prepared surfers stumble aimlessly through cyberspace using hit-or-miss methods in search of useful information, with few results, little substance, and a lot of frustration.

In 1994, the Lycos technology was created by a scientist at Carnegie Mellon University to help those on the Web regain control of the Web. The company's powerful technology is the bedrock underlying a family of guides that untangle the Web, offering a simple and intuitive interface for all types of Web surfers, from GenXers to seniors, from Net vets to newbies.

Lycos (http://www.lycos.com) is a premium navigation tool for cyberspace, providing not only searches but also unique editorial content and Web reviews that all draw on the company's extensive catalog of over 60 million (and growing) Web sites.

Lycos designed its home base on the premise that people want to experience the Web in three fundamentally different ways: They want to search for specific subjects or destinations, they want to browse interesting categories, or they want recommendations on sites that have been reviewed for the quality of their content and graphics. Traditionally, Internet companies have provided part of this solution, but none has offered a finding tool that accommodates all degrees and types of curiosity. Lycos has.

Lycos utilizes its CentiSpeed spider technology as the foundation for finding and cataloging the vast variety of content on the World Wide Web. CentiSpeed processes a search faster than earlier technologies, featuring Virtual Memory Control, User-Level Handling, and Algorithmic Word Compaction. This advanced technology allows the engine to execute more than 4,000 queries per second. CentiSpeed provides faster search results and unparalleled power to search the most comprehensive catalog of the World Wide Web. Lycos uses statistical word calculations and avoids full-word indexing, which helps provide the most relevant search results available on the Web.

In mid-1995, Lycos acquired Point Communications, widely recognized by Web veterans for its collection of critical reviews of the Web. Now an integrated part of the Lycos service, Point continues to provide thousands of in-depth site reviews and a thorough rating of the top Web sites throughout the world. The reviews are conducted by professional reviewers and editors who rate sites according to content, presentation, and overall experience on a scale of 1 to 50. Reviews are presented as comprehensive abstracts that truly provide the user with subjective critiques widely heralded for their accuracy and perceptiveness. In addition, Point's top five percent ratings for Web sites receive a special "Top 5% Badge" icon, the Web's equivalent to the famed consumer "Good Housekeeping Seal."

And for Web browsers who don't need a touring list of well-reviewed sites but who may not be destination-specific, Lycos offers its Sites by Subject. Organizing thousands of Web sites into subject categories, Lycos Sites by Subject gives the cybersurfer at-a-glance Web browsing, including sports, entertainment, social issues, and children's sites. A compilation of the most popular sites on the Internet by the Lycos standard—those with the greatest number of links from other sites—the directory provides Web travelers with a more organized approach to finding worthwhile places to visit on the Web.

Lycos was originally developed at Carnegie Mellon University by Dr. Michael "Fuzzy" Mauldin, who holds a Ph.D. in conceptual information retrieval. Now chief scientist at the company, Dr. Mauldin continues to expand the unique exploration and indexing technology. Utilizing this technology, Lycos strives to deliver a family of guides to the Internet that are unparalleled for their accuracy, relevance, and comprehensiveness. Lycos is one of the most frequently visited sites on the Web and is one of the leading sites for advertisers.

The Lycos database is constantly being refined by dozens of software robots, or agents, called "spiders." These spiders roam the Web endlessly, finding and downloading Web pages. Once a page is found, the spiders create abstracts which consist of the title, headings and subheading, 100 most weighty words, first 20 lines, size in bytes, and number of words. Heuristic (self-teaching) software looks at where the words appear in the document, their proximity to other words, frequency, and site popularity to determine relevance.

Lycos eliminates extraneous words like "the," "a," "and," "or," and "it" that add no value and slow down finding capabilities. The resulting abstracts are merged, older versions discarded, and a new, up-to-date database is distributed to all Lycos servers and licensees. This process is repeated continuously, resulting in a depth and comprehensiveness that makes Lycos a top information guide company.

Online providers or software makers can license Lycos—the spider, search engine, catalog, directory, and Point reviews—to make them available to users.

Lycos, Inc., an Internet exploration company, was founded specifically to find, index, and filter information on the Internet and World Wide Web. CMG Information Services, Inc. (NASDAQ: CMGI) is a majority shareholder in Lycos, Inc. through its strategic investment and development business unit, CMG@Ventures. CMGI is a leading provider of direct marketing services investing in and integrating advanced Internet, interactive media, and database management technologies.

**This book consists of two parts.** Part One is a directory of World Wide Web sites and other Internet resources, listed by category, with a brief description of the company, or the content of the site. Part Two is a guide to help you get started investing in common stocks, focusing on using the computer and the Internet as useful tools to help you in your investing.

Throughout this book, there are several icons used to describe items of particular interest:

 *High Yield Links* are sites of significant interest and value to individual investors in their respective categories. These Web sites meet minimum criteria of design, layout, usefulness of information presented, and/or general relevance to the topic they address.

*The Web Swami* is an Internet wizard, and he provides helpful hints on using the Web and other Internet resources. The all-knowing Swami will show you how to use your browser, as well as what to watch out for on the Internet.

 *Upticks* are tips, facts, or suggestions that you can use in your investing.

 *Downticks* are warning notes; cautionary tips about potential pitfalls and unfortunate obstacles you may encounter in your investing.

*Ask Doug* is where you'll find detailed answers to common questions, as well as side trips to briefly explore other interesting investing topics.

Part Two is not meant to be a complete textbook for investing in stock—many books on that subject have been written by more financially astute men and women than I. If you've never invested in the market, the strategy outlined in this section should serve as a quick starter. If you're a more experienced investor, you should find some interesting ways to use the Web in your investment analysis and portfolio management.

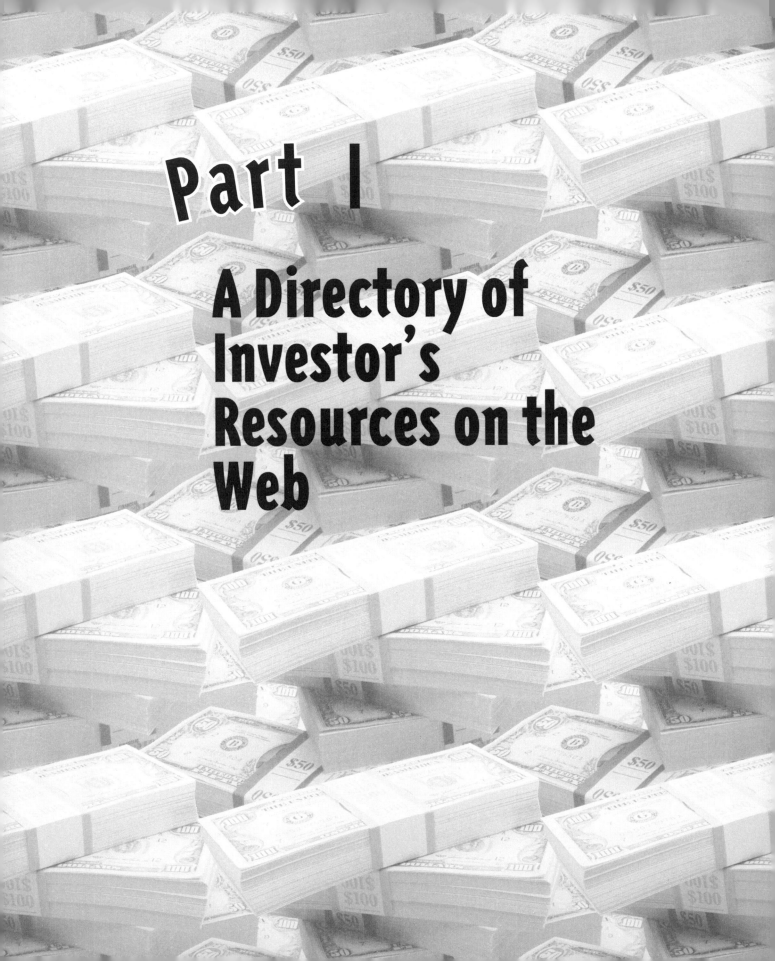

# Part I

# A Directory of Investor's Resources on the Web

EDUCATIONAL SITES

THE STOCK MARKET

MUTUAL FUNDS AND BONDS

FUTURES, OPTIONS, AND DERIVITIVES

NEWS AND ADVICE

TOOLS FOR INVESTORS

AGENCIES AND ASSOCIATIONS

INVESTMENT TALK

INTERNATIONAL INVESTING

PERSONAL FINANCE

# Chapter 1
## Educational Sites

"Every young man should have a hobby; learning how to handle money is the best one."

—Jack Hurley

**Every investor** was once a beginner. And every investor can tell you the tale of his or her first foray into the markets and the eventual outcome of that first purchase—whether a profit was realized or a lesson was learned the hard way.

Getting started in the market still presents a significant hurdle to many people. For many decades, the prevailing attitude in our country seems to have been that investing was a pastime for the wealthy. Our schools completely ignore teaching us to balance a checkbook, complete a tax return, or budget for a household, much less plan for retirement or invest.

As usual, there's nothing like a crisis to raise people's awareness, and the predicted demise of the Social Security system has at least started Americans thinking about how they'd like to spend their golden years. At the same time, many people are beginning to realize that taking control of their financial destiny isn't so hard after all.

Of course, the banks, brokers, insurance companies, and mutual fund companies, always keen to exploit a trend, are providing many of the means by which the average Joe can be transformed into a market player (albeit on a small scale). Commissions at deep-discount brokers are lower than ever, and mutual fund companies willingly take the responsibility of extracting dollars from an investor's bank account and investing them each month (at no charge!). Names like Peter Lynch, the Beardstown Ladies, and the Motley Fools have entered the vernacular of American language, serving as the standard bearers of a new generation of investors who realize there's no such thing as a small investor—only investors with small amounts to invest.

What's key to this movement is the free flow of information now available to investors. Arguably, the Internet has been responsible for much of the increase in access to financial research and news that was previously the domain of investment professionals. The Internet has surely been responsible for

reducing commissions below $10 per trade. At this writing, a firm offers a $9.95 flat rate commission for up to 5,000 shares, the lowest regular commission offered by a brokerage firm online or off. Companies realize real cost savings by providing online access to their customers. Instantaneous (or nearly instantaneous) access to news and quotes is available to investors on the World Wide Web, as are research reports, fundamental data, charts and analysis. Discussion forums and newsgroups give investors a cyberspace version of the office water cooler—a place to talk, ask questions, and trade hot tips.

Although this abundance of information can overwhelm a novice investor, the Internet offers plenty of support for individuals just getting started. In fact, it's possible for an investor to learn nearly everything he or she needs to know to chart a course for a successful financial future using online resources.

# INVESTING GLOSSARIES

Financial professionals speak a language of their own. From a dizzying array of acronyms and abbreviations to a dazzling compendium of ratios and phrases, an investor needs to be able to interpret and understand the lingo in order to buy stocks, funds, bonds, or any other investment, for that matter.

Fortunately, the Web offers the necessary translators. Turn here when you need to know about leverage or beta or candlestick charts.

## American Association of Individual Investors Glossary
**http://www.aaii.org/glossary.html**
AAII is a national membership organization for investors, and their glossary defines 130 common terms, mostly regarding portfolio management, investing styles, and security valuation techniques.

*the*
**swami speaks**

I sense confusion. Come closer as the Web Swami explains how Web pages are built. Pages on the World Wide Web are written in Hyper-Text Markup Language, or HTML. These files are nothing more than text files with special tags that specify certain attributes, such as the size, color, alignment, and weight of text, a page's background color, the width and spacing of a table, the position of images, and so on. Your browser interprets these files and displays them on your screen. The Hyper-Text part of the name refers to the ability of Web pages to offer links to other parts of the same page, other pages on the same server, or other pages on other servers anywhere in the world. Links are usually (but not always) underlined, and if you click on a link with your mouse, you'll be whisked away to more information on the topic at hand.

## The Art of Investment Glossary of Investment Terms

**http://www.aofi.com/glossary/index.html**

The companion Web site to the Canadian television series "The Art of Investment," created in association with the Canadian Bankers Association and the Canadian Securities Institute. Substantial hyperlinks enhance this well-organized dictionary, which includes many terms and organizations unique to Canada.

## Campbell Harvey's Hypertextual Finance Glossary

**http://www.duke.edu/~charvey/fintb.htm**

Harvey is Professor of Finance at the Fuqua School of Business at Duke University. His "Financial Toolbox" includes a comprehensive hyperlinked, cross-referenced dictionary of investing terms. Although the frame-based layout on the pages is a little quirky even for frames-enabled browsers, the extensive hypertext element of this glossary is extremely helpful. For instance, since you can't understand "Total debt to equity ratio" without understanding "current liabilities" or "shareholders' equity," Harvey provides links to those definitions from the "Total debt to equity ratio" page. Also available on his site is his "Original Extended Finance Glossary" focusing on futures and options. Traders will be interested in his "Guide to Futures and Options Quotations" and "Options Pricer" pages, too.

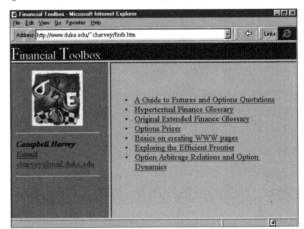

## Chicago Mercantile Exchange Glossary of Future and Options Terms

**http://www.cme.com/market/glossary.html**

The "Merc" is the world's largest financial exchange, where currencies, interest rates, stock indices, and agricultural commodities are traded. Their lexicon is a good source for investors interested in trading futures and options contracts.

### Chicago Board Options Exchange Glossary of Options Related Terms
http://www.cboe.com/intro/glossary.html
This page might not pass the censors—even though the term "naked writer" has nothing to do with clothing or a lack thereof. It covers the basics of options trading.

### CNNfn Glossary of Business Terms
http://www.cnnfn.com/researchit/ referencedesk/glossary/
CNN's sister financial news network offers a Reference Desk, with a business glossary that can be helpful in deciphering a company's financial statements. Provided by Dearborn Financial Publishing, this glossary is big and technical, but Dearborn hasn't quite gotten around the problem of definitions that raise more questions. Here's an example: accrual accounting is defined as "A method of reporting income when earned and expenses when incurred, as opposed to reporting income when received and expenses when paid." Got that?

### Craig E. Buck's Real Estate Dictionary
http://www.homeowners.com/dictionary.html
Buck is a real estate attorney and chairman of the Northern Virginia Association of Realtors Standard Forms Committee, and his dictionary is a simple hypertextual document. Nothing fancy here, but plenty of cross links and bare bones descriptions of real estate terms.

### E-Muni Glossary of Municipal Bond Terms
http://www.emuni.com/glossary.html
Electronic Municipal Statistics, a firm that provides news and financial information about the bond markets, offers a glossary of jargon and terms related to tax-exempt securities. Zane B. Mann, publisher of the *California Municipal Bond Advisor*, prepared the glossary.

### Federal Reserve Bank of Chicago Glossaries
http://www.frbchi.org/frinfo/about/ welcome.html
The Chicago Federal Reserve Bank (FRB) offers eight short glossaries of highly specialized terminology, mostly related to the banking industry and monetary policy. They include Consumer Credit Terms, Financial Regulators and Institutions, Foreign Banking Terms, Investment Terms, Monetary Policy Terms, Payment Mechanism Terms, and Securities Credit Terms. The entries are all highly technical, but this is the place to go to learn what a *discount rate* is. The glossaries themselves are not in hypertext but are merely text files on the FRB server.

### Fidelity Investments' Investment Dictionary
http://wps.fid-inv.com/fir/ime/ime-id.htm
Mutual fund giant Fidelity Investments includes a short dictionary in their "Investing Made Easy" area. (While investing may be easy, making money at it is a little harder!) As expected, the glossary primarily covers mutual funds and annuities, but with just a few terms and in very little detail.

### International Financial Enclopaedia
http://www.euro.net/innovation/Finance_ Base/Fin_encyc.html
It can be hard to make sense of this site from Information Innovation, a financial consulting firm. Its layout and design hearken to the early days of the Web: gray backgrounds, sparse graphics, extremely long pages, little or no apparent navigational structure. Still, their

**ask doug!**

**Q:** What is a P/E Ratio?

**A:** A Price/Earnings Ratio (P/E Ratio) is the current price of a stock divided by its earnings per share. Earnings per share (EPS) can be calculated from the last four quarters (trailing or actual earnings), the next four quarters (projected or estimated earnings) or the last two quarters plus the projections for the next two quarters. P/E Ratios are the most commonly used analytical ratio in investing. Sometimes known as the *multiple*, the P/E Ratio tells you how much investors are willing to pay for a share of a company's profits.

You can use a stock's P/E Ratio as a stand-in for its share price, to see how the market values that stock compared to the market in general or to other companies in its industry group. P/E Ratios can differ significantly from industry to industry, however. You can also compare a stock's current P/E Ratio to its historical record to get a sense of its *relative value* in light of that stock's past trends.

"Financial Encyclopedia" impresses, not only by its sheer size, but also by the amount of financial and technological information it contains. A primary focus of the compendium is financial technology and transaction processing, so individual investors may find this a little overwhelming. One interesting feature is that you can look up a country and find out what its currency is (in Mongolia, they use the Tugrik).

### Investor's Galleria Glossary of Technical Analysis Terms
**http://centrex.com/indicate.html**

More descriptions of primary technical analysis terms await you on this page. Given the graphical nature of the Web these days, it's surprising that a page like this doesn't take advantage of illustrations; a picture of a candlestick chart would probably replace several descriptive sentences. This page is not for novices; "Investor's Galleria" uses a technical approach to defining technical terms, which can sound like double-speak to a beginner.

### Investor's Galleria Glossary of Financial & Trading Terms
**http://centrex.com/terms.html**

A few misspellings and a few not so accurate definitions mar this simple and otherwise readable page. An "Annual Report" is defined in part like this: "SEC rules require that it be distributed to all shareholders. A more detailed version is called a 10-K." Well, that's not exactly what a Form 10-K filed with the Securities and Exchange Commission is…. Otherwise, this is a good general reference.

### Kiplinger's 101 Investment Terms You Should Know
**http://www.kiplinger.com/faq/faq101.html**

The Editors of Kiplinger's publications have put together a glossary of the most important investing terms, and it's written in plain English. By its very name, it is clear this is not intended to be the penultimate reference work, but it is a handy page to bookmark.

## Lebenthal & Co. Bond Terms

http://www.lebenthal.com/bond_terms.html

A comprehensive lexicon of terms related to municipal and corporate bonds, from the leading municipal bond broker.

## The Money Mentor's Glossary of Investing & Trading Terms

http://www.moneymentor.com/mm_gloss.html

The Money Mentor is a sprawling financial Web site, and their glossary claims to offer definitions of "popular technical and fundamental terms." However, it's really focused on the technical angle. If you're wondering about Bollinger Bands, Fibonacci Studies, McClellan Oscillators, or Tirone Levels, then detailed descriptions of these indicators and trading terms await you here. Unfortunately, many of the terms in the index are not included in the actual glossary.

## MoneyLine Corporation Bond Glossary

http://www.moneyline.com/mlc_glos.html

MoneyLine is a provider of real-time fixed income information, including U.S. Treasury bonds, notes and bills, money markets, corporate bonds, and other fixed income securities. Their glossary, naturally, deals with bonds, from Accrued Interest to Zero Coupons. Frequent examples and well-thought-out definitions make this a high yield page.

## MoneyWorld Glossary

http://www.moneyworld.co.uk/moneyworld/glossary.htm

MoneyWorld is a personal finance site for citizens of the United Kingdom, so their glossary emphasizes British financial terminology. If you ever need to know what a *gilt* is, this is the site!

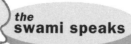

**the swami speaks**

On the Web, no one can hear you scream, so there's no sense getting frustrated about the fact that lots of sites don't seem to like your particular Web browser. The history of HTML standards is a long and sordid tale. The upshot of it is that most of what you see on Web pages these days isn't part of an official standard but rather the result of conventions established by the two major browser developers, Microsoft and Netscape. As a result, you'll often run across sites that recommend Microsoft Internet Explorer or Netscape Navigator. For optimal Web browsing, you'll want to make sure you have the most recent version of one or both browsers, which you can download from their respective Web sites.

## Prudential Securities Glossary

http://www.prusec.com/glos_txt.htm

Prudential Securities has established a Virtual Branch Office on the Web, with a Virtual Financial Advisor who can help you better understand investing, investments, and financial goals. Their glossary is a collection of terms, largely related to financial, estate, and retirement planning, where you'll find phrases and acronyms such as Inter Vivos Trust, laddered portfolio, and REMICs clearly explained.

## The Syndicate Municipal Bond Terms

http://www.moneypages.com/syndicate/bonds/muniterm.html

The Syndicate is Bill Rini's labor of love for the benefit of individual investors. A former stockbroker and current Web programmer, Rini has constructed a site that rarely disappoints. One of the many gems to be found on his site is this short lexicon of municipal bond terms, ranging from Ad Valorem Tax to Mello Roo's.

### *Research:* Glossary of Investment Terms
**http://www.researchmag.com/investor/glossary.htm**

*Research:* is a magazine read by most stockbrokers across the country, so it's not surprising that this very short glossary covers the basics of stock trading. Margin accounts, bid and ask, odd lot, and street name are a few of the terms defined. This lexicon is particularly good for beginners.

### Savoy Discount Brokerage Investment Glossary
**http://www.savoystocks.com/glossary.htm**

There comes a time in every investor's life when that first trade has to be made. A phone call must be made to a broker (or, these days, an order form filled out on the brokerage's Web site). A decision has been carefully made to buy shares in a particular company, and money is ready to be spent. Suddenly, a flurry of abbreviations brings you to a dead stop. AON? GTC? DNR? Fortunately, Savoy Discount Brokerage has provided a glossary of terms and ac-

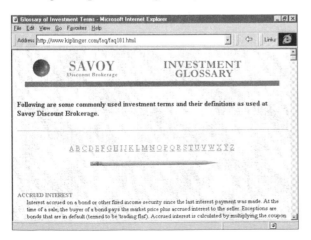

ronyms that an investor is likely to come across in dealing with a broker. Using this glossary, it won't be long before you can say FOK with the best of them! This page also includes appropriate links to Savoy's own further explanations of particular items.

### Stein Roe Mutual Fund Glossary
**http://networth.galt.com/www/home/mutual/steinroe/glossary.html**

This single page of terms offers the nitty-gritty on mutual fund phraseology. The definitions are short and precise, but you won't find certain terms, like index fund, included (Stein Roe doesn't offer any).

### U.S. Department of Housing and Urban Development Home Buyer's Vocabulary
**gopher://gopher.gsa.gov/00/staff/pa/cic/housing/hmvocab.txt**

This plain text file (on a gopher server, no less!) is dated March 1987, but it is still a useful document. It defines the full gamut of terms that a home buyer is likely to encounter in purchasing a property.

### Vanguard Mutual Funds Investor Education Glossary
**http://www.vanguard.com/educ/glos.html**

Vanguard covers a wider array of terms than their arch-rival, Fidelity, though still focused on funds. Vanguard attempts to cover the terms an investor would encounter in opening an account, from Joint Tenants with Right of Survivorship to Tenants in Common, as well as more general mutual fund phraseology.

### Wall Street Directory's Glossary
**http://www.wsdinc.com/pgs_idx/w_indi.shtml**

The Wall Street Directory is one of the largest financial catalogs on the Web, and their glossary covers a substantial number of investing terms in appropriate detail. Both technical and fundamental terms are included.

## The WashingtonPost.com Business Glossary

**http://www.washingtonpost.com/ wp-srv/business/longterm/glossary/ glossary.htm**

This nicely done glossary defines 1,250 business terms, organized and cross-referenced for convenience. Users can search the glossary for a particular word and its definition or search the full text of the glossary to find every reference to a word or phrase anywhere it appears in the glossary. Or, users can browse the glossary by letters of the alphabet. The cross-references within the definitions are particularly helpful.

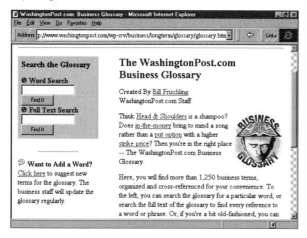

## Web Investors' Dictionary

**http://www.Webinvestors.com**

This site's raison d'être is to provide a "fast, easy way to learn investment concepts on the Web." While the goal is admirable and the dictionary shows much promise, the content is apparently still in development. For instance, there are no terms included in this dictionary that begin with the letter R. Hopefully,

the creators, a couple of stock and commodities traders, will keep working until they get to the end of the alphabet! The terms the dictionary does include are nicely defined, and a few are enhanced with links to sites on the Web that pertain to the topic under discussion, a nice touch.

# TUTORIALS AND SITES FOR NEW INVESTORS

If you're just getting started, the Web can provide the necessary information to kick-start your investing plan. These sites offer tutorials and other information geared for beginning investors to help educate them about many different facets of finance.

## American Association of Individual Investors

**http://www.aaii.org**

The American Association of Individual Investors (AAII) is a national membership organization that aims to help individuals become better investors. Their Web site provides information taken from their monthly publications *AAII Journal* and *Computerized Investing* as well as from details of membership. A highlight of their site is a version of their printed *Information Guide*, which is a directory of regulatory agencies, exchanges, NASD offices, financial journals, data sources, and places for investors to take complaints. The online version of their guide is not in hypertext format, however (the URLs of listed resources aren't available as hyperlinks). The "Investing Basics" section offers a handful of articles of interest to beginners. "Basic Investment Principles of Risk and Return" and "Building Toward an Investment Plan Starting From Scratch" should be read by all new investors. Their Reference Shelf holds a library of articles about where to find information on specific topics, such as annuities, closed-end funds, ADRs, dividend reinvestment plans, and discount brokers.

## A Brief Guide to Closed-End Funds
**http://www.icefi.com/tutorial/**

Though closed-end funds are not nearly as popular as their open-end cousins, they still offer plenty of advantages for savvy investors. Since the capital structure of a closed-end fund doesn't support the extensive marketing that other mutual funds typically undertake, and since no one has a vested interest in the success of a closed-end fund, there are fewer resources available for investors who wish to learn more about this particular vehicle. The Internet Closed-End Fund Investor is the best source of information on the Web when it comes to closed-end funds, and they provide "A Brief Guide to Closed-End Funds" on their site. But calling this guide brief is something of a misnomer, since it contains seven chapters, ranging from "The Basics " to "A Deeper Look at Discount/Premium." It is quite comprehensive in scope. The guide gets high marks for readability, as well.

## The Beginner's Guide to Microcap Investing
**http://www.financialWeb.com/guide.html**

This tutorial, from The SmallCap Investor ("The Unofficial Directory of Nasdaq® SmallCap Stocks on the Web"), is an introduction to investing in companies with market capitalizations of less than $25 million. Author Jeffrey Grossman offers straightforward advice for investors interested in very small publicly traded companies.

## Characteristics and Risks of Standardized Options
**http://www.cboe.com/options/contents.html**

With most investments, the amount that could be lost is limited to the amount invested. A stock, for instance, can become worthless, rendering a shareholder's investment a 100 percent loss. However, options traders are at risk of losing more than the amount of their initial investment, and most financial disaster stories you're likely to hear about probably involve an options strategy gone amok. That's why, prior to buying or selling options, the Securities and Exchange Commission (SEC) requires that investors receive a copy of *Characteristics and Risks of Standardized Options*, a comprehensive guide that details these risks. The Chicago Board Options Exchange presents a hyptertext version of the publication on their Web site, as well as an Adobe Acrobat version. Though it's not easy reading, any investor considering investing in options should study this guide carefully.

## Chicago Board Options Exchange: Education
**http://www.cboe.com/intro/whatis.html**

CBOE provides information on various educational resources for options traders. It includes their Options Toolbox Software, educational seminars, a guide to understanding stock options, and a recommended reading list.

## CNBC Ticker Guide
**http://www.cnbc.com/tickerguide/**

On Wall Street, tickertape is no more. Replaced by computer terminals, tickertape is relegated to the archives of financial history, which made for some pretty interesting items being tossed out office windows during the tickertape parade held for the Yankees after they won the World Series. But vestiges of the tape remain, in computer versions often seen in broker's offices, and on financial television news programs. CNBC, the financial network, offers this guide to "reading the tape," 1990s style.

### EduStock

**http://tqd.advanced.org/3088/**

EduStock is an educational Web page designed to teach about investing through tutorials on the stock market and how to pick stocks. It also includes a real-time stock market simulation, and users can create and track their own portfolios. Confused about what to buy? Sample profiles of a few companies are included. But what's most interesting about this site is that it was created by three high school students from Potomac, MD and was the first prize winner in the 1996 ThinkQuest Internet competition. ThinkQuest is a contest to challenge students to create innovative learning tools using the Internet. The EduStock team should be heartily congratulated!

### Equity Analytics, Ltd

**http://www.e-analytics.com/techdir3.htm**

Charles J. Kaplan's firm, Equity Analytics Ltd., provides fee-based trading recommendations, primarily to institutional clients. The company's Web site is rough-hewn, yet with gems to be found for surfers who persevere. New investors may want to check out the educational articles about stocks, technical analysis, futures and commodities, and bonds.

### Fleet Bank Investing Primer

**http://www.fleet.com/abtyou/persinv/**

Fleet's Investing Primer is a concise guide that describes various kinds of investments—how they work, their benefits, and their risks. Unfortunately, clicking on any of the included links for more information about a term only takes you to a sales pitch for a Fleet Bank product. "Building your own Definition of Risk" is an interesting discussion of the various risks involved with many kinds of investing. Other articles include "The Top Five Financial Mistakes" and an Investing FAQ.

### InvestorGuide

**http://www.investorguide.com**

This online reference guide offers a selection of educational articles that encourage individuals to get into the market, including "Why You Can Do It Yourself" and "Why You Should Do It Yourself." My favorite title is "Advice on Taking Advice," cautioning investors to be wary of people with hidden agendas who may be touting a particular investment, product or service, especially online.

### InvestorWEB

**http://www.investorWeb.com**

InvestorWEB, a site that helps companies reach investors, offers a few good articles for beginners in their Beginner's Investment Checklist, including "Good Books for Beginners," "Asset Allocation for the Absolute Beginner," and "Investment Style."

### Making Sense Online

**http://www.makingsense.com**

Making Sense is an online financial guide directed specifically at kids and their parents. The site includes a glossary of investing terms, financial calculators, articles about investing, and links to plenty of other resources.

### Merrill Lynch Investor Learning Center

**http://www.ml.com/investor**

The venerable brokerage firm of Merrill Lynch, Pierce, Fenner & Smith Incorporated has set aside two areas of their Web site devoted to education and personal finance. The Learning Center first offers tips on getting organized, household budgeting, and record keeping. Next, they provide basic investment information, an explanation of the professional help that can help an investor make financial decisions and a handbook of definitions and concepts. The Personal Finance Center contains more in-depth information about specific financial challenges, customized by an investor's age.

### The Motley Fools
**http://www.fool.com**

Tom and David Gardner are "The Motley Fools." They have parlayed their successful AOL forum into a best-selling book, regular television appearances, and now, a Web site filled with educational materials, all derived from the Foolish philosophy. To the Motley ones, to call an investor Foolish is the highest compliment, since in their eyes the "wise" folks who write financial newsletters, manage mutual funds, or broker securities only seem to be able to generate sub-par returns for their clients. The Fools counsel individuals to take control of their own financial destinies and outline several strategies for equity investing. Their Fool's School is a great introduction to investing for novices, and Fool Classrooms offers further instruction.

### Mutual Funds Interactive
**http://www.fundsinteractive.com/newbie.html**

New to mutual funds? Mutual Funds Interactive provides a basic entree into fund investing with Funds 101: Mutual Funds for the New Investor. Topics include how mutual funds work, who runs the funds, and "The Ten Commandments of Mutual Fund Investing." After perusing this introductory article, surfers can check out the rest of this site's

commentary, links to funds, funds newsgroup, news, and other resources.

### National Association of Investors Corporation
**http://www.better-investing.org**

If you are totally new to the market, your first stop on the Web should be the National Association of Investors Corporation (NAIC). Best-known for its support of the formation and operation of investment clubs, NAIC also has an individual membership category for those who are not members of a club. NAIC's Computer Group has put together an excellent Web site to provide information and educational resources for individual investors. But you don't have to be a NAIC member to benefit from the plethora of resources available here. The site offers complete information on every aspect of the organization: membership, publications, study tools, books, and software. You can find reprints of many articles from NAIC's excellent monthly magazine, *Better Investing*, and from its sister computer publication, *BITS*. You can also download demo versions of NAIC software programs for fundamental analysis, screening, or record keeping. You can find out about local NAIC activities in the nearly 90 regional councils across the country, where classes, workshops, and Investors Fairs® are held on a regular basis.

Membership in NAIC is $39 a year, and includes a subscription to *Better Investing*, as well as discounts on investing books and other products. But perhaps the biggest benefit of membership is NAIC's Low Cost Investment Plan. It is a way to get started in the stock market with very little money. NAIC has arranged for its members to be able to purchase a single share of stock in any of about 150 companies, for a $7 fee above the purchase price. Once the first share transaction is completed, the investor can buy additional shares of that stock directly from that company's dividend reinvestment plan, with little or no commission and in increments as small as $10 to $25. The NAIC Web Site has complete details on the plan, along with information about participating companies.

The NAIC Web site strives to go beyond merely providing information about the organization, though. In conjunction with its companion e-mail discussion mailing list, the I-CLUB-LIST, a whole cyber-community of investors has been formed who all share NAIC's approach to stock investing.

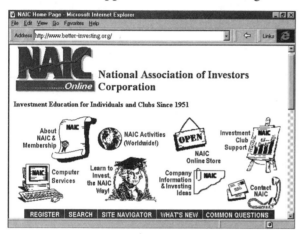

## Niké Securities
**http://www.nikesec.com/whatuit.html**

Niké Securities L.P. is the sponsor of the First Trust® Family of Unit Investment Trusts (UITs). They offer a very short "Investing 101-A Course in the Basics," consisting of a few paragraphs about risk and return. Perhaps of more interest, though definitely of more limited appeal, is their essay on the advantages of UITs, "What is a Unit Investment Trust?" UITs are like mutual funds, in that they hold other securities, but a UIT's portfolio is fixed at its creation and no further buying or selling is done until the trust matures. Fixed income investors, as Niké Securities points out, can often find UITs to be desirable.

## PC Financial Network
**http://www.pcfn.com**

PC Financial Network is a discount broker that has been offering online trading for years on the Prodigy Network. Now they've moved to the Web, and this guide is part of their extensive collection of information and research. Provided by Standard & Poor's, *How to Invest* contains seven chapters of advice, definitions, and strategies for the new investor.

## *Research:* Magazine
**http://www.researchmag.com**

*RESEARCH:* Magazine has built a section in its Web site, "Getting Started," with some reprints of SEC publications, a glossary, and other articles. "How's Your Portfolio Doing? Ways to Help Figure it Out" sheds some light on the tricky subject of calculating returns on an investment.

## T. Rowe Price
**http://www.troweprice.com**

Mutual Fund giant T. Rowe Price offers a three-step plan towards more effective investing in mutual funds: defining goals, understanding risk, and then finding the funds to meet your objectives. They also stress the importance of diversification. T. Rowe Price's approach can be helpful to investors interested in any asset, not just funds. Once you've studied their plan for getting started, you can access their Insights Library, an extensive collection of articles that supply general information (including "The ABC's of Investing"), investment strategies ("Dollar Cost Averaging," "Growth Stock Investing," "Value Investing"), and guidelines for investing in just about every type of investment: high yield junk bonds, emerging market securities, global bonds, mortgage-backed securities, and more.

### Vanguard Funds Investor Education Center
http://www.vanguard.com

Vanguard Mutual Funds sponsors an extensive Investor Education Center on their Web site, including a section they call The Vanguard Online University. Like a real college, the University offers a series of educational courses designed to help investors learn about mutual fund investing in a structured, step-by-step format. "The Fundamentals of Mutual Funds" walks through the process of building a fund portfolio, and "Retirement Investing Seminar" describes tools and strategies for investors planning for their golden years. The Vanguard Online Library presents Vanguard founder John C. Bogle's perspectives on the fund industry, indexing, and investing in the 1990s. International investing and emerging markets are two of the topics in the Plain Talk Series.

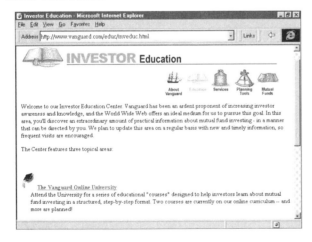

### *Worth* **Online**
http://www.worth.com

*Worth* magazine has set aside an area on their site especially for new investors, Investor 101. Topics covered include reading financial statements, understanding P/E ratios, the basics of technical analysis, and other articles to help investors build a solid foundation of investment knowledge.

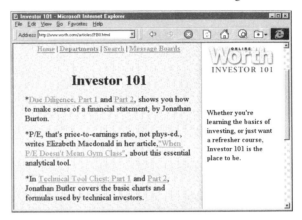

# FAQS: FREQUENTLY ASKED QUESTIONS

FAQs are an Internet tradition, spawned in Usenet newsgroups by users who were tired of seeing the same old questions posted time after time by new users. FAQ is an acronym for Frequently Asked Questions, and these investment-related FAQs are required reading even if you never set foot in a newsgroup.

### Futures FAQ
http://www.ilhawaii.net/~heinsite/FAQs/
futuresfaq.html

If there are futures in your future, this FAQ is for you. Topics covered range from placing commodity and future orders to the collapse of Baring's Bank due to derivatives trading.

New Usenet subscribers are well advised to read the appropriate FAQ prior to posting a question in any newsgroup. If you don't, you risk being "flamed" by other members demanding that you "read the FAQ!" Flaming is the act of sending highly inflammatory (hence the name), highly insulting messages via e-mail. Don't fall victim to a flame-thrower; stick to the FAQs.

### Investment FAQ Home Page
http://www.cs.umd.edu/users/cml/invest-faq/

The Investment FAQ began as the FAQ for the newsgroup misc.invest (now known as misc.invest.misc) and answers common questions on investment and personal finance topics, including stocks, bonds, options, discount brokers, information sources, retirement plans, and life insurance. Mutual funds have their own FAQ (see below). The Investment FAQ is representative of one of the strengths of the online community; the FAQ is composed solely of contributions from investors who share common-sense advice, personal experiences, and instructions. As compiled by Christopher Lott, the Web version is nicely hyperlinked, making navigation easy. This FAQ is required reading for all new investors. Bookmark this site and refer to it first for all your investing questions.

### Mutual Funds FAQ
http://www.moneypages.com/syndicate/faq/

Like its broader investment counterpart, the Mutual Funds FAQ deals with the most common questions asked about funds, ranging from "What is a mutual fund?" to "What is the difference between yield and return?" Bill Rini now maintains the FAQ as part of his excellent syndicate Web site.

### Technical Analysis FAQ
http://www.wiwi.uni-frankfurt.de/AG/JWGI/FAQS/tech-faq.htm

Though this FAQ is no longer actively maintained, a version of the FAQ for the misc.invest.technical newsgroup remains on this server at the University of Frankfurt. Since it was last updated in 1994, some of the information in the FAQ may be irrelevant. Enough of the basics of technical analysis are explained to make this a worthwhile stop for investors interested in this method of stock trading.

# INVESTMENT CLUBS

In the past three years, the number of investment clubs in the U.S. has more than doubled, according to the National Association of Investors Corporation (NAIC). This is the not-for-profit organization that supports the formation and operation of investment clubs.

An investment club is nothing more than a small group of individuals, usually comprised of friends, coworkers, church members, neighbors, and family members, who meet on a regular basis for the

purpose of pooling their funds and investing in a club portfolio.

While these clubs are certainly interested in making a profit, members also find that investment clubs are a great way to learn about investing. In fact, NAIC recommends that clubs focus on education first and foremost. If club members are too concerned about having their portfolio show lots of big numbers in the profit columns, especially when they're first starting out, their stock selection is likely to suffer. Clubs that follow this advice and maximize the educational aspects of their meetings usually find that profits follow.

With an educational component in the forefront, investment clubs can be a great vehicle for beginning investors. Clubs offer the structure and support that many people need to get started investing, and clubs make it possible to get into the market without a big initial investment, another incentive for new investors.

### National Association of Investors Corp.
**http://www.better-investing.org/clubs/clubs.html**
Want to start an investment club? Look no further! NAIC has been helping folks to start investment clubs for over 45 years, and their Web site presents much of their accumulated knowledge.

### NAIC's Investment Club Mailing List
**http://www.better-investing.org/computer/maillist.html**
NAIC Online sponsors a discussion mailing list for investment club members (and other investors and NAIC members interested in growth stock analysis). Discussions on the list include particular stocks and industries; investment club operations; questions about the Stock Selection Guide or other NAIC tools; using NAIC software; and announcements

NAIC reports that the number of investment clubs who are NAIC members has reached an all-time high (including 64 clubs that have been in existence for more than 40 years). What's more, 42.9 percent of these clubs outperform the S&P 500, a feat the majority of professional mutual fund managers can't beat.

about upcoming Investors Fairs and NAIC workshops. To subscribe to the list, you can use the form on the above Web page, or you can send an e-mail message to listproc@better-investing.org. In the body of the message, type the following: SUBSCRIBE I-CLUB-LIST "YOUR FULL NAME" but replace "YOUR FULL NAME" with your first and last name, without the quotation marks. Do not include a subject in the header, or a signature in the body of the message. If your mail program requires a header, enter a blank space.

## INVESTMENT CLUBS ONLINE

The explosion of the online world has had a considerable impact on the investment club community. The Pioneer On-Line Investment Club (POLIC) is generally acknowledged as the world's first online club, formed in 1991 on CompuServe's NAIC Forum by a group of investors who had never previously met in person. The club has no set monthly meeting date but operates continuously as members post messages on the Forum throughout the month. At the end of the month, members vote by e-mail on ballot items, including buy and sell decisions. The club maintains bank and brokerage accounts and elects officers annually, in every respect operating like a typical investment club, with the sole exception that all communications are done electronically.

As a member and past-president of the Pioneers, I'm happy to report that today we have a $35,000 portfolio, and members in Japan, California, Colorado, Tennessee, New York, Massachusetts, Maryland, New Jersey, Nebraska, District of Columbia, and Texas.

To observe the Pioneers in action on CompuServe, go to the NAIC Forum (GO NAIC) and look for their section of the Forum. You can download a copy of their partnership agreement, bylaws, and information about their club from the Forum's I-Club-Information Library. Search on the keyword POLIC.

Many other clubs have followed in POLIC's footsteps. Investment clubs have sprung up on other commercial online services. Many other online clubs include far-flung family members who use e-mail to invest as a group. These virtual clubs are the latest incarnation of the modern investment club movement.

But a club doesn't have to be virtual to take advantage of online tools. Club members can use e-mail for sending copies of meeting minutes and agendas prior to monthly meetings, or to keep members apprised of news about stocks in the club portfolio. And there are more than a few resources on the Web that are helpful for investment research.

**ask doug!**

**Q:** How do I find an investment club to join?

**A:** Most clubs are relatively private affairs, formed by family members, friends, co-workers or church members, which makes it hard to find an existing club to join. Since the Securities and Exchange Commission sees investment clubs as unregistered securities, clubs are unable to advertise for new members. Unfortunately, NAIC, which has over 25,000 member clubs, is unable to refer individuals to specific clubs, either. This all adds up to mean that it's very difficult to find a club to join, even if that club is looking for new members. One of the best ways to find a club is by networking—attend local investor events held in your area by one of NAIC's 85 local councils. Each council holds regular meetings, workshops, model clubs, and other events. By meeting other investors and club members, you may find a club that's willing to accept you as a member. Or, you might find other investors who are looking for a club and you can all start your own.

## RESEARCH: Magazine Club Portfolio Tracking

**http://www.researchmag.com/investor/naic.htm**

*RESEARCH:* Magazine offers a unique club portfolio tracking feature on their site. The club treasurer enters the club's portfolio into the service, and other members can access the portfolio at any time to check their holdings (but only the treasurer can make changes). Future promised enhancements include

broadcast e-mail new alerts to all club members. While you're visiting this site, be sure to take advantage of their array of research on stocks and funds.

Other clubs have taken their educational focus to another level. They maintain Web sites with information about their activities and portfolios to provide not only a central resource for exiting members but to share their experiences with outsiders.

## Gateway Eagles Guide to Personal & Club Investing

http://members.aol.com/byington/gweagles/gweagles.html

The Gateway Eagles was begun in March 1996 by a group of McDonnell Douglas engineers (who work on the F-15 Eagle) in St. Louis (the Gateway to the West). Their site includes an overview of how to start an investment club, information about Dividend Reinvestment Plans, investment strategies, as well as links to numerous stock quote services, stock news services, electronic brokers, and other investing sites. While you're here, don't forget to check out the Gateway Eagles Investment Club portfolio, too.

## High Seas Traders Investment Club

http://www.hst.org

High Seas Traders is an online investment club formed by commissioned officers of the sea services of the United States Armed Forces. They conduct all their club business via e-mail and their Web site. Visitors can get a peek at their club portfolio, stock analyses, watch list, and training materials.

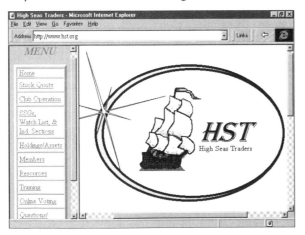

## REAP Investment Club

http://members.aol.com/dougnrobyn/reap.html

REAP stands for Retire Early And Party, so this Virginia club obviously has fun while still taking their investing seriously. Be sure to check out the results of their stock picking contest, and the Photo Gallery. You'll also find their club portfolio, with links to the sites of the companies they own, and information about club operations.

## SAIG

http://www.afn.org/~afn01170/SAIG.html

The SAIG investment club was formed by employees at the University of Florida. Their home page was one of the first club pages on the Web. A sample partnership agreement and outline of their investing guidelines are highlights of this site.

# OTHER INVESTMENT CLUB WEB SITES

The following is a list of investment clubs who have established Web pages to promote the club concept. Their members are happy to share their experiences and spread the word that clubs are a great way to learn about investing and plan for a more secure financial future for all involved.

## The 100 Club

http://www.isl.net/~follese/100_club.html

Minneapolis, MN

## AEA Investment Club

http://sdf.laafb.af.mil/~gowerj/clubs/invest.html

Los Angeles, CA

## The AUG Investment Club
http://www.shadow.net/~brolston
Cupertino, CA

## Aviano Investment Club
http://www.ets.it/personal.pgs/sparks/aic.htm
Aviano Air Base, Italy

## BAI Club
http://ourworld.compuserve.com/homepages/
ernest_moosa_jr/
Columbia, MD

## Boardwalk Investors' Group (B.I.G.)
http://www.gis.net/~vsanthony/big.html
Boston, MA

## Black Monday Investment Group
http://www.gordian.com:80/users/
blackmonday/
Santa Ana Heights, CA

## Blue Chip Posse
http://www.interport.net/~gerlach/bcp.html
New York, NY

## Blue Heaven Investment Club
http://www.unc.edu/~sherman/bhic/
Chapel Hill, NC

## Blue Horseshoe Investment Club
http://www.xnet.com/~gidding/bht.html
Aurora, IL

## The Browncroft Investment Club
http://www.vivanet.com/~alby/bic.htm
Rochester, NY

## Cent Sational Stockers
http://www.wolfenet.com/~baus/
stockers.html
Seattle, WA

## Cherokee Prospectors Investment Club
http://home.ptd.net/~mercker/cheok.html

## Chuma Investment Club
http://www.afrinet.net/~hallh/ic.html
Cyberspace

## Doubter's Investment Club
http://www.dfw.net/~ggrosh/dic/
Fort Worth, TX

## Dynavestors
http://www.wavefront.com/~sullivan/dyna/
dyna.html
Roseville, MN

## Financially Rewarding On-Line Investment Club (FROLIC)
http://pages.prodigy.com/RVPP30A/frolic.htm
Cyberspace

## Fortune 8 Players Investment Club
http://ourworld.compuserve.com/homepages/
Fortune8Players/
Los Angeles, CA

## G.O.L.D. Investment Club Online
http://members.aol.com/AristotleM/gold.htm
Cyberspace

## Greater Kansas City Investment Club
http://www.qni.com/~dkcamer/
Kansas City, MO

Occasionally, both online and off, you may come across an investment club that seems to operate more like a small money management firm, with an advisor who receives compensation for managing the club's portfolio, while other investors are passive. These arrangements may be legal, but they are not what is generally understood to be an investment club. Genuine clubs are distinguished by the fact that all members are all active in the operation of the club. That's what makes them so educational.

### Green Horn Stock Market Investment Club

http://granby.mtl.net/moreau.html

Eastern Townships, Quebec

### Hanover Investment Club

http://www.hanover.edu/econbus/hic.html

Hanover, IN

### In the Black Investment Club

http://www.panix.com/~okolo/invest/invest_drum.html

Cyberspace

### Investors Plus Investment's Club

http://www.cloudnet.com/~brixius/invplus.html

St. Cloud, MN

### Kubera Investment Club

http://www.ultranet.com/~nagi/kubera/index.htm

Marlboro, MA

### Maximum Securities Investment Club

http://www.avana.net/pages/personal/jimb/index.htm

Dunwoody, GA

### Millennium Investments

http://www.tc.umn.edu/nlhome/m113/bisc0016/millpage.html

Minneapolis, MN

### The Mint Collectors Investment Club

http://www.voicenet.com/~jsarnese/

Philadelphia, PA

### National OnLine Investment Club

http://www.gehlken.com/olic/index.html

Cyberspace

### Northern Virginia Stock Yards Investment Club

http://ourworld.compuserve.com/homepages/Ray_Anderson/

Washington, DC

### Oglethorpe Group Holdings

http://www.geocities.com/WallStreet/3498/

New York, NY

### Professional Risk Investment Club

http://ourworld.compuserve.com/homepages/EWilliams/price.htm

Evansville, IN

### Profiteers Investment Club

http://www.netcom.com/~xochi/profiteers.html

Fresno, CA

## Rags to Riches Investment Club
http://www.ghgcorp.com/cabrown/

Houston, TX

## REAP Investment Club
http://members.aol.com/dougnrobyn/
reap.html

Northern Virginia

## Royal Oak Investments
http://www.westol.com/~rbigley/index.htm

Scottdale, PA

## Santa Clara United Monies
http://www-leland.stanford.edu/~aubuchon/
SCCUM/

Santa Clara, CA

## Skyhigh Stock Club
http://www.netcom.com/~muzdad

Harrisburg, PA

## $LY Investment Club
http://www.ncn.net/~dougadams/
slyinvestclub.html

Sac City, IA

## South Jersey Investment Club
http://www.jersey.net/~mountaindog/sjic/
sjic.htm

New Jersey

## Stockbytes Investment Club
http://www.teleport.com/~radforj/
stkbytes.htm

Portland, OR

## Trails End Investment Club
http://www.cyberhighway.net/~karla/

Salem, OR

## Up Your Assets Investment Club
http://www.geocities.com/WallStreet/1168/

Foster City, CA

## Valley Investment Partners
http://www.geocities.com/CapitolHill/2320/
vip.html

Huntsville, AL

## Wild Capital Investment Club
http://www.computerland.net/~missouri

Columbia, MO

## Windy City Investment Club
http://pages.prodigy.com/wcic/home.htm

Cyberspace

# MARKET GAMES, SIMULATIONS, AND CONTESTS

Some investors may find that it's best to practice a bit before committing their hard-earned dollars to the market for the first time. Others may want to test the waters with a new or modified trading strategy. Still others might just be looking for some fun.

These market games and simulations run the gamut from stock-picking contests, to brokerage simulations geared towards professionals that provide third-party verification of a model portfolio's performance, to software and companies that develop predictive trading models.

## Auditrack Simulated Brokerage
http://auditrack.com

Auditrack is a full-service, fee-based simulated brokerage firm. Geared towards money managers and other institutional traders, Auditrack manages accounts that operate just like real brokerage accounts. A professionally staffed order desk determines in

One problem with investment games, contests, and simulators is that they inevitably reward short-term performance and sheer luck. If you're a long-term investor, there is no effective way to test a five-year investing strategy in real time.

real-time the precise purchase and sale prices of every trade, as if the trade was actually made in the open market. Auditrack can provide regular statements and performance reports.

### E*TRADE Stock Market Game
http://www.etrade.com/html/visitor_center/game.htm

E*TRADE Securities, the online broker, runs an on-going stock market game. Each month, a new game allows users to trade stocks and options using real market prices and a portfolio of $100,000 in game money. Portfolio and transaction records are updated automatically, and the top ten players are posted daily.

### Final Bell
http://www.finalbell.com

Build the winning portfolio in this stock market game and win $10,000. Chat with other players in The Forum, and try your hand at some other bonus games to win additional dollars to add to your portfolio.

### MarketPlayer Hedge Hog Competition
http://www.marketplayer.com

MarketPlayer offers a set of professional investment tools that help investors identify up-and-coming growth stocks and attractive market sectors. The HedgeHog Competition allows participants to build

their own one million dollar hedge fund stock portfolio using MarketPlayer's tools, competing with other contestants for prizes in a test of financial acumen.

### Profits Warning
http://www.team17.com/TGR/

Profits Warning is an online British stock market game available from The Games Room, hosted by Team 17 Software. This new share trading game runs in three-month cycles and requires additional software that is downloaded from their Web site. Trades are based on the value of real shares. It costs £25 to play, but prizes include a BMW328si or £25,000 in cash.

### Market Skill-Builder
http://www.starbyte.com/msb

Belgian Richard King offers this $295 Windows program to help build technical trading skills in a realistic market environment. King's premise is that forecasting financial markets is impossible, but identifying what will probably happen next is easy. His chart-based program is intended to provide the necessary practice to make it possible for investors to increase the likelihood of being right when trading currencies, metals, agricultural commodities, financial futures, or stocks.

### MockStock Investment Challenge
http://www.inforel.com/~eharland

The MockStock Investment Challenge is a financial simulation game for college students who invest in stocks traded on the NYSE, Nasdaq, and AMEX. Prizes reward the best performing portfolios, and a small fee is required for registration.

### nVestor Stock Market Simulation Game
http://investorsleague.com

Sponsored by the League of American Investors, nVestor allows users to invest $100,000 in game money to buy 20 stocks in a model portfolio. Stocks must be chosen from a list of "participating companies," and investors receive updates from those companies while their portfolios hold their stocks. All accounts are assigned an International Investors Ranking that shows performance compared to portfolios of other members, and all participants are eligible to win $100,000 of stock in participating companies in their StockPIX contest. nVestor is free to participants.

### Raspberry Hill Publishing Market Games
http://www.raspberryhill.com/marketgames.html

Rapsberry Hill produces several market games, where participants buy and sell shares of sports teams, race car drivers and politicians. Registration is free, and cash prizes are offered.

### Rogue Market
http://www.roguemarket.com

Rogue Market is a stock market game with a twist; instead of buying and selling companies, players buy and sell shares in celebrities from entertainment, sports, and business. Is this a fun diversion, a satire on popular culture, or a market simulation? One thing is clear: the laws of supply and demand that govern equity markets are in full force on the Rogue Market. It's free to play the game, and prizes are offered as an added bonus.

### Sierra On-Line Stock Market Challenge
http://smc.sierra.com

This is a Web-based stock market trading game. By devising a successful strategy in trading stocks, you can increase the value of your "challenge" portfolio. Players have an option to pay an entry fee to become eligible to win prizes.

### SMG2000: The Stock Market Game
http://www.smg2000.org

SMG2000 is the online version of an electronic simulation of Wall Street trading that's been used in schools since 1977. Designed for both students and adults, SMG2000 helps users understand the stock market, the decision-making process, and economic concepts. Students enter transactions using the Internet, and they access their portfolios online, too. Teachers can participate in training workshops to learn how to use the program in their classrooms.

### Stock-Trak
http://www.stocktrak.com

Stock-Trak is a fee-based market simulation service popular with college finance and investment courses. Students call an 800 number to trade a portfolio of $100,000 in play money as part of their course

### the swami speaks

Why is it that so many sites require registration? For sites that offer paid services, of course, registration is how the Web site can collect payment. But other sites provide information only to registered users, requiring a password and user name in order to access the service. Sometimes they ask for personal information. This is usually so they can generate demographic statistics for advertisers who are footing the bill for the information you receive for free. Other sites provide customized services, like portfolio tracking, so they need to know who you are in order to provide the right portfolio. Some sites like to know how surfers use their resources, and registration assists them in this effort. In any case, most Web publishers keep all this information confidential. It's often the price users have to pay in order to receive the bountiful information provided on the Web.

work, managing a model portfolio of stocks, options, futures, bonds, or mutual funds. Stock-Trak also offers individual investors the chance to open a portfolio and test an investment strategy, learning about the financial markets in the process. The $24.95 registration fee also enters account holders in Stock-Trak's quarterly national competition. Financial professionals can also use Stock-Trak to develop a track record with an independent third party.

### University of Iowa Electronic Markets
**http://www.biz.uiowa.edu/iem/index.html**
During presidential election years, the University of Iowa Electronics Markets also grabs its share of headlines as futures trading on the various candi-

dates heats up through caucuses, primaries, and the general election. A few days before the last election, futures paying $1.00 to the winner were going for a nickel on Dole and $.95 for Clinton. In fact, the IEM has predicted the last several presidential elections closer than any of the polls. This is a real-money futures market in which contract payoffs depend on economic and political events, such as elections. Participants are students from colleges and universities all over the world who trade in accounts ranging from $5 to $500. Students then learn first-hand about the operation of financial markets and market and trader behavior.

### Wall Street Simulator for Windows
**http://www.larax.com**
Larax Software markets this shareware program as a way to learn how to invest without risk. Wall Street Simulator for Windows simulates a real brokerage account with an opening value of $500,000, and where it goes from there is left to the investor's acumen. The program supports margin trades, short sales, configurable broker call rates, and money market funds rates. The ticker shows the latest prices of securities in the portfolio, though quotes must be imported from an outside source. WSW will keep you honest, too. Once you've entered a transaction, you can't delete it! Registration is just $17.

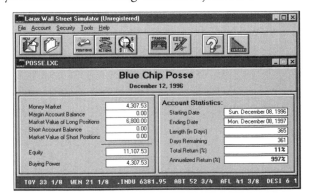

# GLOSSARY

BEAR—An investor who believes that a stock or the market in general will decline. A bear market is an extended period of falling prices in the overall market.

BLUE CHIP STOCK—Stock in a well-established, financially-sound and stable company that has a very good record of paying dividends.

BOND—A bond is a promise made by the government or a corporation to repay funds loaned by investors at a specific rate by a specific date.

BULL—An investor who thinks the market or a specific security or industry will rise. A bull market is an extended period in which the market consistently rises.

BROKER—An individual or company that charges a fee or commission for buying and selling securities. Brokers must register with the Securities and Exchange Commission as well as with states in which they do business.

BUY AND HOLD—A long-term investing strategy in which an investor's stock portfolio is fully invested in the market all the time.

COMMISSION—The fee paid to a broker to buy or sell securities. A commission increases the tax basis of the purchased security (thereby reducing the eventual capital loss or gain). Commissions vary widely from broker to broker.

COMMON STOCK—A class of stock in a company, normally with voting rights. Corporations may have several classes of common stock, as well as preferred stock, or they may have a single class of common stock. Common stockholders are on the bottom of the ladder in a corporation's ownership structure and have rights to a company's assets only after bond holders, preferred shareholders, and other debt holders have been satisfied.

FUNDAMENTAL ANALYSIS—A method of evaluating stocks based on fundamental factors such as revenues, earnings, future growth, return on equity, and profit margins, to determine a company's underlying value and potential for future growth.

MUTUAL FUND—An open-ended investment company that manages a portfolio of securities and offers shares to investors. Shares are issued and redeemed as per demand, and the fund's Net Asset Value per share (NAV) is determined each day.

SECURITY—According to the Securities Exchange Act of 1934, this is the definition of a security: "The term 'security' means any note, stock, treasury stock, bond, debenture, certificate of interest or participation in any profit-sharing agreement or in any oil, gas, or other mineral royalty or lease, any collateral-trust certificate, preorganization certificate or subscription, transferable share, investment contract, voting-trust certificate, certificate of deposit, for a security, any put, call, straddle, option, or privilege on any security, certificate of deposit, or group or index of securities (including any interest therein or based on the value thereof), or any put, call, straddle, option, or privilege entered into on a national securities exchange relating to foreign currency, or in general, any instrument commonly known as a 'security'; or any certificate of interest or participation in, temporary or interim certificate for, receipt for, or warrant or right to subscribe to or purchase, any of the foregoing; but shall not include currency or any note, draft, bill of exchange, or banker's acceptance which has a maturity at the time of issuance of not exceeding nine months, exclusive of days of grace, or any renewal thereof the maturity of which is likewise limited." Got that? A simpler definition is that a security is a piece of paper that can be assigned a value and sold, or any investment made with the expectation of a profit.

STOCK SYMBOL—A unique symbol assigned to a security, also known as the ticker symbol.

STOCKBROKER—A licensed representative who places orders to buy and sell securities for customers.

TECHNICAL ANALYSIS—A method of evaluating securities by analyzing data of a stock's market activity, generally price and volume. Technical analysts use charts to identify patterns that can suggest future activity.

# Chapter 2
## The Stock Market

"The safest way to double your money is to fold over once and put it in your pocket."

—F. McKinney Hubbard

**When you compare** the potential risks of investing in stocks to the potential rewards, common stock investing generally provides the best returns with the smallest downside. That's why some U.S. government officials recently floated an idea to invest some of the holdings of the Social Security system, traditionally invested in safe and secure bonds, into a vehicle with potentially higher returns—the stock market.

Individual perceptions of the stock market vary. Some people don't see much difference between the stock market and casino gambling, with the potential for a huge windfall but an even bigger opportunity to go bust. Others think of *playing the market* as if it were nothing more than a Monopoly board with a real payout to the winners.

Disciplined investors who take the time to learn about investing in stocks, though, see the real potential in the stock market. It's the chance to own a piece of America's best companies while securing their own financial futures.

The Web provides many (if not all) of the tools and information every investor needs to research, select, and follow common stocks.

## SUPERSITES

Nowhere is the adage "you get what you paid for" more true on the Web than at these sites. There is an inverse relationship between the quality of data and the price; free data often isn't worth what you paid for it. In order to get reliable and unbiased research, sometimes you have to invest in information. In the past few years, the cost of such research, often touted as professional quality or institutional quality, has dropped to the point where it's accessible to the average individual investor.

*SuperSites* are investors' one-stop shopping centers for financial information. Typically subscription-based, the SuperSites offer quotes, charts, fundamental or technical data, news, commentary, portfolio tracking and other services and information, with additional charges for premium features. They often offer free services to draw traffic to their sites, or a free month's subscription to sample their wares, and savvy investors should gladly take them up on their offers!

### INVESTools
### http://www.investools.com

While many investing SuperSites excel at providing financial data, none come close to INVESTools when it gets down to investing analysis. INVESTools began as an online financial library, with reports and newsletters from vendors such as Morningstar, Standard & Poor's, Hussman Econometrics, and the Prudent Speculator available on either a per-issue or subscription basis. INVESTools grew by adding portfolio tracking, news, quotes, charts, and discussion forums. Still, the panorama of investing opinion provided by INVESTools makes this an excellent Web destination for investors. And what could be an easier way to get a complete rundown of news and commentary about a particular security? Enter the ticker symbol and INVESTools displays a list of all available research, news stories, research reports, and headlines. I tried the ticker of one of my favorite undiscovered small-cap stocks and turned up over 40 separate items and reports that INVESTools could provide. Not only did the list contain reports from S&P and Zack's, and news from Reuters, but also links to issues of newsletters that mentioned my stock. All were available for purchase. INVESTools offers subscription and pay-as-you-go plans to meet every investor's needs, whether it's researching a new potential investment or following stocks and funds in an existing portfolio. When you're looking for the "why" and not just the "what," this site delivers.

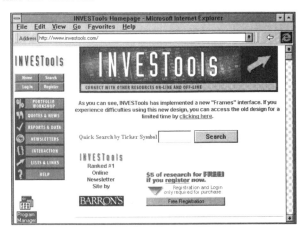

## Investors Edge
http://www.investorsedge.com

You'll know for sure when you've arrived at Investors Edge—every nook and cranny of your screen will be filled with moving tickers, scrolling headlines, and blinking ads. Besides quotes, news, and current market indices, Investors Edge has added a new twist to their personal portfolio tracker: an auto-refresh feature that automatically updates the portfolio every few minutes. This makes it possible to sit at your desk and watch your net worth increase and decrease with the daily market fluctuations! Investors Edge provides free comprehensive company reports for about 45 publicly traded companies and more succinct (but still free) reports on any other publicly traded company. Via a partnership with IPO Online, the site also offers monthly calendars of new stock offerings. Investors Edge offers Nelson Company Research Summaries on a subscription or pay-per-view basis, ranging from $29.95 a month down to $0.50 per report in quantity. Nelson's reports include detailed consensus earnings estimate information (upgrades, downgrades, actual results),

but the most useful feature of the Summaries may be the lists of brokerage and investment firms who cover the stock. Also included is the date of the last report and recent research report headlines. For a dollar or less, these reports are a great value.

## NetWorth
http://www.networth.galt.com

Part of the Quicken Financial Network, NetWorth is a free site primarily focused on mutual funds, but with a growing collection of equity investing resources. The Mutual Fund Market Manager provides information on nearly 20 fund families, including American Century, Dreyfus, Montgomery, Kaufman, and Vanguard. Investors can download prospectuses, get information on any of these funds, or look up current and historical net asset values for any fund. NetWorth offers free Morningstar profiles on any mutual fund, too, and a screening program allows users to search the Morningstar database on a dozen criteria to find the best funds to fit their goals. No investor should purchase a fund without checking NetWorth first. The Equities Center offers a free portfolio tracker, for up to 50 securities, quotes, and links to over 2,000 publicly traded companies. But the best feature of NetWorth's site is the Advanced Graphing function. Users can build a customized price graph of a single stock or fund (or a comparative percentage graph for up to four tickers) for the past one to 100 days, with up to three moving averages from the past five to 200 days. The colors of grid lines, text, chart background, and of each data series can be selected.

## Portfolio Accounting World WideFinancial Network
http://www.pawws.com

Portfolio Accounting World Wide (PAWWS) is an elaborate online financial network.

Portfolio tracking is the cornerstone of the PAW-WS network, with online trading available through several brokers: The Net Investor, National Discount Brokers, Herzog Heine Geduld JRP, Securities Inc., or Jack White & Company. Going much beyond what other vendors offer up as portfolio tracking (simply tracking the issues in a portfolio), PAWWS provides *cost basis tax lot portfolio accounting*. The basic $8.95 a month subscription (free for customers of their broker partners) provides for up to 50 securities in each of three separate portfolios, and the simultaneous display of quotes for up to 150 stocks and funds in an unlimited number of watch lists. Reports can be e-mailed daily. Some general data is included for each stock, but additional reports are available for a fee from vendors such as Griffin Financial Services; Ford Investor Services; Stock Market Index, Inc.; and Hoover's. The advantage of PAWWS's approach is the ultimate in convenience—recordkeeping, portfolio tracking, portfolio management, and tax reporting, as well as actual trading, are combined in one bundle. PAWWS offers limited free services, such as quotes and some market commentary.

## Quicken Financial Network
### http://www.qfn.com

Quicken is the leading personal finance software from Intuit, Inc., and Quicken Financial Network (QFN) is their Web-based center of financial information and services. The site is divided into several centers, mostly comprised of services from Intuit's other Web sites and other providers, repackaged for QFN. The Investments area links to NETworth, providing mutual fund and stock information and to Intuit's Investor Insight service, for fee-based portfolio tracking. Click on News and you can set up a free customized Newspage provided by Individual, Inc. (headlines and summaries only; full-text news is an additional cost) or read current news organized

### the swami speaks

How would you like a cookie? You might not have the chance to refuse, because these aren't the home-baked variety. *Cookies* are bits of data that some Web sites deposit into a text file on your hard drive. Sites use cookies for a number of reasons—advantages for you—such as remembering your name, customizing content for you, remembering the last time you visited a site, storing your personal preferences, or allowing you to bypass a logon process. While cookies can be handy, some users object to having an outside computer secretly writing data to their own hard drive. Some browsers can be set to notify you whenever a site tries to pass you a cookie, though rejecting cookies may cause some sites to work unexpectedly. Other software is beginning to appear on the market to allow you to circumvent the whole cookie process. Despite the potential for abuse, most users will be happy to accept the benefits of cookies.

by industry. Electric Library provides free business and financial information, and a plug for a monthly subscription to access general reference information in the full Electric Library. Quicken InsureMarket offers real-time life, automobile, and home policy quotes, agent referrals, and quote comparisons from the nation's leading insurance companies. The Banking Center includes links to banks and financial institutions that offer online banking services that integrate with Quicken software. The Retirement Planning section is built around an online planner that helps to create a strategy for a comfortable retirement. The QuickenStore links to information about Intuit's products for personal finance. QFN's overall focus is on personal finance, rather than investing, but the site does provide convenient access to helpful services.

## Quote.com
**http://www.quote.com**

Establishment in 1993 makes Quote.com one of the oldest Web-based financial services companies. As you would guess from the company name, Quote.com specializes in quotes. They are one of the major providers of quote servers to other financial Web sites and offer free delayed quotes for all visitors, though registration is required to partake in any of their services, free or paid. Earnings, yield, P/E ratio, and 52-week high and low prices are provided with each quote as an added bonus. A limited portfolio tracking system allows investors to follow only seven securities, though real-time and historical news headlines are provided. Non-customizable technical analysis charts, market index charts, tables of daily market movers, and industry groups round out Quote.com's complimentary package. Subscriptions range from $9.95 to $42.95 and include multiple portfolios, customized charts, historical data, research reports, and news stories, in increasing quantities. Reports from Disclosure, Nelson's, Standard & Poor's, Trendvest, and news wire feeds are also available in subscription plans or a la carte. The variety of resources that Quote.com serves up is staggering, and it's possible to run up a hefty monthly tab here, but if price is no concern, this site has almost everything you need.

### Research: InvestorNet
**http://www.researchmag.com**

*Research:* is a trade magazine for the financial community. Besides providing an online version of their publication, the site is divided into three main sections: InvestorNet, BrokerNet, and InstitutionNet. The last two are open only to financial professionals, but InvestorNet is targeted at individual investors and offers some terrific (and I hesitate to say it) research! Enter a stock's ticker and *Research:* provides a company profile, shareholder news, stock chart and quote, brief revenue, and income statistics and link to the company's Web site, all for free. Want more information? *Research:* has designed their own single page, tear sheet-style "Investment Report," with financial history, business summary, and graphs. Users can download this report in Acrobat format for a fee. For subscribers, they also offer Wall Street Analysis, a summary of analysts' earnings estimates for the stock, as well as one of the best reports available on the Web, their own "Research Report" devised with Standard & Poor's. The Research Report is eight pages of detailed financial information and analysis and can be viewed in Adobe Acrobat or HTML versions. (Similar mutual fund reports are available, too.) *Research:* has a corporate clientele—publicly traded companies that are trying to tell their stories to the investment community—and so throughout the site you'll find prominent links to featured companies. Many of these are blue chips or industry leaders, and the paid reports on them are offered at no charge. As part of their free services, *Research:* offers one of the best online stock and fund

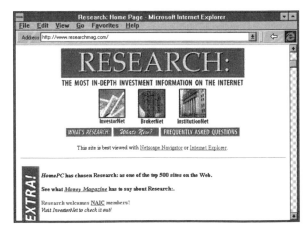

screening programs, as well. Investors can search the *Research:* database for stocks that meet any of more than 25 criteria; the results are displayed with links to the charts and reports available on their Web site. Fund screening is just as simple and full-featured. A free portfolio feature allows an unlimited number of portfolios and an unlimited number of investments to be tracked online. You can also enter other personal assets, such as real estate and automobiles, though you'll have to update those values yourself. A separate watch list keeps tabs on stocks you're actively following. Rounding out the impressive array of information on the *Research:* site are industry spotlights, a depositary receipt directory, information about precious metals, current news headlines (full-text stories available by subscription). This is one site that lives up to its name.

## Reuters Money Network on the Web
### http://www.moneynet.com

The Web version of Reuters Money Network offers free portfolio tracking, quotes, current news, and price history charts. Premium research reports are available for a fee, as are real-time quotes. Inc.Link is MoneyNet's online investor relations service, which includes basic fundamental data for all companies and expanded reports for client firms.

## Thomson MarketEdge
### http://www.marketedge.com

Thomson Financial Services is a leading global provider of financial information and services, primarily to an institutional clientele. Investors may be familiar with many Thomson subsidiaries, such as First Call, CDA Investnet and Securities Data Publishing. MarketEdge is Thomson's online service focused on individual investors. The site features company reports, screening programs, price charts, quotes, and commentary from experts such as insid-

Investors who come to the Internet in search of a bonanza of free financial information will soon realize that free information is often worth just what you pay for it—nothing. To be sure, there are plenty of exceptions to this rule, but serious investors who want timely, reliable, and convenient research at some point will have to be willing to shell out a few dollars. Some SuperSites bundle lots of information into one monthly subscription fee, making them a smart shortcut.

er trading guru, Bob Gabele. In particular, the company and fund reports are value-packed; company reports feature four years of income statement and balance sheet items, insider and institutional trading activity, earnings consensus estimates, ratio performance figures, and summaries of major brokerage research reports. The mutual fund reports are just as complete. A portfolio tracking features allows users to manage several different portfolios, and when you've finished your research, bulletin boards give you the chance to trade tips with other MarketEdge members. Monthly subscriptions start at $7.95, a relative bargain for the professional-quality investment research that MarketEdge provides.

## Wall Street City
### http://www.wallstreetcity.com

This site from Telescan, Inc. has all the promise of being "The Investors Supersite on the Web," as they immodestly bill themselves, but it's still very much a work in progress. Dial-up users will find the site a bit too graphics-intensive for frequent use. Wall Street City offers an array of services for investors, some for free, but most on a subscription basis, ranging from $9.95 to $34.95 per month, and even more for other surcharged services like S&P MarketScope or Market Guide detailed financial reports. The basic subscription includes current and historical quotes, news, price and news e-mail alerts, and Telescan ranking graphs, among others. More expensive subscriptions include reports such as Zack's Earnings Estimates or Vicker's Insider Trading Reports. All investors can benefit from the site's free services, including a couple of neat Java applets. One displays your customized portfolio in a ticker running across the main page of the site, another displays industry group performance charts based on the ticker symbol you enter.

### Yahoo! Quotes

**http://quote.yahoo.com**

If you invest in stocks, bookmark this site now. Yahoo!, the leading Web directory, has built a site-within-a-site just for investors. Besides a quote lookup feature, Yahoo! will track multiple portfolios (including cost basis of each security) and offer links to detailed quotes, one-year historical chart, news stories, and a company profile courtesy of Hoover's. From the profile, links are available to search the Securities and Exchange Commission's EDGAR database of corporate filings and to search the Alta Vista Web index for references to the stock elsewhere on the Web.

# QUOTES AND PORTFOLIO TRACKING

Nearly every financial site on the Web now provides a link to a quote server. Getting a quote for your stock (or mutual fund or option) has never been as easy as this. Just enter your ticker symbol, click a button, and you'll see your security's market price as of 15 or 20 minutes ago.

If you wanted to check on the prices for a whole portfolio, however, it might be a little tedious to enter ticker symbol after ticker symbol day after day. That's why a number of sites provide custom portfolio services, so you can track your holdings online quickly and conveniently.

## QUOTE SERVERS

It's probably safe to say that the single piece of financial information most sought after by investors is the quote. Always happy to oblige, nearly every provider of financial content on the Web offers free delayed stock and end-of-day fund quotes. Stock quotes are delayed 15 or 20 minutes due to restrictions and fees imposed by the exchanges, and that's fine with most investors.

There have been plenty of innovations in the delivery of quotes to investors via the Internet. Besides the simple Web-based quote lookup, services offer end-of-day and intra-day e-mailed quotes. They also offer stock tickers that scroll quotes across a computer screen, as a Java applet, stand-alone application, or as part of a portfolio tracking program.

Delayed quotes may not fit the needs of investors on the fast track. If that's you, check out some of the providers of real-time quotes now available on the Web. Before the popularity of the Internet, real-time quotes required a separate piece of hardware on the desktop. Since the Internet is a perfect way to transmit data, many vendors now provide up-to-the-tick quotes online. But be warned. Real-time quotes are not cheap, and in addition to paying a subscription to the provider, monthly exchange fees are also required. Users must not be financial professionals, either. The exchanges require brokers, investment advisors, and others in the industry to pay higher fees for real-time quotes.

Many online brokers also offer real-time quotes to clients, including Ceres Securities, PCFN, CompuTel

Securities, Charles Schwab, and Pacific Brokerage Services. Some charge additional fees for the service, but some provide it at no cost to all account holders.

### Data Broadcasting Corporation
http://www.dbc.com

Besides offering free delayed quotes on their Web site, Data Broadcasting Corporation (DBC) is the provider of Signal and QuoTrek, two premium real-time market data solutions. On the Web, DBC offers MarketWatch, with real-time access to securities listed on American exchanges, and delayed quotes for futures, equity options, and international exchanges; foreign exchange rates; mutual and money market fund quotes; and bulletin board stock data. Investors can create personal portfolios on DBC's secure server, view historical charts, and review real-time market news. Skeleton fundamental data is also provided on stocks, and MarketWatch is integrated with online brokers such as CompuTel and E*Trade. If this isn't enough for $29.95 a month, DBC also throws in the latest sports scores!

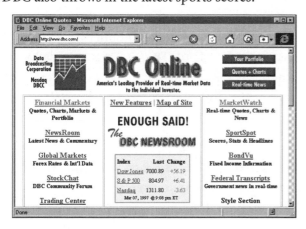

### InterQuote
http://www.interquote.com

InterQuote offers real-time and delayed tick-by-tick quotes on a monthly subscription basis, ranging from $19.95 to $69.95 per month before exchange

fees. Using their software and any Internet connection, investors can log on to InterQuote's servers and get a continuous feed that includes every trade as it occurs. Lower-priced options include real-time quote lookup (instead of a continuous feed) or a continuous feed that's delayed 15 minutes. The software also includes graphing capabilities to build historical and intra-day charts.

### MoneyLine Corporation
http://www.moneyline.com

Moneyline is a provider of live, real-time fixed income market data, analyses, and news for the capital markets community. The service offers broker prices, dealer offerings, indicative and end-of-day prices for Treasury and corporate bonds and other fixed income issues. Aimed at professionals, subscriptions begin at $100 per month.

### PAWWS Financial Network
http://www.pawws.com

PAWWS and North American Quotations provide real-time quotes that work in conjunction with PAWWS's online services for investors. For an additional charge of $50 a month, PAWWS will give investors access to real-time quotes in all of their portfolio accounting services.

### PC Quote
http://www.pcquote.com

PC Quote offers free delayed quotes and two levels of real-time quotes for a Web-based quote lookup service, plus a dynamically updated service that requires separate software. MarketSmart (as low as $23 per month when paid on an annual basis) provides real-time bids, asks and sizes, as well as customized charts and portfolios. PC Quote 6.0 for Windows provides a continuous feed of quotes, charts, alerts, and news, and includes dynamic Nasdaq Level II market maker screens that show trades being matched. Depending on the level of service and the number of exchanges selected, this level ranges from $75 to more than $300 per month.

### PC Quote Europe
http://www.pcquote-europe.co.uk

The European division of PC Quote offers the same PC Quote 6.0 for Windows package as their American counterpart. In addition, their SnapForex Service provides real-time foreign exchange rates for 25 currencies. This browser-based service is £6.00 per month for unlimited usage. PC Quote Europe is also working towards offering real-time quotes for European exchanges. This site also provides delayed and end-of-day quotes for a wide array of global exchanges.

### Quote.com
http://www.quote.com

Quote.com's Real-Time Quotes Service offers access to quotes for securities and options on the major U.S. exchanges for a monthly subscription of $34.95. Canadian and futures exchanges are also available at additional cost. Subscribers can configure a single portfolio of 50 securities that is updated automatically but are limited to 1,000 quotes per day. Stock price alarms can be delivered automatically via e-mail, and continuously streaming Java-enabled quotes are promised for the near future. Quote.com also offers free quotes, charts, and news headlines to registered users.

### RealTime Quotes
http://www.rtquotes.com

RealTime Quotes provides delayed or real-time tick-by-tick trading information, real-time news head-

While it can be fun (or frustrating) to check your portfolio's prices a couple of times a day from these free quote servers, you can't really formulate a trading strategy based on these prices. That's because the stock exchanges require quotes to be delayed 15 or 20 minutes before being transmitted, unless the end user has filed the proper forms and paid additional fees. By the time those prices end up on your desktop, the pros on Wall Street have already had plenty of time to react.

lines, watchlists, symbol and news search, e-mail, chat sessions, alerts, and quotes downloading, beginning at $35 per month. The service requires the use of RealTime Quotes' Corona software, which carries an additional charge.

### Reuters Money Network on the Web
http://www.moneynet.com

The Web version of Reuters Money Network offers real-time quotes for $29.95 a month ($15.45 plus exchange fees of $14.50). The service is provided a single quote at a time for stocks, call options, and put options. Free portfolio tracking and quotes are also available.

### Standard & Poor's ComStock on the Net
http://www.spcomstock.com

The ComStock division of Standard & Poor's offers continuously updated real-time market data, including quotes, news, charting, and analysis. Using the ComStock software and a link to the Internet, users have access to over 256,000 stocks, options, foreign exchange, commodities and indices, starting at $175 per month.

## PORTFOLIO TRACKING

Every investor wants to keep up to date on news affecting his or her portfolio. That used to mean scouring the next day's newspaper to find out why a particular stock tanked the day before. With services like the ones below, you can simply click to reach a Web site that follows your portfolio for you or get an alert message in your e-mail. All of the SuperSites described at the beginning of this chapter provide portfolio management services of one kind or another, too.

### Closing Bell from Mercury Mail
http://www.merc.com

Mercury Mail is unique among most of the Internet's financial service providers because it relies on e-mail to deliver content to its subscribers. Closing Bell is the company's news and quotes service, and users receive daily or weekly updates of their portfolio, with quotes and summaries of market-making news on up to 200 securities. If you need more information on a particular headline, Closing Bell provides a link to the full text of the article on their Web site. Other options include news alerts during the day, currencies and commodities reports, your choice of price and volume formats, and an attached ASCII quotes file that can be imported into Quicken or a spreadsheet. What is the price for all

this? It's free, supported by unobtrusive ads that accompany each e-mail message. It's one of the best bargains on the Web.

### Cable News Network Financial Network
http://www.cnnfn.com/markets/quotes.html

The Web site of Cable News Network's financial network provides delayed quotes for stocks, mutual funds, and money market funds. Enter one or more tickers at a time and get a snapshot of 52-week performance, as well.

### GrayFire on Wall Street
http://www.grayfire.com

GrayFire is a fee-based personal portfolio service that includes recent news stories. Members also have access to stock research resources: search for news by ticker symbol; see a 90-day historical closing price graph; view the latest price with last trade detail; calculate a wide range of indices; and view a 60-day pricing history.

### iGuide
http://www.iguide.com/work_mny/stocks/

This guide to the Internet provides a free portfolio tracking service, including number of shares owned and cost basis, and a single quote lookup function.

### InvestLink
http://www.investlink.com

InvestLink's free Personal Portfolio Manager and Stock Watch service let you track your holdings online with quick gain/loss summaries and up-to-date valuations. Stock Watch keeps an eye on all the stocks you are following on one convenient page. Some fundamentals are provided in the portfolio screens, in addition to price updates.

### Kiplinger Online

**http://www.kiplinger.com/cgi-bin/getstock3**

The Kiplinger Online quotes service provides delayed data on stocks (Canadian and U.S.), mutual funds, money markets, and bonds, one ticker at a time.

### Net Profit

**http://www.MyAgent.com/signup.htm**

Net Profit offers free quotes for a ten-stock portfolio of stocks and funds, e-mailed to you each day.

### Market Watcher for Windows

**http://www.marketwatcher.com**

Micro Trading Software, Inc. offers this software to manage a portfolio on the Internet. Market Watcher updates your portfolio with news, quotes, and performance from the Web or CompuServe. The program provides complete portfolio analysis with graphs, reports, and alerts.

### Microsoft Investor

**http://investor.msn.com**

This site from the Microsoft Network (MSN) is a free online portfolio manager, using Microsoft's ActiveX controls. Enter your stocks and funds into the system, and then check your portfolio's daily performance. You can also get historical performance results and news from the past 30 days related to your holdings. Microsoft Investor integrates with some online brokers, so you can trade right from the program, as well.

### Money Online

**http://www.money.com**

Money Magazine's online edition provides a portfolio service to track purchase price and number of shares of up to 30 U.S.-traded stocks and mutual funds so that a portfolio's entire value can be instant-

Many of the portfolio trackers in this section also have the ability to download quotes to your personal computer in a format that can be imported into personal finance software like Quicken or a spreadsheet. This feature can save you the time and effort of manually entering quotes into another software program.

ly updated throughout the day. Their quote lookup service provides delayed quotes for individual tickers.

### My Yahoo! Ticker

**http://my.yahoo.com/ticker.html**

The folks at Yahoo! have built a free applet that puts a scrolling ticker on your desktop, displaying news, quotes, weather reports, or sports scores. The applet is integrated with Yahoo!'s personalized service, My Yahoo! and also allows a search of the service from the ticker bar.

### NetStock

**ftp://ftp.jaxnet.com/private/henrik/netstock.zip**

NetStock is a free program to access quotes and other data for stocks and mutual funds from several Internet quote providers. Users can export data to Quicken or other formats.

### New York Times

**http://www.nytimes.com/yr/mo/day/business**

The *Times*'s free portfolio service will let you track seven securities and adds a few pieces of fundamental data to the display, but it's basically just a saved ticker list for their quote lookup function rather than a portfolio tracker. Worse, portfolios are deleted if not accessed in 30 days.

## QuoteGrabber
http://www.zoom.com/mito/quote

This free Java application provides continuously updated quotes for one or more portfolios on a 20-minute delay. Charts and news are also provided.

## Quote Ticker Bar
http://www.starfire-inc.com

Starfire Software's Quote Ticker Bar is a floating ticker application for Windows that displays scrolling quotes on your desktop. The program can access stock, fund, or index prices from any of nine free Internet quote servers and will set off an audio alarm when a pre-set price alert is reached. Quote Ticker Bar will also export quotes in a variety of formats.

## Personal Stock Monitor
http://www.clark.net/pub/aivasyuk/psm

This shareware program retrieves stock quotes for you and brings them to your desktop. Instead of having to go to a quote server on the Web, Personal Stock Monitor will automatically retrieve the current price of each stock in your list. The program also exports data in Quicken and other formats, builds graphs, and notifies you when a preset price alert is reached.

## Primate Software
http://primate.com

Primate Software's Quote Monkey data downloading program accesses a database of 130,000 symbols on stocks, bonds, mutual funds, indices, futures, and options, for end-of-day or historical quotes. A monthly subscription also includes Windows charting software, Chart Monkey, with over 14 technical studies, and free fundamental stock data.

## ProStream
http://www.ps-group.com

PS Group, Inc. develops Internet broadcasting products, and ProStream is their free stand-alone Windows application that delivers quotes directly to your desktop. The software retrieves quotes on all stocks from the NYSE, AMEX, and NASDAQ exchanges on a 20-minute delayed basis.

## Standard & Poor's Equity Investor Services
http://www.stockinfo.standardpoor.com

S&P offers a free portfolio management service for an unlimited number of portfolios and funds. The system is integrated with S&P's online research, providing access to over 250,000 reports that are available for purchase. Market news is also provided, but the emphasis is on S&P's array of quality equity research.

## StockSmart
http://www.stocksmart.com

StockSmart offers a free Personal Portfolio Manager for stocks, mutual funds, money markets, closed-end funds, and indexes. Holdings are linked to a comprehensive corporate profile page that includes data and charts, and users can receive e-mailed updates. A separate quote lookup lets users enter 12 tickers at a time or retrieve stock quotes by industry.

## StockVue
http://www.alphaconnect.com/stockvue

Alpha Microsystems has built a stand-alone ActiveX-based Internet application to help investors manage their portfolios. The program downloads stock quotes from the Web, plus news and Securities and Exchange Commission (SEC) filings at scheduled times, allowing you to set price alerts and export data to Quicken or Excel. A nice touch is that

There's a big difference between portfolio tracking and recordkeeping. Most of the portfolio tracking services on the Web allow you to watch the news and price changes of the securities in your portfolio, but they don't provide the recordkeeping you'll need in order to determine the cost basis or tax liability of your security transactions. For that, you'll need software like Managing Your Money, Microsoft Money, Quicken, or NAIC Personal Record Keeper.

SEC filings and news articles can be exported in Microsoft Word format.

### StockWatcher

**http://www.wayfarer.com/demonstration**

Wayfarer Communications built StockWatcher as a demonstration program for their QuickServer software for Internet client/server applications. StockWatcher lets you select from stocks listed on the NYSE, NASDAQ, and AMEX exchanges and to view updates throughout the trading day as they scroll across your screen. The program works as a stand-alone application or as a Web browser plug-in.

### Virgil Corporation's StockCenter

**http://www.stockcenter.com**

Surfers can get free, delayed quotes on Virgil's Web site or can download their Internet StockTracker program. StockTracker is a stand-alone Windows portfolio manager for use over the Web. The program retrieves free end-of-day quotes from Virgil's Web site, or subscribers can receive delayed quotes during the day.

### WashingtonPost.com Business Section

**http://www.washingtonpost.com/wp-srv/business/**

WashingtonPost.com is one of the most interesting online news sites sponsored by a newspaper. Their business section offers research resources, portfolio tracking for up to 40 securities, news, charts, quotes, and excellent commentary from Post columnist James Glassman.

### WinStock

**http://www.teleport.com/~magoldsm/winstock**

WinStock is a shareware program that grabs quotes from any of several Internet quote providers, and then displays the results in a rolling ticker on your screen and in a spreadsheet format. The program supports price alerts, ticker symbol lookup, and printed reports. It will export to or import from Quicken and retrieve news articles for your securities.

## STOCK ANALYSIS

In time, each investor develops his or her individual approach to the market. Fundamentalists look at the company itself and try to find value overlooked by the market. Technicians look at how market forces and their relationship direct the movement of a particular security's price. Some investors combine both disciplines to build their own unique strategy. The Web abounds with information on both technical and fundamental analysis.

### FUNDAMENTAL ANALYSIS

Fundamental analysis is the evaluation of a stock based on factors such as revenues, earnings, return on equity, and profit margins. The aim is to determine a company's underlying value and potential for future growth. These sites provide the news, data, and reports needed for investors to carry out their own analysis and selection of stocks.

## Active Investment Research
### http://www.stockresearch.com

Bob Bose is a Vermont money manager who has built a substantial Internet following with his insightful analysis of long term, fundamentally sound stocks, selected in part using the principles of Warren Buffett. Bose offers a free e-mail newsletter as well as detailed recommendations on the Web site (along with historical performance of his picks compared to the S&P 500), and he lets his record speak for itself. No hard sell is to be found here.

## Annual Report Gallery
### http://www.reportgallery.com

As more and more public companies establish a presence on the Web, it's only natural that they begin to publish a full array of investor relations resources online, as well. This site features a comprehensive listing of companies who have published their annual reports on the Internet. Especially well-designed reports are acknowledged. Lists of technology companies and blue chips are provided, too.

### ask doug!

**Q:** What is Adobe Acrobat format?

**A:** The Adobe Acrobat format is a file format associated with an application in which you can create and view documents in their originally created format. The document maintains a standard viewable format without requiring the specific software application that the document was created in (for example, Word, Power-Point, Illustrator). Many times, documents on the Web will be in Acrobat format for quick viewing. All you need to view an Acrobat file is the Adobe Acrobat Reader, which you can obtain from the Adobe Website at http://www.adobe.com.

## The Berkshire Hathaway Home Page (Unofficial)
### http://www.transarc.com/afs/transarc.com/public/abh/html/brk/

Or, Everything You Wanted To Know About Warren Buffet, But Were Afraid To Ask. This page is an amalgam of links, news clippings, excerpts of writings, and annual reports, all featuring the legendary value investor, Warren Buffett. His firm, Berkshire Hathaway, is a diversified holding company; since Buffett took control of Berkshire 31 years ago, he has increased the book value of its Class A shares from $19 to $14,426 (a rate of 23.6% compounded annually). With a recent share value of somewhere over $30,000, Buffett is neck and neck with Microsoft's Bill Gates to hold the title of the richest man in America. But enough of Warren Buffett here. If you want to know more, this site is the place.

### Deloitte & Touche PeerScape
http://www.peerscape.com

Accounting and consulting firm Deloitte & Touche has build a powerful financial resource on the Web with PeerScape, offering industry and company research in Adobe Acrobat format. PeerScape calls its reports investment bank analysis, and they surely are among the most comprehensive reports available online or off. They have graphs, historical data, performance comparisons between companies and the S&P 500 and their peers, and more.

### Global Financial Data
http://web.calstatela.edu/faculty/btaylor/globalfd.htm

Global Financial Data has extensive long-term historical data on stock markets, interest rates, exchange rates, and inflation rates from around the world. Their database provides historical data on over 50 countries and goes back to the 1690s. (Yes, that's the 1690s.) While the firm's data is available for purchase, they do offer a selection of free downloadable files, including 700 years of data on inflation, 200 years of data on stock markets, and 100 years of data on exchange rates.

### Graham And Doddsville Revisited
http://Web.idirect.com/~telcomm

In this ongoing series, investment advisor Reynolds Russell is taking an updated look at Benjamin Graham and David Dodd's classic investing text, *Security Analysis*. Russell himself is a value investor, following principles set forth by Graham, applied to the circumstances of today's economy, equity markets, and tax code. He uses valuation methods such as those employed by Graham's disciple and the wealthiest living investor, Warren Buffett, CEO of Berkshire Hathaway. Surfers can check out past issues of Reynolds's commentary.

### Investorade
http://www.dfw.net/~rajivroy/

This handy online utility instantly displays balance sheet and income statement summaries from reports filed with the SEC's EDGAR. Simply type in the name of the company you're researching and Investorade returns a list of filings. Click on a filing, and that company's income statement and balance sheet summary are displayed.

### Hoover's Online
http://www.hoovers.com

Hoover's provides free capsule reports on over 10,000 public and private companies, with company contact information, recent financial results, Web site addresses, and links to recent news from Hoover's partners (which include CNNfn, infoSeek, *Fortune*, *Money*, *Time*, the *Los Angeles Times* and the *Washington Post*). Links are also provided to major Internet search engines to continue with your research of a particular company. More extensive profiles for 2,500 companies are available on a subscription basis.

One of the biggest mistakes investors make in investing in stocks is thinking that they can time the market, buying when the market is low and selling when the market is high. There are thousands of professionals who are trying to do the same thing, and only a handful of them ever come close to predicting the market's performance. In fact, according to the *Wall Street Journal*, if you were out of the market on the ten best trading days of the 1980s, you missed one-third of the market's total return. For individual investors, unless you have a crystal ball, you'd better stay away from attempts at market timing.

## INVESTools
http://investools.com

INVESTools is unique among financial content providers on the Web, not only in the scope of opinion and commentary it provides, but in the way users can purchase reports on demand. Just enter a ticker symbol and let INVESTools show you what's available: reports from S&P, Zack's, and Morningstar, among others, or commentary from some of the best investment newsletters currently analyzing the market. No monthly subscription is needed; you can pay as you go. A variety of samples, specials, free offerings (like the INVESTools Newsletter Digest, a weekly summary of opinion from some current publications) and a free portfolio tracking service make this an invaluable tool for investors.

## Legendary Investor Selections
http://worthnet.com/www/13f

This page looks at 13D, 13F, and 13G reports filed with the SEC by famous money managers such as Warren Buffett, George Soros, Mario Gabelli, and Michael Price to see what stocks they're buying and selling. The SEC requires that large shareholders report large purchases or sales of publicly traded stock on these forms. Users can access lists of stocks recently bought or sold by hedge funds, value investors, and growth investors, by stock, or by fund manager. Or, search the SEC database for recent filings.

## MarketGuide, Inc.
http://www.marketguide.com

MarketGuide is a leading data provider to the online community, and their site includes a wealth of investment and financial information. The company offers a variety of research reports on over 8,300 publicly traded companies. The basic Company Snapshot report is free, as are daily lists of the hottest (and the worst) sectors, industries, and stocks. More comprehensive reports are available for a fee or by subscription. MarketGuide also has a Windows-based stock screening application, StockQuest, which uses datasets downloaded from the Web (on a subscription or single-purchase basis). StockQuest allows users to search for stocks that fit any of 50 customizable variables. The company plans to provide Web-based screening in the future.

## National Association of Investors Corporation
http://www.better-investing.org

The NAIC, already mentioned in Chapter 1, is an educational organization that aims to help individuals learn about investing in the stock market. NAIC Online offers demos of software for fundamental analysis; articles about investing; sample stock studies done using NAIC software; software data files for featured companies; archived discussions of stock studies from the group's popular mailing list, the I-CLUB-LIST; and a growing collection of educational resources for those interested in long-term, growth stock investing.

### Public Register's Annual Report Service
**http://www.prars.com**

The Public Register's Annual Report Service (PRARS) distributes reports for over 3,200 publicly traded companies. Users can order reports from the PRARS Web site and have them delivered by mail within a day or so. While not every publicly traded company is included, there is a good chance that the company you're looking for is among the 3,200 PRARS clients. Users can select by alphabetical lists, or, in a nice touch, by *industry*, as well. Also on their site is a PaceSetters Database, a screened list of stocks that meet certain fundamental criteria.

### *Research:* Magazine InvestorNet
**http://www.researchmag.com/investor.htm**

The free company profile pages that *Research:* offers for nearly all public companies are worth a look. The comprehensive S&P Research Reports are a gold mine of information; the Company Profile is a detailed look at a firm and its operations, and the Wall Street Analysis is a roundup of analyst opinion. Most reports are available free for featured companies and otherwise for a fee.

### Securities and Exchange Commission EDGAR
**http://www.sec.gov/edgarhp.htm**

EDGAR is an investor's best friend. EDGAR is the acronym for Electronic Data Gathering And Retrieval, which is the SEC program under which companies make required filings electronically. There are actually several EDGARs; a number of commercial and educational organizations also distribute SEC filings on a value-added basis, such as providing data on the filing date for a fee. But the SEC's EDGAR is probably sufficient for most investors, with filings available within 24 hours of receipt by the SEC. Investors can download quarterly and an-

nual reports (10-Q and 10-K Reports, respectively), as well as a host of other filings, for nearly all publicly traded companies. The SEC's EDGAR files are just text files filled with codes and often formatted in ways that makes them difficult to read. Once you get the hang of navigating a 10-Q in your browser, you'll find this site to be one of the most valuable tools in your investing toolbox.

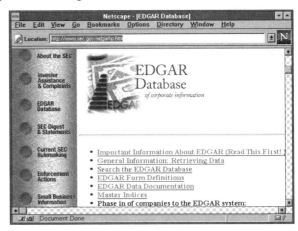

### Standard & Poor's Equity Investor's Service
**http://www.stockinfo.standardpoor.com**

Investors can purchase individual S&P Stock Reports from Standard & Poor's Web site, as well as set up a personal portfolio to track their holdings. Online, S&P also offers subscriptions to many of their publications, lists of recommended stocks, and company news reports.

### Value Investing Forum
**http://worthnet.com/www/value/**

Value money managers like Buffett, Gabelli, and others have written extensively about their methods and reasoning behind their purchases and sales. This site provides excerpts from the required public SEC filings filed by these managers, giving users insight into their methods. A bulletin board provides the forum for users to discuss value investing concepts and related topics.

## The Value Investor
http://www.msn.fullfeed.com/~sequel/value.htm

This free investment newsletter, from the manager of the Value Advisor stock fund, is targeted at equities that are significantly undervalued by the market, based on screening for stocks that have favorable price/earnings ratios, dividend yields, balance sheets, and growth rates. Each month they feature up to five stocks that successfully meet these criteria, as well as update selections from previous newsletters that are still good values.

## Value Point Analysis Financial Forum
http://www.eduvest.com

The Value Point Analysis Financial Forum is a terrific example of the power of the Internet. Forum members have built a community of investors who share their stock picks and analysis using a common valuation model. Visitors evaluate their own stocks using a 13-field fundamental analysis model and post the results so others can provide comments and additional insight. If you think someone is way off the mark, you can instantly do your own analysis, modifying the original assumptions. Then, surf over to the VPA bulletin board and discuss your stock study with other Forum members. The Value Point Analysis computer model was designed in 1979 to evaluate a stock's worth in terms of its fundamental economic and financial factors and the general condition of the money market. The site is free, but there is plenty of value available here.

### ask doug!

**Q:** I downloaded a 10-Q report from EDGAR, but when I tried to print out the file, it was practically unreadable. What gives?

**A:** If you try to print an EDGAR file from your word processor, you're likely to encounter strange page and line breaks, unreadable tables, and special codes. This is because EDGAR's files are preformatted text files, with additional field codes that help EDGAR's computers interpret the files. But to your word processor, a large portion of these files look like nothing but gobbledygook. Here are some tips: The first and last sections of any EDGAR filing contain search keywords, and you can ignore these parts of the document. To view a file on your screen, you may need to reduce the size of the fixed-width font in your browser. To print a file in your word processor, try widening the margins in the online document to 0.5 inch and reducing the font in the document to 10 pt. or lower. You'll still have to manually adjust the tables to get them to fit. The SEC provides a utility that converts EDGAR files to WordPerfect format, which might also help.

## WallSt.com
http://www.wallst.com

From the folks who brought you Wall Street by Fax comes this site, presenting free portfolio tracking and investment reports for purchase and download. Using Adobe Acrobat, users can retrieve an S&P Stock Report, a First Call Earnings Report, or any of a plethora of other financial reports, and in minutes have a wealth of research at their fingertips.

### Zack's Analyst Watch
**http://aw.zacks.com**

Zack's Investment Research, a leading provider of analysts' consensus earnings estimates, offers an on-line research service composed of five distinct services: daily e-mail alerts of changes in analysts' opinions, company reports, custom screening, Research Marvel software that screens an offline database and builds custom reports, and brokerage research reports. This package is available on an annual subscription basis. Zack's also provides a no fee zone on their Web site, with free quotes, consensus earnings estimates, daily earnings, surprise news, and lists of brokerage research for any publicly traded company.

## TECHNICAL ANALYSIS AND CHARTS

Market technicians can put these sites to good use. You'll find online charting, technical newsletters and advisories, and data sources for all your technical analysis needs.

### AlphaChart
**http://www.alphachart.com**

AlphaChart has created two Java-based technical analysis charting applets that are available free to users of their Web site. Among the customizable chart types are Bollinger Bands, MACD, SAR,

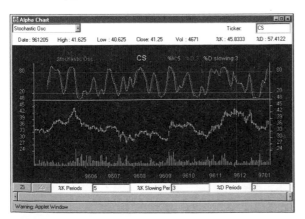

Momentum Chaikin Oscillator, Directional Movement, OBV, Williams %R, RSI, Moving Averages, Accumulation/Distribution, Candlestick, and Stochastic Oscillator. The graphs are nicely executed and easy to read.

### ASK Research
**http://www.askresearch.com**

This site wraps services provided by other providers, such as INVESTools and DBC Corp., into one free package. Users can create customized charts on 10,000 stocks and 4000 mutual funds, read daily stock market commentary and analysis, and check quotes and news.

### Avid Trading Co. Insight Information
**http://www.avidinfo.com**

Avid Trading Co. aspires to be the "premier online source of technical market opinion," and their Web site provides plenty of fuel for the avid trader. Avid's analysts offer free daily and weekly opinion and commentary on the stock, bond, currency, precious metals, and world markets. Other features, such as a weekly stock-picking contest and a chat area, add to the appeal of the site. Avid Trading invites surfers to create their own personal research staff with a complement of subscription-based trading advisories focusing on specific approaches, such as short-selling, short-term trading, or sector momentum timing signals.

### The Burmese Tiger
**http://www.nito.com**

NiTo (New Innovative Technical Opinion), an advisory firm, offers free daily updated technical trading signals, analysis, and recommendations for foreign exchange (Forex), bonds, and stocks.

Investors may subscribe to extended services that offer further commentary and updates via e-mail, including support and resistance levels for major currencies.

## Cognotick Market Service
http://www.cognotick.com

Cognotick Market Service uses proprietary indicators to pinpoint price reversals on the S&P 500 Index and Nasdaq market. Available as a subscription service, Cognotick publishes daily market timing indicators, complete with graphs and commentary.

## Data Broadcasting Corporation Charts
http://www.dbc.com

Data Broadcasting Corp. (DBC) provides free 180-day bar charts with 50-day moving averages for most stocks. Their subscription-based MarketWatch service offers 90-day, 180-day, or 1-year daily bar, candlestick, or line charts for stocks and funds, as well as downloadable historical price data.

## Elliott Wave International
http://www.elliottwave.com

Ralph Nelson Elliott developed his wave principle by discovering 13 recurring patterns (waves) of directional movement discernible in the market. With this understanding, Elliott built a rational system of market analysis. Elliot Wave International offers books, newsletters, software, and conferences for individual and institutional investors. Their Web site features an online learning center, with plenty of educational material, and excerpts from other commentary about the Elliot wave principles.

## Espin Stock Charts
http://www.arrakis.es/~pacoespin/charts.htm

From Spain comes this free daily service, offering technical analysis charts of international stock indices. The charts feature moving averages and relative

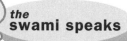

### the swami speaks

If you want to give your browser a jolt of caffeine, Java will do the trick. No, this Java isn't brewed from beans—it's a programming language that extends your browser's capabilities, particularly in the graphics area. It's not an acronym, either, but is really named after the hot beverage that computer programmers drink so much of! Many of the charting services on the Web now use Java applets (as the programs are called) to create interactive stock graphs. There's a catch, however. In order to use the applets, your browser must be Java-enabled. You'll need to check to make sure your browser and your operating system can support Java applets (the latest versions of Netscape Navigator and Microsoft Explorer will probably handle it nicely).

strength indicators and are updated daily. Also available for downloading is a free Windows application that calculates the percentage difference between two figures.

## First Capital Corporation
http://www.firstcap.com

Two free online newsletters are available at this site: *Stock Market Timing*, a short-term technical approach to the stock and bond markets; and *Global Viewpoint*, a weekly technical analysis of world markets, including interest rates, foreign exchange, spot stock indices, and commodities. Back issues of both are online, and each offers plenty of recommendations, tips, illustrations, and charts for traders.

### Global Market Strategists, Inc.
http://www.gmsresearch.com

This newsletter provides to personal investors and institutions a blend of fundamental and technical analysis of U.S. and global stocks, interest rates, currencies, precious metals, and commodities on a daily, weekly, and monthly basis. The Web site offers samples in Acrobat and HTML format.

### The Growth List
http://www.growthlist.com

The accountant who runs this site, Geri Crane, analyzes the markets for stocks whose fundamentals demonstrate growth potential, but specifically targeted for technical analysts. Each week, Crane offers two lists of 30 to 50 stocks each for purchase, giving technical analysts a manageable database from which to begin charting.

### Interactive Quote
http://www.iqc.com

Interactive Quote offers free charting and analysis tools for investors in bar, line, and Japanese candlestick formats. They include daily, weekly, and monthly charts for 9,000 U.S. stocks and indices. I.Q.Tracker is a user-customized applet that gener-

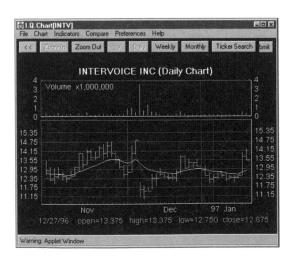

There are those who contend that technical analysis is fundamentally (if you'll pardon the irony) flawed, that there is little if any relationship between a security's past patterns and its future performance. Some say that even if there is a correlation between a stock's past and future performance, there is no cause and effect relationship between them to justify trading on the basis of a chart alone. This controversy, like most, will probably never be resolved.

ates and automatically updates intra-day charts in up to four different portfolios. A portfolio service monitors your holdings, and nicely illustrated tutorials about technical indicators and Japanese candlestick patterns are helpful to those just getting started in technical analysis.

### International Federation of Technical Analysts
http://www.ifta.org/~ifta

International Federation of Technical Analysts (IFTA) is an international organization with members in 26 countries. Their Web site consists of pointers to IFTA member chapters around the world and information about conferences and other events.

### InvestmentWizard
http://www.ozsoft.com

Online Intelligence is the name of the firm behind the Investment Wizard, an online database of Wall Street analysts' recommendations and technical indicator signals. The service covers over 11,000 stocks and mutual funds for subscribers, backing up technical signals with fundamental opinions from Wall Street analysts.

## INVESTools

http://www.investools.com/cgi-bin/charts.pl

INVESTools provides free, customizable online charting in bar, line, or candlestick formats, with 5- to 200-day moving averages and other adjustable settings.

## Kuber's Trading Desk

http://www.best.com/~mwahal/invest

Mudit Wahal has put together an extensive site that features intra-day (delayed 15 minutes) and end-of-day charts for major indices, high volume option-able stocks, financial futures, and funds.

## Market Technicians Association

http://www.mta-usa.org/~lensmith/

A national non-profit professional organization for market technicians, the Market Technicians Association is dedicated to education about technical analysis. Their Web site includes information about the organization, a member database, archives of their discussion mailing list, and a handful of technical analysis charts.

## Mendelsohn Enterprises, Ltd.

http://www.profittaker.com

Louis B. Mendelsohn developed one of the first commercially available futures trading programs for the personal computer. Today his firm today offers software that employs technical analysis and intermarket analysis, neural networks, moving averages, and price forecasts for trading futures and commodities, including agriculturals, interest rates, meats, stock indices, softs, currencies, metals, or energies. A very large archive of Mr. Mendelsohn's past articles on futures trading is available and well worth studying.

**ask doug!**

**Q:** What's a moving average?

**A:** Many stock charts include a line for a 200-day (for instance) moving average of the stock's price. This average is calculated by adding up the stock's prices from the past 200 days, plotting the point on the graph, and continuing for each day on the chart. This technique smoothes out the jigs and jags of a line, and offers a potentially clearer view of a trend. Some technical analysts look for stages when a security's price crosses its 50-day or 200-day moving average lines in certain directions.

## NETworth Graphs

http://quotes.galt.com/cgi-bin/stock_grapher

NETworth's user-definable online graphing feature offers 5- to 200-day moving averages, control of all graph colors, 1- to 200-day graphs and adjustable gridlines, or four-stock comparative percentage graphs.

## Planetary Cycles

http://novatech.on.ca/planetary_cycles

Over 5,000 years ago, civilization was dependent on the cycles of nature—drought, rain, feast, and famine. Merchants became wealthy and kings gained power when they were able to recognize these cycles, and so a body of knowledge formed. Planetary Cycles applies this ancient wisdom to the technical study today's commodities markets. Sample market comments are published on their Web site, but other publications and educational courses are available for a charge.

### Prophet Information Services, Inc.
http://www.prophetdata.com

Prophet Information Services is a leading provider of online financial data. Various subscription packages provide charts and data going back to 1959 on thousands of futures contracts, equities, indices, options, or funds, from 250 worldwide markets. Prophet offers Web-based graphs with moving averages, in candlestick or semi-log format. They also provide downloadable data for technical analysis software programs and their own stand-alone QuickCharts application that grabs data from their site.

### Cees Quirijns' Technical Analysis Home Page
http://www.globalxs.nl/home/q/quirijns/

Cees Quirijns is a trader in The Netherlands, and his home page is an attempt to reach out to other investors around the world. Every month Cees poses a proposition on a subject such as technical analysis theory or system testing, inviting responses from visitors. He then posts the responses on the site. Surfers can also download his free trading system and check out some links to other technical-related sites.

### Remedies
http://remedies.com

Remedies provides free daily charts of major indices, futures, and stocks in the Dow Jones Industrial Average. The Remedies Newsletter Network provides links to financial advisories, many of which are focused on technical analysis.

### R&W Technical Services, Ltd.
http://www.econonet.com/rw-technical

R&W is the developer of the MarketMaster Trading System, a series of software programs for trading Eurodollars, foreign currencies, Treasury bonds and the S&P 500 Index. Their site provides information on the system.

### S&P 100 Index Master Blaster
http://www.pixi.com/~marvel/zig.htm

Besides technical analysis charts of the S&P 100 index, this site provides free graphs of the Nasdaq 100, Nasdaq Composite, Dow Jones Industrials, and several other bonds and futures indices, all updated daily. Some technical market opinion is also proffered.

### StockMaster
http://www.stockmaster.com

Originated by Mark Torrance at the Massachusetts Institute of Technology's artificial intelligence lab, StockMaster now stands alone on the Web, providing investors with free delayed stock and mutual fund quotes and historical charts. Graphs represent a security's 12-month performance against the Standard & Poor's 500 Index.

### The Stock Room
http://loft-gw.zone.org/jason/stock_room.html

Jason Martin and Digigami, Inc. have teamed to provide free graphs and quotes of U.S. and foreign stock market indices, bond yields, metals, currencies, advance/decline and breadth indicators, interest rates, producer price indices, Fidelity sector fund relative strength, and custom graphing options. Technical analysts will be especially interested in the interactive comparison of any index against any other index, with closing prices, up to two moving averages, and a moving average oscillator.

## Technical Analysis of Stocks & Commodities
### http://www.traders.com

This monthly magazine provides traders with information on how to apply charting, numerical trading, and computer trading methods to trade stocks, bonds, mutual funds, options, and futures. The site includes excerpts from current articles; a Novice Trader's Notebook, which is a tutorial of technical analysis techniques; and an extensive search engine of related Web resources.

## Technical Securities Analysts Association of San Francisco
### http://www.ifta.org/~ifta/TSAA/ tsaahome.html

The membership of the Technical Security Analysts Association is made up of both professionals and lay individuals dedicated to the study of classic technical analysis. The site includes information about the organization, newsletters, events, and membership information.

## Telescan Investment Center
### http://www.telescan.com

Telescan is a leading provider of investing software and financial data. Subscribers can receive comprehensive financial market information, including charts, quotes, financial reports, and news. Telescan's software suite includes modules for equity screening, charting, and analysis. The Telescan database offers statistical and textual information on more than 77,000 stocks, mutual funds, bonds, options, futures, commodities, industry groups, and market indexes, dating back to 1973. (Note: Web surfers may be more interested in Telescan's Wall Street City Site.)

Some investors combine fundamental and technical analysis, using a company's fundamentals to determine if a stock is a solid investment, then using technical analysis to buy at an opportune moment. Also, looking at a company's chart from a technical perspective can indicate potential problems with a particular stock. Another advantage of this technique is that you'll always be buying when other technicians are buying, helping your stock to go up!

## TeleStock
### http://www.teleserv.com

This site, in both English and German versions, allows users to access free quotes and charts of more than 60,000 stocks, bonds, and options from around the world. It does take some study in order to understand how to use their *stock tags*, the constructs that make it possible for their system to understand on which global exchange a particular ticker symbol is listed. Data from the past two years can be displayed in table or chart format.

## Timely.com
### http://www.timely.com

Each day, the folks at the Timely Investor Corp. post charts of major U.S. and global stock indices with technical indicators that include stochastics, Bollinger Bands, and Moving Averages.

## The Trader's Corner
### http://www.halcyon.com/tcorner

*The Trader's Corner* is a newsletter that makes aggressive recommendations on small-cap, high-growth stocks, primarily on the Nasdaq exchange. Their Web site offers chat boards for fundamental and technical analysis that are open to any investor, plus past picks and analysis.

### Trend Analysis, Ltd.
**http://www.trend-analysis.co.uk/index/**
This London firm has a team of technical analysts who provide research on the world's major foreign exchange, financial futures, and commodities markets via an online newsletter.

### Turtle Traders
**http://www.turtletrader.com**
Turtle Traders are long-term trend followers, not predictors. The Turtle Traders site offers a classic technical trading system for purchase, for use with stocks, funds, options, and commodities. Their methods are derived from the mathematical disciplines of game theory and statistics and require strict adherence to the trading rules developed as part of the system. Commodity traders will be interested in downloading free data files for most major U.S. futures contracts dating back to the early 1960s.

### Wall Street Web
**http://www.wallstreetweb.com**
Using Java's unique graphic capabilities, Wall Street Web has built a charting service that's powerful and easy to use. Charts are customizable, and subscribers can create personalized lists of tickers. Users can also use a Castanet version, with the Castanet Tuner from Marimba, which speeds performance considerably.

## SPECIALIZED ANALYSIS

Online investors often specialize in particular segments of the market. Two of the most popular are technical stocks and small-cap stocks, including

Here's a simple rule of thumb for most investors: Don't ever invest in anything you don't understand. While this doesn't mean you need an electrical engineering degree to buy a semiconductor stock, you can still learn enough about a company, its products, and its competitors to make a knowledgeable investment decision. Reading a company's press releases, visiting its Web site, studying its SEC filings with the SEC, and searching for related information on the Internet are some good first steps.

penny stocks. Both require a slightly different investing touch than other common stocks, but there are numerous sites that are happy to indulge these predilections.

## TECH STOCKS

Inveterate Web investors and tech stocks seem to go hand in hand. Here are the sites that cater to surfers looking for big returns in high-tech stocks.

### @tvantage
**http://www.atvantage.com**
The Gartner Group, a leading high-tech consulting firm, provides insight into the information technology industry on their @tvantage site. Directed at professionals, the site brings together a selection of research and analysis from Gartner Group and other sources, mainly to discern long-term industry trends. Users can access a limited number of sources for free, but most are only available by subscription or on a pay-as-you-go basis.

## Chip Directory

http://www.hitex.com/chipdir/chipdir.html

Chips, chips, chips! This directory is intended as a technical reference, and doesn't boast many graphics or any navigational structure to speak of. But it does have lots and lots information about chips, including Web pointer, company addresses, products, and much more.

## Dataquest Interactive

http://www.dataquest.com

Dataquest publishes market analysis, statistics, and data for the information technology sector. Much of Dataquest's research is available only for paying customers. However, all users can access daily news stories punctuated with expert commentary and updates on the firm's New England Dataquest 100 High Technology Stock Index or Dataquest/KNTV Silicon Valley 100 High Technology Stock Index. The first reflects trends and fluctuations in New England's 100 leading high-technology companies; the latter tracks Silicon Valley's 100 leading high-technology companies.

## Electrical Engineering on the World Wide Web

http://www.e2w3.com

This site offers extensive lists of companies, products, and publications as a resource for electrical engineers. Investors may want to search the E2W3 site for links to companies involved in all aspects of the computer industry.

## Electronic Buyers' News

http://techWeb.cmp.com/ebn/current

This site is a leading source of electronics and computer industry information on the Web, from the editors of *Electronic Buyers' News*, a weekly trade newspaper. The site features daily news and searchable archives of the print and online versions of the publication. *Electronic Buyers' News* is a good source of insight into many segments of the computer industry, including semiconductors, computer equipment, and manufacturing.

## The Electronics Industry Association of Japan

http://www.eiaj.org

Electronics and technology have been at the forefront of the Japanese economy for a long time. In fact, the Electronics Industry Association of Japan (EIAJ) trade association was formed in 1948. The site features a home page on semiconductors that focuses on global issues revolving around the chip industry (such as anti-dumping measures and import/export agreements). Investors interested in semiconductor stocks will find important background information about the sector at this site.

## The Final Test Report

http://www.ikonix.com

Jim Mulady has published this newsletter dedicated to semiconductor testing equipment and systems since 1985. The highly technical monthly publication is available to subscribers on the Web, and nonsubscribers can check out summaries of products and companies involved in the subsector.

## Hambrecht & Quist

http://www.hamquist.com

Hambrecht & Quist (H&Q) is one of the Silicon Valley's best known and most successful venture capital firms. On their Web site, the company offers research reports on trends in the computer, technology, and Internet sectors. The firm also provides updates on the H&Q Internet Index and H&Q

Technology Index, both created by the firm to track the performance of the two sectors.

### INFRASTRUCTURE
**http://www.infras.com**

This Web site provides links and investment analysis on companies in the semiconductor, semiconductor equipment, and flat panel display industries, via daily and monthly subscriptions. The site features company descriptions, charts, and Web site pointers for stocks in these sectors, plus back issues of their publications.

### Interactive Age Digital
**http://techweb.cmp.com/ia/iad_web_/**

This self-proclaimed "Online Source for the Internet Industry" is the Web version of the weekly trade magazine, *Interactive Age*. The digital version features daily news about the Internet business, a regular column on Internet investments, and the Internet Stock Index.

### Inter@ctive Week
**http://www.zdnet.com/intweek/**

*Inter@ctive Week* is another trade publication encompassing the Internet industry. Tech investors will be interested in their @Business coverage, including the *Inter@ctive Week* Internet Index of stocks involved in the sector. Besides current quotes on all the components of the index, the site also provides option strike data and links to corporate home pages. The rest of the *Inter@ctive Week* site is filled with news, commentary, and data about online companies and trends.

**ask doug!**

**Q:** What's the *book-to-bill* ratio?

**A:** In the semiconductor industry, the book-to-bill ratio is a commonly used fundamental indicator of how well the sector or a particular company is faring. The ratio compares new chip orders (indicated by orders booked by the manufacturer) to prior chip sales (represented by orders billed by the manufacturer to its customers). If a company's book-to-bill ratio is 1.1, then it received $110 in new orders for every $100 in shipments made the prior month. Ideally, this ratio should be greater than 1.0, representing growth in the sector.

### ionTech
**http://www.iontech.com**

ionTech offers a downloadable list of more than 1,800 high-tech companies, company classifications, and Web site addresses to help investors find information, compare companies, create indexes, and track industry trends. The service is fee-based, though the site features an extensive list of company URLs.

### Mercury Center
**http://www.sjmercury.com**

This site is provided by the *San Jose Mercury News*, a leading newspaper in the Silicon Valley. Surfers can access the paper's substantial archives of technology-related stories, as well as current news, or check out the offerings in their Stocks department, including updates on the Silicon Valley 150 index and "Good Morning Silicon Valley" news briefs. The site features a portfolio service along with quotes and MarketGuide fundamentals.

## Red Herring
### http://www.herring.com

Online site of the slightly irreverent (but usually squarely on target) magazine of the technology and entertainment business. Company reports, news, and analysis, as well as searchable archives of the magazine, are highlights of the site.

## Semiconductor Equipment and Materials International
### http://www.semi.org

Semiconductor Equipment and Materials International (SEMI) is an international trade association that represents semiconductor and flat panel display equipment and materials suppliers. They publish monthly statistics on the North American semiconductor equipment industry book-to-bill ratios, a necessary bit of information if you're buying chip stocks. Archives of *Channel*, the group's monthly magazine, are online for all to peruse; other publications are available for a fee.

## SemiWeb
### http://www.semiWeb.com

A global semiconductor-related resource and exposition center that provides the latest in company and product news, employment opportunities, connections to related sites, research references, and much more.

## The Silicon Investor
### http://www.techstocks.com

This site provides comprehensive coverage of more than 250 hi-tech stocks. Besides charts, custom stock groups, financials, links to company Web sites, and company profiles, there are discussion forums. Investors from around the world meet to trade tips and get the dirt on their favorite high-tech stocks.

## TechInvestor
### http://techweb.cmp.com/investor

Check current stock quotes, look up company information, research trends, track portfolios, and get expert opinions—all at no cost. A key component of TechInvestor is the TechWeb 250, which covers top technology stocks ranging from OEM, to channel, to enterprise, to home computing. TechInvestor also features a Java-enabled stock ticker of the TechWeb 250, 15-minute delayed stock and mutual fund quotes, and continually updated financial and product news.

## U.S. Semiconductor Industry Association
### http://www.semichips.org

This trade group offers an array of statistics, forecasts, and background about the semiconductor industry. Most of the site is presented in a non-technical way, including articles such as, "What's a Semiconductor?" Monthly book-to-bill statistics are also provided.

### Upside
http://www.upside.com

This monthly magazine offers an "unflinching insiders' view of the world's leading technology companies." Focusing on the business of high-tech, both the publication and Web site cover the financial aspects of the industry with in-depth articles. The online edition adds Java charting, sector comparisons, the "Upside 200" top tech companies, and profiles of both private and public firms.

### Wired
http://www.wired.com/wired/

This online magazine features a monthly tech stock portfolio, TWIT$ (The Wired Interactive Technology Fund), that focuses on tech stocks. Be sure to search the site or check the archives for the "Follow Your Money" column for the accompanying analysis of the TWIT$ portfolio. Otherwise, *Wired* covers technological trends, businesses, and personalities that can be helpful in researching stocks in the sector.

## SMALL-CAP AND PENNY STOCKS

Known by a number of monikers, such as small-cap stocks, micro-cap stocks, penny stocks, or emerging stocks, these investments carry higher risk than securities but also promise higher rewards if you make the right picks. Unfortunately, information on these companies can be difficult to come by.

The sites focusing on small-cap investing tend to fall into two categories: newsletter and advisory services that make selections for subscribers, and public relations companies who are paid to disseminate information on their clients.

### Berkshire Information Services, Inc.
http://www.growth.com

This site features small, publicly held, aggressive, growth companies with complete analysis, financial reports, press releases, equity research, daily comments, and market quotes. A subsidiary of an investment banking firm provides financing for the companies presented. Users can visit for free, but registration is requested.

### Demontigny Devlin Investment Newsletter
http://www.ddin.com

This monthly investment newsletter focuses on small caps and special situations. Current and past editorials and stock picks are available on the site.

### Global Penny Stocks
http://www.pennystock.com

This advisory service recommends stocks under $5.00 to its subscribers, in a twice-monthly online newsletter. A handful of research reports are available on their Web site, for which the service is paid to publish.

### Griffin MicroCap Service
http://pawws.secapl.com/griffin

Griffin offers free tear sheets on select Nasdaq Bulletin Board and Small-Cap stocks, as well as Hot Stock Picks, for companies who paid for inclusion in their listings.

### H$H Investment Forum
http://hh-club.com

Members of the H$H Investment Forum trade tips and receive recommendations on fundamentally sound NASDAQ mini-stocks (priced below $1.25). The leaders of the Forum have constructed a set of

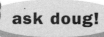

**ask doug!**

**Q:** I'm new to investing and looking for some inexpensive stocks to buy. Where can I find out about penny stocks?

**A:** Hold it! Just because penny stocks sell for a dollar or so doesn't mean they're "cheap." In fact, a stock's price and its value have little to do with each other. A 15 percent return on your investment is the same whether you own 1,000 shares of a $1.00 stock or ten shares of a $100.00 stock. Penny stocks are notoriously volatile and probably not suitable for investing novices. With today's dividend reinvestment plans, direct purchase programs, and deep discount brokers, it can be an inexpensive proposition to begin your investing career with a portfolio of blue chips.

buyer's guidelines they follow religiously when making purchase decisions, and their approach apparently works. These stocks are extremely volatile, but H$H Forum members are taught to *average down* on price drops if a company's fundamentals are still sound, generating above-average returns. The Forum operates on a mailing list and Web discussion board, with company profiles posted on their Web site as well.

## Investment Reporter Magazine
http://members.aol.com/investrptr

*Investment Reporter Magazine* covers undiscovered companies that are overlooked by the general media. Their focus is on micro-cap companies, and the site provides fundamental and technical information about a handful of companies.

## Investors Guru Small Cap Stock Observer
http://home.istar.ca/~invguru

The Investors Guru tracks thousands of small-cap stocks, primarily of Canadian resource and technology companies. From this group a series of Stock Watch lists is culled and posted on the site, and research reports are e-mailed to subscribers. Subscriptions are free.

## Kostech SmallCap Research
http://www.kostech.com

Kostech offers subscribers e-mailed research and bulletins about high-growth companies with new and innovative products and services, trading under $10 per share. Their Web site offers archives of past alerts and recommendations.

## *MicroCapitalist* Research Report
http://www.hh-club.com/microcap

This subscription-based research report focuses on micro cap stocks the publishers feel have a firm foundation and a better than average chance for upside movement. The newsletter is printed, but subscribers can access a special area of their Web site to discuss the picks and micro-cap investing in general.

## The *MicroStocks Review*
http://www.microstocks.com

The *MicroStocks Review* is an all-electronic financial magazine that concentrates on reviews of companies with a market value of less than $25 million. Published every three weeks on the Internet, the *MicroStocks Review* provides subscribers with analysis, insight, and judgment on these companies. The site also includes some helpful articles about small-cap investing and risk.

There are substantial risks in trading penny stocks. The spread between bid and ask prices is usually quite large, and prices are very volatile. An increase of a mere dime in the price of a share of stock purchased for $0.75 is a 13.3 percent return on your investment, but if the price drops, your loss is just as big. A good broker can often be an important asset in getting the best bid and ask prices for your penny stock purchases and sales.

### Penny Stock Journal
**http://www.accent.net/nffc**

The *Penny Stock Journal* recommends emerging public companies that sell for less than a dollar and have long-term potential, though this site doesn't appear to be currently active.

### PrimeQuest Market Monitor
**http://www.cyberdeas.com/primequest**

Suggested for the "prudent investor and astute speculator," the PrimeQuest Market Monitor focuses on junior companies with good capital appreciation potential in the mining and resources sectors. Their newsletter and archives are available on this site.

### Pristine's *Small Cap Review*
**http://www.pristine.com**

Pristine Capital Management publishes the *Small Cap Review*, a weekly letter dedicated to finding undiscovered stocks priced under $10 that have upside potentials of greater than 100 percent within 12 months. The newsletter is a companion to their *Pristine Day Trader*, which provides daily recommendations for active traders.

### The Rampaging Bull
**http://www.rampagingbull.com**

The Rampaging Bull clearly announces on its main page that it is a service of a financial public relations firm. The research reports on the site describe each of a half-dozen or so companies in condensed form.

### The Red Chip Review
**http://www.redchip.com**

Oregon-based analyst Marc Robbins has created a unique, independent publication committed to finding promising, small-cap companies long before they show up on Wall Street's radar. Robbins and his staff focus on 300 companies from 28 industries, many based in the Pacific Northwest region. Non-subscribers can access Red Chip analysis reviews on the site for $5 apiece, while subscribers get online access to the latest news and analysis for the companies in the Red Chip universe.

### Small Stock News Network
**http://ssnn.com**

The 40 or so small-cap companies that sponsor the Small Stock News Network provide users with e-mailed press releases, news updates, and stock research reports, as well as charts and quotes.

### The SmallCap Investor
**http://www.financialweb.com**

Billing itself as "The Unofficial Directory of Nasdaq SmallCap Stocks on the Web," The Small-Cap Investor provides links to small-cap company Web sites along with brief company summaries and direct links to stock prices, graphs, and SEC filings. A beginner's guide to investing in micro-cap stocks is worth studying, and the updates about new stocks trading on the Nasdaq small-cap market can be helpful. All in all, there is plenty of useful information for small-cap investors on The SmallCap Investor.

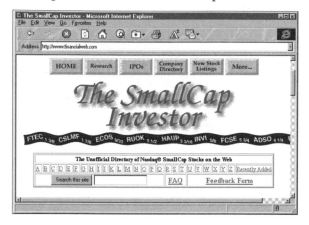

## SmallCap StreetSmart
http://www.smallcap.com

SmallCap StreetSmart is a direct-from-the-company multimedia report providing all of the information you need to know about selected small-cap companies. The site provides access to their database of stocks and allows retrieval of reports in Acrobat format.

## Robert Speirs' Small-Cap Stock Analyst
http://chebucto.ns.ca/~ab304/scsa.html

This Canadian financial consultant provides information about a handful of small-cap Canadian stocks.

## The Stock Spectator
http://www.stock-spectator.com

The Stock Spectator offers corporate profiles of a handful of emerging growth companies, with financial data and press clippings. The site also features Real Audio broadcasts of The Financial Hour, a syndicated radio show.

## StockGuide
http://www.stockguide.com

StockGuide is a resource for OTC Bulletin Board and other small NASDAQ stocks, with an online database that includes contact and ticker information for more than 5,000 companies. Users can get free delayed quotes or extensive profiles on a few featured companies. Two monthly e-mail newsletters focusing on small-cap stock picks are also available.

## StockHouse Online Journal
http://www.stockhouse.com

StockHouse provides fairly extensive information, news, and commentary about micro/small-caps on NASDAQ and Canadian exchanges. The attractive site offers news stories; press releases; online newsletters; quotes and charts; a database of small-cap companies with ticker symbols, addresses, Web site URLs, e-mail addresses; a directory of public companies on the Web; and corporate profiles from companies who pay for the service.

## LeRoy Stockman Forum
http://emporium.turnpike.net/~dpd/stocks/homesite

LeRoy Stockman leads a group of analysts and individual investors who discuss specific low-priced stock picks and small-cap analysis via an Internet mailing list. The group uses what Stockman calls a *position style investing philosophy*, and the Web site offers a rundown on this approach, as well as links to quotes, charts, and other financial services.

## Wall Street Small Cap Report
http://www.wallstreetsmallcap.com

This site provides past issues of a newsletter featuring recommendations of high-growth, small-cap stocks. Subscribers receive news, up-date reports, background commentary, corporate information, and stock quotes.

### Westergaard Online
http://www.westergaard.com

Westergaard Online provides investment research and analysis on investor-owned U.S. and Canadian micro-cap companies of less than $300 million market capitalization. Founder and Editorial Director John Westergaard and his staff have provided over 500 pages of investment research and political and economic commentary about micro-cap stocks.

# PUBLICLY TRADED COMPANIES

Thousands of publicly traded companies have set up shop on the World Wide Web. In addition to information relating to each company's business operations, many of these sites also provide news and services for shareholders and potential shareholders. Even if they don't, it's still not a bad idea to check out a corporation's home page to get an understanding of its business operation before investing in its stock.

There are a handful of directories that make quick work of finding a particular company's Web site.

### Cable News Network Financial Network Web Connection
http://www.cnnfn.com/researchit/
referencedesk/companies/search.html

This feature of the Cable News Network Financial Network's (CNNfn) Web site lets users search for official company Web sites, by company name or ticker symbol.

### Companies Online
http://www.companiesonline.com

A joint venture between Lycos and Dun & Bradstreet, Companies Online provides information on 60,000 public and private companies, including background summaries and links to their corporate Web sites.

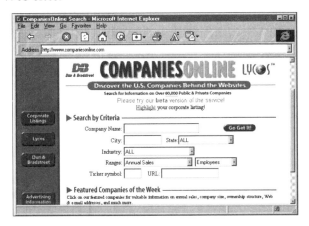

### The Company Library
http://www.colibrary.com

The Company Library is a virtual library of documents and hotlinks with information on public and private companies from around the world. If available for a particular company, investors can access regulatory filings, annual reports, marketing materials, press releases, catalogs, manuals, newsletters, biographies, and other information. A link to a company's home page is also provided.

### NETWorth Investor Relations Resource
http://networth.galt.com/www/home/equity/
irr/

NETWorth lists the home pages for over 2,250 public companies, along with its ticker symbol and a short description of the company.

## Hoover's Online

http://www.hoovers.com

Hoover's offers free company capsules for more than 10,000 companies, including a description of the company, address, officers, sales and employment figures, and hyperlinks to more information, like their corporate Web site, financial reports, stock quotes, SEC filings, and news searches.

## InvestorWEB

http://www.investorWeb.com

InvestorWEB lists publicly held companies with an Internet presence but then rates each site as to how much investor information is provided.

## Wall Street Research Net

http://www.wsrn.com

Research a company on Wall Street Research Net, and you'll be presented with links to news, quotes, charts, and Web sites related to that company. The service has catalogued over 140,000 links relating to public companies and mutual funds.

## The Web 100

http://www.w100.com

A comprehensive ranking of the 100 largest U.S. and the 100 largest international companies, by revenue, with a corporate presence on the World Wide Web. Updated monthly, The Web 100 provides a glimpse of how business's heavy hitters are grappling with this new medium.

## Yahoo! On the Money

http://biz.yahoo.com/news/

Yahoo!'s new business-oriented site offers news, quotes, and company profiles for nearly every publicly traded company. Simply search for your company name, or select from alphabetical lists, and you'll be presented with an array of information about that corporation.

# GLOSSARY

ANNUAL REPORT—A corporations's annual statement of financial operations, typically a glossy, colorful publication. Annual reports include a balance sheet, income statement, auditor's report, and description of a company's operations. The SEC requires that publicly traded companies file an annual report, called a Form 10-K, with the Commission. The 10-K contains more detailed financial information than many annual reports.

AUTHORIZED STOCK—Every corporation is permitted to issue shares of its stock up to the number authorized in the corporation's charter. The number of authorized shares can be changed only by a vote of the company's shareholders.

BASIS—Also known as cost basis or tax basis. A security's basis is the purchase price after commissions or other expenses and is used to calculate capital gains or losses when the security is eventually sold.

CAPITAL GAIN—The profit made when a security is sold for greater than its original cost basis.

CAPITAL LOSS—A capital loss occurs when the security is sold for less than its cost basis.

CAPITALIZATION—Also known as *invested capital*. The sum of a corporation's stock, long-term debt and retained earnings.

CYCLICAL INDUSTRY—An industry, such as manufacturers of durable goods, whose performance is closely tied to the business cycle of the general economy.

DIRECT PURCHASE STOCK—Many public companies have registered with the SEC to sell shares of their stock directly to investors. Investors typically participate in that company's dividend reinvestment plan.

DIVIDEND REINVESTMENT PLANS—Abbreviated as DRIPs or DRPs. These are plans offered by many corporations for the reinvestment of cash dividends by purchasing additional shares or fractional shares, on the dividend payment date, occasionally at a discount from market price. Many DRIPs also allow the investment of additional cash from the shareholder, known as an *optional cash payment* or *optional cash purchase* (OCP). The DRIP is usually administered by the company without charges or with just nominal fees to the participants, and many allow additional purchases of as little as $10.

DOLLAR COST AVERAGING—A technique of buying a fixed dollar amount of a particular investment on a regular schedule, regardless of the share price, thus purchasing more shares when prices are low and fewer shares when prices are high. Over time, the average cost per share of the security will become smaller. This method attempts to lessen the risk of investing a large amount in a single investment at the wrong time. Usually used with mutual funds and dividend reinvestment plans.

GROWTH RATES—The compounded annualized rate of growth of a company's revenues, earnings, dividends, or another figure.

INDUSTRY—One of any number of categories used to describe a company's primary business activity, usually determined by the largest source of a company's revenues. Can be broad (such as consumer cyclical companies) or specific (quick-service hamburger restaurants) or some category in between.

LONG—Or *long position*. Describes the owning of a security. An owner of shares of McDonald's Corp. is said to be "long McDonald's" or "have a long position in McDonald's."

MARKET CAPITALIZATION—The total dollar value of all outstanding shares, calculated by multiplying the number of shares times the current market price.

MARKET MAKER—On the NASDAQ system, a broker-dealer willing to accept the risk of holding a particular number of shares of a particular security in order to facilitate trading in that security. Over 500 firms act as NASDAQ market makers, displaying buy and sell quotations for a guaranteed number of shares.

MARKET TIMING—An attempt to sell a stock or portfolio when a market is at a high and buying at a low. Generally an exercise in futility.

MARKET VALUE—The price at which investors buy or sell a security at any time.

OVERBOUGHT\OVERSOLD—Technical analysis terms that try to define when a market's prices have moved too far and too fast in either direction than are justified by the fundamentals.

QUOTATION—Or Quote. The current price being offered for a particular stock.

RELATIVE STRENGTH—Calculated by dividing the performance of a stock's price over a period by a market index. Used to determine a stock's performance relative to the market and other stocks.

# Chapter 3

# Mutual Funds and Bonds

"The way to stop financial joy-riding is to arrest the chauffeur, not the automobile."

—**Woodrow Wilson**

**Besides stocks,** there are two common vehicles investors use to meet their financial goals: bonds and mutual funds. In recent years, mutual funds have kept growing in popularity. The largest fund company, Fidelity, has over $400 billion in assets under management. In addition, it may surprise many investors to learn that the value of the overall bond market is many times larger than the entire equities market.

There are now plenty of sites on the Web that offer guidance and data for fund and bond investors, ranging from subcription-based services to free information resources.

# MUTUAL FUNDS

For millions of Americans, mutual funds are the chosen vehicle for their investment dollars. Funds offer plenty of advantages: diversification, professional management, conveniences of recordkeeping, lower expenses, high liquidity, and the ability to focus on specific sectors or objectives. The mutual fund industry has embraced the World Wide Web, offering a number of newsletters, services, information, analysis, and software specifically for fund investors.

### 100% No-Load Mutual Fund Council
**http://www.galt.com/www/home/mutual/100/**
No-load mutual funds do not charge their shareholders any sales, redemption, or marketing charges. The 100% No-Load Mutual Fund Council is an industry group made up of these no-load funds, and their site makes available a directory and profiles of their members. The profiles contain facts and figures about each fund family, including contact information and fund objectives. Lots of educational articles about mutual fund investing are also included on the site.

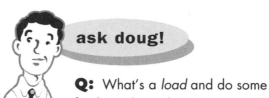

**ask doug!**

**Q:** What's a *load* and do some funds not have them?

**A:** In mutual fund parlance, a load is a front-end sales commission you pay when you buy a fund, and it can be as high as 8.5 percent over the net asset value of the fund. Some funds are *no-load* funds, which means their funds are available to you without a sales commission.

There are other charges associated with mutual funds that you should be aware of. All funds charge a management fee. You'll never have to write a check to cover this expense, though; it's paid to the fund advisors off the top, before the fund's net asset value is calculated. Typically, this charge is in the ballpark of 1 percent to 3 percent of a fund's assets, and it goes towards the salaries of the management staff, office rent, printing and mailing statements to shareholders, and the usual costs of running a business.

Another charge you'll run into in some funds is a 12b-1 fee, also called a distribution fee. This strange-sounding fee is nothing more than a charge for marketing and advertising expenses borne directly by the shareholders, instead of by the management.

Some mutual funds charge redemption, or *back-end*, fees when you sell your shares. Sometimes these redemption charges decrease the longer you hold a fund and are really meant to encourage you to invest for the long term.

A fund's prospectus outlines all the charges made by that fund, so be sure to read it carefully before you invest.

## Advisor Software Inc.
http://www.advisorsw.com

Advisor Software makes two Windows software programs, Mutual Max and Mutual Fund Advisor. Mutual Max lets you track your mutual fund portfolio, calculate performance figures, and match your funds to your asset allocation target. The program comes with a database of 5,200 mutual funds. Advisor offers access to a more comprehensive database by subscription, or you can import data from Morningstar's funds software.

Mutual Fund Advisor adds professional-level features to the package, such as multiple portfolios, geared to the needs of money managers and advisors.

## The Association of Mutual Fund Investors
http://www.amfi.com

The Association of Mutual Fund Investors is a research organization dedicated to helping its members beat the stock market by investing in mutual funds. Subscribers receive monthly research reports for growth funds, bond funds, and sector funds. Members can also purchase investment manuals and talk to the association by telephone hotline.

## Bull's Eye Funds Forecaster
http://www.citilink.com/~bullseye

This mutual fund service provides fund forecasts, rankings, and ratings for the 40 largest no-load funds in the country. Subscribers can receive twice monthly reports on 6-star and 7-star funds, with the Bull's Eye Forecaster's independent ratings, which are marketed as "a cut above Morningstar." The site includes a free section for all investors, which includes Forecast Rankings and updates of the Forecaster's strategies, as well as background information on the no-load funds covered by this service.

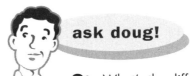

**ask doug!**

**Q:** What's the difference between a closed-end fund and a mutual fund?

**A:** Closed-end funds are publicly traded investment companies that invest in other securities (like open-ended mutual funds) but have a fixed number of shares and trade on a market exchange (like stocks). On the other hand, mutual funds issue shares to any investor who wants to buy into a fund. Closed-end funds typically trade at a discount or a premium to their net asset value, depending on the market's perception of how well the fund will perform, as well as supply and demand for that closed-end fund. Mutual funds must be prepared for shareholders who wish to redeem their shares, and so most maintain a significant position in cash or cash equivalents. The downside of this is that a portion of a mutual fund's portfolio isn't really working towards the fund's objective. Since closed-end funds trade on an exchange, their advisors don't have to worry about shareholder redemption and thus can fully realize a particular investment strategy. This is why closed-end funds often invest in highly volatile, illiquid, or long-term strategies.

## The Closed-End Fund Investor
http://www.icefi.com

The Closed-End Fund Investor focuses on this often overlooked area of investing, with a comprehensive site offering information and profiles on closed-end funds. Subscribers can access charts, data, and customized reports on over 500 closed-end funds. All users can join in the discussion on the site's bulletin board, get a cursory profile on any closed-end fund, or study a very good tutorial on investing in closed-end funds.

## EagleWing Research Gold Funds Page
### http://www.eaglewing.com

Prospecting for some gold to add to your portfolio? Perhaps a gold fund would pan out well for you! The monthly *EagleWing Research Newsletter on Gold Funds* focuses on gold and precious metals funds, covering global trends and events that affect these funds. Subscribers also receive access to weekly updates on their Web site. The site provides back issues, links to gold fund sites and charts, and performance rankings.

One of the advantages of mutual funds is that your investment dollars are being managed by professionals. One area in which this advantage is particularly important is in global investing. Experts say that investors should diversify their portfolios with securities from outside the U.S., but investing in international stocks brings its own risks. Most investors aren't capable of properly assessing the currency risks, political risks, or economic risks of buying foreign stocks. International funds have expertise and knowledge about foreign markets that make them a better choice for most investors looking for some global exposure.

## FundAlarm
### http://www.fundalarm.com

This free site, run by CFA/CFP Roy Weitz, helps individual investors make the decision to sell a mutual fund holding. The service looks at how well funds have performed against the Vanguard 500 Index Fund in the past one-, three- and five-year periods; turnover in fund management; and significant changes in the size of a fund's assets. This site may prove to be a real eye-opener for many fund holders. At the end of 1996, FundAlarm covered 522 funds

and rated 45 percent of them (234 funds) as 3-Alarm funds, serious candidates for sale! Commentary and highlights complement the performance tables and data.

## Fundscape
### http://www.fundscape.com

Fundscape is a free mutual funds updating service that automatically updates your data to produce timely and valuable reports about your mutual fund investments. Using stand-alone software, users can download price information for a large selection of funds and then calculate precise rates of return and other customized reports.

## John Grenier's Mutual Fund Company Directory
### http://www.cs.cmu.edu/~jdg/funds.html

John Grenier's directory of funds lists links and telephone numbers for most of the fund families in the U.S. and Canada, as well as funds from other countries.

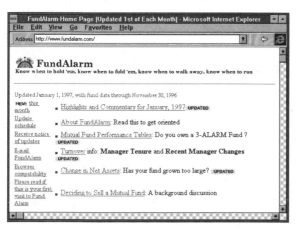

### IBC Financial Data, Inc.
http://www.ibcdata.com

IBC publishes a dozen different money fund industry newsletters that cover over 2,400 money market and bond funds. All of the newsletters are available to subscribers on the Web, and other users can access free money market mutual fund and bond fund yield rankings, commentary, news, special reports, and a helpful primer on money fund investing.

### Interactive Nest Egg
http://nestegg.iddis.com

This online financial planning publication features the Tradeline Mutual Fund Center. Each week, you can get the latest performance results of the country's largest funds, with charts and graphs, as well as lists of focus funds from a particular objective or fund family. A Mutual Fund Directory lists contact information, fund style, and portfolio managers for over 8,300 funds.

### INVESTools
http://www.investools.com

Morningstar is widely recognized as the leading source for unbiased, insightful mutual fund information. As part of a wide array of reports, data, and newsletters available on this site, INVESTools of-fers Morningstar Mutual Fund Reports OnDemand, allowing users to purchase and download reports for any of the 1,500 funds that Morningstar covers. Users can search for funds by annual return, annual yield, objective, or Morningstar's star ratings, a handy and free way to narrow your search for the right fund.

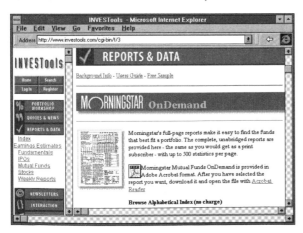

### Manhattan Analytics, Inc.
http://www.manhattanlink.com

Manhattan Analytics is the developer of Monocle, Monocle Plus, and Tax Tracker software for mutual fund investors. Monocle follows 1,000 funds with daily updates; Monocle Plus ups the total to 2,500. Both follow complex quantitative and technical analysis indicators and allow performance ranking and screening. Tax Tracker, from the No-Load Shareholders Association, enables funds investors to monitor the tax liabilities of their portfolios.

### Mark Pankin Investing Page
http://www.dcez.com/~mdp/invest.htm

Fidelity's Select group of mutual funds focuses on specific sectors: technology, retailing, natural gas, electronics, energy, air transportation, and 30 more. But since these funds are not diversified, they are more volatile than most equity mutual funds. Dr. Mark Pankin aims to reduce the risks in Fidelity sector fund investing with his Select Switching System. His site offers information on the system and the research Pankin has done, as well as time-delayed trades Pankin executes for himself and his clients.

### Market Timer Report
http://www.mtreport.com

The Market Timer Report is a market timing system for mutual fund investors. Subscribers to the report receive weekly market analysis and recommended mutual funds for aggressive and conservative model portfolios. The MTR Timer Index carefully tracks interest rates; Federal Reserve Board policy; and market sentiment, volume, momentum and breadth—and then signals when conditions are best for stock market appreciation. For non-subscribers, the Market Timer Report provides a list of recommended funds in its free weekly Fund Watch, along with a sample of the previous issue of the newsletter.

## Market Timing for Mutual Funds
http://www.qadas.com/~jwalker

Here's a free e-mail newsletter that generates market timing signals for mutual funds. *The Walker Market Letter* is published monthly by Jeff Walker, based on his Master Timing Module, an intermediate term timing system that is implemented in two model portfolios. An aggressive portfolio switches between the Rydex Nova fund, the Rydex Ursa fund, and a money market fund. The conservative portfolio switches between the Vanguard Index Trust 500 and a money market account. Users can check out trading histories for both portfolios on the site.

## The Mutual Fund Cafe
http://www.mfcafe.com

Want an inside look at the mutual funds industry? Grab a stool at the counter in the Mutual Funds Cafe, a veritable smorgasbord of mutual fund information, analysis and opinion, all directed at fund business and marketing professionals. A weekly "Blue Plate Special" provides commentary and analysis. "Bean Counters" addresses accounting issues. "Legal Stew" looks at regulatory issues. This cleverly designed site is worth a visit by individual investors, if only to be reminded that the mutual funds business is, after all, a business.

## Mutual Fund Info Center
http://www.pawws.com/Mfis_phtml/

The Mutual Fund Info Center provides a select list of mutual funds from which investment kits and prospectuses can be ordered, including the ARCH Family of Mutual Funds, the CGM Group, Guinness Flight, INVESCO, John Hancock Mutual Funds, the Kaufmann Fund, Montgomery Funds, and Value Line. A page on mutual fund investing outlines basic information about how funds operate, risk and return, and the benefits of owning mutual funds.

## The Mutual Fund Investor's Center
http://www.mfea.com

The Mutual Fund Education Alliance, a trade group of no-load funds, presents this site in order to help investors use funds to reach their financial goals. It features extensive information about investing for children, links and information about funds that are members of the Alliance, and educational features to help you understand mutual funds. In the Bookstore, investors can order free or low-cost materials about mutual fund investing and financial planning. Unfortunately, the site's design will be annoying to many users, since it only uses a 640 x 480 screen resolution no matter what the size of your monitor's display.

## Mutual Fund Investors Resource Center
http://www.fundmaster.com

The sponsor of this site, Sentra Securities Corp., will send free prospectuses and applications on over 2,700 mutual funds to surfers who request them. A page devoted to fixed income funds, a few financial calculators, and a short list of frequently asked questions about mutual funds complete the site.

### Mutual Funds Interactive
http://www.fundsinteractive.com

This expansive site is filled with news and features for fund investors. In addition to daily mutual fund news and quotes, Mutual Funds Interactive includes regular features such as fund manager profiles, "Funds 101," and "Expert's Corner," as well as discussion areas for various topics related to fund investing.

### Mutual Funds Made Simple
http://members.aol.com/plweiss1/mfunds.htm

The home page of Patricia L. Weiss aims to educate beginners on the basics of mutual fund investing. A "Personal Mutual Fund Selection Guide" helps beginners to define their risk tolerance and clarify personal goals, and a glossary of mutual fund terminology provides definitions that often stump novices.

### *Mutual Funds Magazine* Online
http://www.mfmag.com

The companion site for this publication from The Institute for Econometric Research offers Web investors a family of tools for researching and evaluating mutual funds. Register for free to receive unlimited access to current and all back issues of the magazine, a weekly e-mail newsletter and use of their fund and load performance calculators. A char-

ter membership program gives investors closing quotes, performance rankings, fund profiles on over 7,000 funds, and custom screening of their database for just $4.99 a month.

### NETworth Mutual Fund Market Manager
http://networth.galt.com

NETWorth plays host to a number of mutual fund families on the Web, providing profiles, prospectuses, and quotes for offerings from American Century, Dreyfus, INVESCO, The Kaufmann Fund Scudder, T. Rowe Price, and The Vanguard Group, among others. The Mutual Fund Market Manager area of their site also provides recent and historical prices for all funds, as well as profiles from Morningstar, a leading analytical service for mutual funds. You can screen the Morningstar database using Fund Search, specifying your desired investment objective, or a dozen other fund performance and cost criteria. Occasional articles about mutual fund investing are also highlighted on the site. Users must register to use certain areas of the site, though there are no charges to access NETworth's services.

## Pick's Fidelity Review
http://www.metrolink.net/pfrfunds/

This page offers a free issue of *Pick's Fidelity Review*, a monthly newsletter that tracks and analyzes Fidelity's family of Select funds. This printed publication gives investors a simple approach to sector fund investing using Fidelity's family.

## Research: Magazine InvestorNet
http://www.researchmag.com/investor/imutual.htm

Know what you're looking for in a mutual fund but don't know how to find it? *Research:* magazine's free fund screening features let you select a fund from over 3,500 in the database by inputting your own criteria. Choose from over two dozen criteria, and *Research:* presents you with a list of candidates. For more information, you can subscribe to purchase *Research Mutual Fund Reports*, comprehensive four-page studies with performance data and commentary. (If you're lucky, perhaps one of your chosen funds will be a Research Featured Fund, with a free report available.) Other feature articles, as well as lists of the top performing funds in the top performing sectors, are available free on the site.

## Roger Hagan's Market Timing In a Spreadsheet
http://www.halcyon.com/rhagan/

Using just eight pieces of data entered daily into a spreadsheet, Hagan's mutual fund market timing system generates signals that claim to outpace the averages. His videocassette, *Mutual Fund Timing With Your Computer*, illustrates the complete setup and use of the system with any spreadsheet program. On the Web site, you'll find Hagan's persuasive arguments in favor of market timing, essays, and regularly updated graphs and observations about the market.

## Rich's MONEYFLO Funds, Inc.
http://www.harborside.com/home/m/moneyflo/fundsigs.htm

Richard Calkins writes a daily e-mailed market timing report for growth, index, bond, and gold funds. Strategies are presented for conservative, aggressive, and defensive investors. Calkins presents plenty of other material about technical analysis, market timing, signals used in his system, and the comparative performance of his "Nifty 50" and "Terrific 20" growth funds using his model.

## Select Timing System
http://www.dollarlink.com

Timing Laboratory and DollarLink Software have created an aggressive mutual funds switching system that shoots for 40 percent to 45 percent annual returns by timing the market and switching between Fidelity Select sector funds. This very short-term system identifies trends and integrates elements of chaos theory and statistics, triggering monthly fund switches. Subscribers receive updates via e-mail; a free trial is available from the Web site.

## Sensible Investment Strategies
http://www.seninvest.com

Financial planner Jack L. Piazza's motto is "A good plan builds wealth," and his Sensible Investment Strategies offers a low-cost way to develop your own investing plan. For a small one-time fee, Piazza will customize a plan just for you, with recommendations from highly ranked 100 percent no-load mutual funds. Simply answer the questionnaire on the Web site, include your credit card payment and in short order you'll receive a complete strategy, including asset allocations and specific funds. Piazza includes some other articles on the site about the advantages of no-load fund investing and mutual fund investing risk.

### the swami speaks

Free, or not so free? That is the question. There still exists on the Internet remnants of a time when online commerce didn't exist and all information was free. But today, sites likely fall into one of these broad categories: sites promoting an offline or online product or service; advertising-supported sites; subscription-based sites; or individual user home pages. A knowledgeable investor knows who is behind a particular Web site, and what, if anything, they're selling. Don't be afraid to take advantage of the freebies, but exercise common sense as well.

## Standard & Poor's Managed Funds Ratings

**http://www.ratings.standardpoor.com/funds/**

So you think all money market funds are alike, huh? This site is bound to be an eye opener, then. This division of S&P service rates money market funds, bond funds, local government investment pools, and unit investment trusts, evaluating the funds on a series of criteria and assigning ratings accordingly. After you've checked out the ratings and rationale, compare your money fund to the fund indices available on the site. Standard & Poor's Managed Funds Ratings also provides a customized portfolio monitoring service designed for use by fiduciaries and fund management.

## Windsor Financial Advisors, Inc.

**http://www.nerc.com/~wfa**

Windsor Financial Advisors publishes *The Sector Report*, a weekly newsletter devoted to trading and analyzing Fidelity's Sector Funds and available by e-mail or fax. Their system tries to identify sector funds that are likely to remain in established up trends, and then always to be invested in one of the top-performing sectors. Users can sign up for a four-week free trial or review sample issues on the Web.

## MUTUAL FUNDS ONLINE

If you're a fund investor, you'll find a bonanza of mutual fund companies on the Web. At the best of these sites, you can immediately download a prospectus and fill out an application online (and send your check later). Or, if you're already a shareowner, get access to your current funds and check on their current Net Asset Values and distributions.

## AAL Mutual Funds

**http://www.aal.org/CMC/**

The AAL Mutual Funds is a family of mutual funds offered exclusively to Lutherans, offering money market, bond, municipal bond, utilities, capital growth, mid cap stock, small cap stock, and international funds. The site provides daily share and NAV updates, but no online prospectuses or account access. Lutheran investors can request more information via an online form.

## AIM Funds

**http://www.aimfunds.com**

AIM account holders can obtain the share balance and market value of their holdings on this site. Visitors can check daily NAVs or view prospectuses online, or drop in on the AIM Investor Education Center, which has helpful articles on investing topics, as well as market commentary.

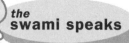

## the swami speaks

You have always heard that the Internet is a big circus, but you never thought you'd find so many Acrobats online. The Web Swami hastens to explain: Adobe Acrobat is a software program in common use to publish documents on the World Wide Web. The advantage of using Acrobat is that the original document can be viewed by users no matter what computer they use or fonts they have installed on their system, and each user will see exactly the same document. Mutual fund companies often provide applications and prospectuses in Acrobat format, so that the online versions look exactly the same as their pre-printed counterparts available by mail. The Acrobat reader program is free and can be downloaded from Adobe Systems' Web site at http://www.adobe.com. Every Web investor should have a copy in his or her toolbox.

## American Century Funds
http://www.americancentury.com

Following their merger, Twentieth Century Mutual Funds and The Benham Group became known as American Century Funds. Shareholders can access their accounts or get daily NAV prices via the Web site. If you're shopping for a fund, download a prospectus in Acrobat format. Comprehensive educational resources on the site include materials relating to retirement planning, investing for a child's education, and other topics.

## Ameristock Mutual Funds
http://www.ameristock.com

This no-load, value-based, domestic equity-income mutual fund invests in large cap stocks. Surfers can view a prospectus for the fund, get a current NAV, evaluate the fund's holdings, and review the fund's investment philosophy.

## Calvert Group
http://www.calvertgroup.com

Calvert Group invests according to socially responsible principles. Many (but not all) of the funds in their family are profiled on their Web site, accompanied by prospectuses, or you can request more information via an online form. Current Calvert shareholders can check their account status on the site, too, and find daily NAVs in the Fund Performance at a Glance section. Calvert devotes quite a bit of bandwidth to the topic of socially responsible investing and how it relates to their fund picks.

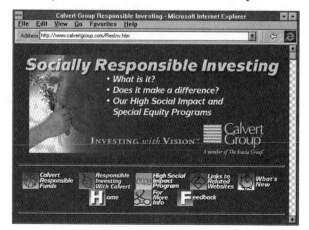

## California Investment Trust
http://www.caltrust.com

This San Francisco-based 100 percent no-load mutual fund family offers seven money market, bond, and equity index funds. Their Web site includes an overview of each fund, but you'll need to fill out a form to receive a prospectus.

### CGM Realty Fund

http://www.cgmfunds.com

This site is nothing more than a brochure inviting investors to become a shareholder, with an application to receive a prospectus and more information via the mail.

### Colonial Mutual Funds

http://www.lib.com/colonial/colonial.html

This family of 40 mutual funds is available through investment professionals. Colonial is a subsidiary of Liberty Financial Companies, and this pointer page directs users to a toll-free number for further information.

### Compass Capital Funds

http://www.compassfunds.com

Point your browser towards Compass Capital Funds and scope out complete profiles on their family of 28 mutual funds. Download a prospectus in Acrobat format or review daily NAVs, fund objectives and strategies, Morningstar ratings, and fund manager profiles.

### Crabbe Huson Funds

http://www.contrarian.com

The online profiles of each of Crabbe Huson's contrarian funds are jam-packed with information, including the fund's objectives, investment guidelines, current NAV, average annual returns, top ten holdings, portfolio diversification, and links to view a prospectus online or in Acrobat format. Click on the name of one of the portfolio managers and get a short bio; Real Audio comments from portfolio managers are an added touch.

### Baxter Financial Corporation

http://www.netrunner.net/~philfund/

Not too many funds can boast the history of the Philadelphia Fund. This fund was established in 1923, and is still going strong today (though not under the same management), aiming for long-term capital growth and income. Its sister fund, Eagle Growth Shares, sticks with capital appreciation and a portfolio of growth stocks. Users can download a prospectus for either of these funds from the investment advisor.

### Fidelity Investments

http://www.fid-inv.com

As you might expect from this mutual fund giant, Fidelity has established a strong presence on the Web, offering everything from Web-based trading for current accountholders to market news, data, and commentary; investment planning information and tools; performance and investing information for Fidelity funds; and resources for researching and trading stocks and bonds with Fidelity through their brokerage services. Fund profiles are clear and comprehensive, and prospectuses are available for downloading for many (but not all, oddly enough) of Fidelity's funds. Their educational materials and planning tools are worth perusing by any investor.

### Gabelli Funds

http://www.gabelli.com

Gabelli Funds owes their investment philosophy to Benjamin Graham and David Dodd, the founders of modern security analysis. Their family of funds follow Graham's and Dodd's principles. Investors can retrieve one-page fund summaries, daily closing prices, and quarterly reports and prospectuses in Acrobat format. The Shareholder Information Center provides Gabelli Funds owners access to current and historical account information.

## Global Asset Management Funds
http://www.usinfo.gam.com

Global Asset Management (GAM) provides Web investors with performance fact sheets and prospectuses in Acrobat format for their eight regionally focused global funds.

## GIT Investment Funds
http://www.gitfunds.com

Investors can choose from nearly a dozen of GIT's equity and tax-free funds and get daily share prices or lists of the securities in each portfolio. For more information, request a packet using their online form or download a prospectus. If you've decided GIT's funds are right for you, fill out an application form right online and send in your check.

## IMS Capital Value Fund
http://www.imscapital.com

The no-load IMS Capital Value Fund uses a value-oriented, contrarian investment philosophy and invests primarily in blue chip companies. IMS provides a prospectus, an application online, and a form for more information. Archived issues of their quarterly publication, *The Contrarian Viewpoint*, are also available.

## Investa Management Co.
http://www.investa.com/invmgmt.html

Investa Management Co. is offering three new funds: the Super Index Fund, a mutual fund which uses options to enhance the return of the S&P 500 Index; the Woman's Fund, a mutual fund that invests in stocks of companies which promote women to senior management positions more readily than others; and the InvestmentWizard Fund, a mutual fund invested according to buy and sell signals generated by technical indicators. Since the funds are new, there is no further information on the Web site about any of them.

## Janus Funds
http://www.janusfunds.com

This leading fund family provides a comprehensive site, including online account access for shareholders, daily NAVs and performance figures, printable application forms, a chat area, and profiles of funds, with brief information on the fund's manager. Prospectuses are available for download in Acrobat format. A sprinkling of other articles completes the site.

## Lutheran Brotherhood Family of Funds
http://www.luthbro.com

The Lutheran Brother Family of Funds includes seven mutual funds, each with its own objective ranging focused on growth, income, tax-exempt income, stability, or some combination thereof. Besides offering fund profiles, a prospectus in Acrobat format and daily share values, the fund sponsor has added some rather fun interactive tools to determine your risk tolerance and to demonstrate the importance of starting to save for retirement today. Educational articles and information about the Lutheran Brotherhood's other activities are also provided.

## MFS Mutual Funds
http://www.mfs.com

MFS is the country's oldest mutual funds organization, with over 50 funds under its umbrella. Check out fund and manager profiles, fact sheets, and Acrobat prospectuses for all the funds. The MFS Investor Education Center offers helpful articles in addition to market commentary.

### Munder Funds
http://www.munder.com

Munder Capital Management is home to the Net Fund, one of the first mutual funds to invest solely in companies involved with the Internet, as well as a full family of funds with more conventional objectives. Also available are prospectuses in HTML and Acrobat format, fund profiles, a Portfolio Snapshot of each fund's asset allocation and sector weighting, top ten holdings, and monthly commentary from fund managers. Tech investors should be sure to check out their "Guide to Investing in the Internet," with links to publicly traded companies involved in the Internet sector and other resources of interest.

### Nations Fund
http://www.nationsbank.com/mutual_funds

The Nations Fund family, from NationsBank, consists of 49 no-load mutual fund portfolios. The site includes descriptions of all funds, downloadable prospectuses and applications, and financial planning tools and information. An online application form is provided. The fund profiles are a nice overview of each fund's objectives and holdings.

### The New England Mutual Funds
http://www.tne.com

The New England Life Insurance Company offers a family of mutual funds as part of the vast financial services the firm provides. Unfortunately, there is no information about their funds available on their Web site.

### Nicholas-Applegate Mutual Funds
http://www.nacm.com

Though the complex layout of this site makes it somewhat difficult to navigate, the site does provide complete information for Nicholas-Applegate's eight funds, with online prospectuses, daily NAV reports, and fund profiles.

### Numeric Investors
http://www.numeric.com

Numeric Investors has been in the vanguard of the movement to apply quantitative analysis techniques to the markets. They offer three funds using their computer-based models of stock selection. Surfers can download prospectuses or check fund profiles on their site.

### Piper Capital Management
http://www.piperjaffray.com/money_management/

This division of Piper Jaffray offers a family of mutual funds, but this page provides no information on them, referring users to local brokers instead.

### Polynous Growth Fund
http://www.polynous.com

The Polynous Growth Fund invests in mid-cap stocks with annual revenue growth of between 15 percent and 30 percent. The site offers daily NAV updates, a profile of the fund, and a form to request a prospectus and other information.

## Prudent Bear Fund
**http://www.tice.com**

This fund, from David W. Tice and Associates, aims to be profitable in both "up" and "down" markets, by reacting to the fund manager's perception of the current market valuation. The prospectus, as well as the most recent semi-annual and annual reports, current quotes, a 52-week price chart, and account application form, is online and in Acrobat format.

## Prudential Mutual Funds
**http://www.prusec.com/Prudential/ prumutfd.htm**

Since Prudential's funds are mainly available through their network of full-service brokers, they apparently didn't see the need to include prospectuses on their Web site. Fund and manager profiles are provided for the portfolios in Prudential's family, but for any more information than that, you'll need check with your nearest Prudential representative.

## Robertson, Stephens & Company
**http://www.rsim.com**

Robertson Stephens really wants to make sure investors hear their message—they've employed Real Audio to provide commentary by their fund managers. This feature is part of the company's strategy to open lines of communications between fund managers and shareholders. Profiles of managers are offered, along with online prospectuses and daily NAV reports for the Robertson Stephens funds. Tech investors will be interested in their Information Age Fund, which invests in companies in the information technology sector. An online portfolio manage-

ment program lets you input stocks as well as funds and get regular updates on your holdings.

## SchwabFunds
**http://www.schwab.com**

Schwab clients can select from 15 no-load Schwab-Funds, covering the range of investment objectives. Each fund is covered in a profile, and prospectuses are provided.

## Stein Roe Mutual Funds
**http://www.steinroe.com**

Stein Roe offers 18 no-load equity, bond, and money market mutual funds. Their Web site provides online prospectuses in Acrobat format, market insights, a mutual funds glossary, and news about the funds. Fund managers are profiled, along with each fund's performance and holdings. One of Stein Roe's unique products is the Young Investor Fund, a mutual fund focused on, obviously, young investors. Links to the Young Investor site are provided for more information on this fund and on investing and kids in general.

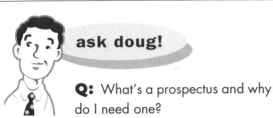

**ask doug!**

**Q:** What's a prospectus and why do I need one?

**A:** A mutual fund prospectus is a formal document that mutual fund companies must provide to investors before accepting an investment into their fund. The prospectus outlines the objectives of the fund, its policies, its management, its past financial performance, and a complete rundown of all the expenses, fees, and charges associated with the fund. Investors should read the prospectus carefully before investing (especially the part about fees and expenses).

### Strong Funds
**http://www.strong-funds.com**

Featuring their family of no-load funds, Strong Funds provides on this attractive site nearly everything an investor needs to know about investing in funds. Besides daily prices, fund profiles, and downloadable prospectuses, surfers can listen to a Real Audio market report, updated three times each

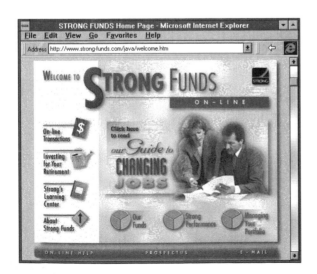

day. The Strong Learning Center provides interactive tools—quizzes and calculators to help you understand how to best meet your financial goals. Each month, one of Strong's fund managers tackles an investor's question in "Ask the Portfolio Manager." Online access for Strong shareholders is also provided.

### SunAmerica Mutual Funds
**http://www.sunamerica.com/products/mutfunds.htm**

SunAmerica is a financial services firm that specializes in retirement savings products. Their family of 12 mutual funds is available from financial advisors and brokers across the country, but you won't find any information about the funds on their Web site, beyond this brief list.

### Third Avenue Value Fund
**http://www.mjwhitman.com**

Martin J. Whitman's Third Avenue Value Fund is a value-oriented fund with a long-term perspective. His site provides a capsule profile of the fund, including top holdings and sectors, as well as an online prospectus and application forms.

### The Timothy Plan
**http://www.timothyplan.com**

The Timothy Plan is a so-called "morally responsible" fund that avoids investing in companies involved in certain activities identified by several Christian ministries as immoral. The site provides a fund profile, report on portfolio holdings, current NAV, and downloadable prospectus for the Timothy Plan, as well as a list of brokers who sell the fund on a strictly commission basis.

## T. Rowe Price Funds
http://www.troweprice.com

T. Rowe Price offers a variety of free services on their Web site, from a personalized mutual fund watch list to free stock quotes. Investors can get complete information on T. Rowe Price funds, including profiles, daily prices, and performance information, and then download or request a fund prospectus. The site also includes plenty of educational material related to fund investing and retirement planning, perfect for beginners and helpful to experienced investors. Information is also provided on the company's discount brokerage services.

## Touchstone Funds
http://www.touchstonefunds.com

Touchstone provides applications, prospectuses, and annual reports for its funds in Acrobat or HTML format, as well as daily NAVs and manager profiles.

## Van Eck Global Mutual Funds
http://www.vaneck.com

Van Eck's funds focus on global opportunities, particularly in Asia, and hard assets, such as gold. Their site describes each portfolio's manager, holdings and performance, and offers downloadable prospectuses. However, the information is not conveniently organized, and there are no profiles of the individual funds.

## Vanguard Mutual Funds
http://www.vanguard.com

This elegantly organized site is a perfect example of how companies can effectively use the Internet as a business tool to convey information to both potential and current clients. The site is easy to navigate, and the graphics enhance the site without becoming overbearing. Areas of the site are devoted to five topics or functions, with Vanguard's mutual funds at the center. Fund profiles are thickly layered with detailed information, written in "plain English," and with easy access to online or downloadable prospectuses. Planning Tools offers interactive, online tools to help determine your investment personality and plan for retirement. The Education Center is a top-notch resource for novice investors interested in learning about investing. The Vanguard Group is a leader in keeping fund operating expenses low, and the site reflects Vanguard's personality—it's not frivolous, to the point, and very rewarding.

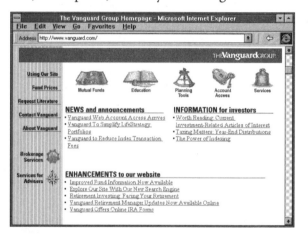

## Waddell & Reed, Inc.
http://www.waddell.com

Investors can review information about the more than 20 funds available from the United Group and Waddell & Reed Mutual Funds at this site. A very brief profile of each fund is available, as well as daily price updates for the entire family, but you'll have to ask for a prospectus to be sent by mail if you'd like any further details.

### WWW Internet Fund

http://www.internetfund.com

The WWW Internet Fund was the first fund to invest solely in stocks of companies participating in the Internet industry. The site provides an online brochure, prospectus, account application, and information about the fund advisor and investment strategy, as well as daily NAV updates and performance comparisons to the Internet indices.

### Zaske, Sarafa & Associates Funds

http://www.zsa.com

Zaske, Sarafa & Associates, a Michigan-based financial advisor, offers a no-load Asset Allocation Fund that seeks growth and income. The site offers a prospectus by mail to users who make a request from their feedback form.

# BONDS

No matter who issues it—public corporations, the U.S. Treasury, or local governments—a bond is really nothing more than an IOU, a promise by the issuer to pay back the debt at a future date and to pay interest along the way. Investors seeking income usually turn to bonds, building a portfolio based on a desired yield and individual risk tolerance. Bond investors have many options from which to choose.

The U.S. government is considered by many to be the most reliable borrower in the world. That is why

## MUTUAL FUND GLOSSARY

12b-1 FEES—Charges paid by shareholders for marketing and distribution costs.

DISTRIBUTION—A payment of dividends, capital gains, and other income made to shareholders of a mutual fund.

INDEX FUND—A mutual fund that attempts to match the performance of a particular market index (like the Standard & Poor's 500 Index) by holding the same securities as that index.

INVESTMENT TRUST—Commonly known as a closed-end fund. Closed-end funds invest in other securities (like a mutual fund does) but have a fixed number of shares and are traded similarly to stocks. The market price may exceed the net asset value (NAV) per share, in which case the fund is selling at a *premium*. When the market price falls below the NAV, the fund is selling at a *discount*.

LOAD—Commission charged by a fund to buyers of its shares. Some funds charge a back-end load when shareholders sell their holdings in the fund.

MUTUAL FUND—An open-ended investment company that manages a portfolio of securities and offers shares to investors. Shares are issued and redeemed as per demand, and the fund's Net Asset Value per share is determined each day.

NET ASSET VALUE—Abbreviated as NAV, this is the value of a mutual fund's investments, calculated each day, and usually expressed as a per share amount.

PROSPECTUS—A formal written statement that discloses the terms of a public offering of a security or a mutual fund. The prospectus is required to divulge particular essential information to investors about the proposed offering.

SECTOR FUNDS—Mutual funds that invest in a specific industry or market sector.

TAX-FREE FUNDS—Bond funds that pay tax-free distributions to shareholders by investing in municipal bonds. Generally suitable for people in the highest tax brackets despite their lower yields.

the 30-year Treasury bond is known as the *benchmark* by which all other bonds are measured. U.S. Treasury bonds provide maximum safety.

State and local governments often issue their own bonds to pay for schools, highways, or construction projects. These are known as *municipal bonds*, and they are often exempt from federal, state, and/or local taxes. Due to the tax exemption, the interest rate offered by municipal bonds may be somewhat lower than comparable corporate bonds.

Some corporations issue bonds in lieu of bank loans to finance their growth. Corporate bonds are riskier than government bonds, but usually offer higher yields.

Government agencies can also use bonds to raise funds. The best known agency bonds are *mortgage-backed bonds* offered by Ginnie Mae, Freddie Mac, and Fannie Mae. These bonds are backed by pools of mortgages and offer both higher risk and higher interest rates than government bonds.

But aren't bonds boring? Not on these Web sites, where investors can find expert analysis, data, and information on fixed-income securities. While the bond market is still dominated by institutional investors, there are a number of resources directed at individual investors, too.

## The Blue List

http://www.bluelist.com

This division of Standard & Poor's publishes the primary source of municipal and corporate bond offerings in the U.S. Each day, an online print version of *The Blue List* publication is available by subscription on the Web, providing information on over 8,000 municipal and corporate bond offerings. Visitors can get a taste of the service via a demonstration area, as well as yield scales, commentary, and other live reports.

## Bonds Online

http://www.bondsonline.com

Twenty-First Century Municipals, Inc. sponsors Bonds Online, a collection of links, articles, and commentary about Treasury, corporate, and municipal bonds, as well as bond funds. Have a question about fixed income investing? Ask the Bond Professor and you may get an answer! (It does appear he's been on sabbatical lately; the Frequently Asked Questions list is a pretty good substitute, however.) Regular commentary from such distinguished names as Bondtrac, Fitch Investors Service, and Interactive Data Corp., as well as yield curves, educational articles, and a bond map to search for municipal offerings in your state, combine to make this a good stop for bond investors.

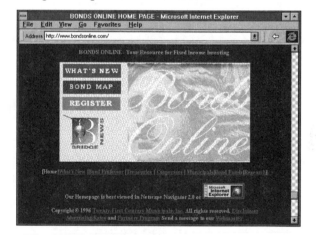

## Bondtrac, Inc.

http://www.bondtrac.com

Bondtrac's services are available by subscription to licensed broker/dealers only. Bondtrac provides information on the municipal, corporate, and government bond markets, listing the inventories of hundreds of broker/dealers. The Web site allows users to search for bond offerings that meet particular criteria.

Unlike stockholders, who are the owners of a corporation, bondholders are creditors who must be repaid. That means that if a company goes bust, bondholders have a better chance of getting a piece of what's left of a company's assets (which might not be much, but it's a lot more than common stockholders would receive).

## BradyNet Inc.

**http://www.bradynet.com**

Brady Bonds are relatively new securities, made up of loan debt from countries in Asia, Africa, Eastern Europe, and Latin America. BradyNet is the self-proclaimed pioneer provider of Brady Bond information through the Internet. Users can get free daily pricing and yields of Brady bonds, Eurobonds, exotics, short-term instruments, Mexican Peso forward markets, South African bonds, and other indices. There's also lots of commentary from traders and dealers about Brady markets and events that affect them. A number of discussion boards provide investors with an outlet to ask questions and share research with other Brady Bond investors.

## Bureau of the Public Debt Savings Bonds

**http://www.publicdebt.treas.gov/ sav/sav.htm**

If you want information about U.S. Savings Bonds, it makes sense to go right to the source. This site at the Bureau of the Public Debt is a comprehensive resource for information on Savings Bonds, including buying them, calculating their value, and redeeming them. The site also includes the Savings Bond Wizard, a free Windows program that calculates current

redemption value and earned interest and generates inventory reports of bonds you own.

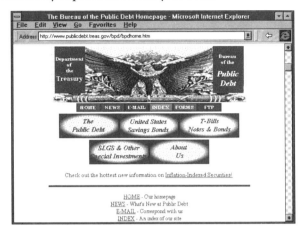

## Bureau of the Public Debt T-Bills, Notes, and Bonds

**http://www.publicdebt.treas.gov/sec/sec.htm**

The Bureau of the Public Debt offers information about inflation-indexed securities; upcoming Treasury Note, Bond, and Bill auctions, and past results; details on the Treasury Direct program; and answers to common questions about T-Bills and other federal issue bonds.

## Capital Access Corp

**http://www.interactive.net/~cac**

Capital Access provides consulting, market research, and data resources for fixed-income issuers, underwriters, broker/dealers, and market-makers. The company publishes the annual *Derivatives Desk Reference* in book form or on CD-ROM.

## Chapman Securities, Inc.

**http://www.tyrell.net/~munis/**

Full-service investment firm specializing in tax-free municipal bond investing, located in the Kansas City area and specializing in municipal bonds in Kansas and Missouri. Explanations of bond swapping, laddered maturities strategies, and a glossary of terms are available on the site.

## Cutter & Co. Brokerage, Inc.
http://www.stocktrader.com

Cutter & Co. is a discount broker with a nice collection of resources for bond investors. They provide a daily chart of the U.S. Treasury Yield Curve and a monthly chart of the long-term Treasury Bond yields, along with some articles on the risks of the bond market.

## Duff & Phelps Credit Rating Co.
http://www.dcrco.com

Duff & Phelps is a credit rating agency that provides ratings and research on bond offerings and other corporate financing vehicles. This site offers a Rating Guide of U.S. and international companies' corporate bonds, preferred stock, and other debt issues, which includes S&P and Moody's ratings as well as Duff & Phelphs's; a list of all rating changes in the past 90 days; and a list of all companies on a ratings watch. Users can download, in Adobe Acrobat format, the most recent edition of *Credit Decisions*, their weekly news publication focusing on fixed income markets around the world.

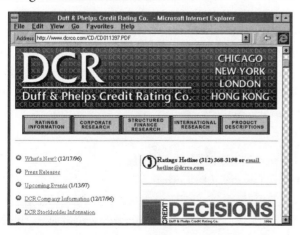

## E-Muni (Electronic Municipal Statistics)
http://www.emuni.com

Electronic Municipal Statistics (E-Muni) is an organization that provides documents, news, developments, and financial information about the municipal bond market. Their Web site contains an assortment of free resources for muni bond investors. An Electronic Library contains data pertaining to municipal bond issuers and issues, accessible alphabetically or by CUSIP. Articles reprinted from other publications and a glossary are also included.

## Federal Reserve Bank of New York
http://www.ny.frb.org

Treasury Direct is a program that provides investors the opportunity to purchase Treasury securities (bills, notes, and bonds) directly from the Federal Reserve Bank or the U.S. Treasury Department. The New York Reserve Bank provides detailed instructions and information about the program, along with recent Treasury auction results and dates. Web investors can print out tender forms for the Treasury Direct program that can be mailed with payment. The site also includes information about U.S. Savings Bonds.

## First Chicago Capital Markets
http://www.fccm.com

First Chicago Capital Markets is one of the nation's leading tax-exempt bond dealers, specializing in underwriting debt securities. Unfortunately, most of the Research, Deals, Forecasts, and Current Events on the site had not been updated in more than two months, limiting its usefulness.

Investors can buy Treasury Bills, Notes, and Bonds with no commission charges directly from the U.S. Treasury via the Treasury Direct program (although there is a $25 annual maintenance fee for investors who hold over $100,000 of bills, notes, or bonds). Individuals must submit a *non-competitive tender* indicating how many bills, notes, or bonds they wish to purchase along with a check for the full par value of the bonds. On auction day, the Treasury first fills all competitive bids, mainly from institutional investors, starting with those closest to par value, until the quota is filled. Then it averages all the accepted bids and sells bills to non-competitive bidders at that price, refunding the difference.

## First Miami Securities, Inc.
http://www.firstmiami.com

First Miami Securities, a broker specializing in fixed income investments, offers several free services on their Web site. Their Muni-Trac system provides e-mailed portfolio reports for investors interested in tracking their municipal bonds. Online forms let users ask for lists of bond offerings, information on particular offerings, or free publications of interest such as their *Bond Talk* quarterly newsletter (which, unfortunately, isn't available online). They do provide tables and charts on their site that list current yield rates for AAA, AA, and A-Rated bonds in 10-, 20-, and 30-year maturity ranges.

## Fitch Investors Service L.P.
http://www.fitchinv.com

Fitch is a credit rating agency that provides ratings and research on taxable and tax-exempt bond issues. Investors will find lists of recent rating actions the company has taken on issues in municipal and corporate markets and an index of reports Fitch has released, updated quarterly. Free four-week trials are available for a few of the company's services.

## Fixed Income Investment Research
http://www.well.com/user/tonydelo/

Over 200 daily reports for institutional bond investors, from Strategic Investment Consultants.

## GovPX, Inc.
http://www.panix.com/~govpx

GovPX is a wholesale provider of Treasury market data to many distributors. However, visitors can study a quarterly report on the Treasury market issued by the company.

## Government Financial Advisors, Inc.
http://www.gfa.com

This firm serves as an advisor to local governments who are raising capital in the debt markets, primarily in Florida. Their Web site offers some rather outdated information about offerings in Florida.

## C.W. Henderson & Associates, Inc.
http://www.cwhenderson.com

This investment counseling firm specializes in tax-exempt municipal securities and provides surfers with a bit of free short and incisive market commentary, as well as a good-sized list of Frequently Asked Questions (with answers, of course). If you already own a few munis, Henderson will provide a complimentary analysis of your current portfolio.

## Jones Hall Hill & White
http://www.jhhw.com

This law firm's practice is specifically focused on serving local governments in connection with their municipal bond and financing needs. Their Web site includes a number of technical articles about legal issues surrounding municipal debt issuance and related matters.

### Lebenthal & Co., Inc.
**http://www.lebenthal.com**

Need a good idea for your municipal bond portfolio? Check out the "Bond of the Week" on Lebenthal's Web site. The leading municipal bond broker, Lebenthal & Co., also provides a glossary of bond terms, an up-to-date issue of their newsletter and daily lists of the firm's bond inventory. Don't miss "Gammon's Economic Outlook," regularly updated forecasts from the president of Lebenthal Asset Management.

### Legg Mason, Inc.
**http://www.leggmason.com**

Legg Mason is an investment firm and broker, and their site provides information primarily related to stocks and funds. Their article, "How To Create A Bond Ladder," is worth a look by bond investors, however.

**ask doug!**

**Q:** What's a *bond ladder*?

**A:** A bond ladder contains a number of bonds that mature in successive years, to protect the portfolio owner from adverse changes in the bond yields. For instance, a ten-year laddered portfolio would have bonds that mature in each of the next ten years. Each year, when a bond matures, the investor then buys a new ten-year bond to maintain the ten-year ladder. The advantage of this strategy is that the investor gets a ten-year maturity interest rate, but with just an average five-year maturity. Any changes in the interest rate are averaged out over time. While you can do this yourself, at least somewhat through the Treasury Direct program, it's a lot easier and not that expensive to have your bank or broker handle the laddered transactions.

### MMRSoftware's EEBond
**http://www.mmrsoft.com**

EEBond, for Windows or DOS, maintains a complete database of all your Series EE and Series E Savings Bonds and U.S. Savings Notes. It includes all savings bonds from 1942 to the present. You can also compute the values of your Series EE Savings Bonds at MMRSoftware's Web site, using their online calculator. Updated savings bond valuation tables for the software are available.

### MoneyLine Corporation
**http://www.moneyline.com**

MoneyLine provides real-time information on fixed income markets to a subscription clientele composed mainly of financial professionals. Their services cover

Pay close attention to credit ratings if you're investing in municipal or corporate bonds, for these ratings have a big impact on a bond's return. A bond with lower credit quality will provide a higher return, but you must be able to tolerate the additional risk of the issuer being late with interest payments or even defaulting on the bond.

Another factor that you should consider when determining the income you can realize from your bond investments is your own time frame. Bonds with longer maturities usually have higher yields, but the underlying value of the asset or fund will be more volatile. Bonds with shorter average maturities provide less income, but are more stable in the near term. Make sure your investing horizon matches the bonds you purchase.

U.S. Treasury bonds, notes and bills, Agencies, money markets, corporate bonds, emerging markets, and other fixed income securities. Web site visitors will find their free Bond School, a series of educational lessons and glossary, to be a very good primer on fixed income investing.

### Moody's Investor Service
http://www.moodys.com

Moody's is a leading provider of credit ratings, research, and financial information about capital markets. Their Web site features an array of free services for investors, including a searchable database of rating actions and featured rating actions; executive summaries and/or full reports of recent credit research issued by Moody's; and expert commentary on the credit markets. Investors should definitely check out the information about Moody's approach and process of making credit ratings.

### J.P. Morgan & Co., Inc.
http://www.jpmorgan.com

The Web site of this major investment bank offers some interesting research for bond investors. For instance, users can peruse *Government Bond Markets Outline*, a reference manual of information about bond issues made by 16 countries; or *The Govern-*

*ment Bond Index Monitor*, a summary of J.P. Morgan's monthly analysis of world government bond markets (in Acrobat format). Similar information is available for emerging markets bond indices. Users can also download daily and historical data sets of global bond indices.

### The Munibond Guy
http://www.themunibondguy.com

Marco T. Godwin is The Munibond Guy, a California broker who specializes in fixed income investments. Surfers can check out Selected Bond Offerings or Bond Offerings of the Week (corporate and municipal). An interactive form lets you request bids on your current holdings.

### municipal.com
http://www.municipal.com

This Web-based service from financial publisher R.R. Donnelley Financial provides data for and about the municipal securities industry. Access to the Municipal Securities Disclosure Archive is available by subscription, but investors can download in Acrobat format current and past issues of *Moody's Municipal & Government News Reports*" for free. These reports cover more than 9,000 bond issuing municipalities and government agencies.

## National Association of Bond Lawyers
http://www.nabl.org/nabl/

This group of attorneys works in the field of law relating to state and municipal bonds and other obligations. On their Web site, they provide a list of publications and upcoming seminars and workshops.

## Northwest Municipal Information Corporation
http://www.bondbyte.com

Northwest Municipal Information (NMI) publishes *Bond Byte*, an online reporting service offering investors information on municipal bonds in the Pacific Northwest. The Forum section of their site includes a few articles on various aspects of the bond market in the region.

## Nuveen Research
http://www.nuveenresearch.com

John Nuveen & Co. maintains the largest research department in the industry devoted to the analysis of tax-exempt securities. Their Web site is overflowing with research reports, on topics such as Municipal Credit Information, Investment Strategies, and Bond Market Comments. Users can also access New Issue Summaries or download prospectuses for Nuveen's tax-free mutual funds.

 While it's possible to invest in bonds directly, it's probably a whole lot easier for most investors to go through a broker or a bond mutual fund. A bond fund can potentially offer a better rate of return with less risk by diversifying and adjusting the fund's average maturity, while providing much greater liquidity.

## The Odd Lot Machine
http://www.oddlot.com

From Daiwa Securities America Inc. comes "the oldest and largest automated fixed income trading system." This unique site is designed to provide an efficient and cost effective method for trading U. S. Treasury securities in amounts less than $10 million. Daiwa account holders require telnet client software to access the system.

## PC Trader
http://www.fixedincome.com

PC Trader, from Market Broadcasting Corp., provides real-time 24-hour coverage of treasuries, foreign exchange, and currency markets on the Internet. The subscription-based service uses a separate Windows program to deliver market news and real-time fixed income quotes. Visitors to the PC Trader Web site can check out current headlines and Treasury bond and bill quotes.

## Piper Jaffray
http://www.piperjaffray.com

Piper Jaffray is a full-service investment firm, and among its free offerings for Web surfers interested in the bond markets are monthly economic commentary, a muni-bond calendar, weekly interest rate report, and daily fixed income market commentary.

## Prudential Securities

**http://www.prusec.com**

Prudential Securities, the full-service broker, has appointed a "virtual financial advisor" to lead visitors through their site, giving visitors a selection of articles on many investing topics. If you're interested in bonds, you can peruse the article "Why Invest in Fixed-Income Securities?" and continue with explanatory discussions of U.S. Treasury securities, municipal bonds, certificates of deposit, zero-coupon bonds, and mortgage-backed securities. Each trading day, you can get morning, afternoon, and closing bond market commentary, or order a copy of *MuniPulse*, with Prudential's insights to the municipal bond marketplace.

## Public Securities Association

**http://www.psa.com**

The Public Securities Association is the bond market trade association. Their Web site presents an extensive collection of data, statistics, links, news, and reports relating to regulatory and legal issues. Their Research Desk is the bond investor's best bet, however—it's filled with freely downloadable reports and tables.

## PublicFinance

**http://www.publicfinance.com**

When launched, this site promises to offer disclosure documents for municipal securities and related economic and financial data for state and municipal governments throughout the United States and Canada.

## Ryan Labs, Inc.

**http://www.ryanlabs.com**

It's an age-old match-up: the battle of stocks vs. bonds. And Ryan Labs is the scorekeeper in the stock/bond game, tracking total returns for the S&P 500

Be aware of credit risks when investing in bonds. Two factors affect yields: a borrower's credit quality and the bond's maturity. So-called "junk" bonds, also known as non-investment-grade bonds, are of lower credit quality and so offer higher yields to compensate investors for the added risk that the company may be late with interest or principal payments or default on the bond altogether. As a result, if a bond's yield is rising and its price is falling, and interest rates overall are not rising, it may be an indicator that a company's financial situation is worsening. Don't chase after high yields without understanding the real risks involved.

Index vs. the 15-year Treasury Strip and publishing the results on their Web site (and in other venues). You may be surprised at the results. Ryan Labs is a fixed income research and investment management company specializing in government bonds.

## Standard & Poor's Ratings Services

**http://www.ratings.standardpoor.com**

Standard & Poor's Ratings Services is the largest global bond rating agency, specializing in evaluating credit risks in the world's capital markets. Users can freely download Acrobat editions of *Corporate Ratings Criteria* and *Municipal Finance Criteria*, publications that highlight the key areas of S&P's ratings analysis. Or, check out recent Credit Wire announcements of newly assigned ratings.

## Stone & Youngberg LLC

**http://www.styo.com**

This California investment bank specializes in underwriting local government debt, buying and selling municipal bonds, and managing government, individual and corporate investment portfolios. The firm provides weekly market commentary on their Web site or through a free e-mail subscription.

## The Syndicate: Bonds
http://www.moneypages.com/syndicate/bonds/

The bonds section of this general investing reference site features a bond glossary and articles on topics such as "The Anatomy of a Bond Swap" and "Buying at the Treasury Auction."

## Thomson MarketEdge
http://www.marketedge.com

A division of global financial company Thomson Financial, the subscription-based MarketEdge features

a Municipal Bond Center. Members can access *Regional Review*, news and analysis from the municipal markets, including a regional review of activity, supplied by The Bond Buyer. An excellent *Municipal Bond Guide* addresses most of the common questions, designed to introduce novices to bond investing.

## Thomson Municipal Market Monitor
http://www.tm3.com

Thomson brings together nearly all of the most-respected names in the municipal bond industry for this online service geared for municipal bond professionals. Subscribers get access to continuously updated municipal news, leading market indices, and U.S. Treasuries and money markets. They also get data analysis from Muller Data/MuniView,

## BOND GLOSSARY

BOND—A bond is a promise made by the government or a corporation to repay funds loaned by investors at a specific rate by a specific date.

CALLABLE BOND—A bond that can be redeemed by its issuer before the date of full maturity.

COUPON RATE—A bond's interest rate.

DEBT FINANCING—A company can raise working capital by issuing bonds or notes to individuals or institutions, along with a promise to pay interest as well as to repay the principal. The other major way of raising capital is to issue shares of stock in a public offering.

INTEREST RATE—The percentage of a bond's par value paid on a regular basis.

MATURITY—The date when a bond is due to be repaid.

MUNICIPAL BOND—Munis are issued by local governments and are exempt from federal income taxes. State and city governments also exempt the

interest from their own muni bonds from taxes for their own citizens.

PAR VALUE—The dollar amount of a bond that will be repaid at maturity.

STRIP—Also known as a zero-coupon bond. Issued by the U.S. Treasury, Strips pay no interest while the bond is maturing. Instead, they pay a lump sum at maturity.

TREASURY BILLS—T-Bills are short-term securities issued in 3-, 6-, or 12-month maturities, with a minimum par value of $10,000.

TREASURY BONDS AND NOTES—T-Notes and T-Bonds are long-term issues with maturities of two to ten years and greater.

YIELD—The return on investment.

ZERO COUPON BONDS—Instead of paying interest in installments, zeros pay a lump-sum at maturity.

Municipal Market Data, CDA Spectrum, CDA Wiesenberger; and they get additional services from Dalcomp and Red Book.

## Treasury Direct
### http://www.publicdebt.treas.gov/sec/ sectrdir.htm

Treasury Direct is the program operated by the U.S. Department of the Treasury to provide investors the opportunity to buy T-Bills, Bonds, and Notes directly from the Treasury. The Treasury Department's site outlines all the steps necessary to participate, including opening an investor account; prices, rates, and yields; completing and submitting a tender; and an online form to order the necessary applications and other paperwork.

## Wall Street Net
### http://www.netresource.com/wsn/

This free service allows investors to search for financial deals (stock offerings, new bond issues, or any other financial instrument), by investment bank, instrument type, industry, coupon rate, or share value. Wall Street Net's monitoring service will send e-mail notification of new deals in the industry or by the bank of your choice.

## Winstar Government Securities Co.
### http://www.winstarsecurities.com

Winstar is a major market maker for over 400 U.S. Treasury Bills, Notes, Bonds, and Zero coupons for an institutional and brokerage firm clientele. An online discussion board is available for questions about government securities, as well as links to other information on the Web about the Treasury market.

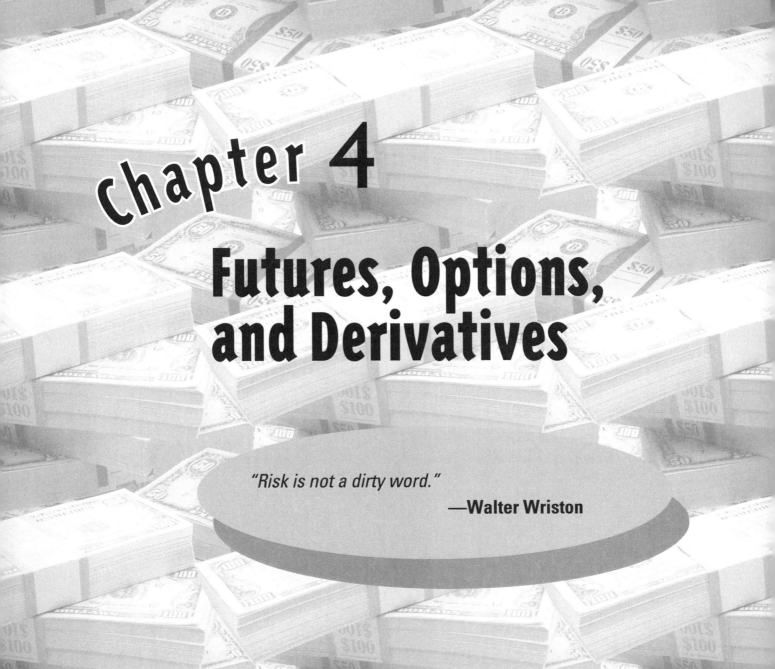

# Chapter 4
# Futures, Options, and Derivatives

*"Risk is not a dirty word."*

**—Walter Wriston**

**Today's commodities** extend much beyond the agricultural products and raw materials we traditionally think of when we hear the term. Besides pork bellies, you can find gold, silver, copper, palladium, sugar, coffee, frozen concentrate orange juice, black tiger shrimp, soybeans, corn, wheat, heating oil, natural gas, foreign currencies, Treasury bills and bonds, stock indices, and Government National Mortgage Association certificates (GNMAs), all trading on and off exchanges.

The Web can provide the educational tools, the advice, the news and data, and the brokers to let you explore the world of futures and options. But pay close attention—the structure of many of these vehicles is complex and the use of leverage increases your risk as well as your rewards.

# FUTURES, OPTIONS, AND DERIVATIVES

Need advice on trading commodities or options? Soothsayers abound on the Web, with pundits offering their systems and recommendations, for a price, of course. Or you can get the raw data for yourself and come up with your own approach. At any rate, here are the providers of software, newsletters, data, charts, and educational tools you can use in trading your favorite futures.

### Applied Derivatives Trading
### http://www.adtrading.com
Applied Derivatives Trading is a free monthly online magazine "written by derivative traders for derivative traders." Regular features include a beginner's column, book and software reviews, market commentary, and pithy editorial from

the U.K.-based publishers. "Jargon Solutions," their glossary of trading terms, is a nice addition.

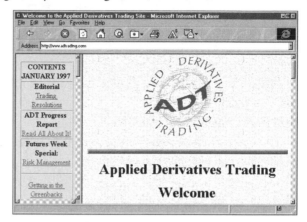

### Astrikos
### http://www.astrikos.com
Do you see your futures in your stars? This financial astrology site provides e-mail and fax newsletters that recommend stock, option, index option, and futures trades. The site also offers various articles on astrology and investing, stock reports, nightly forecasts, and a library of charts.

### Bruce Babcock's Reality Based Trading Company
### http://www.lloyd.com/~babcock
Babcock is a professional trader, the founder of Commondity Traders Consumer Reports and the

author of several books on commodity trading. His site includes a variety of his educational articles, a weekly trading idea, and a section entitled "Commodity Futures Trading for Beginners." For beginning commodity traders, this site is a must-see.

### The Barclay Group
**http://www.lisco.com/barclay**

This site, from the publisher of the Barclay Managed Futures Report, the Barclay Institutional Report, and the Barclay Hedge Fund Report, is directed mainly at the managed futures industry. An extensive library of publications is online, separated by area of interest: individual investors, institutional investors, or futures professionals.

### Jake Bernstein's Futures Web
**http://www.trade-futures.com**

Bernstein, a veteran futures trader and former psychologist, offers an impressive array of advice and commentary on this site, along with his catalog of his books, newsletters, software, and audio tapes. He also answers frequently asked questions from traders about futures.

### Gibbons Burke's Wahoo!
**http://www.io.com/~gibbonsb**

Burke writes "The Computerized Trader" column for *Futures Magazine* and archives back issues of his work on this site, along with spreadsheet templates and shareware mentioned in the articles. He also maintains a list of Internet resources for futures traders, dubbed "Wahoo!"

 Don't be fooled into thinking that you can protect yourself from an adverse price change just by placing a stop-loss order. A stop-loss order is a standing order for your broker to sell your position if the price drops below the stop price. However, commodity prices can quickly drop through your established price level with no chance for your stop order to be executed. Your losses could be much greater than you anticipated.

### Canadian Derivatives Clearing Corporation
**http://www.cdcc.ca**

Jointly owned by the Montreal, Toronto, and Vancouver stock exchanges, the CDCC guarantees the integrity of the Canadian derivative market. The site offers lists of Canadian options and other information about their organization.

### CISCO
**http://www.cisco-futures.com**

CISCO is a research, database, and trading company that offers futures and commodities data, as well as a home study course, "New Market Analysis." Don't expect glitz or glamour from this site's design, however—it's distinctively utilitarian.

### Club 3000—Commodity Traders Network
**http://ison.com/club3000**

This network of computerized commodity traders has been in existence for over 15 years, providing a forum for discussion of all aspects of commodity trading. Members contribute commentary to a newsletter published 20 times a year; a sample issue is online.

## Commodity Futures Trading Commission

**http://www.cftc.gov**

The Commodity Futures Trading Commission (CFTC) is the independent agency mandated by Congress to regulate commodity futures and option markets in the United States. Their very dry site includes transcripts of speeches by commissioners, news releases, details of enforcement actions, online editions of CFTC publications, statistical data, and information about filing claims against brokers for reparations.

## Commodity Traders Advice

**http://infomatch.com/~adas/adv.html**

This subscription service provides end-of-day updated quotes and charts on all futures and options commodities traded on U.S. markets, along with futures market analysis, agricultural weather reports, and specific daily trading recommendations.

## Commodity Traders Resource Center

**http://www.futures-trading.com**

This page provides links to news and quote services for commodity traders.

## The CommStock Report

**http://www.siouxlan.com/commstock**

From Iowa (where else?) comes The *CommStock Report*, a blend of commentary and market analysis aired on Iowa radio stations for years and described variously as the Mark Twain/Paul Harvey/Rush Limbaugh of commodities. Created by a full service commodities brokerage, the report is now available on the Internet for subscribers.

---

*the*
### swami speaks

You are in need of a shortcut, I see. This tip may save a few keystrokes in typing those extended URLs in your browser. If you're using a current version of Microsoft Explorer, you can omit the "http://" when typing in an address (instead of typing "http://www.investorama.com", you can simply type "www.investorama.com"). Netscape Navigator takes this time-saver one step further. Not only can you omit the http:// from the URL, but if the domain is a commercial site (with a .com extension) and uses the standard www. prefix, you can just type the domain name itself—for example, investorama—and Navigator will figure out the rest!

---

## CMA Reports from T. Young and Co., Inc.

**http://www.cyberfutures.com/cmareports**

*CMA Reports* is an online newsletter rating the performance of leading commodity trading advisors and managed futures programs for sophisticated investors. T. Young & Co. is one of the nation's oldest firms in the managed futures industry.

## CTS Financial Publishing

**http://cts.dearborn.com**

CTS offers charts and analysis for commodity options and futures and for stock options. From six product lines, subscribers can create the package that best fits their needs. All information is transmitted via the CTS Web site in Acrobat format.

One of the reasons commodities trading is so risky is that prices are volatile. Many factors affect the price of a commodity: weather, strikes, inflation, foreign exchange rates, new technology, politics, transportation, storage, natural disasters. All of these uncontrollable, unpredictable circumstances increase the risk that you won't realize a profit on a particular trade.

## Dynatach
http://www.dynatach.com

Dynatach provides trading systems that work with Omega Research, Inc.'s TradeStation software for trading commodities.

## The Edge
http://www.pnc.com.au/~mako

From Australia comes this professional pit trader's option trading and risk management program, The Edge. It's used extensively on and off the floors of the Sydney Futures Exchange.

## EzTrade
http://www.eztrade.com

The Java-based EzAnalyzer program automatically scans stock, futures, or index option trades, seeking those with the highest probability of success and the best risk/reward ratios. Subcribers can access EzTrade's extensive options pricing and volatility database, which is updated daily, to create graphs and determine the most profitable trades. The site also includes very helpful options tutorial and interactive learning tools for beginners.

## Frankfurt Money Strategist
http://www.fmstrategist.com/fms

The Frankfurt Money Strategist is a research report focusing on the German Bundesbank, aimed at global investors seeking a deeper understanding of Deutschmark and DM-linked currency, bond and derivatives markets, and the European Monetary Union. Weekly and monthly synopses appear on the Web site, and subscriptions are available for e-mailed versions in Acrobat format.

## FutureLook
http://www.wp.com/futurelook

FutureLook provides intraday analysis on five of the most active financial futures contracts. Java-based charts outline optimal entry/exit strategies to the end of day.

## Futures 101: An Introduction to Commodities Trading
http://www.xensei.com/users/squantum

This site provides information on an impartial beginner's book on how commodity markets work. The book is available for purchase online.

## Futures and Options Contracts Database
http://finance.wat.ch

This Web site from Switzerland provides a database of international futures and options contracts. Each contract datasheet provides specifications and descriptions, such as the underlying asset, trading dates, tick size, and value and currency it trades in. A directory of world stock and commodity exchanges is also available on the site.

One of the factors that makes commodities trading so risky is what also makes it so profitable when it works: leverage. To trade commodity futures, a customer needs to make only a relatively small cash outlay. This amount (the initial margin) controls a commodity futures contract worth a much larger amount of money. Just a small change in the price of the commodity has a much larger impact on the original investment, either leaving you with a terrific return or requiring you to ante up additional margin payments.

**ask doug!**

**Q:** What's the difference between European-style and American-style options?

**A:** An American-style option contract can be exercised prior to the expiration date. (All stock options are American-style, as are most other options that trade on an exchange.) A European-style option contract can only be exercised on the expiration date itself.

## The Futures Group
http://www.futures-trader.com

The Futures Group presents Scott Krieger's *How to Become a Realtime Commodity Futures Trader—From Home*, a popular A-Z guidebook used by both beginning and experienced traders. Also available are software add-ins for Omega TradeStation that follow the methodology outlined in the book.

## Future Options Pricing Made Easy
http://www.dirs.com/invest/shaw

This page advertises a pocket reference book to help you calculate option prices on futures using newspaper quotation tables. But you can't order online; you must print the order form and send it in with a check.

## Futures Magazine
http://www.futuresmag.com

The online edition of the magazine provides market and industry news, feature articles, and interviews from current and past issues. Futures Talk is their online discussion forum, and the Learning Center is their list of educational resources (books, software, videotapes, conferences).

## Futures Truth Company
http://www.ison.com/truth

Futures Truth reports the results of over 150 commodity trading systems, regularly updated for subscribers in their monthly newsletter. Detailed reports and private opinion letters on particular systems are also available for purchase. The site lists the Top Ten systems tracked by Futures Truth and a listing of all programs they follow. Before you purchase a trading system, it's worth checking out what Futures Truth has to say about it.

## FutureSource
http://www.futuresource.com

FutureSource is a real-time data and software vendor for the futures, options, and cash markets. Users can download demos of their software from the Web site and get delayed quotes on 20 contracts, as well as delayed news from *Future World News*.

### Harris-Mann Company
http://www.quiknet.com/harris

Come rain or shine, Harris-Mann specializes in medium-to-long range weather predictions for U.S. and international agriculture, as well as highly detailed forecasts for agricultural commodities and other markets. Daily reports are provided on the Web for subscribers, along with a quarterly printed edition. The firm also offers Elliott Wave technical futures market analysis.

### INO Global Markets
http://www.ino.com

This comprehensive site includes just about everything under the sun related to futures and options, including quotes and charts (intraday, daily, or weekly), industry news and events, daily market reports, calendars of events, and links to exchanges and industry organizations. INO offers on-line editions of newsletters covering financial markets and a market bookstore stocked with financial titles. A selection of feature articles highlights trading techniques and approaches. Don't forget to click on Rover's Home Page for a selection of "free stuff," offers, and trial subscriptions to various services and products.

### Intraday Dynamics
http://www.intraday.com

The Daily Technical Review is Intraday Dynamics's daily market information service for professional futures traders. The site aims to provide floor traders and short-term speculators with a commentary, support and resistance numbers, and Intraday Dynamics's own proprietary time frames. Free historical futures charts are available on the site for all users.

### Investment Crossroads
http://www.investaweather.com/investaweather

Roemer Weather, Inc. offers a monthly newsletter and a daily weather service for commodities traders, employing global agricultural and energy commodity weather analysis. Forecasts are based on detailed meteorological analysis, using satellite and computer technology, as well as one hundred years of historical and cyclical data. Non-subscribers can access several articles for free on the site each month, including "Ask Weather Jim," a weather advice column.

### Investment Enhancing Systems, Inc.
http://www.ies-invest.com

Though most options are thought to be "risky," Investment Enhancing Systems (IES) claims that covered-call options are effective, conservative hedges that can be used to improve investment returns. Their Windows-based software steps through the analysis and selection of specific stocks suitable for covered-call options writing. Each month, three stocks analyzed with their covered-call options software are presented on the Web site for consideration. If you're unfamiliar with covered-call options, read through their "Short Course," a thorough but succinct explanation.

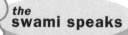

### the swami speaks

On the Web, just as with your investments, you must sometimes learn to backtrack. Pages on Web sites change frequently, so sometimes the URL you've discovered for a particular page won't work. If the address you've got for a Web site returns the dreaded "File Not Found" message to your browser, delete the end of the URL back to the nearest slash character (/) and press the Enter key on your keyboard. If your browser still doesn't display a page, delete the next bit of the URL to the next slash and keep going until you get to any working page. Then try navigating to the location of the new page, if you can.

## Investment Reference
**http://home.earthlink.net/~irfutures/**

Investment Reference is a teaching and consulting firm for professionals in the futures industry. They offer classes and document preparation to assist candidates in taking the Series 3 National Commodity Futures Exam, as well as consulting for existing firms with an emphasis on compliance. A few articles and a short question-and-answer column are available for visitors.

## Ipso Facto Daily Commodity Trade Recommendations
**http://www.ipso-facto.com**

Olympic Research, Inc. presents Ipso Facto ("by the fact itself"), a commodity trading and daily recommendation page. The trading portfolio analyzes on a daily basis 32 U.S. futures markets with three distinct technical trading systems. Directed at speculators,

the advisory service is free, with charts, seasonal tables, and contract specifications all nicely presented.

## LimitUp!, the Futures Trading Simulator
**http://members.aol.com/vqlabs**

Before you jump into the commodities trading pits, perhaps you should try your hand at LimitUp!, a shareware program from Vision Quest Labs. This futures trading simulator is a good tool for beginners to use to learn about commodities. Once you understand how futures trading works, you can use it to practice trading multiple markets in real or compressed time. A sample chapter from "Futures Shock: An Introduction to Commodities Trading" provides good reading.

## Managed Futures Association
**http://www.mfahome.com**

The Managed Futures Association (MFA) is a membership organization of professionals who provide investment services to clients around the world. The latest edition of their newsletter, *MFA Reporter*, is online, along with information about the Association and its activities.

## Market Research, Inc.
**http://www.barchart.com**

The Daily Market Service from Market Research, Inc. (MRI) gives subscribers access to more than 650 bar charts with five underlying studies. Also offered are 18 months of data in over 60 futures markets, trending information, daily prices and statistics in futures and options, weekly charts, price movers, and daily and weekly chart books for downloading and printing. Samples of all charts and data are available.

## Market Systems Newsletter

**http://www.ison.com/mktsys/**

Greg Meadors has published his stock market timing guide for ten years, using technical analysis, cycles and scientific methods to give short-term recommendations for trading the S&P 500 and OEX Options. Investors can subscribe to the newsletter or call the MRI hotline for updates.

## Paul McKnight's Scale Trading Information Page

**http://www.best.com/~au/psm/scaling.htm**

Scale trading is a method of buying and selling commodity futures, and trader McKnight has assembled a collection of links and resources for traders interested in this technique. He also provides some of his own writings on the topic.

## Monthly Profits

**http://www.napanet.net/vi/monthlyprofits**

Monthly Profits explains the technique of writing covered calls and helps investors use it through a trading manual, monthly newsletter, and an e-mail service. You can learn more about this technique, and their services, at the optimistically named Monthly Profits site.

## NetPicks Stock Option Investment Advisory

**http://www.netpicks.holowww.com**

If you're an aggressive trader, NetPicks's advisory service claims to be designed to yield triple digit annual returns. Focusing exclusively on stock option trading, the service provides subscribers with a daily Interactive Portfolio, updated via e-mail. Visitors can sign up for a free two-week trial.

## NumaWeb

**http://www.numa.com**

Numa Financial Services has built a complete derivative resource center on the Web. Among the vast array of information and utilities included on the site are calculators to analyze options; convertible bonds and warrants; an interactive guide that teaches how to place futures and options trades; an expert system that evaluates options strategies; a derivatives bookshop; and libraries of derivatives-oriented shareware and spreadsheets. Be sure to check out NumaWeb's derivatives FAQ and dictionary of over 200 Derivatives Acronyms.

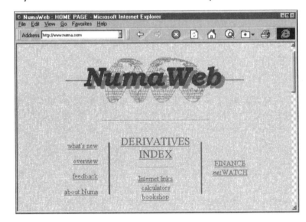

## The Office for Futures and Options Research

**http://w3.ag.uiuc.edu/ACE/ofor/aboutofor.html**

Based at the University of Illinois at Urbana-Champaign, the Office for Futures and Options Research (OFOR) promotes scholarly research on futures, options, and derivative markets. Their site includes working papers by faculty members, reading lists, links to related Web sites, and information about their undergraduate and graduate programs.

## Prophet Time Systems

http://www.wwa.com/~ron1/ptimer

Prophet Time provides subscription-based timing analysis for actively traded futures, using time to determine entry/exit periods. But be warned—the site is a frenetic jumble of animation and graphics.

## The Option Fool

http://optionpage.com/fool.htm

Hubert Lee is The Option Fool, a self-styled "zealous debunker of classic Wall Street mysticism and secrecy." Lee publishes a free e-mail newsletter focusing on options trading, where he humorously knocks down the over-hyped snake oil salesmen on Wall Street, while providing down-to-earth commentary and instruction to an eager audience. He also reviews software and books, and offers copies of his book, *Dear Option Fool*. After you've checked out his archives of questions and answers, it's practically guranteed that you'll want to join the mailing list!

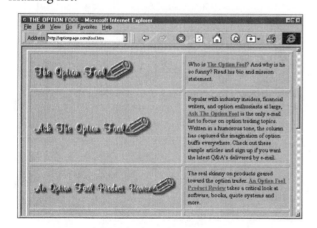

## The Option Page

http://www.optionpage.com

The Option Page is a guide to educational and trading resources, with a list of hotlinks pointing to content by option theorists, professional traders,

writers, and other experts. It's a good starting point for investors interested in trading options.

## The Option Strategist

http://www.dirs.com/invest/tos/

This page is home of Lawrence G. McMillan, author of the book, *Options as a Strategic Investment*. It provides information on his newsletters *Daily Volume Alert*, a fax alert focusing on stock trading, and *The Option Strategist*, a printed publication directed at equity, index, and futures options. Excerpts and samples are available on the site.

## The Options Industry Council

http://www.optionscentral.com

The Options Industry Council is comprised of the five U.S. exchanges that list options. The site provides delayed options trades and quotes, a directory of publications, software and educational resources to help investors learn about options trading, and answers to frequently asked questions about options. Don't miss the Strategy of the Month, an article that discusses a particular technique of option trading.

## PitStar BBS Quote Page

http://www.serve.com/pady

This free site provides daily listings of 77 commodity futures, available by e-mail or on the Web site.

## Prophet Information Services, Inc.

http://www.prophetdata.com

Prophet Information Services is a leading provider of charts and data going back to 1959. Subscribers get access to tens of thousands of up-to-date historical charts on futures from around the world. CD-ROMs of historical data on nearly 250 worldwide markets are also available. Subscribers can receive daily e-mail data updates or retrieve them from

**ask doug!**

**Q:** What is hedging?

**A:** Have you heard of the saying, "hedging your bet?" Well, it's not much different in the world of finance. Hedging is a risk-management technique to help protect the value of assets in a portfolio and limit opportunity losses. If you held Treasury Bonds and thought that interest rates would decline in the future (thus lowering the value of your bonds), you might sell (go short) U.S. Treasury bond futures. If rates do rise, your futures will provide a gain to help offset the loss on the value of the bonds in your portfolio. If rates don't rise, the increase in the value of the bonds makes up for your loss on the futures contracts.

Prophet's FTP server or via the Web. Visitors can sample back-adjusted continuous futures contracts on nearly any commodity for free. If it's data you're after, Prophet surely has what you need!

## Robert's Online Applications
**http://www.intrepid.com/~robertl**

Dr. Robert Lum has built a number of interactive applications, some using Java, to price options, derivatives, and loans and commissions, among others. The user inputs the variables into the applets, and the program calculates the results.

## Strasser Futures
**http://www.strasser.com**

Strasser Futures has a full catalog of educational products on commodities trading, including books,

charting software, and videotapes. The company also offers seminars, courses, and complete trading systems. The Web site has articles on commodity trading and Strasser's monthly newsletter.

## TradeComp International
**http://tribeca.ios.com/~tradecmp**

TradeComp is a fee-based simulated futures brokerage firm where traders of all levels can learn to trade, improve a trading system, or develop an independent track record in a real-time market scenario. The company is set up like a real futures brokerage house, and investors call or fax orders to their account representatives. Orders are filled at "real" prices, and clients receive monthly account statements. TradeComp also sponsors trading competitions.

## Trader Gizmos
**http://www.tradergizmos.com**

Trader Gizmos is a trading superstore with a large collection of trading gizmos available for purchase— books, charts, data, publications, videos, and audio tapes. Their products cover everything from how to get started to sophisticated strategies. Visitors can check the Tips and Techniques section for a daily tidbit of wisdom from one of Trader Gizmos's super-traders.

## TraderScan
**http://www.traderscan.com**

TraderScan is an interactive Web site for the managed futures industry, including Commodity Trading Advisors, asset allocators, and financial publishers. It provides advisor performance data and disclosure materials, as well as other information on futures, options, and related financial instruments.

## Trading Places
**http://www.net-link.net/~dward**

Donovan Ward offers his "Ops" system for commodity trading. On his site he presents a running tally of the system's trades and profits.

## Trendy Systems
**http://www.trendysystems.com**

Trendy Systems offers subscribers a neural network-enhanced, computerized, short-term position trading model for S&P index futures. It is distributed nightly via e-mail and the World Wide Web. Users can also download software to generate their own graphs and signals.

## Trident Trading Systems Limited
**http://www.trident-trading.com**

Trident Trading Systems is the developer of Tracker IV, futures trading software, which works in conjunction with the company's advisory newsletter, *Ticks & Tactics*. The newsletter and software cover all major futures contracts that are traded on the U.S. exchanges.

## Waldemar's List
**http://apollo.netservers.com/~waldemar/list.shtml**

Waldemar Puszkarz, an astronomer and individual investor, maintains this sorted collection of links to futures sites, in categories such as Services, Institutions, Charts, and Reports, along with links to articles and educational resources.

## The Wolf
**http://www.flinet.com/~fgl/wolf.htm**

The Wolf scans the options tables daily looking for unusual trading volume that can be the tipoff of an impending explosive move in a stock and option.

Subscribers can receive updates via fax, e-mail, or telephone.

## XYZ for Commodities
**http://www.fastfwd.com/xyz**

XYZ for Commodities's software uses artificial intelligence to catch trends in 35 primary markets, generating signals for trading or hedging commodities or currencies, in the spot or futures market.

# COMMODITY TRADING ADVISORS AND BROKERS

If you want to trade commodities, you'll need a broker. You can surf the Web sites of many of these advisors and companies, ranging from boutique firms to global conglomerates. Some sites even provide daily recommendations for visitors, so you can test their market approach. Others provide brochures and educational articles to help you learn about investing in commodities and futures.

## AIS Futures Management Inc.
**http://www.aisgroup.com**

AIS is a registered investment manager offering a diversified managed futures portfolio consisting of the S&P 500 Index, U.S. Treasury bonds, Japanese Yen, metals, agricultural, and energy investments. The company provides an elegant presentation of their methodology and services on their site.

## Alaron Trading Corp.
**http://www.alaron.com**

Alaron is a registered Futures Commission Merchant based in Chicago. Their Web site includes information on their services, along with a futures calendar,

The titles and acronyms of individuals and firms in the commodity business can be dizzying. There are Commodity Trading Advisors (CTAs), Commodity Pool Operators (CPOs), Introducing Brokers (IBs), and Futures Commission Merchants (FCMs). But these complicated names are all the result of the firms or individuals having registered with the Commodity Futures Trading Commission. Registration means these companies and their representatives must comply with certain regulations, and customers can contact the CFTC to check the background of any registered entity.

Too often, traders don't consider the risk/reward ratio of futures trading carefully enough. It's possible to end up in a position where your maximum potential profit is $2,000, but your losses could easily reach $20,000. Be sure to understand the risk characteristics of any instrument before you invest, and keep the balance in your favor.

order pricing guide, futures and options expirations charts, and a few pieces of commentary.

## American Futures Group, Inc.
### http://www.afg-inc.com

This full-service commodities broker provides weekly trade recommendations and an economic calendar for visitors to their Web site.

## Astor Financial Inc.
### http://www.astorinc.com

This discount futures brokerage has offices in New York, Chicago, and Los Angeles. They provide clients with free charting software and free daily trading recommendations. An alphanumeric pager service connects you to news and quotes from the world markets 24 hours a day. Visitors can click on "Trade Alerts" to get updated recommendations from the firm.

## Barkley Financial Corp.
### http://www.barkley.com

Don't miss Barkley's "Plain Language FAQ," 26 plain-language answers to frequently asked questions about buying options on futures as an investment. This Florida broker offers a free audiotape and newsletter to potential clients.

## Ceres Trading Group, Inc.
### http://www.cerestrading.com

Ceres Trading Group is a broker that specializes in speculative investments in the commodity futures and options markets. The site provides current recommendations and a list of their offices around the country.

## Jack Carl Futures
### http://www.jackcarl.com

Jack Carl is recognized as one of the country's leading discount futures brokerage. The site includes price quotes, commodity calendar, contract specifications, margin requirements for commodities, and Web links related to futures. Don't miss Jack Carl's MarketLine commentary, posted each day.

## Commodities, LLC
http://www.trading.com/commodities.llc

This Oregon firm is a full-service futures and options brokerage, via self-directed and managed accounts. Their site is set up as a starting point for Web explorations of futures research, though some information is provided on the firm's principals (if you can find it).

## Commodity Resource Corporation
http://www.commodity.com

Commodity Resource Corporation is a full-service futures and options brokerage and trading firm based in Nevada. Visitors can review the trade of the month and weekly agricultural forecasts.

## Commodity Specialists Company
http://www.commodityspec.com

This subsidiary of Pillsbury specializes in beverage and food processing by-products (no surprise there). You can get current prices, details on its brokers, and links to other agricultural business sites.

## Compass Financial
http://rampages.onramp.net/~maddin/

Compass Financial is a full-service futures and options firm offering discount commissions and a 24-hour trade desk at their Texas headquarters. Prospective clients can download an application to open an account; all visitors can check out their collection of links.

## Ira Epstein & Company Futures
http://www.iepstein.com

This leading futures brokerage offers an array of services and software for futures traders. Visitors to the site must register but then can download free demo-versions of their software, get delayed quotes on all futures markets, daily quotes on all futures contracts, and special market reports on major futures markets. Of course, you can also get information on commissions and accounts and download application forms. Account holders can download free market price data for futures and stocks. They can also access purchase and sales statements, updated margin schedules, and special market reports (via a Telnet connection). Audio and video clips from Ira punctuate the site.

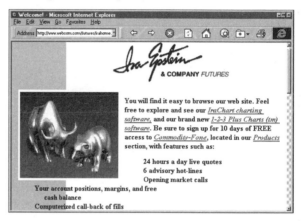

## First American Discount Corporation Custom Brokerage Services
http://members.aol.com/fadccbs

This affiliate of First American Discount Corporation (FADC) offers a full spectrum of services for traders of futures and options on futures. Their Web presence is just a single page with contact information, however.

## First American Discount Corporation
http://www.fadc.com

This discount futures clearing firm was founded by a former Chairman of the Chicago Board of Trade and offers discount and full-service access to the markets. The site includes trade recommendations, quotes, charts, trading calendar, and stock ticker. Account holders can access records of their transactions, fill reports, and personal quotes using a separate BBS system. Visitors can request free literature and account applications using an online form.

### Fortune Management Group
**http://www.johnfortune.com/fmg**
This Atlanta-based registered Commodity Trading Advisor specializes in short-term stock index and financial futures trading. Their site includes information on the firm and its programs.

### FuturesCom
**http://www.futurescom.com**
William Chippas brings his many years of futures industry experience to this site dedicated to the trading and analysis of commodity futures and options. Visitors can request a free trial of his mailbox service, including a *Daily Advisory Newsletter* and Mid-Day Flashes.

### Michael P. Glorioso Investments Co.
**http://www.lookup.com/Homepages/56704/**
Glorioso is a full-service commodities broker in Louisiana, and his site tells you all about his services and commissions. E-mail him your address and he'll send a free booklet on trading commodities.

### Great Pacific Trading Company
**http://www.gptc.com**
Great Pacific Trading Company is a full-service commodity brokerage offering services to beginning traders with no experience in the markets at all, as well as advanced traders who are just looking for fast, efficient executions. For the former, the firm has developed a Paper Trader's Survival Kit, a complete how-to guide to paper trading. For the latter, Great Pacific has a discount desk with low-fee trading. For their Web site visitors, the firm provides a Traders Almanac, and Seasonal Strategems, an ex-

planation of how to use the basic supply and demand cycle of commodities in a trading program. The pleasant, homespun design of this site is an added bonus.

### Harris Capital Management, Inc.
**http://www.newpower.com/bcharris**
Craig Harris is a registered Commodity Trading Advisor and full-service futures broker. He also writes a daily e-mail market letter and will send you a four-week free trial. Some sample articles are available on his site.

### John W. Henry & Company
**http://www.jwh.com**
John W. Henry & Company, Inc. is an established leader in the managed futures industry, primarily for an institutional clientele. They provide regularly updated performance reviews of their investment programs and news about their firm.

### Institutional Advisory Services Group, Inc.
**http://www.iasg.com**
Institutional Advisory Services Group, Inc. (IASG) provides institutional and brokerage clients and high net-worth individual traders with access to the

world's futures and foreign exchange markets through managed futures, brokerage, and clearing and execution. They also provide other consulting services to institutions. They have their own rankings of managed futures advisors on their site.

## Island View Financial Group, Inc.
http://www.derivative.com/dmg/ivf/

Island View is a Commodity Trading Advisor offering three managed futures account programs. Principals Charles LeBeau and David Lucas are experienced professionals who are experts in futures trading. They have authored the book *Computer Analysis of the Futures Market*. The site provides information and some outdated performance reviews of their programs.

## Lind-Waldock & Co.
http://www.lind-waldock.com

Lind-Waldock proudly proclaims itself the world's largest discount futures brokerage firm. Their Web site is a veritable smorgasbord of news, data, market updates, charts, report schedules, and much more. Clients can trade online in real-time using Lind On-Line trading software; Web investors can download application forms from the site. This site's snazzy design and logical layout are also commendable.

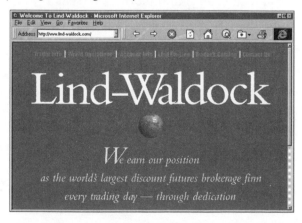

## Linnco Futures Group, LLC
http://www.lfgllc.com

Linnco Futures Group, LLC is a Futures Commission Merchant serving affiliate brokers across the country. Proprietary research is available to clients of these brokers, and yesterday's news is online for guests.

## Lloyd, Stevens & Co.
http://www.lloydstevens.com

Lloyd, Stevens offers futures trading services, managed futures analysis, selection, and surveillance, and managed equities portfolios. On their site, they present information on their firm and programs, as well as copies of their newsletters and other educational articles.

## Bill Lucas Futures
http://www.pcis.net/wglucasfutures

This is Lucas's simple pointer page for his full service futures and futures options trading services. It includes a few links to other financial sites.

## E.D. & F. Man International, Inc.
http://www.edfman.com

E.D. & F. Man is a global leader in futures and options clearing execution services, serving individuals, brokers, and institutions. You'll find information on their business services on this site.

## E.D. & F. Man Metals Team
http://www.iolweb.com/edfman

The Man Metals Team specializes in metals price risk management for the principal producers, processors, fabricators, consumers, and dealers of traded metals.

**ask doug!**

**Q:** How many shares of stock are in an option contract?

**A:** For stock options, each contract represents 100 shares of the underlying stock.

## Margil Capital Management

http://www.margil.com

This site provides an introduction to Margil Capital Management, an international commodity futures and options broker. They offer an introduction to trading commodities article, and users can request a free copy of the book *Trading Tactics of Professional Traders* (though a couple of sample chapters are online). Clients have access to a wide selection of commentary and charts on the site.

## Midstates Commodities

http://www.midstates.com

This Oklahoma firm is one of the first to offer online futures trading. Account holders can place orders, review current closed and open positions, get current market prices, and more. Surfers can access closing prices for futures and options free.

## Moore Research Center, Inc.

http://www.mrci.com

Moore Research provides computerized analysis of futures, stock, and cash prices for traders, as well as special reports for the Chicago Mercantile Exchange, Chicago Board of Trade, and London Securities and Derivatives Exchange. The company publishes monthly and historical reports, available for pur-

chase on their site. Visitors can access free quotes and samples of their research.

## Newport Commodities

http://www.ypo.com/newport

Newport presents an outline of their business, serving as Introducing Broker for traders of commodity futures and options contracts.

## Niederhoffer Investments, Inc.

http://www.derivative.com/nii

Niederhoffer is a Commodity Trading Advisor directing accounts with futures contracts, options on futures contracts and physical commodities, forward contracts, and other commodity-related contracts traded on United States, foreign, and international exchanges and markets. The site describes their program and provides downloadable client agreements.

## Pacific Rim Futures and Options

http://www.teleport.com/~futures/

From Oregon comes Pacific Rim Futures and Options, a full-service introducing broker. They provide links to plenty of futures resources on the Web. They also offer information on their services, though you'll have to request an account form to be sent to you.

## Pathways to Profit

http://www.ptpnet.com

At first glance, this site appears to be focused on helping investors understand commodities and commodity futures options. And it does deliver some basic information on trading commodities. But click through the offers of free cassettes and newsletters and you'll find a small checkbox asking if you'd like information on setting up a new account.

## Premier Trading Inc.
http://www.premiertrading.com

Premier Trading is a discount and full-service commodity futures and options brokerage. Their site includes a trade calendar, margin requirements, and links to quotes and charts. E-mail them for an account application if you so desire.

## Rafferty Associates, Inc.
http://www.well.com/user/business/
rafferty.html

Gerald Rafferty oversees a mini-empire: GPR, Inc., a full-service futures brokerage; Rafferty Associates, Inc., a long-established NYMEX floor brokerage presence; Rafferty Energy Group, Inc.; OTC and physical brokerage for swaps, basis swaps, and options; and Rafferty Technical Research, Inc., publisher of daily technical market analysis. The site provides cursory information on all aspects of his operations.

## Rand Financial Services
http://www.rand-usa.com

From their headquarters in Chicago, Rand offers futures and options brokerage services for institutions and individuals. The site provides details on the company and its programs, in English, German, or Japanese.

## Robbins Trading Company
http://www.robbins-trading.com

In addition to being an Introducing Broker, Robbins Trading sponsors the annual World Cup Championship of Futures Trading. The Championship gives individual traders the opportunity to pit their trading skills against other competitors from around the world. The company also provides information on their firm and services, including their System Assist Trading Service. Account forms are available for downloading.

## Spectrum Commodities
http://www.mcn.net/~spectrum

Headquartered in Montana, Spectrum is a full-service (or should that be full spectrum?) commodities brokerage. Their market page contains audio commentaries and links to weather maps, and clients can receive a daily technical market update via e-mail.

## STA Research, Inc.
http://www.stafutures.com

STA Research is committed to informing their clients of market-moving news events as they occur. Their Web site presents an array of economic and agricultural information. Each day, their Morning Financial Call Report and Agricultural Call Report (each an information-packed, one-page call sheet) are updated on their site. Other fundamental and technical information related to the futures industry is also available, and users can download an application kit to open an account. While the reports STA provides are filled with information, they are scanned images of printed reports, not HTML pages, so they may load slowly.

## Surge Trading S.A.
http://www.surgetrd.com

Based in Geneva, this company specializes in commodities and financial futures, options, and forex, with competitive rates and guaranteed stop-loss accounts. They serve private investors, introducing brokers, fund managers, and institutions. The Surge Trading Web site includes daily commodity and forex reports, and they also offer a free daily e-mail report. Novices should definitely review the educational articles in their Learning Center, including a glossary and details on placing futures and options orders.

### Time Leverage Capital
http://futures.netstations.com

It's possible to get quite lost while exploring Time Leverage Capital's Web site. This says good things, I guess, about the amount of material that's available, but it's not so complimentary when it comes to the site's layout. Visitors can access most of the site, but the really interesting information requires a password, which entails calling or e-mailing the firm. Still, the software, charts, commodity reports, and futures strategies worksheets seem almost worth the effort. Time Leverage Capital is a Guaranteed Introducing Broker, and potential clients can download account applications from the site.

### Treasure State Futures Inc.
http://www.digisys.net/futures

This Montana Guaranteed Introducing Broker offers information on its services and links to futures-related services.

### Toni Financial
http://www.primenet.com/~gunther

Toni Financial provides commodity brokerage services, managed accounts, commodity funds, and seminars from their North Hollywood offices. Clients can access daily recommendations on their site. A brief Beginner's Corner is also worth a glance.

### Rudolf Wolff
http://www.rwolff.com

Rudolf Wolff is London's leading metals broker; investors can subscribe to the online *Daily Wolff Metal Report* for full analysis of the metals markets.

### Worldwide Trade Brokerage
http://wwtrade.com

This global marketing consulting firm brings together buyers and sellers in the international commodities trade business.

### Woodriff Trading Company
http://www.woodriff.com

Woodriff Trading offers their Global Programs, with an innovative futures trading approach. Their site provides updates of actual performance, positions and graphs, and background on the programs.

# COMMODITY EXCHANGES

Every day, billions of dollars worth of commodities are bought and sold on the trading floor of the world's commodity and futures exchanges. And though electronic trading is beginning to take its place in the market, most of the action still occurs in the pits, with traders wildly gesturing and screaming at one another. The apparent chaos is really the efficiency of the open outcry market at work, with buyers and sellers bidding openly on a particular commodity.

Here, then, in the somewhat more civil arena of cyberspace, are the Web sites of the leading commodity and futures exchanges. Many of these sites provide excellent educational materials, quotes, data, and charts for investors.

### Chicago Board of Trade
http://www.cbot.com

The Chicago Board of Trade (CBOT) is the world's leading futures and options on futures exchange. Guests can read the history and overview of CBOT, take a virtual tour of the trading floor, and get a comprehensive introduction to options, futures, and hedging. MarketPlex is a one-stop information resource for current commodities news, featuring CBOT Internet Radio in RealAudio format, quotes, charts, data, and commentary from a variety of sources.

### Chicago Board Options Exchange
**http://www.cboe.com**

The Chicago Board Options Exchange (CBOE) is the index options market, since it has more than a 94 percent share of the U.S. index options market. Their Education Center provides lots of good material to help you learn about options, or you can order their Options Toolbox software for Windows. The CBOE publication, *Characteristics and Risks of Standardized Options,* is a must-read for every inves-

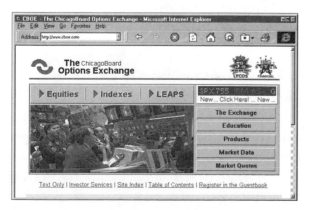

**ask doug!**

**Q:** What's a LEAP?

**A:** LEAPS are Long-term Equity AnticiPation Securities. They are long-term options that provide the owner the right to purchase or sell shares of an individual stock (or the value of selected indices) at a specified price on or before a given date up to three years in the future. If you're bullish on a particular stock, LEAPS calls can provide you with the opportunity to participate in the upward movement of a stock without buying it outright. On the other hand, LEAPS puts can provide a hedge for a stock you already own in the event its share price declines. The Chicago Board Options Exchange <http://www.cboe.com> has info on LEAPs, as does the American Stock Exchange <http://www.amex.com>.

tor thinking of investing in options, and a copy is conveniently provided on the site. Special sections of the site are devoted to LEAPS and index options. You can get delayed market quotes for options, too.

### Chicago Mercantile Exchange
**http://www.cme.com**

Known as The Merc, the Chicago Mercantile Exchange is an international marketplace for futures contracts and options on futures. The site provides daily settlement prices for currency, interest rates, stock index and agricultural contracts, and daily and weekly charts. Some of the strategy and research papers are online in their educational section, but they tend to be very technical.

### Coffee, Sugar, and Cocoa Exchange
http://www.csce.com

The Coffee, Sugar, and Cocoa Exchange (CSCE) is located in New York City. It is an exchange for the coffee, sugar, cocoa, milk, cheddar cheese, butter, and nonfat dry milk futures and options markets. You can learn the history of the exchange and how it works or view news releases, daily market reports, quotes, historical data, and charts. Users can also download SOFTSware, interactive options strategy software for beginners and experts.

### Hong Kong Futures Exchange
http://www.hkfe.com

This fast-growing exchange provides an efficient, diversified futures and options market for investors to take advantage of Asia's growth. Home of Hang Seng Index Futures, the Hong Kong Futures Exchange also offers options on individual stocks. The site provides background on the exchange, with current data and news, and a form to order more information.

### Kansas City Board of Trade
http://www.kcbt.com

The Kansas City Board of Trade (KCBT) is the world's predominant marketplace for hard red winter wheat, the major ingredient in the world's bread. Western Natural Gas futures and options are also traded on the KCBT, as well as Value Line stock index futures. You can learn about these products, and about the KCBT, on their site.

### London International Futures and Options Exchange
http://www.liffe.com

The London International Financial Futures and Options Exchange (LIFFE) is the leading futures and options market in Europe. The site offers contract statistics and a description of the operation of the Exchange, as well as press releases, details of educational courses, information on LIFFE's publications, charts, prices, and historical data.

### MarchÈ ‡ Terme International de France
http://www.matif.fr

One of the world's foremost financial futures and options exchanges, their products include a complete range of franc-denominated futures and options contracts on the French franc yield curve, as well as European Currency Unit-denominated products. Data and statistics about the contracts are provided on the site.

### MEFF Renta Fija
http://www.meff.es

Based in Barcelona, MEFF Renta Fija is the Spanish futures and options exchange and clearinghouse. Their publications library is available online in a variety of formats. There are also news and statistics here.

### MEFF Renta Variable
http://www.meffrv.es

MEFF Renta Variable is the Spanish Equity Derivatives Exchange, clearing and trading options and futures on the IBEX-35 and options on Spanish stocks. The site provides an overview, in English or Spanish, along with historical data and lists of contracts traded.

### MidAmerica Commodity Exchange
http://www.midam.com

The MidAm gives you the basics and introduces you to the world of futures trading. You can download their multimedia brochure for even more details or delve into the pit yourself with their interactive trading simulation.

## Minneapolis Grain Exchange
http://www.mgex.com

The Grain Exchange is the largest cash exchange market in the world, trading a daily average of one million bushels of grain including wheat, barley, oats, durum, rye, sunflower seeds, flax, corn, soybeans, millet, and milo. It is also the world's only seafood complex, trading White and Black Tiger Shrimp futures and options contracts. Get specifications and quotes on all their contracts, plus other information on the Exchange.

## New York Cotton Exchange
http://www.nyce.com

If you're looking to trade potato futures and options, turn to the SPUD. That's the Special Potato Underlying Division of the New York Cotton Exchange (NYCE). Besides cotton and potato futures and futures options, the NYCE and its divisions also trade in frozen concentrate orange juice futures, indexes, and financial futures. Historical charts and daily market reports are provided.

## New York Mercantile Exchange
http://www.nymex.com

New York Mercantile Exchange has two divisions: NYMEX, on which crude oil, heating oil, gasoline, natural gas, propane, platinum, and palladium trade; and COMEX, on which gold, silver, copper, and the Eurotop 100 stock index trade. A highlight of this site for individual investors is How a Commodities Exchange Works, a delightfully illustrated and easily understood description of the commodities trading process.

## South African Futures Exchange
http://www.safex.co.za

One of the younger futures exchanges in the world, South African Futures Exchange (SAFEX) deals in financial and agricultural contracts. The site offers historical data and current statistics, and background on the Exchange.

## Sydney Futures Exchange
http://www.sfe.com.au

This exchange began nearly 30 years ago as the Sydney Greasy Wool Futures Exchange for Australia's largest export product, merino wool. Fortunately, they changed their name, and today the exchange is the largest open-outcry futures exchange in the Asia-Pacific region. The site provides contract specifications and data for products traded on the Exchange.

## Tokyo Grain Exchange
http://www.tge.or.jp

The Tokyo Grain Exchange is a leading futures exchange in Asia, trading azuki, corn, raw sugar, U.S. soybean futures, and options on U.S. soybeans and raw sugar futures. Besides providing information on the exchange and its contracts, users can click on Hot Japanese Word to learn how to say some of their favorite commodity trading terms in Japanese!

# FOREX

Forex, often abbreviated further as F/X, is the global inter-bank currency exchange market, where the trading of currency is taking place at inter-bank rates, 24 hours a day and through the informal global network of banks and dealers, not through the formal exchanges.

Each day, somewhere between $1.3 and $1.5 trillion worth of currencies changes hands. The usual players in the foreign exchange market are banks, corporations, speculators, and money/fund managers. Each participates for different reasons: to profit from short-term fluctuations in exchange rates, to hedge against losses due to changes in exchange rates, or to acquire foreign currency that is needed to buy goods and services from another country.

The retail Forex market has grown substantially, and now individuals can participate along with the world's leading banks. These sites provide tools, as well as professional help, for traders interested in the Forex market.

## Axone's Forex Options Calculator
http://www.axone.ch/calcul/forex/

Provided in both Windows and Java versions, this calculator figures the premium and all the risk factors (delta, gamma, theta, vega, rho) for European or American Forex options.

## The Burmese Tiger
http://www.nito.com

From NiTo Asset Management comes this technical trading system for foreign exchange, bonds, and stocks. Private, corporate, and institutional subscribers receive analysis and trading recommendations.

## Chiprock Limited
http://www.chiprock.com

Behind this somewhat cryptic Web site is a UK-based market analyst who provides forecasts on market movement and specific commentary on currency markets. The firm's clientele is primarily companies involved in import/export, helping those companies to manage their Forex risks and decide when to buy and sell.

## Contingency Analysis
http://www.contingencyanalysis.com

Consultant Glyn Holton's area of expertise is financial risk management, and his site offers hundreds of pages of information on derivative instruments, credit risk management, and financial engineering. The site also features a discussion group. While this material isn't for pure beginners, it's worth exploring for most other investors.

## Currency Management Corporation PLC
http://www.forex-cmc.co.uk

Currency Management Corporation is a London-based independent market maker in Foreign Exchange, offering 24 Hour Foreign Exchange quotations to banks, corporates, investment managers, and individuals. The site offers a daily market report and a *Dealing Handbook* that covers the entire process of transacting a Foreign Exchange deal. The firm also provides online Internet trading using their stand-alone Marketmaker software.

## Custom House Currency Exchange
http://www.customhouse.com

Custom House is Canada's largest foreign exchange brokerage house. They offer daily commentary on the Canadian dollar and the foreign exchange market, online or via free e-mail subscription, and opening mid-market interbank exchange rates between Canadian and U.S. dollars and most major currencies. Traders can open an account online.

## DataFeed International
http://www.hk.super.net/~datafeed/

This Hong Kong financial software house is the Asian distributor of several products for Forex traders.

## Dynex Corporation
**http://dynexcorp.com**

This foreign exchange trading manager specializes in managing currency portfolios for banks, institutions, and high net worth private investors. Dynex Corporation uses proprietary methods to quantify various readings of market psychology, and enters positions based on its contrarian strategy, analysing when market opinion has become, in their opinion, overwhelmingly one-sided. The site also includes a good explanation of interbank trading, performance reports, and account applications.

## 1st Money Garden Corporation
**http://www.forex-mg.com**

1st Money Garden offers 24-hour-a-day trading online with their New York Forex desk for both wholesale and retail traders. Their site offers links to market commentary, real-time prices, charts, and educational materials for traders new to Forex. With the Money Garden Forex Deal Station, you can execute trades online, too.

## FX Week
**http://www.fxweek.com**

This publication focuses on the business of the foreign exchange market, looking behind-the-scenes at the top echelons of the financial industry.

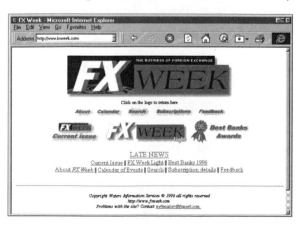

The Web site includes an index of each week's issue, as well as a "light" version that focuses on online developments in the industry. It also includes an excellent collection of Forex links.

## Global Vision Forex
**http://www.gv-forex.com**

This Dun & Bradstreet-rated financial services corporation is dedicated to providing international asset diversification, currency risk containment, and portfolio hedging to the individual or institutional investor based on their needs and financial objectives. Global Vision Forex specializes in managing currency trading for individual investors. Their site includes several articles describing the Forex market, currency investments, and their services.

## International Financial & Trading Network
**http://www.iftn.com**

For over a decade, International Financial & Trading Network (IFTN) professionals have been at the forefront of the trillion-dollar-a-day spot currency trading industry, providing a full range of financial services to individual and corporate investors throughout the world. With their Infinex2000 software, investors can trade in real-time over the Internet. Their site provides live 24-hour quotes, hourly and historical Forex charts, and 15-minute delayed spot currency quotes and Forex charts.

## International Foreign Exchange Corp.
**http://www.ifexco.com**

International Foreign Exchange Corp. (IFEXCO) is a Geneva-based broker in Forex and Forex options, providing services for private investors, fund managers, introducing brokers, and institutions. Check their site for daily charts and market updates and a daily focus report (in Microsoft Word format only).

## MMS International
http://www.mcgraw-hill.com/financial-markets/mms/mmshmpg.htm

MMS is the world's premier provider of real-time market commentary, analysis, and economic forecasts in the global bond, money, foreign exchange, and equity markets. They work through quote vendors such as Bloomberg, Knight Ridder, Reuters, and Telerate.

## M.W. Marshall & Company Limited
http://www.mwmarshall.com

Marshalls ranks as one of the world's leading moneybrokers, with offices worldwide. The company acts as an intermediary between banks and other financial institutions in the Foreign Exchange, deposits, and derivative markets. They offer daily New York Forex trading ranges on their site.

## Olsen & Associates
http://www.olsen.ch

Olsen is a world leader in advanced forecasting technology for the financial markets. The firm provides research, data, forecasts, timing services, trading models, and software for clients. Their

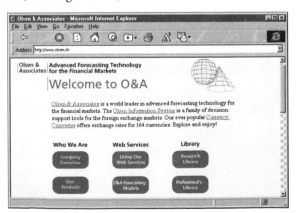

Web site offers free use of an online currency converter with exchange rates for 164 currencies, as well as a research library. Other services are available by subscription.

## Prisma ForeX Internet
http://www.prisma.co.uk

This currency forecasting service is used by international banks to protect their Foreign Exchange risks and manage them more profitably. Prisma also offers their services by subscription to private investors, outlining strategies dedicated to intraday and short-term currency movements, or intermediate and long-term currency movements.

## Trading and Commercial Consulting SA
http://www.tccsa.com

Yet another Geneva-based Forex firm provides asset management and Forex trading services. Check their site for daily market commentary.

## Tueta Gestion Sarl
http://is.eunet.ch/forex

This firm (from Geneva, where else?) specializes in technical analysis in their foreign exchange exposure and hedging advisory service. Traders can subscribe to receive real-time e-mail and fax transmission of our trading signals (using an intraday and medium-term strategy).

## Tullett & Tokyo International Ltd.
http://www.tullett.co.uk

The global network of this international money broker spans Europe, North America, and Southeast Asia. Their Web site provides live commentary, FX rates, and technical analysis, but only to registered clients.

## The Universal Currency Converter
**http://www.xe.net/currency**

Xenon Laboratories supplies this online currency converter that allows users to perform foreign exchange rate conversion. Type the amount of source currency in the input box, then select a destination currency, and the program does the rest. They also provide an interactive currency table that displays a list of currency values relative to a base currency that you select. Users can sign up for a free Currency Update Service to receive free currency table updates automatically by e-mail, in your choice of base currency. The site is also available in Swedish.

# GLOSSARY

**AMERICAN-STYLE OPTION**—An option contract that can be exercised at any time before the expiration date.

**AT-THE-MONEY**—When the strike price of an option equals the price of the underlying security or contract.

**CALL**—An Option contract that gives the buyer the right (but not the obligation) to buy the underlying security at a specified price (the strike price) during a specified period.

**COMMODITY**—A product or raw material that can be bought or sold.

**COMMODITY POOL**—A managed portfolio in which a number of individuals contribute funds for the purpose of trading futures or options on futures.

**COMMODITY TRADING ADVISER**—A individual or firm who advises others, either by recommendations in written publications or other media, or by overseeing a client's account, on particular futures contracts or commodity options

**COVERED CALL OPTION WRITING**—A strategy in which one writes (sells) call options at the same time as one owns an equivalent position in the underlying security, commodity, currency, index, or futures contract.

**DAY TRADING**—Opening a futures or options position and closing it the same day.

**DERIVATIVE SECURITY**—One whose value is determined from the value and characteristics of another, underlying security.

**EUROPEAN-STYLE OPTION**—An option contract that can be exercised only on its expiration date.

**EXERCISE**—The action to buy (in the case of a call option) or sell (in the case of a put option) the underlying security.

**FOREX**—An over-the-counter market where buyers and sellers conduct foreign currency trading.

**IN-THE-MONEY**—When the strike price of a call option is below, or the strike price of a put option is above, the price of the underlying contract.

**LEAPS**—Long-term Equity AnticiPation Securities. Stock or index options, available in calls or puts, with expiration dates up to three years in the future.

**LEVERAGE**—The ability to control a large dollar amount of a commodity with a comparatively small amount of capital.

**MARGIN**—The funds (or other collateral) deposited by a customer with his broker for the purpose of insuring the broker against loss on futures contracts. The margin is not partial payment on a purchase. The initial margin is the amount of margin per contract required by the broker when a futures position is opened. The maintenance margin is the amount that must be on deposit at all times.

MARGIN CALL—A request from a brokerage firm to a customer to deposit more funds in an account to restore margin levels, usually because of losses.

OPTION—A contract giving the buyer the right to buy or sell a specific quantity of a commodity or security at a specific price in a specific period of time.

OPTION PREMIUM—The price that the option buyer pays to the option seller for the rights contained in the option.

OUT-OF-THE-MONEY—When the strike price for a call is higher, or the strike price of a put option is lower, than the underlying security.

PUT—An Option contract that gives the buyer the right (but not the obligation) to sell the underlying security at a specified price during a specified period.

SPOT MARKET—The cash market price for a commodity that is available for immediate delivery.

STRIKE PRICE—The predetermined price at which an underlying security can be purchased (in the case of a call) or sold (in the case of a put) if the option holder chooses to exercise the option contract.

# Chapter 5
# News and Advice

"High finance isn't burglary or obtaining money by false pretenses, but rather a judicious selection from the best features of those fine arts."

—Finley Peter Dunne

**First comes the news.** No longer do you have to wait for the six o'clock news or tomorrow's newspaper for the scoop on the news that affects you. The Internet provides investors with nearly instantaneous access to top stories, delivered to your computer. You can read the news, watch the news, hear the news, or search the news. Every investor needs the news, to monitor stocks in your portfolio or on your watch list, or to track interest and exchange rates, or for any of the thousand other reasons that we pay attention to the news.

Next, you need to put the news to work. Along with all the other research and knowledge you accumulate as you invest, you'll need to develop your approach to the market. There are plenty of investing systems being plied on the Internet, some of which just might be the ticket to financial success for you. Sometimes it helps to have some additional insight from a professional. No matter what your interests, from just getting a bit of market commentary, to subscribing to an advisory service, to having your account managed by a professional, the Web has sites to explore.

# FINANCIAL NEWS

Every investor needs to stay on top of the holdings in his or her portfolio. You can get news on the Internet in a variety of ways. Some services will bring news to you via e-mail or a software program. Some customize the content according to your preferences. Other sites are the equivalent of electronic newspapers, where you scan the headlines and then zero in on stories of interest.

If nothing else, the Web certainly gives you options. Check out these sites and find the ones that best fit your needs and habits.

## NEWS SERVICES

These sites offer current news headlines and stories in formats ranging from wire news services to daily newspapers. Investors can get the details of the day's market activity from these sources or catch the buzz on why your stock is falling through the floor.

### Atlantic Broadcasting System
http://www.abslive.com

Hear the news, don't just read about it. Atlantic Broadcasting System (ABS) provides real-time audio commentary on the U.S. stock market during market hours. Using RealAudio, ABS tracks major market averages, individual stocks, futures, and sectors. Their commentators link moves in the fixed income, currency, and overseas markets to U.S. equities.

### Bloomberg Personal
http://www.bloomberg.com

The Bloomberg terminal is a fixture in brokerage firm offices. Now individual investors can get a taste of the news and analysis, previously available only to the pros, on the Bloomberg Personal Web site. Updated continuously throughout the day, the site provides news headlines and summaries for world and U.S. markets. Users can listen to WBBR radio on the site using the Streamworks or

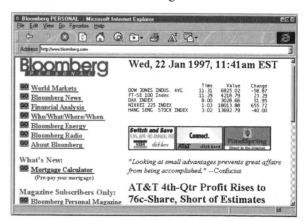

If you are a buy-and-hold investor, hearing bad news on a stock you own is not necessarily cause to sell. It is cause to take a new look at a company's fundamentals, though. In the course of your investigation, you may determine that the bad news is symptomatic of a company's deteriorating fundamentals, and selling your stock is the right thing to do. On the other hand, you may discover that the bad news is just a temporary setback, and you now have the opportunity to buy more shares at a bargain price.

RealAudio players or check in with the latest in sports, horoscopes, lottery results, trivia, or weather.

## Briefing.com
http://www.briefing.com

Briefing.com provides live market insight each day, available by subscription. The company attempts to reach beyond news, telling investors what's important and why. A staff of experienced professionals provides concise market analysis on the bond, stock, and foreign exchange markets. Look for headlines, downgrades, upgrades, earnings calendar, tech stock analysis, economic data, and more. Briefing.com gets the scoop online faster than nearly any other Web news source.

## Business Wire
http://www.businesswire.com

Business Wire is an international media-relations wire service that disseminates full-text news releases for public and private companies. On their Web site, investors can check out the Corporate News section for news from Business Wire's corporate clients or set up a Personal Web Box (for a fee) to automatically pull news releases in preset keywords or categories

onto a personalized page. Today's News and High-Tech News are also available.

## Canadian Moneysaver
http://www.altamira.com/altamira/moneysaver/

This site offers a very short selection of articles from Canada's leading personal finance magazine.

## CDA Investnet Insider Watch
http://www.cda.com/investnet

Insider trading (no, not the illegal variety) can be an indicator of a company's future prospects. That's because insiders, the people who work for or are on the board of a corporation, ought to know best how that company is likely to perform. When insiders are buying, it's a bullish indicator, but when lots of them are selling, look out! Bob Gabele's *Insiders' Chronicle* is the leading newsletter devoted to tracking this activity. If you'd like to follow the action, too, you can download a sample copy from the site, or subscribe to a four-week trial. Also available and free to users are editions of Gabele's nationally syndicated column, "Periscope," a daily tip, and commentary on insider activity to watch.

## Closing Bell from Mercury Mail
http://www.merc.com

Lots of investors like Closing Bell for the quotes they receive, e-mailed daily to them free. But the news summaries provided for each stock in your portfolio are a great way to keep up to date on your holdings. Closing Bell will even e-mail you throughout the day with breaking news, or send you a Morning Call with a summary of each day's kick-off market action. Check out their Internet Daily report, with news on the sector, too.

## Cable News Network

http://www.cnn.com

The 24-hour news network offers a Web site that's overflowing with the day's news. For the biggest news stories, Cable News Network (CNN) offers expanded online coverage. The site offers news in several departments, including U.S., World, Weather, Technology, Style, and Show Biz. Video Vault offers QuickTime clips from current and past stories.

## CNNfn

http://www.cnnfn.com

CNNfn is the financial network of parent CNN, and surfers can get full-text news and photos on the Web soon after it hits the tube. QuickTime clips of news stories enhance the day's events for those with a super-fast Internet connection. "fn to go" is a Javascript application that puts a second small browser window on your desktop that tracks top news headlines and stock market developments reported by CNNfn while you're looking at other sites. A reference section offers links to public companies and other research tools on the Web. Stock and fund quotes are also available.

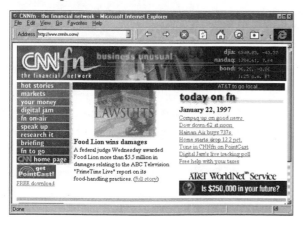

## the swami speaks

Reading words and viewing pictures on the Web may be sufficient for some, but I sense that you seek a richer online experience. Many sites now offer audio and video capabilities that may satisfy you, with names like Acrobat, RealAudio, TrueSpeech, QuickTime, and Shockwave. In order to take advantage of these capabilities, however, you'll need some additional software, most of which can be downloaded free from the Web. When you encounter a file on a Web site that needs a special viewer, the site will probably direct you to a page where you can download the necessary program.

In the most recent incarnation, many of these applications are *plug-ins*, which means they plug into your browser and work directly with the browser to present specific content to you. For instance, the Adobe Acrobat reader can work just like another application in its own window. Or, it can be installed as a plug-in, turning your Web browser into an Acrobat reader when you download an Acrobat file.

## Freeloader

http://www.freeloader.com

Freeloader works with your browser to retrieve Web sites to your computer's hard drive according to your schedule so you can browse your favorite sites at your convenience. Freeloader also works with content providers such as MSNBC, ZD Net, Yahoo!, Infoseek, Excite, Hotwired, *USA Today*, AT&T, GeoCities, Sportsline, Macromedia, and Newspage to provide current news and information. As the name implies, the software and news are free!

### IBM InfoMarket NewsTicker

http://www.infomarket.ibm.com

InfoMarket is a research service that lets you buy valuable information on a per-document basis delivered through IBM's Cryptolope containers. These containers are secured files built to be transmitted over the Internet. But even more interesting is Info-Market's free NewsTicker, a stand-alone program that provides headlines in a continuous ticker running across your screen. Click on a story and get the full text of that news article. NewsTicker works with several providers of news on the Internet and is configurable according to your own preferences.

### Market News Online

http://www.vlcn.com

If you're the type who likes your news to come to you rather than having to search for it, perhaps you should subscribe to Market News Online. Each day, the service will e-mail you the news on stock splits, earnings announcements, stock buybacks, and analysts' picks. You'll also get access to their Day Trader's newsroom, for up-to-the-minute updates. Try the service free for two weeks and see if it fits your needs.

### Market Voice

http://www.ino.com/marketvoice/

Top market analysts provide daily stock, bond, futures, options, and other market commentary in RealAudio format on the MarketVoice site. Listen to an analyst's opinions—and if you've got a response, click to send them an e-mail message.

### MSNBC News

http://www.msnbc.com/news/default.asp

MSNBC covers breaking stories throughout the day. Jump to their Commerce section for financial news, including daily earnings digests, quotes, the day's top stories, and feature articles. A summary of each day's business news is available in RealAudio format, too.

### My Yahoo! News Ticker

http://my.yahoo.com/ticker.html

My Yahoo! offers a free customizable page to all Web surfers, with news, quotes, weather, and sports scores customized to your interests. Their News Ticker program runs on your computer desktop, in your task bar, or in its own window. It delivers the latest news, prices and scores. Double-click and your browser jumps to the Yahoo! server for the full story.

### NewsPage

http://www.newspage.com

If you can't hire a personal editor to cull tens of thousands of pages of news from 630 sources each day for stories that might be of interest to you, then NewsPage may be the next best thing. Create your own NewsPage for free and get daily access to news briefs for the stories that matter to you. For full-text articles, you'll need to subscribe, starting at just $3.95 a month.

### Personal Finance Network

http://www.wwbroadcast.com/pfn

Listen up! The World Wide Broadcasting Network offers a schedule of RealAudio commentary and analysis, on topics such as retirement planning, taxes, mutual fund investing, women and pensions, insurance company annuities, Social Security, and Washington developments that will affect your financial security.

### PointCast Network

http://www.pointcast.com

Rather than surfing the Web for news you can use, why not sit back in your chair and let PointCast de-

One of your stocks has just released its quarterly earnings, a few pennies shy of what the analysts were expecting. Now the share price is dropping like a bombshell. It's a fact of the market that many, if not most, stocks are earnings-driven. "Missing their estimate" can lead to precipitous price drops. Just look on the bright side: when your stocks come in with earnings higher than analysts' estimates, their share prices are likely to jump.

liver news to your desktop? Download the PointCast software, then fire it up to retrieve the latest from the sources you select, including *Time, People, Money*, Reuters, PR Newswire, BusinessWire, Sportsticker, Accuweather, CNN, CNNfn, *Wired, Chicago Tribune* and *Miami Herald*. Stock quotes, charts, EDGAR filings of public companies, and news releases are brought to you for the companies in your portfolio. PointCast can run as a screensaver or be configured to dial up an Internet connection as needed.

## PR Newswire
http://www.prnewswire.com

PR Newswire's Company News On-Call is a leading distributor of news releases for publicly traded companies, available free on their site. They also provide industry commentary.

## WorldFlash News Ticker
http://www.scroller.com

WorldFlash News Ticker is a free Windows 95 program that lets you see personalized, up-to-the-minute scrolling stock quotes, news headlines, incoming e-mail headers, and weather updates in a separate window while surfing the Web. News

sources include Reuters News, CNN, *The Nando Times*, ClNet News, *USA Today*, CMP TechWeb, Wired News, *San Francisco Examiner, Boston Globe, Chicago Sun-Times*, MSNBC News, *Philadelphia Daily, Washington Post, Seattle Times, Miami Herald, Arizona Star, New York Post*, and *Los Angeles Times*. Double-click on a headline to get the full text of an article.

## Yahoo! On the Money
http://biz.yahoo.com

Yahoo!, a popular Internet directory, offers a collection of financial resources that should appeal to any investor. Each day, their U.S. News and Stock Report provides hourly updates of new stories about the stock markets and other financial topics. Click on Industry to read articles sorted by market sectors for the past two months, or select Business for the day's top stories. If you don't have time to scan the headlines, you can search for stories about a particular subject. If you click the Company link, you can scroll through alphabetical lists of news stories sorted by company, and then access quotes and company profiles provided by Hoover's as well as news. To follow the stocks you own, select Quotes and create your own portfolios. Each time you check your portfolio, you'll see if there are new stories related to your holdings.

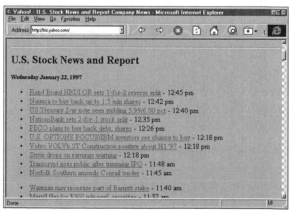

## FINANCIAL NEWSPAPERS AND MAGAZINES

Most print publications have seen the future and know that it lies in the online medium. Thus, newspapers and magazines have been migrating to the Web, in one form or another. While many haven't quite found the right formula for publishing on the Web, others have flourished. Financial and business publications have taken the lead online, so investors can find lots of near-replacements for their daily newspapers.

### Barrons
http://www.barrons.com

The online version of the esteemed financial weekly offers a graphically intense experience that's sure to satisfy your hunger for market news. The site provides access to all of *Barrons* editorial content each week, *Barrons* archives and daily performance reports for U.S. stocks, international stocks, bonds, commodities, interest rates, exchange rates, and mutual funds. A highlight of the site are the *Barrons* Dossiers, which are comprehensive news and performance information about a particular stock or fund. Each dossier includes fundamental historical data, price charts, performance graphs, news stories, and relevant *Barrons* commentary. The site will eventually be available on a subscription basis, though it is free for now.

### Better Investing
http://www.better-investing.org/bi/bi.html

The National Association of Investors Corp. (NAIC) is a leading membership organization for individual investors, as well as investment clubs. NAIC members receive *Better Investing* magazine as part of their membership; non-members can also subscribe (though membership is a better deal). The NAIC Web site offers a growing collection of reprints from the magazine, which focuses on educational articles and growth stock investing.

### Crain's Cleveland Business
http://www.crainscleveland.com

Crain's Cleveland version provides stock quotes for local firms, daily news, links to Northeast Ohio businesses, and archives of old issues.

### Crain's Detroit Business
http://www.crainsdetroit.com

The Detroit edition of this business weekly offers a daily briefing, summaries of weekly news, and editorials in their online version.

### Crain's New York Business
http://www.crainsny.com

The New York edition of Crain's offers current and historical economic statistics about New York City and the metropolitan area, weekly features from the printed publication, and a Small Business Section and Business Survival Guide with resources for business people.

### The Economist
http://www.economist.com

The highbrow political/business weekly, *The Economist*, has established an experimental Web site, offering tidbits of their global perspective in selected articles from the print edition and a summary of each week's issue. Archives provide the same smattering of content from the print edition, although a hypertext version of *The Economist Review*, focusing on books and multimedia, is a nice touch. Users can sign up for free weekly summaries of business and politics around the world, sent via e-mail.

## The Electronic Newstand
http://www.enews.com

The Electronic Newstand showcases a large variety of business and financial magazines, offering samples of content, links, and a customized newstand to keep track of your favorite magazines. Users can search their site and even subscribe online.

## The *Financial Times*
http://www.usa.ft.com

Don't expect the Web site of London's *Financial Times* to be pink like the print edition. The Web edition does offer full-text highlights of the day's news with color photos and a nice selection of market reports. It includes company snapshots of key financial people and fundamental information for more than 11,000 companies worldwide; closing spot rates in London for 38 currencies; daily closing price of 3,000 equities on the London Stock Exchange; and fund and index prices. Two discussion groups provide forums for users to discuss the news and what it means to them.

## *Financial World*
http://www.financialworld.com

*Financial World*, America's oldest business magazine, offers the cover story from each issue and articles from recent issues on a Web site that's high on promise but short on delivery. The magazine's unique ratings of stock and mutual funds are presented, sorted, and screened by several criteria. Unfortunately, the data is too stale to be of much use.

## Forbes
http://www.forbes.com

Each day, *Forbes* updates its site with new articles, adding to it a collection of insight from "The Capitalist Tool." Investors should take a good look at the

Many companies are beginning to make their quarterly earnings announcements after the close of market hours. It's not uncommon for trading in a stock to be halted while news announced during market hours is disseminated. Companies contend that by making their announcements after the markets have closed they are helping individual investors. However, exchanges in other countries may be open, and trading in the growing after-hours market may also be accessible to institutional traders. As a result, companies are handicapping individual investors by forcing them to wait until the following day to act on the announcement.

site's investment primer, a collection of advice from past pages of the magazine. *Forbes*'s ratings of mutual funds and public companies and features like "The 200 Best Small Companies in America" are bound to keep investors returning for more.

## *Fortune* Magazine
http://www.fortune.com

Besides articles from the magazine, *Fortune*'s site includes the complete data set of the Fortune 500, available for downloading in spreadsheet format. Or you can peruse the tables online sorted in a variety of ways. The Global 500 is also provided. Users can search for articles of interest from the site or join in a discussion forum to chat about financial topics.

## *Inc.* Online
http://www.inc.com

If you're thinking of starting your own business, or you already have, *Inc.* Online is the Web site for you. Over 5,000 articles from the magazine's archives are online, including the current issue. But *Inc.* Online uses the medium to offer interactive worksheets, searchable databases, software libraries, and bulletin boards. Users can create their own page on the *Inc.* site, too.

## *Individual Investor* Interactive
**http://www.individualinvestor.com**

The Web site of this snappy monthly offers users a chance to chat with experts about the magazine's picks in discussion forums. Regular updates of companies in the *Individual Investor* Magic 25, their annual selection of hot stocks, are also provided.

## Investor's Business Daily
**http://www.investors.com**

The Web edition of the newspaper offers stories from all of the regular departments in its print edition. But with no archives and no search engine, the site is a bust for research purposes. Daily volume tables list the most actives on the U.S. exchanges, and include the magazine's proprietary ratings, as well. The Investment Education Course is a step-by-step explanation of the basics of the stock market and the CANSLIM approach to investing.

## *Kiplinger* Online
**http://www.kiplinger.com**

The online center of *Kiplinger*'s kingdom of business and finance commentary features articles from *Kiplinger's Personal Finance Magazine.* They are summaries of current issues of the Kiplinger business letters. Investment tools, such as lists of top funds, stock quotes, and an impressive array of financial calculators, make the site a useful addition to an investor's hot list.

## *Money Magazine*
**http://www.money.com**

The online edition of *Money Magazine* shares little content with its printed sibling. A few feature articles are provided, along with quotes, a portfolio tracking service, and bulletin boards for users. The Financial Toolkit has some handy tools to compute your net worth, portfolio return, or adequacy of retirement savings. Subscribe to Money Daily free and get e-mailed news each day in your mailbox.

## The *New York Times*
**http://www.nytimes.com**

Where can you get all the news that's fit to print, on the World Wide Web? Here at the *New York Times* site, of course. The site includes all the day's news, along with market quotes, lists of most actives and industry groups, and a portfolio tracker. Users can search the site for articles of interest, and a stock market forum provides the opportunity for reasoned (or not so reasoned) discourse.

## San Jose Mercury News
**http://www.sjmercury.com**

From the heart of Silicon Valley comes this daily newspaper's cyber edition. Surfers will find the complete text of news articles each day, along with features like a regular insider trading report of

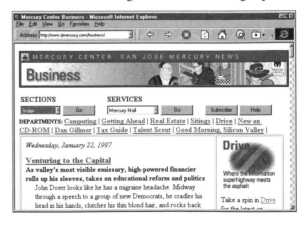

selected stock transactions involving publicly held companies in Silicon Valley or market information on Silicon Valley's top 150 companies. A personal portfolio service is also provided.

## USA Today
**http://www.usatoday.com**

*USA Today* Online provides the same brisk coverage of business and finance as its daily paper version. The usual stock quotes capability is here. Added features include a list of the coming week's IPOs; retirement, car, mortgage, and tuition calculators; and commentary from the Motley Fool.

## U.S. News and World Report Online
**http://www.usnews.com**

*U.S. News and World Report* expands upon the coverage provided in the print edition with this attractively organized site. Offered are daily news updates, in addition to columns and departments of the magazine. Search the archives for past or current stories, too.

## The Wall Street Journal Interactive Edition
**http://www.wsj.com**

Available only by subscription, the *Wall Street Journal* Interactive Edition brings its extensive financial coverage to the online community. Daily updates of the world's major markets, with quotes, charts and tables, are provided, as well as personal portfolio tracking and quotes lookup. But the most useful feature of the site may be the Company Briefing Books. These comprehensive guides are available for most public companies; they provide background, news, press releases, fundamental data, and stock performance graphs.

 Another good source of news about a particular stock is that company's own Web site. Often, companies make their own press releases available on their sites.

## The Web Newstand
**http://www.web-newsstand.com**

The Web Newstand provides links to news sites on the Internet, including magazines and newspapers in several different categories, such as Business, Politics, or Computers.

## Worth Online
**http://www.worth.com**

*Worth* is the magazine of "financial intelligence," and the Web site lives up to the name. Besides excerpts from the print edition and a complete archive (including all of Peter Lynch's columns), *Worth* Online boasts special features, personal finance FAQs, a great beginner's course, and online events. Message boards let you chat with other like-minded investors, and a free weekly newsletter is available.

# FINANCIAL ADVICE

Need some guidance building your portfolio? You've got two options: do it yourself, or bring in a pro. Either way, a bit of expert advice can't do much harm—or, when it comes to investing, can it? At any rate, the Web is home to a host of pundits, gurus, and average Joes who are willing to offer some wisdom, sometimes on a cash-only basis and sometimes just for a tip of the hat.

## ADVISORY SERVICES AND MARKET LETTERS

The Internet's market letters bear little resemblance to their printed cousins. Investors can receive e-mailed buy and sell signals from an advisory service nearly instantaneously or log on to a Web site and check out the latest charts and picks. These services run the gamut from general market commentary and advice to specific systems for investing.

### A.S.K. Financial Digest
http://www.askd.com

Investment advisor Dan Kirchen writes this monthly letter for traders of stocks, bonds, and mutual funds. His letter analyzes the markets as well as the economy. Samples and subscription information are provided.

### Accelerating Growth Stockselector
http://www.dirs.com/invest/ags

Looking for growth companies with explosive stock price appreciation potential? Who isn't! The *Accelerating Growth Stockselector* newsletter is published monthly, with regular picks of fast-growing over-the-counter stocks. Subscribers to the print publication also receive e-mail or fax updates.

### Alaska's Voice of the North
http://www.ptialaska.net/~voice/

This firm offers a monthly newsletter providing the results of their financial forecasting research on growth stocks and special situations.

### Alternative Wealth Strategies
http://aws.net

If you're the type who always has to be different, how about trying some of these alternative investment opportunities: hardwood timber ownership, offshore trust accounts, life insurance buyouts, or fine arts. This free newsletter and Web site offer tips and advice for adventurous investors.

### American Stock Report
http://www.awod.com/gallery/business/asr/

Available in print or by e-mail, the *American Stock Report* gives investors concise reviews of selected growth stocks. The *Report* tracks leading financial publications and condenses the results into a monthly journal. Feature articles are also included.

### Aurex Market Masters
http://www.aurex.com

This online investment newsletter looks for near-term winners, using sophisticated models to pick stocks that are likely to outperform. Their goal is to provide information, tools, and strategies to help the speculator. Users can sample their offerings on the site before subscribing.

### Bob'z Personal Investing
http://www.tiac.com/users/bobz/

Got a quick question about personal finance? Bob and his crew of professional advisors are here to lend a hand. Bulletin boards are provided for your questions, and feature articles will help enlighten and educate you.

### Cabot Money Management's Investment Advisory Services
http://www.cabotm.com/cabot.html

*The Cabot Market Letter*, published 24 times a year, gives advice on buying and selling fast-growing stocks of lesser-known companies and is now available by e-mail as well as in print. The site presents a Tip of the Month, current issue highlights, and the chance to sign up for a free trial of the e-mail edition.

## J. Patrick Calby Newsletter

**http://www.2020tech.com/pcalby**

Florida-based investment advisor Pat Calby offers a susbcription-based e-mail newsletter of long-term and short-term recommendations. Users can check out his archives on the site.

## The Contrarian's View

**http://www.assumption.edu/HTML/ContraView/about.html**

Nick Chase publishes a monthly newsletter with essays and model portfolios for a limited number of subscribers. Archives of past issues are available to Web surfers, or you can request a subscription if your viewpoint is as contrarian as Chase's.

## Day Traders On-Line

**http://www.daytraders.com**

Day traders look to profit by very short-term discrepancies in the market, and this service provides subscribers with market research that is directed at intra-day trading and broadcasted in e-mail. Their site offers stock chat rooms, examples of their service, and a two-week free trial.

## The Directors Chair

**http://www.cdrgrp.com/dcwelcome.html**

The Cedar Group offers investors a custom strategy for investing in your 401(k), 403(b), or 457 retirement account. Users subscribe to their service, then access the site for statistical analysis specific to their retirement plan.

## Thomas Doll & Co. Doctor's Report

**http://www.ispot.com/TDC/**

This California CPA firm offers financial planning and consulting specifically for doctors and dentists. The *Doctor's Report* is their monthly advice newslet-

**ask doug!**

**Q:** What's a contrarian?

**A:** A contrarian is an investor who invests against the crowd, buying stocks that are unpopular with the majority of investors. Contrarians operate on the theory that things are rarely as bad as they seem, that the herd mentality of Wall Street leads investors to overreact on bad news, pushing a particular stock's price down further than is really warranted. That's when a contrarian starts buying.

ter for medical professionals, available free online. Current issues and archives are on their site, and much of the information is applicable, even if you only play a doctor on TV.

## Dogs of the Dow

**http://www.dogsofthedow.com**

You can't ask for a much simpler market strategy than the Dogs of the Dow provide. Buy equal amounts of the ten highest yielding (and therefore usually worst-performing) stocks in the

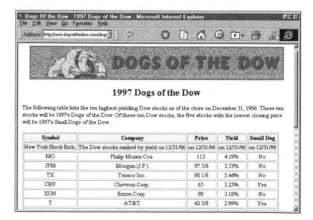

Dow Jones Industrial Average. Hold for one year. Then sell them all and repeat. That's it. Since advocated by Michael O'Higgins, this strategy and its variants have proven to be an easy way to beat the market. Analyst Pete Grosz maintains a site devoted to the Dogs of the Dow, providing free information about the system and also a well-organized group of investment research tools.

## Equities Day Trading

### http://kwicsys.com/investmentresearch

Need help keeping an eye on the market during the trading day? This subscription e-mail newsletter offers trading suggestions during the day, such as announcements of upgrades and downgrades, from various market timers and major brokerage houses. The service also provides the biggest winners and losers at the market close.

## F.X.C. Investors Corp.

### http://www.fxcinv.com

This rather drab site is home to investment advisor Frank Curzio and his newsletter service, but don't be fooled. Curzio is credited by the *Wall St. Journal*, CNBC, the *Washington Post*, ABC, CBS, and other media for calling the 1987 stock market crash. His newsletter is consistently ranked in the top five by *Hulbert's Financial Digest*. Investors can sign up on the site for a subscription to the printed monthly.

## The Financial Center

### http://www.tfc.com

The Financial Center is the home of Wall Street's "Market Mavens," including such pundits as Frank Capiello, John Bollinger, Bob Gabele, George Putnam, Bill Donaghue, Ben Zacks, and many others. Each week, users can get a sampling of wisdom from each of the mavens and then find out more about the newsletters or services each provides. The site is jam-packed with information, and the obvious quality of the contributions makes up for the somewhat over-designed site.

## First Advisors

### http://firstadvisors.com

Subscribers to the First Advisors service receive notification of actual buy and sell transactions, as well as portfolio advice on their selected portfolio style. Using e-mail or fax, money managers including Gabelli Asset Management and Edgar Lomax generate signals in different portfolios: Arbitrage, Large Cap Value, Small Cap Growth, Small Cap Value, and Tactical Fixed Income. Sign up on the site for a 30-day free trial.

## Green Mountain Asset Management Corp.

### http://www.stockresearch.com

For an investing approach modeled on Warren Buffet's, try this free e-mail newsletter, with stock recommendations, updates, and weekly economic commentary, provided by a Vermont money manager. Sensible, straightforward, and market-beating advice awaits on this Web site.

## The Greenwich Report

### http://www.greenwichreport.com

Each week, *The Greewich Report* offers unconventional, yet thorough, advice and insights on stocks, commodities, currencies, precious metals, and the market in general. Users can access the reports free on their site, though registration is required to read some of the most recent editions.

## Green On Money
### http://www.green-on-money.com

Peter Green is a widely recognized market maven who has been publishing *Green On Money* for a dozen years. Published every third week, the newsletter features stock market and economic forecasts, particular stock recommendations, and other topics to help individuals realize financial independence. Sample issues may be requested online.

## The *Holt Stock Report*
### http://turnpike.net/metro/holt

The *Holt Stock Report* provides an incredibly comprehensive composite of market activity at the end of each trading day, including advancers, decliners, stocks reaching new highs and lows, most active stocks, and much more. An intra-day report provides an overview of the market's mid-day position. Past issues of the *Holt Stock Report* are archived on the site, as well. Users can choose to have the reports delivered by e-mail, or can access them on the site.

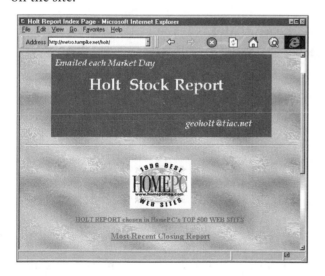

## Hulbert Financial Digest
### http://cybersurfing.com/hfd

The esteemed *Hulbert Financial Digest* newsletter provides objective ratings of over 160 newsletters and the 450 portfolios they recommend. Their Web site provides a list of all the newsletters tracked by the service, answers to FAQs, and an introductory offer. Before you try any newsletter, you might want to see what Hulbert has to say about it.

## INVESTools
### http://www.investools.com

If you're having trouble deciding which stock market newsletter to subscribe to, click directly to the *INVESTools Newsletter Digest*. This free weekly report summarizes the findings from more than 20 market letters and advisory services. If you like what a particular guru has to say, click on over to the INVESTools newsletter index and check out a sample issue. If the vibes are right, you can purchase the most recent issue right online, or even sign up for an electronic subscription. INVESTools includes many of the leading newsletters covering financial markets.

## INVESTORS
### http://www.angelfire.com/free/ INVESTORS.html

This weekly e-mail investment newsletter covers stock markets in the United States, Canada and overseas. An overview of the market is presented, along with a detailed analysis of a particular investment. This short Web page doesn't do the letter justice, however. You'll have to subscribe for a three-month trial and see for yourself how valuable *INVESTORS* really is.

Once you've found a system for investing with which you're comfortable, don't second-guess it. If you're paying an advisor or service to advise you, let them advise you. If you're not consistent in your approach, you'll only end up sabotaging your returns.

## Investors Newsletter Digest
### http://www.investorsnews.com

Taking a *Reader's Digest* approach to financial commentary, *Investors Newsletter Digest* summarizes the opinions and recommendations of many top financial newsletters. Each monthly publication also offers original articles, live market reports, specialized reports, and investment tips. The site provides a stock quote server and portfolio management service, as well as links to financial Web sites.

## Investor's Nightly Journal
### http://www.libertyresearch.com

Each evening, Liberty Research Corp uses technical analysis to filter through thousands of stocks to create lists of stocks to be held long term or traded actively. The *Journal* gives automatic buy/sell signals for these very strong stocks on both a short-term and long-term basis. It also has annotated charts and text to help the reader anticipate the direction of the stock market for tomorrow from both a fundamental and a technical point of view. Subscribe or get a sample issue from the site.

## Jack's Picks
### http://www.jackm.com

Jack's waiting for you, with stock advice, winners, losers, and other market commentary you won't find anywhere else. This site doesn't look like any other, either, with its wild array of colors, fonts, and musical accompaniment. Sign up for Jack's service and get his unique perspective, directed mostly at novices.

## Jag Notes
### http://www.jagnotes.com

Jag Notes is a daily national service with up-to-date information about the stock market; major Wall Street firms' buy, sell, or hold recommendations; technical perceptions; computer trading trends; and option moves. Reports are transmitted to subscribers by fax or the Web; yesterday's report is available for free on their Web site.

## Lombard Street Research, Ltd.
### http://www.demon.co.uk/lombard/

Lombard Street Research offers a domestic (U.K.) advisory service and an international advisory service primarily for institutional investors. This page provides their address for more information, and brief descriptions of the services.

## Market-$mith
### http://members.aol.com/jjeess1/index.htm

Market-$mith provides free predictions for over 100 stock and bond sectors, and for the U. S. dollar, looking three days, one month, three months, and 12 months into the future. Predictions are updated two or more times weekly.

## Market Timing
### http://www.mindspring.com/~edge/timing.html

If you're desperate to avoid a bear market, this stock market timing service claims to offer buy and sell signals to help you do just that. The publisher of this e-mail newsletter has developed two models to generate his signals. Subscribers receive weekly updates.

## the swami speaks

Listproc, listserv, majordomo. These are among the software programs that make Internet mailing lists possible. All are in common use, and they all work by responding to specific commands issued to them via e-mail messages from users. Once you've found a list you'd like to join, you'll need to know a few things in order to participate.

Internet mailing lists exist to allow a group of people to come together to talk about a common topic (a discussion list) or occasionally to allow a single person to send messages to a regular group of users (a broadcast list).

To join a list, you have to subscribe. This doesn't typically entail any money; it's just the act of joining the group. To subscribe or unsubscribe to a particular list, you need to follow the given instructions precisely, sending an exact command to the list software. Usually, the command you send must be in the body of your message, and not in the subject line. (That typically will cause an error.)

Once you've joined, you'll get a confirmation message from the list software and instructions on how to use the list and the separate e-mail address to which you'll send messages. Save these instructions. They contain the information you'll need to someday get off the list, as well as other settings you can select. For instance, some lists have a *digest* feature, by which you can elect to receive a single daily message that includes all the individual messages transmitted over the list each day. This can keep your mailbox a little neater. Some lists are *moderated*, which means a live person has to approve all the messages that are sent to the list, to make sure they are appropriate.

Finally, don't forget these rules of list etiquette:

**1** Don't write in all capital letters. THIS IS THE ONLINE VERSION OF SHOUTING!

**2** Don't excessively quote the message to which you're responding. It's proper to include a snippet of the original post in your reply to help continuity, but prune the original message liberally.

**3** Keep your messages on topic. If you post a question about upgrading RAM to an investing list, you're liable to get some nasty responses. Likewise, keep the idle chatter to a minimum, and fight *thread drift*—the propensity for discussions to continue to the point where they have nothing to do with the original issue. If you're having a nice chat with a particular person but you're getting off topic, it's appropriate to take the message to private e-mail.

**4** Don't post messages to the list about using the list, or unsubscribing. Each list has a list owner, and the instructions you receive when you first subscribe contain the address of the person you should contact if you're having trouble.

**5** Be nice! And a corollary: ignore people who aren't. People who publicly flame other users on lists are usually trying to stroke their own inflated egos, so don't let anyone draw you into an online shouting match. You'll both just end up looking like idiots.

### MathVest

http://www.proaxis.com/
~mathvest/Mvst/index.html

MathVest is a personalized portfolio service based on a unique mechanical system developed by a mathematician. The system gives precise buy-stop and sell-stop orders in certain stocks based upon their market action. Specific positions and results are updated on a regular basis on their site.

### MoniResearch Newsletter

http://www.transport.com/~access/mr.html

Who keeps track of the people keeping track of the market? The *MoniResearch Newsletter* does! Each issue ranks the performance of over 60 market timers and asset allocators, from Paul Merriman to Marty Zweig. Published every other month, the newsletter is filled with tables and data to help you find the hottest advisors out there.

### Mojena Market Timing

http://members.aol.com/smartlet/home.htm

Here's a timing model that detects new stock market cycles and issues buy or sell signals. The system switches investments between index-based stock funds and money market funds. The free Web site includes weekly results, quarterly updates, switch alerts, and a description of the model.

### The Napeague Letter

Bob Davis, a financial consultant, provides free, in-depth research using fundamental analysis tools to identify growing yet undervalued small-cap companies. He then uses technical analyses to identify potential buy and sell points. His reports are then available free to anyone who requests them. To subscribe, e-mail a request to him at rmdavis1@ix.net-

com.com with "subscribe" in the body of the message.

### Newsletter Access—Investments

http://www.newsletteraccess.com/subject/
invest.html

If you're an investor who likes to have a wide selection offered before making a decision, then check out Newsletter Access's searchable and browsable directory of over 5,000 newsletters, including 430 directly related to investments. Addresses, phone numbers, URLs, and subscription details are provided for each publication.

### Newsletter Network

http://www.margin.com

Users can set up an account with the Newsletter Network to purchase the most recent issue of any of dozens of market letters that are included in the service. Samples are free, and you can subscribe online if you find the newsletter that's right for you.

### Northwest News and Market Report

This daily stock market report features performance data focused on stocks from the Pacific Northwest. To subscribe, send a request to charterhar@aol.com.

### PM Hot Stocks Newsletter

http://www.class.mb.ca/class

George Chelekis is a Canadian newsletter writer who publishes a widely followed list of hot stocks. This e-mail newsletter recommends daily buys and sells for each stock on the list, using their Portfolio Manager software tool and a proprietary price performance algorithm. Check out sample issues on the site or request a free monthly trial.

## J. Michael Pinson's *Investment Digest Newsletter*

### http://www.tfc.com/pinson

Pinson's well-respected newsletter features economic indicators, market data, insider trading activity, Fidelity Sector mutual fund outlook, conservative and speculative growth stocks, no-load mutual funds, closed-end country mutual funds, asset allocation tables, monitored stocks for current recommendations, and global markets in review. Lots of sample issues are on his Web site in Acrobat format.

## The Pitbull Investor

### http://com.primenet.com/pitbull

The Pitbull Investor is an online service that focuses on low-cost, low-risk but aggressive growth stock investment, options trading, and high-performance stock shorting systems. Subscribers receive trading manuals (also available on a one-time purchase basis) and regular stock selections.

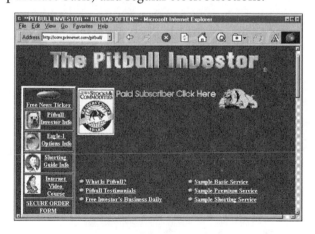

## The Privateer

### http://www.the-privateer.com

The Privateer is an electronic Australian private market letter for the individual capitalist. The publication is global in scope, comprehensive, and "devoid of any trace of political correctness."

**Q:** What's an Investment Advisor?

**A:** Anyone who provides investment advice professionally is required to register with the Securities and Exchange Commission and is then known as a "registered investment advisor." But there are no qualifications or prerequisites for registering, so the title itself confers no evidence of a particular individual's knowledge, only that he or she has registered with the SEC as legally required. Many states also require investment advisors to register.

Recommended stocks in its model portfolios trade on the Australian exchanges.

## Profit Investor Services Group

### http://www.li.net/~profit/index.html

Profit Publishing offers systems and strategies for trading options, IPOs and other securities, as well as newsletters.

## The Profit Letter

### http://www.stockgroup.com/PROFIT.html

The Profit Letter is an independent, unbiased advisory service that provides specific buy and sell advice on selected common stocks, with a preference for junior companies. Past issues are online.

## Rolling Stocks Report

### http://www.itsnet.com/~quantum/

A rolling stock gathers no moss, but can certainly generate a lot of profits! That's the contention of The

*Rolling Stocks Report*, at any rate. The weekly newsletter identifies the hottest rolling stocks (those that regularly cycle between a particular high and low) for e-mail subscribers.

### The Savvy Investor

**http://www.websellerinc.com/savvy/**
**index.htm**

This is a ten-page, monthly newsletter that specializes in undiscovered and undervalued stocks that have tremendous potential for dramatic appreciation.

### Sensible Investment Strategies

**http://www.seninvest.com**

How would you like a list of highly ranked mutual funds customized for your individual preferences and needs for a one-time low fee? That's exactly what Sensible Investment Strategies provides: a plan created by a certified financial planner just for you, using only the best performing no-load mutual funds. You can even purchase your plan online using a secure Web server.

### SGA Goldstar Reseach

**http://sgagoldstar.com/sga/**

SGA Goldstar Research publishes a daily financial newsletter offering opinions and recommendations from successful stock market experts. The advisory tracks a wide array of vehicles: stocks, bonds, options, futures, securities, gold, the NYSE, American and NASDAQ stock exchanges, Dow Jones, over-the-counter stocks, and Canadian stocks. Reports are accessed on the Web site each day; a free two-week trial is available.

 Many advisory services and newsletters on the Internet are nothing but the online equivalent of infomercials. Companies pay to have research about their stock distributed to investors. It doesn't mean this information is inherently suspect, but you should always try to determine if an advisor or service is independent or is being remunerated by the companies being touted.

### Spencer Financial Corporation

**http://www.spencerletter.com**

The *Spencer Financial Newsletter* is published quarterly, reporting on various business investment opportunities in the publicly traded market.

### Stock/Fax

This free monthly e-mail newsletter gives speculators up to six companies to watch, primarily from Canadian exchanges. It also provides news flashes when a company is making a move or appears about to. E-mail stockfax@skybus.com for details.

### Stock Market Secrets

This is a daily market commentary. To subscribe to *Stock Market Secrets*, send an e-mail request to smi-request@world.std.com with "subscribe smi" in the body of the message.

### The Stock Market Advantage

**http://members.aol.com/stocksystm**

This online newsletter uses a proprietary stock market trading system to try to generate above-average returns with below-average risk. The site includes online editions of the newsletter and real-world portfolios. Buy and sell signals are available. All the information is provided free of charge.

## Stock Sector Analysis Newsletter

**http://ourworld.compuserve.com/homepages/ssan/**

This newsletter is focused on the industry sectors that make up the stock market and on the Fidelity Select sector mutual funds. Every 15 days, subscribers receive e-mail or faxes with Fidelity sector fund recommendations and information important to the short-to-medium-term prospects for the industry groups and Fidelity Select funds.

## StockLogic Research

**http://www.accessone.com/~logical**

This site is the home of The Stock Farmer, whose motto is "We grow stocks." The Stock Farmer is a stock selection and timing service that looks for market leaders with accelerating earnings and then analyzes major indices for specific signs of turning points. Sentiment indicators, such as the numbers of bullish vs. bearish advisors and the short interest ratio, are also considered. Results are updated regularly on the site.

## Stocknet Mutual Fund Timing Report

**http://www.consulan.com/stocknet/**

This report sends e-mail signals to subscribers on buying and selling mutual funds and on the S&P 500 index. Check out the model's performance history on the site and subscribe online.

## Street Tips

**http://user.mc.net/dougp/st/aaasa.html**

This bimonthly e-letter specializes in low-priced and technology stock tips. Sign up for two free issues on the site.

## TJK Market Letter

**http://members.aol.com/taejkim**

Tae J. Kim publishes his stock picks with detailed stock analysis and timely trading notices on this site. It is free.

## Tech 100 Daily Report

This free daily e-mail service provides closing quotes, overbought/oversold indicators, technical chart alert pointers, market wrap-up, specific company news briefs, and more. To subscribe, send a message to baccom@aol.com requesting to be placed on the *Tech 100 Daily Report* mailing list.

## Timing Is Everything

**http://www.ilinks.net/mktimer**

Subscribers to this e-mail newsletter are privy to objective buy and sell signals for stock mutual funds, using a long-term horizon that keeps trades to an average of once per year. The site provides plenty of graphs and a description of the system.

## Thomas Nelson Weekly Market Overview

**http://olis.north.de/~tnelson**

Nelson calls his market wrap "for the serious investor," and there's no fluff here—mostly just statistics for markets around the world. He also profiles a particular stock and offers a bit of commentary. You can access the overview on his site or request an e-mail subscription at no charge.

## Walkrich Investment Advisors, Inc.

**http://www.mo.net/walkrich/wrhome.htm**

Walkrich offers a weekly fundamental neural network appraisal of over 4,500 common stocks, rated on a standardized scale of their own creation. Subscribers can use these ratings to find the most fundamentally underpriced stocks and then apply their own analysis.

### Wall Streetwise Investment Newsletter
**http://www.awa.com/softlock/tturner/wsw/ wsw.html**

This education-oriented investment newsletter, published quarterly, offers stock recommendations in three areas: aggressive, growth, and conservative. Their site offers free financial planner software for downloading, an interactive investment personality quiz, and sample articles from the publication.

### Walter Deemer's Market Strategies and Insights
**http://www.4w.com/deemer**

Walter Deemer generates market strategies for sophisticated institutional investors in daily fax updates or weekly newsletters. He features technically oriented (but long-term) analysis of major market sectors. Past insight is available on the site.

### U.S. & World Early Warning Report
**http://www.subscriptions.com/beacon**

In this monthly newsletter, business and economic analyst Richard Maybury tackles geopolitical trends as they affect stocks, bonds, interest rates, gold, currencies, commodities, real estate, and foreign investments. Read sample commentary or order an information packet on their Web site.

### Yankee Hill Enterprises
**http://www.he.net/~yankee**

Yankee Hill Enterprises takes the art of portfolio management to a new level, allowing users to look over the shoulder of Leonardo da Vinci reincarnated as an experienced private investor. The master manages his personal portfolio, with real-time orders and specific positions, all reported on the site.

## MONEY MANAGERS AND INVESTMENT ADVISORS

When it's time to turn to professional help for your portfolio, you can turn to an investment advisor for assistance. Many of these advisors have established sites on the Web that outline their philosophies and strategies, provide performance results and model portfolios, or expound on the current state of the market. Some even offer educational resources, such as tutorials and glossaries, ready to be mined by prospecting investors.

### Association for Investment Management and Research
**http://www.aimr.org**

The Association for Investment Management and Research (AIMR) is an international, nonprofit organization with a membership that includes securities analysts, portfolio managers, strategists, consultants, educators, and other investment specialists. Their site is focused on the professional services, but diligent investors may want to check out the AIMR standards for presenting performance results followed by most advisors.

### Atlantic Financial
**http://www.af.com**

This full-service financial firm provides clients with objective top-quality advice at deep discount prices. Their VIP Asset Management Account provides a single statement for all your holdings, along with a no-fee debit VISA card, free check writing, and other services. The site provides a financial planning questionnaire and lots of other educational materials.

## Buckhorn Capital Management
http://www.buckhorncapital.com

This Charlotte-based investment management firm is primarily involved with individuals and small businesses in the southeastern United States. They offer to manage pension and profit sharing plans, corporate cash management accounts, endowments, individual accounts, trusts and estates, and Individual Retirement Accounts.

## Clark Capital Management Group, Inc.
http://www.ccmg.com

Clark Capital Management Group is a Registered Investment Advisor that seeks to insure that clients are positioned to take maximum advantage of favorable markets worldwide, while limiting risks related to market volatility and improper asset allocation. Their Navigator programs offer investors the chance to meet these goals. The firm is based in Philadelphia.

## Classic Asset Management
http://www.moneymanagement.com

Classic Asset Management provides discretionary money management services to individual investors, using momentum investing to attempt to generate consistent above-market returns. They also publish a monthly newsletter that details current stock selections and models portfolio performance and market outlook. Access their buy list and model portfolio on their Web site or sign up for a free trial of their newsletter.

## Conscious Investing
http://www.investing.com

Chuck Jones & Associates presents an innovative resource for those interested in personal financial planning and investing. The cleverly designed site provides professional planning tools, knowledge bases, news, and information about the services of the

Many professional investment advisors post current recommendations and research on their Web sites. While they intend to demonstrate their market smarts to potential customers, these sites can be a good source of ideas and insight that independent individual investors can use.

firm. Their Investor Refugee Camp is for individuals who feel they've been mistreated by an investment advisor. Dozens of articles on financial planning and investing await you at Conscious Investing.

## Creative Investment Research
http://www2.ari.net/cirm

Creative Investment Research provides general investment information and information on minority- and women-owned brokerage firms, banks, and thrifts. Their investment advisory services will guide investors in the management of portfolios and the selection and sale of securities.

## Danforth Associates Inc.
http://www.environs.com/wellesley/
DANFORTH/

Started 40 years ago as a way for a Boston family to manage its own investments, Danforth Associates now offers managed accounts to individual investors.

## D.A.C. Davis Investment Counsel, Inc.
http://www.io.org/~davisic

This Toronto-based firm (licensed to do business in the U.S. as well) invests for pension plans and high net-worth individuals, with a particular interest in U.S. small-cap and mid-cap stocks. The site features stock picks from their analysts, speeches and articles by company founder Doug Davis, and insights on the economy, along with some RealAudio highlights.

## DCA Global Investment Management
http://www.dcainvest.com

DCA's strategy is to invest in core asset class funds, then hedge against the market, interest rates, and currency risks. Their goal is optimizing returns, while minimizing volatility. The site includes information on their management team and its style, performance results, and their *Quarterly Review & Outlook.*

## Roger Engemann & Associates
http://www.secapl.com/REA

Here's a site that any investor can find useful. Roger Engemann's Pasedana firm has named its site the Online Investment Advisor, and it's a terrifically designed Web destination. Filled with facts and commentary, the site includes Engemann's growth stock philosophy, the firm's performance record, its current holdings and, as an added bonus, a list of Internet resources for each of the stocks in their portfolio. The Learning Center preaches the virtues of long-term investing in articles like "It Pays to Stay on the Train."

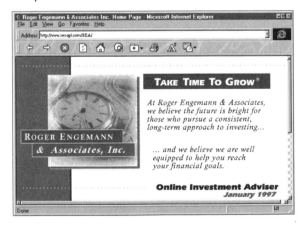

## Green Mountain Asset Management Corp.
http://www.stockresearch.com

Hailing from the Green Mountain State, of course, is Bob Bose and his information-filled site. Find Bose's commentary and recommendations, as well as lots of links.

## C.W. Henderson & Associates, Inc
http://www.cwhenderson.com

C.W. Henderson, in Chicago, is an investment advisor specializing tax-exempt municipal securities. Check their FAQs and municipal market commentary for helpful information about tax-free bonds.

## Heron Capital Management, Inc
http://www.heroncapital.com

Heron Capital Management, in New York City, provides investment services to individuals, trusts, pension funds, and corporations. Their exemplary Web site details their investing methodology and presents current performance results and Standard & Poor's Stock Reports on client holdings, as well as monthly commentary.

## IMS Capital Management
http://www.imscapital.com

IMS uses a contrarian investment philosophy to invest in blue chip stocks. Users can browse the library of their newsletter, *Contrarian Viewpoint*, on the site, or request more information about the firm's services.

## Investment Advisor XChange
http://www.iaxchange.com

The Xchange is an independent center for investment advisors, as well as the general public, and includes a searchable directory of advisors. You'll also find links and articles about advisors and investing in general.

## the swami speaks

You must master the rules of capitalization to make your Web journey most successful. No, the Web Swami isn't talking about market capitalization, but rather the spelling of your URLs and e-mail addresses.

E-mail addresses are not case sensitive. Sending a message to "SWAMI@INVESTORAMA.COM" will work just as well as "swami@investorama.com." Domain names are also not case sensitive. You can type "http://www.investorama.com" or "HTTP://WWW.INVESTORAMA.COM" in your browser and end up in the same most wonderful place. The standard convention is to print URLs in lower case.

However, file and directory names that are part of a URL are case sensitive. Directories are separated by the forward slash character, and any number of subdirectories can be included. In other words, "http://www.investorama.com/FEATURES/terrific_articles.html" and "http://www.investorama.com/features/terrific_articles.html" are not the same. You need to be extra careful in typing in a URL that points to a file in a subdirectory of a Web server.

## Lefavi Financial Center
**http://www.xmission.com/~lefavi/**

Bruce A. Lefavi helps clients to bulletproof their financial futures and reach their financial goals with low-risk strategies. His book, *Bulletproofing Your Financial Future*, helps investors create a personalized worry-free portfolio that maximizes returns and protects from inflation, depression, recession, and personal disasters such as long-term disability. Information on the book and Lefavi's service are available.

Don't become emotionally attached to your investments. If you let sentimental reasons cloud your judgment, you might hold on to an under-performing stock for the wrong reasons. Be strict with your portfolio, and don't be afraid to sell if the situation requires it.

## Lighthouse Investments
**http://www.invests.com**

Lighthouse Investments (which is kind of a funny name for a firm in Kansas) provides their newsletter online for registered users. They also offer free charts and reports on request.

## Macey & Co
**http://www.mindspring.com/~rexmacey**

Macey & Co. positions themselves as investment architects who will outline a financial blueprint based on your own personal goals. The site also includes articles by Rex Macey on general investing topics.

## MainStreet Capital Management Corp.
**http://www.mscapital.com**

MainStreet is a fee-based investment advisor in Maine providing investment advice, research, and portfolio management services concerning stocks, taxable and tax-exempt bonds, options, mutual funds, annuities, CDs, IRAs, 401K, and retirement planning strategies. Their site offers tips on selecting an advisor and a summary of their services.

## Montana Investment Advisory Service
**http://www.mdelano.com**

Each month from his office in Missoula, Montana, Marshall Delano offers investors his insight in a featured article on his Web site, usually focused on his long-term growth stock outlook. He also provides an essay on choosing a portfolio manager that's worth a look.

### McDonald & Company Investments, Inc
http://www.to-invest.com

Private portfolio managers from Cleveland, Ohio offer a model portfolio and the chance to order investment reports from their Web site, along with information about their services.

### Money Manager Review
http://www.slip.net/~mmreview

The *Money Manager Review* is a quarterly guide to the nation's best-performing, independent money managers. Pensions, profit-sharing plans, foundations, trusts, and high-net-worth individuals use the *Review* to locate and identify money managers who fit their needs. The Web site includes a Money Manager Directory, with a capsule profile of several hundred professional management firms and expanded information on featured managers. Also on the site, investors can request a ranking of all the managers in the *Review*.

## ask doug!

**Q:** Who needs an investment advisor?

**A:** Even the most astute investors might benefit from professional help at some point, when it comes to managing their assets. A good advisor will review your goals and your current situation then build a plan with you. Then the advisor will help you implement that plan. Many advisors will only accept clients with net worth of $100,000 or more, and most work on a fee basis. Generally speaking, the people who can benefit the most from an advisor's services are:

**1** Those who lack the experience to successfully invest in the market. It takes commitment and practice to become a successful investor, and some people just won't put the necessary effort into the task.

**2** Those who don't have a clear understanding of their own needs and how they change over time (the "can't see the forest for the trees" syndrome). Sometimes it takes an outside perspective to bring clarity to your goals.

**3** Those who lack broad knowledge about all available asset classes that might be better suited for their portfolio. You might be a great stock-picker, but your portfolio might be better off with a portion of assets in real estate or fixed income securities.

**4** Those independent investors who are looking for a one-stop-shopping solution. Your advisor can provide you with investment research as part of his or her services.

**5** Those who don't want to spend the time managing their portfolio. An advisor will keep you up to date on significant developments in your holdings, and then generate regular performance reports so you can clearly see how well you're doing.

To make sure the performance results advertised by investment advisors are legitimately calculated, the Association for Investment Management and Research publishes guidelines for the presentation of performance that most managers follow. These standards let you know that you're not comparing apples to oranges when evaluating the portfolio performance of several different firms.

## Money Minds
### http://www.money-minds.com

If your personal finance question can't wait, Money Minds has a team of professionals standing by waiting for your call to provide personal financial planning information and advice via telephone. The firm charges per minute (On-Demand information services), per hour (Portfolio Consulting & Financial Planning) or by percentage of assets (in their Summit Investment Management program). The service has been tested and recommended by a number of national financial publications.

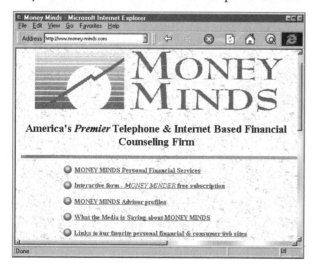

## Nelson Investment Management Network
### http://www.nelnet.com

This Super-Site is a primary source of data on investment managers on the Web, primarily for an institutional audience. Nelson's also hosts manager home pages and provides investment manager performance rankings.

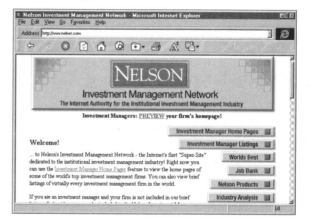

## Newport Pacific Management
### http://www.lib.com/newport/newport.html

This San Francisco-based investment management firm specializes in the Tiger countries of Asia and offers services to institutions, as well as their own mutual fund.

## *Pensions & Investments* Online
### http://www.pionline.com

Updated daily, this site is sponsored by the leading international newspaper of money management. It features breaking investment news and performance data on more than 3,000 investment products and 1,100 money managers. Find out how a particular manager compares to his or her peers.

You must be able to trust your investment advisor if you want to have a successful relationship. When choosing a manager, a good performance history isn't enough. You have to feel comfortable with the staff you are entrusting to make investing decisions on your behalf. Don't be blinded by the red-hot rate of return your advisor boasts.

### Smith Affiliated Capital Corp

http://infoweb.net/sac

This New York-based registered investment advisor boasts $1.3 billion in managed assets. Their specialty is creating fixed-income strategies for institutional and individual clients. Interested investors can e-mail them for more information.

### Joseph Stowell's Money Management Services

http://www.io.org/~mms/stowell/bonds/

Stowell's financial and trading consulting firm specializes in U.S. Treasury Bond futures, cash, and stocks. He is the author of the book *The Essential Characteristics of the Successful Trader* and provides excerpts on his site, along with other articles. Stowell also sells some of his educational videotapes and manuals from the site.

### Steere Investment Counsel, Inc.

http://www.why.net/home/steereic

This Texas investment advisor offers some interesting trend analysis and relative strength graphs and rankings on the site, to help you determine when to acquire stocks, what stocks to acquire, and when to divest them.

### Stendahl Report

http://www.geocities.com/wallstreet/1610/

David C. Stendahl, a registered investment advisor, has written a number of articles explaining some of the trading nuances of investing in today's fast-paced market. Much of the material focuses on index option-related investments, including S&P 500 Index mutual funds and OEX options.

### Turner Investment Partners

http://www.turner-invest.com

This employee-owned investment advisory firm offers equity, fixed income, and balanced account management to corporate, public, endowment, foundation, Taft-Hartley, and high-net-worth individual clients. The site includes up-to-date performance overviews of their managed accounts.

### Wall Street Financial Group

http://www.wallstreetfinancial.com/

Based in Rochester, NY, this firm offers financial planning solutions for their clients.

# GLOSSARY

ANALYST—A professional who analyzes the prices and values of stocks, bonds, industry groups, countries, or the markets themselves, and then provides an opinion as to the suitability for purchase.

ASSET CLASS—A particular category of investment, such as equities, real estate, venture capital, fixed income, and cash equivalents.

ASSET MANAGEMENT—The act of turning over your funds to a professional who is responsible for overseeing and investing in your portfolio on your behalf. Usually charges an annual management fee and/or a share of profits. Also known as money management or portfolio management.

BOTTOM-UP—An investing strategy that looks at a company's fundamentals first, instead of focusing on the overall economic or market situation (the top-down approach).

DAY TRADER—A person who buys and sells the same security on the same day, often at slim profits.

FEE-BASED FINANCIAL PLANNER—A professional who charges a flat fee for advisory services, rather than a commission.

FINANCIAL PLANNER—A professional who advises individuals on the investment and management of their assets. A certified financial planner has been approved to use that designation by the Institute of Certified Financial Planners.

INSIDER TRADING—Buying and selling stocks by management, directors, or other individuals with access to non-public information about a company. Their purchases or sales of that company's stock are regulated by the SEC so as to prohibit them from profiting by this confidential knowledge.

MARKET TIMING—The attempt to predict or detect when a market or security is at a peak (or bottom) and then trading accordingly. A crystal ball is the only sure market indicator.

POWER OF ATTORNEY—A legal form giving another person the power to act on your behalf, such as trading securities in your name.

SECTOR ROTATION—An investing strategy where assets are shifted from economic sector to economic sector based on where the economy is in the business cycle.

SIDELINES—An investor who is not currently invested in the market is on the sidelines.

STYLE—An investor's or manager's approach to the market. Common styles for stock investing include growth, value, sector rotation, market timing, top-down, bottom-up, large cap and small cap.

TOP-DOWN—An investment style where overall economic indicators are primarily used to determine investment strategies, as opposed to looking at a company's fundamentals (a bottom-up approach).

# Chapter 6
# Tools for Investors

"There are two times in a man's life when he should not speculate: when he can't afford it and when he can."

—Mark Twain

**The Internet** is chock-a-block full of tools and educational resources for investors. As you might expect, software developers have been quick to embrace the Web, providing complete specifications, descriptions, and downloadable demos of their programs from their Web sites. Bookstores have been quick to follow, since stocking virtual bookshelves is a lot easier than keep a "real" bookstore full of titles.

Investors who are looking to expand and enhance their understanding of the markets, or who seek new, powerful software tools to help in their investing, can turn to these sites. In most cases, ordering is as easy as using an online form.

# SOFTWARE

No online investor's toolbox is complete without a complementary set of software tools. From screening to analysis, record-keeping to tax reporting, software provides answers to the most common investing problems. A good analytical program can produce new insights into a particular security's performance potential, helping you to make better investing decisions. Software that can sort and screen a database of thousands of mutual funds or stocks can let you discover new investments you never would have found otherwise. At the very least, software can be an enormous time-saver, freeing you from the constraints of record-keeping and letting you spend more time on research, for instance.

These sites include shareware and commercial software developers, online stores that specialize in or feature a wide line of financial software, and Web-based applications, all related to investing.

## American Association of Individual Investors
**http://www.aaii.org**

Members of the American Association of Individual Investors (AAII) can subscribe to *Computerized Investing*, a bimonthly newsletter to help investors make the best use of their computer. The publication includes how-to articles, spreadsheets, and reviews of software and Web sites. AAII also publishes *The Individual Investor's Guide to Computerized Investing*, an annual guide, and *The Individual Investor's Interactive Guide to Computerized Investing*, a multiplatform interactive CD-ROM. The organization has also developed a stock-screening program with a regularly updated database, and low-load mutual fund software to compare funds' most recent performance results.

## Aberration
**http://ison.com/aberration**

Aberration is a commodity trading system that requires just a few calculations each day per commodity to generate trading signals. Even though the system is easy enough to use, a DOS program is also available to automate the process, including the maintenance of historical price files and performance testing in addition to determining buy and sell points. Easy Language code for SuperCharts or TradeStation users is also available.

## AbleSys Corporation
**http://www.ablesys.com**

ASCTrend is an indicator package that contains four indicators for commodities, bonds, stocks, currencies, or options trading. The program works with Omega Research TradeStation or SuperCharts, and a one-month trial is available.

Story stocks are stocks that have a great story behind them or are supported by an exciting concept. Unfortunately, these companies are often fundamentally weak investments. The story usually attempts to validate a stock that is probably already overvalued. If you hear a story that sounds too good to be true, it probably is.

### Advisor Software, Inc.
**http://www.advisorsw.com**

Is the asset allocation of your mutual funds compatible with your own portfolio goals? Mutual Max for Windows can tell you if your funds are staying true to their allocation mix. Mutual Fund Advisor is the company's version for investment advisors. Also available is a Style Spreadsheet, which uses Nobel Prize-winner William F. Sharpe's algorithms to provide a complete style analysis of your mutual funds.

### AIQ's MarketExpert Trendline
**http://www.aiq.com**

MarketExpert uses artificial intelligence to chart and analyze an unlimited number of stocks, indexes, and mutual funds. The software uses over 200 technical rules and indicators, displaying a daily or weekly technical outlook for every security. Investors can download MarketExpert for free, along with a selection of data from Dial/Data.

### AlleyCat Software
**http://localweb.com/alleycatsw**

How's your portfolio doing? Find out with Capital Gainz, a portfolio manager for Windows with the powerful features needed by professional money managers but designed for individual investors.

Besides tracking the securities you own, you can calculate your portfolio's internal rate of return to determine your actual realized performance. Prices can be updated manually, from a file or an online service. A full range of reports is available. The software is free, though no support is currently provided.

### Allomax Asset Allocation Software
**http://www.investmap.com**

Cornerstone Associates Technology Services, Inc. developed this program for investment professionals and individual investors to help determine the most efficient portfolio allocation. Users can also download a free Modern Portfolio Theory Primer from the site.

### The Analyzer
**http://www.dominfin.com/analyze.htm**

The Analyzer is a technical analysis and charting package for Windows that imports data from nearly any available source and creates custom charts. The program also contains a module to generate personalized trading signals based upon user-selected moving average oscillators. A demo version of The Analyzer is available.

### Anderson Investor's Software, Inc.
**http://www.invest-soft.com**

If you're shopping for software to help you with your investments, look no further than Anderson Investor's Software. This Missouri company sells nothing but financial- and business-oriented software, from charting programs to financial forecasting tools. Search from hundreds of available software packages, or browse the inventory by category, then order online. A collection of investing books is also available.

## atOnce Software

http://www.atonce.com/pages/bs-door.htm

atOnce Software specializes in immediate gratification; the company offers hundreds of popular software titles, all available for direct download to your desktop. Their online catalog features a selection of business and financial titles. Choose a title, provide payment info, and then download a fully working program to your own computer.

## Backtest Wizard

http://homepage.interaccess.com/~jas/
backtest_wizard.html

You think you've devised a great system for beating the market? Then you need developer John A. Sarkett's Backtest Wizard to apply your trading strategy to historical securities price data. After you evaluate the results, perhaps you'll find that your system needs a bit more tweaking to be a profitable strategy. The Wizard is a Microsoft Excel template for PC or Macintosh computers and can be used to test technical trading strategies on stocks, options, commodities, and futures.

## Behold!

http://www.bhld.com

For the Macintosh, Behold! is the technical analysis and system development software from Investors' Technical Services. The program allows users to write trading rules in English and then test and optimize the system. A slide-show demo of the program can be downloaded from the site.

## BellCharts Inc

http://www.bellcharts.com

BellCharts offers mutual fund charting and analysis software for Canadian mutual funds. The Daily Bell also provides daily Canadian fund data by subscription, with an option to receive daily pricing information on Canadian and U.S. stocks. A demo version of the program can be downloaded from the site.

## Blue Note Analytics, Inc.

http://www.bluenoteinc.com

bid/OPTIONS Power Pack is a sophisticated tool for the options floor trader, designed to be used on a palmtop computer. The program includes a set of position analysis tools, including what-if analyses, position plots, and Greek distributions.

## BondCalc

http://www.bondcalc.com

BondCalc is a pricing software system for fixed-income securities of all kinds. Popular with bond traders, the program is also heavily used by those on the sell side. A portfolio report and graphing function can plot over 60 statistics and provide many other features.

### Bob Browning's List of Treasury Software

**http://www.textor.com/markets/guide**

Bob Browning's specialized directory is geared for information technology professionals working in the banking industry. It includes listings of over 500 software products for managing front and back office operations, Forex, money markets, capital markets, and derivatives.

### Captool

**http://www.captools.com/captools**

Captool maintains complete records of all portfolio transactions, values your portfolios, tracks cost

basis, computes performance, and generates an array of reports and graphs. A Global Investor version handles multiple currencies and is suited for the international investor. Professional and Individual versions each provide unique functions as needed by these investors. Demos are available for download from the site.

### Chartistics

**http://www.pangsway.demon.co.uk/ pangsway.htm**

Chartistics is a technical analysis program for Windows from Pangsway Limited. The software offers unique charting and statistical analysis for investors

---

**ask doug!**

**Q:** What's the difference between yield, return, total return, annualized rate of return, and all the other different returns I've heard about?

**A:** It's important to be able to calculate the performance of your portfolio and of the individual securities you own to make sure you are reaching your goals. There a number of different return and yield calculations, and each provides key information on performance. Yield is the percentage return on an investment from the dividends paid on a stock or interest paid on a bond or money market fund on an annual basis. Total Return is figured by adding the dividends or interest to the capital appreciation of a security.

Another factor must also be considered, however, and that's the time element. If you calculate that a stock you own has a Total Return of 15 percent, it makes a big difference whether you've owned it for three weeks, three months or three years. So,

the next step is to calculate the annualized rate of return, by taking the number of days you've owned that security and extrapolating that rate of return as if it continued to perform the same way for an entire year.

Here comes the complicated part. Let's say you bought shares of the same stock at two different times in the year, or that you sold part of your holdings in one company. You have to take into account those purchases or sales when calculating your annual return, as well. Next, if you consider your entire portfolio and all of the purchases, sales, interest, dividends, cash withdrawals, and cash deposits, you can see how many separate calculations it would take to figure out your annualized rate of return for your entire portfolio. This is where portfolio management software can help. Your computer can do these calculations much faster and much more accurately than you could do manually.

and momentum traders to analyze stocks, funds, Forex, and commodities.

## ChartSmart Software
http://www.chartsmart.com

ChartSmart is designed to monitor and analyze Canadian stocks, and the program is specifically tailored to assist investors in dealing with junior resource companies and speculative stocks often found on the Vancouver and Alberta Stock Exchanges.

Users can download the software free from the ChartSmart site or view a slide-show demo online. The company also provides subscription data services.

## Computerized Trader
http://www.io.com/~gibbonsb/ct-index.html

Gibbons Burke writes "The Computerized Trader," a column that appears in *Futures Magazine*. Archived on this site are abstracts or full-text versions of all of his articles that have been published in the magazine, focusing on using the computer in trading futures. Also available are spreadsheets that are described in the columns.

## Commodity Trader's Sidekick
http://www.annabec.com

The Commodity Trader's Sidekick is a collection of definitions, examples, and references written in Windows Help file format and geared for the new futures trader. An evaluation version can be downloaded from Annabec Business Services, Inc.'s Web site.

## Customer Service, Inc.
http://www.windowofopportunity.com

Customer Service, Inc. (CSI) offers educational programs and various software packages for traders. Their service includes complete collections of books,

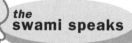

**the swami speaks**

This tangled Web is wonderful for many things, but downloading programs and other files isn't always one of them. One of the Swami's favorite tips for downloading is the right-click trick, which works in Explorer and Navigator and some other browsers. Instead of clicking on a link to download an executable file, like a software demo or a compressed zip file, click with your right mouse button. This will pop up a small dialog box that gives you the option to save the file to your hard drive. You can select the directory and file name, then download the file to precisely the right place on your hard drive. For Mac users, press down on the mouse button and hold it down until the menu appears.

manuals, and videotapes, all designed to be used within the context of a plan the company has devised.

## DollarLink Software
http://www.dollarlink.com/dlink.htm

DollarLink is an intra-day trading program with a sophisticated and comprehensive real-time technical analysis toolbox. It offers real-time customizable charts, quote pages, and technical analysis studies. A free trial is available from the Web site.

## Dynatach
http://www.dynatach.com

Dynatach provides trading systems that work with Omega Research, Inc.'s TradeStation software for trading commodities.

When updating your portfolio in a software program, don't enter stock and fund prices by hand. Use one of the Internet sources for quotes described in Chapter 2 and download a data file to your own computer. Then use the software's import function to automatically update all prices.

### EcoWin

**http://www.ecowin.com**

EcoWin is a time-series analysis package, working in conjunction with a database of the international money, bond, Forex, stock, and commodity markets. The program allows for comparative graphs to be made on a wide range of analytical relationships.

### The Edge, from BulletProof.com

**http://www.bulletproof.com**

The Edge is stock tracking software with other tools for the individual investor, developed by Bullet-Proof.com. The Edge automates stock information gathering, with portfolio management and charting functions. The program can be used to beep your pager about price changes or market news. Built for Windows 3.1 and Windows 95, the software requires a subscription to the CompuServe Information Service for access to quotes, news, and e-mailed alerts. Users can download the program, along with a company database, from the site.

### EEBond

**http://www.mmrsoft.com**

U.S. Savings Bonds are a popular vehicle for many investors who are building a nest egg or saving for a child's college education. But determining what those bonds are worth at any point in time can be a difficult task. EEBond, for Windows or DOS, maintains a complete database of Series EE, Series E Savings Bonds, and U.S. Savings Notes, from 1942 to the present. MMRSoft also provides updated savings bond valuation tables for the software. Users can download a copy of this shareware program from the site.

### ElWave

**http://www.prognosis.nl**

ElWave is a Windows-based software program by Prognosis Software Development designed to apply the Elliott Wave Principle in your security analysis. A working demo version of the software is available.

### Ira Epstein & Company Futures

**http://www.iepstein.com**

Ira Epstein & Company Futures, a leading futures brokerage, offers free demo versions of their Ira-Chart charting software and 1-2-3 Plus Charts software for downloading from their Web site.

### Equis International

**http://www.equis.com**

MetaStock, from Equis International, is the grand-daddy of technical analysis software. This site provides complete information about MetaStock, as well as about Equis's other investing software programs for Windows and DOS, including Option-Scope, The Technician, and Pulse Portfolio. Users with fast Internet connections can enjoy video clips of Equis founder Steve Achelis describing MetaStock and how to get started using it. Current customers will be interested in back issues of Equis International's newsletter; files of tips, system tests, and custom formulas for use with the software; and technical support FAQs. Several demos are available for downloading, as well.

There's a difference between portfolio management and portfolio record-keeping. Portfolio management involves keeping tabs on your holdings to make sure they fit your goals for asset allocation, diversification, performance, and quality. Record-keeping is keeping track of all your transactions, mainly for tax purposes. Some software programs combine the two tasks, but many only fulfill one of these functions.

## ExpressData Corporation

http://www.xprsdata.com

Fixed income investors can put Qwick-Rate right to work, with complete investment accounting and reporting capabilities for Certificates of Deposit. Qwick-Rate (for DOS) calculates and automatically updates your accrued interest figures and allows you to print reports in several formats. ExpressData also provides current CD market data and investment tracking software for financial institutions.

## Ezy Group Stock Market Products

http://www.ezygroup.net.au

From Australia, Ezy Group offers technical analysis software for beginners and intermediate users, including Ezy Chart, a stock market trading program; Ezy Analyzer, to analyze the market for buy and sell signals; Ezy Portfolio Manager; and Ezy Money, a charting and portfolio program in one package. Users can request a demo by e-mail.

## Febo

http://home.earthlink.net/~dataform

Dataform's financial data charting software provides users with the tools to graph stocks, commodities futures, mutual funds, indexes, and other financial investment data. Available for Windows 3.1, a free trial can be downloaded from the site.

## Financial Markets Prediction Services Project

http://www.bio-comp.com/financia.htm

This project of BioComp Systems, Inc. generates predictions of market prices, sales, or demand using their NeuroGenetic technology. Using neural networks, the project has developed market timing models, and it provides links to other systems employing the technology.

## FinancialCAD

http://www.financialcad.com

FinancialCAD is a library of functions for Microsoft Excel covering Forex, equity, interest rates, commodities, forwards, futures, options, swaps, and derivatives. The workbooks included with the program provide enormous power and flexibility in analyzing investment opportunities. A seven-day free trial can be downloaded from the site.

## Fintech

http://www.fintech.ch

Fintech has developed a number of programs, as well as other investment tools, to analyze and optimize a portfolio. Also available on their site are two options pricing applets.

## FlexSoft Software

http://www.flexsoft.com

FlexSoft provides products for the individual and professional investor to aid in the technical analysis of stocks and commodities. Their products, for DOS, are Technical Analysis Scanner and Personal Ticker Tape. Pro-DownLoader is available for Windows for downloading stock, index, bond, and fund

Shareware is software that is provided to users on a "try before you buy" basis. Shareware programs are freely distributed by their developers and by many online sources, and you can download these programs without charge. If you like the program, you can register with the author. Some shareware programs come with some features disabled, like the ability to print, or they only work for a limited time. When you register for the program, those features will be unlocked. Just remember, if you use a shareware program on a regular basis, you are honor-bound to pay for it.

quotes and news from Prodigy. Evaluation versions of the programs may be downloaded.

## FundBuilder

http://www.fundbuilder.com

FundBuilder is a mutual fund management program for Windows that helps investors maximize the rate of return in their mutual fund portfolios. The system uses the market's volatility to generate signals to buy low and sell high. A downloadable demo is available.

## FutureSource

http://www.futuresource.com

FutureSource is a real-time data and software vendor for the futures, options, and cash markets. Users can download demos of their software from the Web site and get delayed quotes on 20 contracts. They can also get delayed news from Future World News.

 ## Gamelan Official Directory for Java (Business & Financial Applets)

http://www.gamelan.com/pages/Gamelan.bf.html

Gamelan is a directory of resources relating to the Java programming language, and their listings of business and financial applets are an excellent place for investors to explore. You'll find links to everything from charting applications to mortgage calculators, retirement planners to derivative valuators, here at Gamelan. Besides links, though, the directory offers brief descriptions of the applets and their programmers. While some of the programs are demonstrations only, you can catch a glimpse at how much of the Web will look in the future on the Gamelan site.

## Hawaiian Label

http://www.maui.net/~label/

Readers of *Investors Business Daily* are likely to follow CANSLIM, the investment technique developed by the paper's founder. Hawaiian Label has developed two programs to rapidly screen market data for patterns and trends used in the CANSLIM approach, Patternfinder and Trendfinder, both for Windows. A Stock of the Month and market commentary are also provided.

## i-Soft, Inc.

### http://www.i-soft.com

StockWiz is a free DOS program that retrieves end-of-day quotes and other data from online sources, then allows you to present this information in any number of report and chart formats. The program will also search its database of 12,000 companies and find any stocks that meet conditions you specify. The program supports price alerts, ranking, screening, a historical price database, stock splits, and data exports to other formats. i-Soft also provides a subscription-based daily data service, and a four-year database on CD-ROM for purchase.

## Inside Track

### http://www.microquest.com

Inside Track from MicroQuest is a Windows-based portfolio management package that enables individual investors to make better investment decisions. The program works with CompuServe or an Internet data provider, collecting data that is sorted and optimally displayed. An Internet Lite edition is available for free from the Web site.

## Insider TA

### http://www.stockblocks.com

Insider TA is a technical analysis program for DOS, using a method known as box charting. In box charting, each trading period's high price, low price, and volume define the plotting coordinates of a box, providing a unique visual interaction with stock data. Downloadable demos of the program are provided.

## InterQuote

### http://www.interquote.com

InterQuote's free software for Windows can be used to access the site's subscription-based end-of-day, delayed or real-time quotes. The program also pro-

While investing systems abound that purport to generate buy and sell signals for a particular investment, don't look for any investing software to be a "black box" analysis tool. Nearly all investing software depends on the judgment, experience, and insight of the user. It's unrealistic to expect your software program to simply be a crystal ball. You have to be willing to invest the required time and effort into understanding all of the analysis tools that you use.

vides portfolio analysis features, as well as graphs and reports.

## Intuit, Inc.

### http://www.intuit.com

Intuit, Inc. is the maker of Quicken, QuickBooks, TurboTax, MacInTax, and other financial software. The site provides an online store, product support, and links to Intuit's online services, such as the Quicken Financial Network and NETworth.

## Investment Enhancing Systems, Inc.

### http://www.ies-invest.com

Many investors shy from options trading because they don't really understand it. Investment Enhancing Systems, Inc. (IES) has developed a system called "Enhancing Portfolio Value with Covered Call Options" that uses software to help investors analyze and select specific stocks suitable for covered-call options writing. Their Short Course explains how covered-call options work and how they can be effective, conservative hedges in any investor's portfolio.

## Investograph Plus for Windows

**http://www.libertyresearch.com**

Investograph Plus is a charting and technical analysis program that uses unique technical indicators, as well as filtering and scanning, automatic buy/sell signals, historical back testing, profit pattern recognition, and user-customizable features. The software supports downloads of historical and nightly updates of price data, and a demo version is online. Liberty Research, the developer of the software, is committed to the education of traders, both in the program and through a toll-free telephone number for users.

## Investor Insight

**http://www.intuit.com/investorinsight**

Users of Quicken will want to investigate Investor Insight, a subscription based service that helps you track, analyze, and manage your investments. Using a stand-alone program, users can retrieve quotes, news, charts, reports, and historical data from the Web and then integrate that information into Quicken's personal finance software.

## Investor's Advantage

**http://www.sacc.com/iawin/iawin.htm**

Investor's Advantage for Windows uses proven technical market indicators to chart individual stocks and market trends. It also generates a weekly report of all the stocks that you track, sorted from strongest to weakest. A demo is available on the site.

## The Investor's Galleria

**http://www.centrex.com**

Shoppers at the Investor's Galleria can check out links and special offers on a variety of products and services. Some highlights include the historical stock and commodities databases on CD-ROMs; Data-

Manager, a Windows utility for maintaining Computrac/Metastock format data files; and Satori for Windows, a candlestick charting program with automatic pattern recognition.

## Jumbo

**http://www.jumbo.com**

Over 93,000 shareware and freeware titles are listed on Jumbo, including a wide selection of business and financial software and spreadsheets. Browse the software by operating system and category, then download the programs that sound like they'll fit your needs. Try out the program, and if you like it, register with the author directly. If you don't like it, delete and forget it!

## Larax Software

**http://www.larax.com**

This Wall Street Simulator for Windows simulates a real brokerage account with an opening value of $500,000, and where it goes from there is left to your skill! This educational program supports all types of transactions, and a scrolling ticker shows the latest prices of securities in the portfolio.

## LimitUp!, the Futures Trading Simulator

**http://members.aol.com/vqlabs**

LimitUp!, from Vision Quest Labs, is a shareware program for the beginning futures trader to learn about commodities. Experienced traders can use it to practice trading multiple markets in real or compressed time. Surfers can download the program from the site.

## LiveWire

**http://channel.isle.net/~cablesoft**

CableSoft's LiveWire program monitors stocks, commodities, and options online in real time. The program generates intra-day, hourly, daily, and weekly historical graphs and calculates the value of multiple portfolios as the market changes. Users can set alerts, compare investments, or build filters. Download a demo to see if the program fits your needs.

## M&C Publications

http://www.ultimate.org/WL123

This California company markets self-help manuals and software, including Your Personal MoneyManager, a personal finance program for Windows.

## Mamdouh Barakat Risk Management

http://www.mbrm.com

For developers of heavy-duty financial applications, MBRM develops analytical toolkits, financial calculators, and source code for the pricing, risk management, trading, fund management, and auditing of cash securities, options, futures, and swaps in the fixed income, commodities, equities, Forex, and money markets. Their software is supplied as Dynamic Link Libraries (DLLs), which can be fully integrated with Excel and Windows. Free 30-day trial versions can be downloaded from the site.

## Managing Your Money

http://www.mymnet.com

MECA Software's Managing Your Money is a long-standing personal finance software package. The program handles everything from paying bills and balancing your checkbook, to tracking investments, estimating taxes, and planning long-term finances. In addition, many financial institutions provide electronic access for customers via Managing Your Money. The site includes downloadable demos as well as product support, FAQs, and utilities.

---

### the swami speaks

If your computer doesn't seem to have enough zip, vim, and vigor, unfortunately the Swami can't help you—you'll have to shop for a new computer on your own. But since we're on the topic, you should know about zipping and unzipping files if you're going to be downloading software from the Internet. A zipped file contains one or more files that have been compressed, both to make the file size smaller and to provide a single package that you download (instead of having to grab 30 files, for instance). Once you download a zipped file, you need to unzip it with a special program. Then, typically, you'll see a text file with installation instructions, and you can run an install or setup program to actually load the software on your computer. A common package for zipping and unzipping files is a shareware program called WinZip (available at http://www.winzip.com). The Mac counterpart to zipping is called 'stuffing.' The StuffIt program is available from Aladdin Systems (http://www.aladdinsys.com).

## Market Mako

http://www.pnc.com.au/~mako

Market Mako is the professional pit trader's option trading and risk management program, used extensively on and off the floors of the Sydney Futures Exchange. The DOS program is built for palmtop computers and can price any option strategy in any market, at any time, anywhere in the world.

### Market Technicians Association
http://www.mta-usa.org/FileResources.htm

The Market Technicians Association (MTA) is a member organization of traders who use technical analysis. They have set up a directory of computer resources for technical analysts that includes analysis software, demos, utilities, technical analysis graphics, artificial intelligence software, data downloaders, and much more. Most of the files are available on their BBS, but many have also been uploaded to their FTP server.

### Market Watcher for Windows
http://www.marketwatcher.com

From Micro Trading Software, Inc. comes this free software to manage your portfolio using the Internet. Market Watcher updates portfolios with news headlines and quotes from StockSmart on the Web or CompuServe and also generates asset allocation graphs, a wide variety of reports, and intra-day price and news alerts. An enhanced version adds an Industry Group Performance window that shows you how the stocks and funds in your portfolios are performing by industry groups, as well as full text of news stories. The free version can be downloaded from the site.

### Media General Financial Services, Inc.
http://www.mgfs.com

Media General Financial Services is a provider of financial data on more than 8,000 publicly traded firms to institutional investors, major corporations, publications, and the academic community. The company provides CD-ROMs of fundamental and technical data.

### Mendelsohn Enterprises, Ltd.
http://www.profittaker.com

Louis B. Mendelsohn developed ProfitTaker software for technical analysis and intermarket analysis, using neural networks, moving averages, and price forecasts for trading futures and commodities. The software can study agriculturals, interest rates, meats, stock indices, softs, currencies, metals, or energies.

### MicroHedge
http://www.may.com

Designed for investment professionals by the investment professionals of May Consulting, Inc., Micro-Hedge is option analysis and risk management software that covers the entire spectrum of derivative instruments. Using a live market feed, the program can display any of 140 columns of information, including full quote data, position data, theoretical values, all of the "greeks" and spreads. The program also concisely displays the current quote information for the underlying instrument.

### Microsoft Money 97
http://www.microsoft.com/moneyzone

Microsoft offers a free trial version of their personal finance software, downloadable from their Web site. Money 97 allows users to pay bills online, connect to their accounts at many banks, as well as perform a full array of personal finance functions.

### Monocle for Windows
http://www.manhattanlink.com

Monocle, Monocle Plus, and Tax Tracker are three software programs designed by Manhattan Analytics for mutual fund investors. Monocle follows 1,000 funds with daily updates; Monocle Plus ups the total to 2,500. Both follow complex quantitative and technical analysis indicators and allow performance ranking and screening. Tax Tracker, from the No-Load Shareholders Association, enables fund investors to monitor the tax liabilities of their portfolios. Users can request a 30-day free trial of Monocle.

## Monte Cristo
**http://www.montecristo-multi.fr**

Monte Cristo is a French developer of multimedia titles, specializing in financial presentations, including products such as Virtual Trading and Interactive Derivatives. This site is in French.

## Most Significant Bits, Inc.
**http://www.msbcd.com**

Most Significant Bits, Inc. is an online store that specializes in CD-ROM software titles. They offer a few business and financial titles.

## Mutual Fund Manager
**http://www.conceptsmfm.com**

Mutual Fund Manager is designed to track mutual fund and stock investments, calculating gains or losses using all IRS-allowed methods. A complete mutual fund database of over 7,300 funds is also included, with complex query capability and custom rating system. From Concepts Software, Inc.

## National Association of Investors Corporation Computer Group
**http://www.better-investing.org/computer/cg.html**

The goal of the National Association of Investors Corporation (NAIC) Computer Group is to increase investment education through the use of computers. Any NAIC member can also join the Computer Group and receive a subscription to *BITS*, their regular publication, and discounts on NAIC software. The NAIC Computer Group also

presents an annual CompuFest, a national event focused on computerized investing. Selected articles from *BITS* are on the site.

## NAIC Software
**http://www.better-investing.org/computer/software.html**

NAIC is a non-profit educational organization that supports individual investors and investment clubs. Their line of software includes packages for fundamental analysis of stocks, screening, and portfolio management (for clubs and individuals). NAIC also offers a subscription to historical data files of fundamental stock data for use in their analysis programs. All programs have downloadable demos.

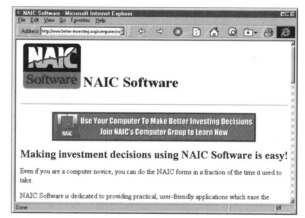

## NetStock
**http://users.southeast.net/~henrik/pages/splitcycle.html**

NetStock is a simple, free program from Split Cycle Computing that retrieves stock and mutual fund quotes from the Internet. The software exports data suitable for import into Quicken.

Minors can't legally own securities. Fortunately, you can transfer cash or securities to a child or grandchild under the Uniform Gifts to Minors Act (UGMA) or the Uniform Transfers to Minors Act (UTMA). Most states use the UTMA format, but a half dozen states provide for UGMAs, which have a few more restrictions on the types of property that can be held in the accounts. The basic format of both UTMAs and UGMAs is the same, allowing you to give money to a minor while retaining control of those funds until the child comes of age. Income is subject to "kiddie tax" rules, and the gift is irrevocable. Once the minor turns 18 or 21, he or she gains complete control of the assets.

## NewTEK Industries

**http://www.loop.com/~variagate**

NewTEK offers the technical analysis program, Compu/CHART, charting software that offers five separate analytical views. The company also develops Commission Comparisons, a software program to compare commissions among discount brokerages for specific trades. Users can order a demo disk from their Web site.

## OmniTrader

**http://www.nirv.com**

Nirvana Systems has designed OmniTrader to make trading simple. The technical analysis software automates the trading process, enabling each trader to quickly scan a universe of stocks, mutual funds, futures, or options to determine the best prospects and generate buy and sell signals. A companion Data Collector helps automate the process of downloading data for the software. A demo version of the program can be downloaded.

## Omega Research

**http://www.omegaresearch.com**

Omega Research offers four software packages for traders and investors: TradeStation, SuperCharts, Wall Street Analyst, and OptionStation. TradeStation is a comprehensive package that lets you develop, test, and automate your own trading systems. SuperCharts is one of the best-selling technical analysis charting programs for Windows. Wall Street Analyst is a charting software package that allows you to use both technical and fundamental analysis to make investment decisions. OptionStation is geared to the serious options trader. It sorts through thousands of possible options positions to uncover those positions that offer the greatest chance of making money. A special freeware edition of Wall Street Analyst is available on the site, along with details about all the programs.

## OptionMax

**http://www.optionmax.com**

OptionMax from DiamondBack Software, Inc. lets you select from any of 38 option strategies for stock, index, or commodities options. The software walks you through the process of creating the most profitable strategy and presents full-color charts of the results. A demo version of the software can be ordered.

## OptionVue Systems International, Inc.

**http://www.optionvue.com**

OptionVue is an advanced options trading program designed to handle every type of option and every type of options analysis. The developer also provides a family of add-in modules to support other functions such as portfolio management. A non-interactive, slide show demo is available on the site.

## Option Wizard

http://homepage.interaccess.com/~jas/option_wizard.html

The Option Wizard harnesses the power of Microsoft Excel to price option puts and calls using the Black-Scholes model. The template is completely customizable and shows premium-time decay at a glance.

## Options Laboratory

http://www.manticsoft.com

Mantic Software created this graphical modeling software for exploring and experimenting with option strategies. A demo version of the Windows program is available for downloading.

## Options Toolbox for Windows

http://www.cboe.com

Provided by the Chicago Board Options Exchange, the Toolbox is an educational tool for newcomers to options trading. The program describes the fundamentals of exchange-traded options and provides an options position modeling feature to simulate the performance under a variety of conditions. An online demo provides a slide show of the program's features.

## Professional Options Package

http://www.pmpublishing.com

PMpublishing offers The Professional Options Package, a risk management system for options traders. The program is designed for use in the pits by floor traders.

## Personal Stock Monitor

http://www.clark.net/pub/aivasyuk/psm

This shareware program retrieves stock quotes and brings them to your desktop. Instead of having to go to a quote server on the Web, Personal Stock Monitor will automatically retrieve the current price of each stock in your list. The program also exports data in Quicken and other formats, builds graphs, and notifies you when a preset price alert is reached. Download your copy directly from their site.

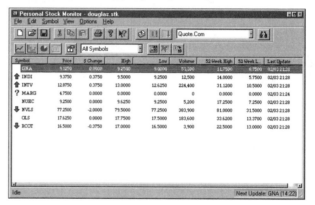

## Primate Software

http://primate.com

Primate Software's Quote Monkey data downloading program accesses a database of 130,000 symbols on stocks, bonds, mutual funds, indices, futures, and options, for end-of-day or historical quotes. A monthly subscription also includes Windows charting software, Chart Monkey, with over 14 technical studies and free fundamental stock data.

## The Portfolio Manager

http://www.class.mb.ca/class

Class Software offers The Portfolio Manager, a tool for tracking, graphing, and analyzing of a mutual fund or stock portfolio. It automatically reports your profits, draws graphs, calculates capital gains, and even gives buy, hold, or sell recommendations based on its proprietary analysis techniques. A 30-day trial version can be downloaded from the site.

## PowerTrader

**http://www.powertrader.com**

PowerTrader Pro is a full-featured program designed for professional trading, with real-time stock quotation and technical analysis features. The software can analyze stocks, equities, options, futures, indices, bonds, money markets, and mutual funds. A standard version of the program removes the capability for intra-day charting; PowerTrader GTX is further limited. CyberCharts is an end-of-day chart viewer and analytic tool with a number of pre-programmed and custom indicators.

## Prime Research Co.

**http://www.fortnet.org/~prime**

Prime Research Co. develops proprietary financial market add-ins for Omega Research TradeStation, including Visual Pattern Designer Professional, Candlestick Consultant, Neural Net Station, and RealTime Option Valuations, for technical analysis of the markets and securities.

## ProStream

**http://www.ps-group.com**

PS Group, Inc. develops Internet broadcasting products, and ProStream is a free stand-alone Windows application that delivers quotes directly to your desktop. The software retrieves quotes on all stocks from the NYSE, AMEX, and NASDAQ exchanges on a 20-minute delayed basis.

## QUANT IX Stock Analyst

**http://www.investorama.com/quantix**

QUANT IX Stock Analyst is a comprehensive DOS program designed to examine the quantitative aspects of risk and return. The Stock Analyst provides computerized investors with the same proven tools professionals use to analyze common stocks, improving risk and return forecasting. It features a comprehensive assortment of fundamental and quantitative analysis tools to help investors determine the *intrinsic value* of common stocks, while identifying when stocks are overpriced or underpriced.

## The QuoteGrabber

**http://www2.zoom.com/mito/quote**

The QuoteGrabber is a stand-alone Java application that provides continuously updated quotes and charts from the Web. The applet was written as an educational project by Louis-David Mitterrand and is freely available.

## Quote Ticker Bar

**http://www.starfire-inc.com**

Starfire Software's Quote Ticker Bar is a floating ticker application for Windows that displays scrolling quotes on your desktop. The shareware program can access stock, fund, or index prices from any of nine free Internet quote servers and will set off an audio alarm when a pre-set price alert is reached. Quote Ticker Bar will also export quotes in a variety of formats and can be downloaded from the Starfire site.

## Quotes Plus

**http://www.webcom.com/~quotes**

Quotes Plus is a Microsoft Windows application that tracks and charts all issues that trade on the major exchanges and NASDAQ. The software consists of a database and several modules that handle charting, downloading, and updating the database. The company also provides daily and historical data for use in the program.

## R&W Technical Services, Ltd.
### http://www.econonet.com/rw-technical
R&W is the developer of the MarketMaster Trading System, a series of software programs for trading Eurodollars, foreign currencies, Treasury bonds, and the S&P 500 Index. Their site provides information on the system.

## Reuters Money Network
### http://www.rol.com/MONEYNET/Products
Reuters Money Network is an online subscription service for investors that features a complete array of financial information, news, and data, including quotes; personalized news; fundamental stock, bond, and mutual fund data; historical pricing graphs; online brokers; and investment alerts. For even more power, try WealthBuilder, a software program that helps you plan and track your personal financial goals. WealthBuilder works with Reuters Money Network to build asset allocation models, timelines, and planning worksheets. Demo versions are available for downloading.

## RRIFmetic
### http://www.fimetrics.com
This Canadian retirement planning software balances assets with lifestyle. The program uses estimates of future assets (including salary, capital gains, and CPP) and calculates an investment schedule that produces a smooth net income stream. For Windows.

---

### the swami speaks

The Swami says it's time for another exploration into the alphabet soup bowl of Internet acronyms. This time, we'll discuss File Transfer Protocol (FTP). As you know by now, dear students, there are many ways to transfer data on the Internet. Two of the most common Internet protocols are the World Wide Web and e-mail. FTP is another way of uploading and downloading files to and from a server somewhere on the Internet. (In other words, it's a protocol for transferring files.) Directories on an FTP server can be set up to require a user name and password, or they can allow a user to access files anonymously. The latter is known as *anonymous FTP* and generally requires a user to use the user name "anonymous" and their e-mail address as the password. Many Web sites use an anonymous FTP server to store demos and programs for users to download. You could use a special FTP program to access these files, but an easier way is just to use your Web browser. In fact, unless you were paying attention, you might not even realize that the file you were downloading from a Web page was actually living on an FTP server. You can also use your browser to access an anonymous FTP server directly (a URL that begins with ftp:// instead of http://) and then navigate up and down the directory tree to see all the available files. Clicking on a file will download it to your hard drive.

### Science in Finance Limited

**http://www.scifi.co.uk**

Science in Finance is a company that uses Artificial Intelligence to develop products for traders. Fuzzy Candlesticks for Windows puts their research to use in a technical analysis package, and they have provided a downloadable demo so investors can test their theorems.

### Sierra Chart

**http://www.sandiego.sisna.com/sierrachart**

Sierra Chart is a Windows 95 charting and analysis program for futures, stocks, indexes, options, or mutual funds. Users can create daily, weekly, and monthly charts for any time period and display and save an unlimited number of charts. Users can download a copy of the program from the Web.

### Shareware.Com

**http://www.shareware.com**

Shareware allows you to try before you buy. Then, if you like the program, you register it with the author, usually at a much lower cost than commercial software. Shareware.com is a project of c|net, and allows you to search for any of hundreds of financial and investing titles. The site offers a brief description of the program to help you decide if you'd like to download it to your computer.

### SOFTSware

**http://www.csce.com**

The Coffee, Sugar & Cocoa Exchange (CSCE) offers SOFTSware, a free interactive options strategy program for both beginners and experts. Available in English or Spanish, the program can be downloaded from the CSCE Web site.

 If you invest in Dividend Reinvestment Plans (DRIPs), you'll want to make sure that your portfolio software can handle reinvestments and fractional shares. DRIPs account for share transactions with as many as six decimal places, and many of the popular commercial personal finance programs only allow two or three decimals to be entered. The resulting tiny inaccuracies can make it difficult to properly reconcile your DRIP account statements.

### Software Systems Boersensoftware

**http://www.net4you.co.at/rlsoft**

This Austrian site offers charting software as well as data from the world exchanges. In German.

### Spreadware

**http://spreadware.com**

Spreadware develops analytical add-in tools for Microsoft Excel. Their products focus on business valuation and forecasting applications.

### Stable Technical Graphs

**http://www.winterra.com**

Winterra Software Group created this technical analysis charting product for Windows, for stocks, bonds, commodities, mutual funds, indexes, and options. Users can download an evaluation version from the Winterra Software Web site.

### SunGard Data Systems, Inc.

**http://www.sungard.com**

SunGard provides a large selection of proprietary investment support systems for financial institutions, from derivatives trading to investment accounting, from retirement planning to securities trading. The site provides summaries of all the available programs.

## Technical Tools
### http://www.techtool.com

Technical Tools ChartBook helps you keep your financial database organized and up to date using ChartBooks. You create your own ChartBooks and then add pages and arrange them in any order for quick and easy access. Technical Tools also offers end-of-day stock, futures, mutual fund, cash, and index data. A self-running presentation demo that describes the software and the data service can be downloaded.

## The Telenium Companion
### http://www.telenium.ca/software/companion.html

Telenium's online service provides access to a range of information services specifically designed for Canadian investors. The Companion is a shareware program built to manage their service's data on thousands of stocks from the major American and Canadian exchanges. The Windows program generates a number of reports and can filter the data based on your criteria. The program can be downloaded from the Web.

## Trader Gizmos
### http://www.tradergizmos.com

Trader Gizmos is an online store devoted to the needs of traders and investors. They offer a comprehensive collection of trading "gizmos": software, books, charts, data, publications, videos, and audio tapes, covering everything from how to get started to complex trading strategies. You can join Trader Gizmos's frequent buyer program and have a personal shopper notify you when new products

become available. Browse their list of software or write your own reviews of products to help other shoppers. The Trader Gizmos software catalog includes most of the popular trading titles currently on the market. Don't miss the Tip of the Day, either, for words of wisdom from one of the Trader Gizmos experts.

## Tradex
### http://www.ilanga.com/ilanga

iLanga, Inc. is the maker of Tradex, which is full-featured technical analysis and portfolio management software for the Macintosh. A shareware version of the program is available from the site.

## Trident Trading Systems Limited
### http://www.trident-trading.com

Trident Trading Systems is the developer of Tracker IV, a futures trading software program, which works in conjunction with the company's advisory newsletter, *Ticks & Tactics*. The newsletter and software cover all major futures contracts that are traded on the U.S. exchanges.

## Virgil Corporation's StockCenter
### http://www.stockcenter.com

Surfers can get free delayed quotes on Virgil's Web site or can download their Internet StockTracker

### ask doug!

**Q:** Where can I find good Mac programs for portfolio management or analysis?

**A:** Unfortunately for you, the vast majority of financial software is built for Windows or DOS, reflecting the much greater use of PCs. If you search long and hard, you will be able to find some software for the Macintosh, such as Behold!, Tradex, and a couple of programs from NAIC Software. Another option is to try SoftPC or SoftWindows from Insignia Solutions, Inc., software products that let Macintosh or Power Macintosh users run DOS and Windows programs.

program. StockTracker is a stand-alone Windows portfolio manager for use over the Web. The program retrieves free end-of-day quotes from Virgil's Web site, or subscribers can receive delayed quotes during the day.

### Wall Street Software
**http://www.fastlane.net/homepages/wallst**
Wall Street Software is an online source for investment-related software. They carry some of the most popular investment-related programs available and also offer downloadable demos and trial versions of many products.

### Watkins Enterprises
**http://www.eden.com/~watkins**
The Tracker family of stock and mutual fund software includes the Wall Street Tracker, the Mutual Fund Tracker, the Tracker Utilities and the Quote

Tracker. These programs offer technical analysis and market momentum to determine when to buy, sell, or hold stocks or funds. All of these shareware programs are available for downloading from the Web.

### What If Software Inc.
**http://www.whatif.org**
What If Software Inc. is designed especially to provide instant tax and retirement planning answers for the individual investor. This Windows program shows the effect on taxes and income of your investment decisions, whether it be in bonds, stocks, or real estate.

### Wilson Associates International
**http://www.wilsonintl.com**
Wilson Associates provides the data and software tools necessary to make informed financial decisions. The firm's products focus on asset allocation, security analysis, and portfolio management. Demos of the programs can be downloaded from the site.

### Window On Wall Street
**http://www.wallstreet.net**
Proclaimed "the world's best-selling investment software," Window on Wall Street offers analysis, data and news retrieval, and charting tools to individual investors as well as professionals. Using technical analysis, the software helps investors manage their portfolio. You can download a free evaluation copy of Window on Wall Street from their Web site.

### WinStock
**http://www.ccnet.com/~winstock**
Myriad Inc. is the developer of WinStock, technical analysis and stock charting software for Windows. The program uses proprietary upward/downward trend reversing analysis to uncover price indicators.

You can download a demo version of WinStock from the site and subscribe to their monthly data service as well.

## Wolfram Research, Inc.
### http://www.wolfram.com

Wolfram Research's flagship product is Mathematica, a technical computing package that is used by many financial analysts. The site includes complete information about the program and many other offerings of Wolfram Research's software.

## XYZ for Commodities
### http://www.fastfwd.com/xyz

XYZ for Commodities' software uses artificial intelligence to catch trends in 35 primary markets, generating signals for trading or hedging commodities or currencies in the spot or futures markets. A demo is available.

# VIDEOTAPES AND AUDIOTAPES

While the Web provides plenty of learning tools for investors, sometimes hearing or seeing a new concept in action makes it easier to digest. Many individuals enjoy listening to audio books on their daily commute or find it easier to sit down to watch a videotape than crack open a book. The following sites provide a smattering of videotapes, audio books, and conference transcripts, related to investing and finance. Some are online stores that cater to the video or audio market. Others provide a single tape or product line of interest to investors.

---

### the swami speaks

Virus alert! The Swami sees computer viruses in your future, unless you take a few simple steps to protect yourself. A virus is a program that sneaks onto your computer by piggybacking on another program, for either malicious or benign purposes. Some viruses do terrible things to your computer when you're not looking; others just exhibit bad behavior. Some recent strains of viruses even hide in Word documents and then execute themselves as macros when you open the file to read it. Unfortunately, you can't protect yourself just by hewing to the straight and narrow of the Internet. Viruses have found their way off the back alleys of the Internet and can be found nearly everywhere. The only protection is anti-virus software, and then only if you use it. (It does no good merely sitting as an icon on your desktop.) Backing up your data regularly isn't such a bad idea, either.

One more important word on this subject: you absolutely, positively cannot catch a virus by reading an e-mail message. An attached file could be infected, which makes it a good policy to never read or execute files mailed to you by strangers, unless they are text files.

---

## AAII Videocourses
### http://www.aaii.org

The American Association of Individual Investors (AAII) produces two home study courses on videotape, "Investing Basics" and "Mutual Funds." Each comes with an accompanying workbook and is designed to provide comprehensive coverage of what is needed to become a successful investor.

**ask doug!**

**Q:** I've heard the phrase "the time value of money" but don't understand what it means. Can you help?

**A:** Most people understand the difference between simple interest and compound interest: put your money in the bank, and it earns interest each month. If you reinvest the interest in the account, it also earns interest. At the end of the year, the interest paid on interest will have compounded the rate paid on your funds. The longer your money is working for you, the larger the return on your initial investment. This is the time value of money at work.

You should also consider the time value of money when figuring the returns on investments in your portfolio. A 90 percent return is terrific, but not if it took 12 years to earn. How long you've owned a particular investment is key to determining your return.

Be sure to consider the opportunity cost of your money, too, when figuring your returns. If a stock in your portfolio gains 5.5 percent in a year, it's not a lot, but at least you've made money, right? Well, not actually. If a one-year certificate of deposit earns 6.0 percent, then you've really lost money compared to what you gave up by not buying a safe CD.

### The Achievement Tape Library
http://www.achievement.com

The Library carries over 1,500 audio and video training programs, all designed for personal growth and business development. Watch and listen to gain insights on how to effectively achieve your goals. Their Building Wealth section features titles by Peter Lynch,

Charles Givens, and David Chilton (author of *The Wealthy Barber*). They also offer a rental program.

### Jake Bernstein's Futures Web
http://www.trade-futures.com

Bernstein, a veteran futures trader and former psychologist, offers an impressive array of advice and commentary on this site, along with his catalog of his books, newsletters, software, and audio tapes. He also answers frequently asked questions from traders about futures.

### Conference Copy Inc.
http://www.xtr.com/CCI/cci.htm

If you can't attend that big national conference, then listening to the key presentations on tape is the next best thing. CCI records seminars and keynote speeches at professional conferences around the country and makes their catalog available on their site. You can browse their directory of keynote speakers or meetings or select a topic such as General Business or Legal/Financial. Organizations such as the Managed Futures Association and the New York University Real Estate Institute have transcripts available.

### Dow Jones/Telerate Technical Analysis Course
http://www.centrex.com/telerate.html

The annual Telerate TAG Conference features some of the world's best traders and speakers who regularly appear on TV or have written best-selling books. Now you can learn the tips and tricks of these masters right at home with these audio cassettes. Recorded at seminars held at the Telerate TAG Conference, these cassettes will help you learn new techniques and improve on old ones. Also available is a four-hour session, "Technical Analysis for New Technicians."

## *Futures Magazine* Learning Center

http://www.futuresmag.com/learning/learning.html

The Learning Center offers a nice selection of videotapes, audio tapes and books from *Futures Magazine*'s acclaimed futures trading conferences, and from their home study course. No online order form is provided, however, so you'll have to call to order.

## Impact Financial Seminar Tapes

http://www.soos.com/mall/impact.html

This single page purports to offer audio tapes that help you develop an investing strategy. Call the toll-free number for more information—if you dare.

## Chuck Jones Financial Planning/ Investing Seminar Tapes

http://www.investing.com/fpstapes/tapes.htm

Chuck Jones, a Registered Investment Advisor and Certified Financial Planner, offers a three-audio tape series of his seminars focusing on financial planning and investing. Each tape comes with a workbook, and the series is designed to provide you with background on the basics of financial planning, such as how to get out of debt and how to budget your household finances. Jones also looks at the fundamentals of investing.

## MediaMart CD-ROM & Video Tape Sales

http://www.mediamart.com/sales

MediaMart carries a selection of Business and How-To titles and offers to match any online price for in-stock products. Several of the videotapes and multimedia titles are related to investing and finance.

Downtick. There's a saying on Wall Street: "Pigs get fat, but hogs get slaughtered." The moral in this message is "Don't be too greedy." If you strive to make a "killing" in the markets, you'll probably end up making mistakes and lowering your returns.

## The Options Industry Council

http://www.optionscentral.com

The Council is an industry group composed of the major U.S. options exchanges. It is devoted to helping investors to understand how to use equity stock options. They offer a free instructional videotape, "The Options Tool," and a guide called "Understanding Stock Options" that they'll send to any Web surfer upon request. Simply fill out their online request form to get your own copy of this handy tool.

## Strasser Futures

http://www.strasser.com

Strasser Futures has a full catalog of educational products on commodities trading, including books, charting software, and videotapes. The company also offers seminars, courses, and complete trading systems.

## Tapeworm Video Distributors

http://www.tapeworm.com

Tapeworm is a source for hard-to-find videos. How-to finance titles like "Demystifying The Stock Market" and "Your Personal Financial Guide" are among the thousands they stock.

### Warren Buffett Talks Business

**http://www.unctv.org/premiums/buffet.htm**

Thanks to North Carolina Public Television, investors can see this rare television appearance by one of America's most successful investors. In an hour-long dialogue, Buffett shares his wit and wisdom with students of the University of North Carolina's Kenan-Flager Business School.

# INVESTING BOOKS AND MANUALS

It's time to face facts. At some point in your investment career you'll need to hit the books, since there is a vast body of financial knowledge still contained in paper pages glued between a front and back cover. The best financial minds of all time, from Benjamin Graham to Peter Lynch, provide a complete financial education to investors in the form of their books.

Investors can browse the cyber-shelves of many online bookstores on the Web, shopping for bargains or looking for specific titles. There are a number of bookstores online that specialize in business, financial, and investing topics, and these can be a great resource for investors. In addition, many entrepreneurs and self-published authors use the Web to publicize their own works.

### Books of Wall Street

**http://www.ambook.org/bookstore/fraser**

Books of Wall Street carries over 600 titles in categories such as banking, finance, commodities, investment techniques, technical analysis, Wall Street history, general business, money, and economics. In operation since 1980, the company offers a selection from their catalog on their site, though you'll have to request a copy of the entire catalog be sent to you.

---

### the swami speaks

How safe are you online? The Swami knows that you've been thinking about security online. Unfortunately, anytime a user transmits information on the Internet, it is theoretically possible for that information to be secretly intercepted by a third party. That goes for every e-mail message and every Web page you load on your computer. For most users, this lack of security is not a problem, since the theoretical invasion of privacy is probably no greater a risk than handing your credit card to a waiter who disappears for 15 minutes before returning with your bill.

However, the most common Web browsers now support encrypted transactions when connected to a server that also supports secure transactions. You'll hear this technology referred to as Secure Socket Layers (SSL), and you'll know that you're connected to a secure server when your browser shows a key in the lower left corner (Navigator) or a lock in the lower right corner (Explorer). Many Web sites use secure servers for their order forms, and you can be assured that your personal information is being transmitted without any risk of interception while in route to the merchant's computer.

### Business & Computer Bookstore

**http://www.bcb.com**

Business & Computer Bookstore is a leading retail and mail-order supplier of computer books. They stock 5,000 current computer book titles, and 5,000 bargain books off the shelf, all ready to ship. Search online or download catalog files to browse offline.

## Business Savvy

http://www.businesssavvy.com

Business Savvy offers thousands of business titles, and hundreds are featured on their Web site. They offer a great selection of finance and investment books, which can be ordered online.

## Change Or Lose: The Bull Is Almost Dead

http://adpages.com/consult/2771.htm

In 1986, Dr. Barry E. Langford copyrighted this detailed, to-the-month prediction of the stock market crash of October 1987. Copies are available from this site.

## ColeNet Info-Source

http://www.colenet.com

ColeNet offers personal finance manuals and software, as well as e-books in digital form.

## Macro-Investment Analysis

http://www-sharpe.stanford.edu/mia.htm

This is a book in progress by William F. Sharpe, Professor of Finance at Stanford University's Graduate School of Business. He is also the winner of the 1990 Nobel Prize in Economics and an originator of the Capital Asset Pricing Model. This investment text is your opportunity to try to digest some intellectual wisdom on securities analysis and asset allocation. Be sure to jump back to Professor Sharpe's home page for links to more article and papers of interest.

## Market Bookstore

http://www.marketbookstore.com/ino

This joint venture of INO Global Markets and Trader's Library carries more than 500 books on subjects ranging from candlestick charting and global trading to marketing timing, currencies, and options.

 One of the least effective investing strategies is the "Some Guy at the Office" Theory (also known as the "Brother-in-Law" Theory). Implementing this system is easy. Every time your brother-in-law or a coworker tells you about a stock that he or she thinks is really going to "take off," buy 100 shares. Don't do any research on the stock. It's amazing how many people have been losing lots of money following this strategy for years and years. You should never buy on the basis of a hot tip from any source without checking it out for yourself.

## Money Blows

http://www.flash.net/~workbook

Money Blows offers books on working, earning, spending, saving, and investing, with book reviews and interviews with authors on related topics. Successful investors, Pulitzer Prize-winning authors, professional money managers, and retirement experts talk with Michael Pellecchia, business book columnist and personal finance writer.

## NAIC Discount Books Program

http://www.better-investing.org/store/books.html

The NAIC offers great discounts on a wide selection of investing books, but you've got to be an NAIC member to order. Books are organized by skill level, author, and title. Summaries and author biographies are also provided.

### New York Institute of Finance Bookstore

http://www.nyif.com/nyifcat/nyifhome.html

The New York Institute of Finance has assembled a comprehensive collection of financial books, providing an in-depth look at the instruments, theories, strategies, and techniques in today's markets. Books are arranged by author and title, and independent study courses are also provided. NYIF has been offering services to financial professionals for over 75 years.

### NumaWeb

http://www.numa.com

NumaWeb is a leading site catering to investors in the financial derivatives. Their bookshop features titles, all dealing with derivatives, from options to warrants to the Barings affair. NumaWeb has a recommended list for beginners, too. All prices are in British pounds sterling.

### Investors' Network

http://www.investorsnet.com

The Investors' Network Resource Center features tools for investors, including books, videos, and audio cassette programs. Over 2,500 titles are listed by category, or you can search their database for the author or title you're looking for. The site also offers news, editorials, and links for investors.

### Gordon Pape's Virtual Bookstore

http://www.gordonpape.com

Gordon Pape is a writer and broadcaster who covers personal finance and investing with a weekly radio program heard across Canada. His bookstore offers his own books and newsletters for sale to Web investors.

### PC Quote Europe Investor's Emporium

http://www.pcquote-europe.co.uk/emporium.html

For investors outside the U.S., PC Quote Europe's Investor Bookshop stocks a very large selection of investment books from around the world on topics such as commodities, options, equities, bonds, metals, Forex, technical analysis, banking, market psychology, economics, and financial markets. They also carry a collection of investing classics and reference books. If you're a voracious reader, check out their frequent buyer program to learn how to get discounts on book orders.

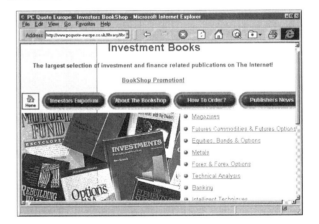

### Trader Gizmos

http://www.tradergizmos.com

Focusing on futures traders, Trader Gizmos is an online store with a wide selection of trading "gizmos": software, books, charts, data, publications, videos, and audio tapes, covering everything from how to get started to complex trading strategies.

### Traders Press Inc.

http://www.traderspress.com

Traders Press is an online bookstore exclusively for investors and traders. Browse their cyber-shelves by author, title, or subject, or drop by the Bargain Basement for great deals on closeouts and remainders. Visitors can read proprietor Ed Dobson's reviews and top 10 picks in many categories, as well as check out the Book of the Day.

### Traders' Library
http://www.traderslibrary.com

Traders' Library offers one of the most complete financial catalogs anywhere, with more than 3,000 pages of information on their Web site. The Fire Sale section lists great deals on closeouts and bargain books, and Bestsellers include the top titles on investing topics. Search for any title you're interested in and read comments from other investors about the book to help you make your decision. If you're in a rush, Traders' Library will ship your book to arrive the next day.

### Traders' Library Canada, Ltd.
http://www.baystreet.com/tlib.html

The Traders' Library catalog of books and investor products lists over 500 titles in 60 pages, but you won't find it here. It's a printed catalog, but you can request a copy be sent to you in the mail. This Canadian company does present their top 10 titles on the site, along with some special offers.

### Tri-Star Book & Software Co.
http://www.tri-star.com/tri-star

This online store offers a small selection of books, software, videotapes, and audio cassettes specializing in personal finance and small business topics, including debt reduction, mutual fund investing, and money management.

### Wall Street Directory, Inc.
http://www.wsdinc.com

Wall Street Directory is the most complete directory of products for investors, with more than 6,500 pages of information. You can search from over 100 categories listing thousands of companies, products, and services or browse their bookstore with 500 titles. Chances are, if it's out there, it's in here!

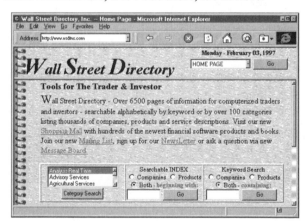

### Windsor Books
http://www.ison.com/windsor

Windsor Books has organized their Investor's Bookshelf into a number of topics, including books for beginners, day trading methods and strategies, commodity spreads, cyclical and seasonal trading, technical charting and techniques, fundamental and market-specific methods, and options trading. They also recommend a selection of must-read titles for futures traders. All orders must be made with their toll-free telephone number, however.

# GLOSSARY

**ASSET ALLOCATION**—The division of a portfolio into different classes of investments, such as equities, bonds, cash, domestic stocks, or international stocks.

**BASIS**—Also known as cost basis or tax basis. A security's basis is the purchase price after commissions or other expenses. It is used to calculate capital gains or losses when the security is eventually sold.

**DIVIDEND**—A portion of a company's profits paid to its shareholders.

**INDICATED DIVIDEND**—The total dividends that will be paid on a security in the coming year, assuming the latest dividend payment rate continues through the year.

**INTEREST**—Payments made by a borrower for the use of borrowed money.

**NOMINAL RETURN**—The actual rate of return realized on an investment, not adjusted for inflation (see Real Return).

**PORTFOLIO**—A collection of investments. An investor could consider his or her entire holdings to be a single portfolio or could divide assets into several portfolios (such as a retirement portfolio or college fund).

**REAL RETURN**—The annual return realized on an investment, adjusted for changes in the price due to inflation. If the nominal return were 15 percent and the inflation rate were 3 percent, then the real return would be 12 percent.

**RECORDKEEPING**—The process of maintaining records of all security transactions, primarily for determining tax liabilities and calculating performance results.

**RETURN**—Also known as the Rate of Return. The percentage gain or loss for a security in a particular period.

**TOTAL RETURN**—Includes all sources of return, including income (such as dividends and interest) and capital gains.

**YIELD**—The percentage return on an investment received from the dividends paid on a stock or interest paid on a bond or money market fund on an annual basis.

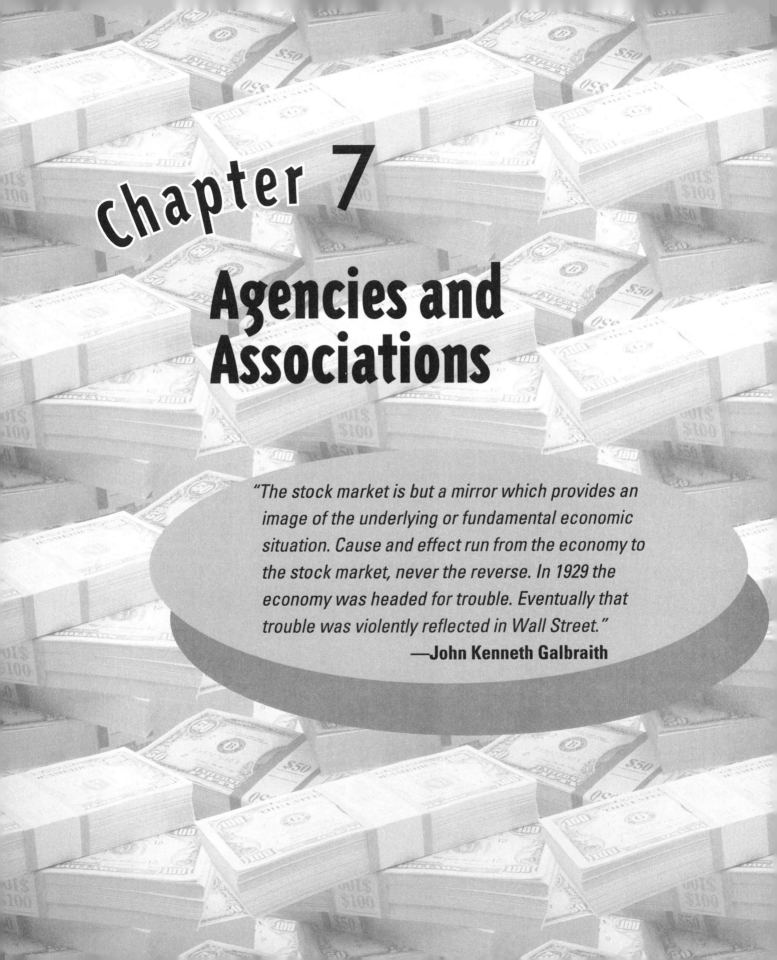

# Chapter 7

# Agencies and Associations

"The stock market is but a mirror which provides an image of the underlying or fundamental economic situation. Cause and effect run from the economy to the stock market, never the reverse. In 1929 the economy was headed for trouble. Eventually that trouble was violently reflected in Wall Street."

—**John Kenneth Galbraith**

**Some of the most useful** information on the Web for investors comes not from companies who are seeking to make a profit, but from government agencies and not-for-profit organizations. For years, organizations like AAII and NAIC have helped introduce new investors to the world of investing, and now the Web provides a new pulpit for these groups to preach to the masses.

Of particular interest to investors is the EDGAR project of the Securities and Exchange Commission (SEC), which provides free access to the required filings made by corporations. Another important effort has been made by the Treasury Department, allowing investors to cut out the middleman when buying T-Bills through their Treasury Direct program. And a law passed by Congress mandates that Federal agencies make public information within their purview available to citizens. Many agencies have found that the Web is an effective means to that end.

Finally, investors can turn to the leading stock markets on the Web for educational information as well as data on listed companies.

# INDIVIDUAL AND PROFESSIONAL ORGANIZATIONS

There's strength in numbers, as the saying goes, and investors have plenty of places to turn for camaraderie and support. The Web is home to a number of organizations that individual investors can join for education and other support services. Often, these groups provide magazines and journals, discounts on books, and software and data services. Some groups also provide advocacy on behalf of individual investors at the state and federal government levels, representing the views of investors to our elected officials.

You'll also be able to look in on the workings of professional organizations, those groups formed specifically for those working in the financial industry. While their Web sites are designed mainly for members, they often provide meaty information that can be helpful to individual investors.

## American Association of Individual Investors
http://www.aaii.org

The American Association of Individual Investors (AAII) is a national membership organization for investors that provides services, software, data, and educational materials. Their Web site is filled with articles reprinted from *The AAII Journal* and *Computerized Investing*, as well as membership information. Unfortunately, users of text browsers or those with slow dial-up Internet access will be frustrated since the only way to access the site is via a large image map.

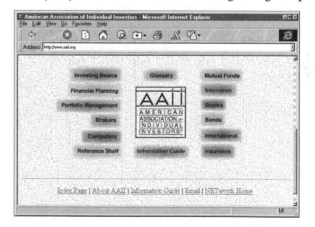

## Association for Investment Management and Research
http://www.aimr.com/aimr.html

The Association for Investment Management and Research (AIMR) is a non-profit organization of investment professionals and educators. The group offers seminars and publications on investment-related topics of interest to investment professionals, as well as advocacy on behalf of the industry.

### the swami speaks

I see that you spend much time thinking about cash. Perhaps you should learn about your cache as well—your browser's cache, that is. Your Web browser uses a cache to optimize its performance, temporarily storing information on your computer's hard drive. Whenever you access a Web page, your browser first checks to see if you have a copy in your cache. If you've been to that page before and a copy is in your cache, your browser loads the page from the cache instead of downloading it from the Web server. You've probably noticed that when you click the Back button on your browser, the page loads very quickly. That's because it was already in your hard drive, sitting in your browser's cache. Sometimes, if you're accessing a site that is frequently updated, your browser will be content loading a page from the cache, even though you're certain that a newer version is on the server.

The only solution here is to clear your cache, going into your browser's setup and finding the option to clear the disk cache (in Microsoft Explorer, this is known as emptying the Temporary Internet Files folder). This will wipe out all the old files in your cache. You can also tweak your browser's performance by adjusting the size of the cache, but just remember a cache that's too big can be a performance drag.

## Canadian Shareowners Association
http://www.shareowner.uwindsor.ca

The Canadian Shareowners Association (CSA) is a non-profit organization that advises on the formation and operation of investment clubs, as well as provides educational tools for individual investors. Through their Low Cost Investing Program, CSA members can build quality portfolios without paying commission. The CSA offers a monthly magazine, an investing manual, computer software, and data and forms licensed from the National Association of Investors Corp. CSA is also a member of the World Federation of Investors.

## Canadian Society of Technical Analysts
http://www.csta.org

The Canadian Society of Technical Analysts (CSTA) is a member of the International Federation of Technical Analysts (IFTA). It provides educational materials and seminars for investors interested in technical analysis.

## International Federation of Technical Analysts
http://www.teleport.com/~ifta/

The IFTA is an international organization with member organizations in 26 countries. Each year, the Federation sponsors an annual conference. Contact information is provided on the site for member chapters around the world.

## Investor's Alliance
http://www.freequote.com

The Alliance is a non-profit membership association for individual investors, formed to enhance the investing skills of independent investors through research, education, and training. By modem they provide fundamental and technical data on CD-ROM

Many securities are required to be registered with the SEC before being offered for sale. Anyone selling a registered security is obligated to provide a copy of the security's prospectus to potential investors, outlining certain financial conditions. However, the act of registration does not mean that the SEC approves a particular investment. Don't be misled into thinking that an investment is safe just because it's been registered with the SEC.

journal published ten times a year that provides specific insights into using NAIC's computer tools. Web surfers can download demonstration versions of NAIC software from the site or get information on starting an investment club. Look for details on subscribing to their I-CLUB-LIST, too, to participate in one of the best investment discussion lists on the Internet.

for 11,500 stocks and 4,500 mutual funds, along with screening software and daily price updates. Users can download a demo of the Power Investor from the site. The site also provides quotes and charts.

## Market Technician's Asscociation
http://www.mta-usa.org

The Market Technician's Association (MTA) is a professional organization dedicated to the furthering of technical analysis. The site includes weekly commentary and monthly charts, their regular newsletter, and membership information.

## National Association of Investors Corporation
http://www.better-investing.org

The NAIC's focus is helping individuals to learn about investing in the stock market, mainly through the support of investment clubs. Focused on education, their site can tell you everything you need to know about getting started in the world of investing. NAIC members receive an excellent monthly magazine, *Better Investing*, as well as discounts on books, magazines, software, study tools, and other resources. Computerized investors should consider joining NAIC's Computer Group. Members receive *BITS*, a

## National Fraud Information Center
http://www.fraud.org

The National Fraud Information Center is a project of the National Consumers League, America's oldest nonprofit consumer organization. The purpose of the center is to help consumers report fraud and learn how to avoid becoming a victim. The NFIC tracks incident reports and refers them when necessary to a variety of federal and state regulatory and enforcement agencies. Their site also provides the "Internet Fraud Watch Daily Report."

## National Investor Relations Institute
http://www.niri.org

NIRI is a professional organization of executives who work in the investor relations field. The group hosts conferences and seminars, issues research publications, and provides links to various Web resources.

## National Association of Securities Dealers, Inc.

http://www.nasd.com

The National Association of Securities Dealers (NASD) is a self-regulating securities industry organization that develops rules and regulations for the operation of securities markets. The NASD's membership includes nearly every broker/dealer that conducts securities business with the public. The organization is responsible for seeing that all members operate under its guidelines and for taking disciplinary action when necessary. The site contains information on NASD's activities, history, corporate structure, and market research and data.

## NASD Regulation, Inc.

http://www.nasdr.com

The NASD is the organization regulating the securities industry and the Nasdaq Stock Market. This site is designed to help investors understand their rights when dealing with financial professionals and how to resolve disputes. You can even learn how to check up on a broker's disciplinary record. Be sure to visit their section What Investors Should Know for informative articles on how the financial industry operates.

## New York Society of Security Analysts

http://www.nyssa.org

The New York Society of Security Analysts (NYSSA) is the leading member organization for senior corporate officials, financial analysts, portfolio managers, and others involved in the investment decision making process. The site provides information on the Society, financial links, and a catalog of transcripts and audio tapes of conferences and presentations.

If a broker you've never dealt with calls you on the telephone with a hot tip and a high pressured sales pitch, be especially wary. Hard-sell tactics violate the spirit of the law, and most professionals won't engage in such conduct. If anyone tries to strong-arm you into buying an investment "right now" or risk "missing out," that's a clear sign that you should run, not walk, from the offer.

## The Public Securities Association

http://www.psa.com

The Public Securities Association (PSA) is the bond market trade association representing securities firms and banks that underwrite and trade debt securities, including municipal bonds, U.S. Treasury securities, corporate bonds, and other instruments. PSA provides information on regulatory and legislative issues, as well as their catalog of publications and continuing education resources. Investors should enter their Bond Market Gateway, with links to hundreds of sites that provide information on the bond industry.

## The Savers and Investors League

http://www.townhall.com/savers

The League believes that increased personal savings and investment is the best way to foster healthy economic growth in the United States. They work to develop tax laws that promote increased private saving and investing, and their site provides details of pending legislative actions.

A unique aspect of the securities industry is that much of the enforcement of federal securities laws is undertaken by the industry itself, through self-regulatory organizations (SROs). Every stock exchange in the country, as well as the NASD, has registered with the SEC and thereby receive the authority (and the obligation) to discipline its members. Nearly all stockbrokers and their firms are members of an exchange, or of NASD, and are subject to fines, suspension, or expulsion if they violate federal securities laws.

## Securities Industry Association

http://www.sia.com

The Security Industry Association (SIA) is the securities industry's trade association representing the business interests of securities firms throughout North America. The site provides information on the Association and its advocacy activities and on programs like their Stock Market Game, used in classrooms since 1977 to teach basic economic concepts.

## Society of Asset Allocators and Fund Timers, Inc.

http://www.saafti.com

Society of Asset Allocators and Fund Timers, Inc. (SAAFTI) is a non-profit association of investment advisors who practice dynamic asset allocation, tactical asset allocation, fund timing, and market timing. Their site provides articles and reprints on these topics. (One such article is titled "Dollar-Cost Averaging Has Its Drawbacks.")

## Technical Analysis Society of Hong Kong

http://home.hkstar.com/~tashk

This non-profit professional body is dedicated to the education of professional and non-professional investors in the methods of technical analysis. The group has a strong representation from Hong Kong's financial community, and the Society is a member of IFTA. Membership information is provided on the site.

## Technical Security Analysts Association of San Francisco

http://www.teleport.com/~ifta/TSAA/tsaahome.html

The San Francisco chapter of the Technical Security Analysts Association (TSAA) is a group of professionals and lay individuals dedicated to the study and practice of timing markets using classic technical concepts and other quantitative approaches. Their site provides articles from their newsletters, meeting notices, and membership information.

## World Federation of Investors Corp.

http://www.wfic.org

The World Federation of Investors is an international group of investing associations. Groups in 16 countries help their citizens to learn about investing by making available study tools, software, and publications to their members. The site includes pointers to all affiliated organizations.

# GOVERNMENT AND REGULATORY AGENCIES

Rules, rules, rules—that's one thing we can always count on from our government. To be sure, the U.S. securities markets are among the most highly regulated in the world (and U.S. investors among the most protected). But the federal government also provides services and information that investors can use. Here, then, is an assortment of some of the sites you could find to be of interest as you research and analyze particular securities or the market.

Beat the Clock and Prepare for Retirement," and "An Introduction to Mutual Funds."

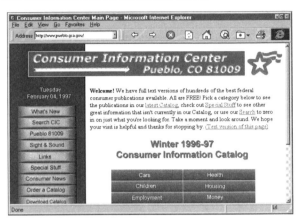

## The Center for Corporate Law
### http://www.law.uc.edu/CCL

From the University of Cincinnati College of Law comes a collection of hypertext versions of U.S. securities laws. Available is the U.S. Securities Act of 1933, often referred to as the "truth in securities" law. It provides that investors receive full disclosure about investments offered for sale, and it prohibits misrepresentations. Also online is the U.S. Securities Exchange Act of 1934, which prohibits behavior such as insider trading and establishes rules for the operation of the markets, including proxy solicitations and tender offers.

## Consumer Information Center
### http://www.pueblo.gsa.gov

The Consumer Information Center distributes federal publications of interest to consumers free or at low cost. Their Web site takes the Center's mission one step further by making available text versions of hundreds of these publications. Their offerings include some very informative publications about financial planning and investing, such as "Investors' Bill of Rights," "Top 10 Ways to

## Federal Deposit Insurance Corp.
### http://www.fdic.gov

Most people have heard the phrase "FDIC Insured" for so long they take the organization for granted. If you want to understand how this independent agency maintains stability in the nation's banking system, then jump to the Federal Deposit Insurance Corp. (FDIC) Web site. You can get the scoop on the laws and regulations applicable to financial institutions, as well as consumer news and banking industry information. They also provide demographic data and financial profiles of each FDIC-insured depository institution.

## Federal News Service
### http://www.fnsg.com

The Federal News Service (FNS) is a private company that provides same-day coverage of White House briefings, congressional hearings, Supreme Court rulings, and other legislative and executive actions. Their Moscow bureau transmits transcripts of press conferences, briefings, statements, and interviews by Russia's political and economic leaders. Users can get a free two-week trial to the subscription service.

## FedWorld

**http://www.fedworld.gov**

The National Technical Information Service (an agency of the U.S. Department of Commerce) maintains FedWorld to provide a central access point for locating government information. FedWorld manages more than two dozen databases, and over 10,000 documents, as well as links to Web sites of other government agencies.

## FinanceNet

**http://www.financenet.gov**

FinanceNet was established by Vice President Gore's National Performance Review. It links financial management administrators, educators, and taxpayers worldwide to reach towards a goal of more productive government. The site includes lists of government asset sales, electronic document libraries, mailing lists, and discussion forums related to the topic.

## Financial Accounting Standards Board

**http://www.fasb.org**

Known by the abbreviation FASB, this is the organization that sets the standards for financial accounting and reporting. The site provides information on their activities and summaries of all FASB standards, as well as their catalog of publications.

## Internal Revenue Service

**http://www.irs.ustreas.gov**

"The Digital Daily" is the Web site of the IRS, and despite their efforts at putting a cheery face on the topic, most investors won't be visiting this site for entertainment purposes. Still, the site beats having to wait on hold for 20 minutes just to order a form. You can download Acrobat versions of all IRS forms and instructions, access filing instructions, and read tax regulations online.

---

*the* **swami speaks**

"Enter your password now." The Swami can guarantee that after spending just a short time on the Internet, you'll have forgotten more passwords than you thought you'd ever need in a lifetime. More and more sites require registration and a logon procedure in order to access their content, so here are a few tips on the subject of user names and passwords.

First, never give out your Internet passwords to anyone. Second, don't use common words when creating your passwords. Use a nonsensical combination of words, like "frogtickle," or a combination of words and letters, like "24ducks." This makes it much harder for a hacker to crack your password. Finally, don't use existing numbers like your telephone number, birthdate, or Social Security number for your password. It's not a bad idea to use different passwords at different sites on the Internet, though that can make it harder for you to remember which password you used at what location.

Microsoft Internet Explorer can automatically remember your passwords and user names for you, if you're the only person who has access to your computer. Otherwise, you'll be consigned to keeping a list of all your logons and passwords to keep them straight. (You might want to save your passwords in a document in your word processor and protect the file with a password.)

When you're wrong, you're wrong. If you realize you've made a bad investment decision, don't try to justify it to yourself and don't become emotionally attached to the investment. Chalk it up to a learning experience and move on.

## International Organization of Securities Commissions
http://www.iosco.org

Over 130 securities agencies from around the world are members of the International Organization of Securities Commissions (IOSCO). The Organization works to promote high standards of regulation in the world's markets, and the site contains their resolutions and lists of public documents.

## Library of Congress
http://www.loc.gov

The Library of Congress presents information and materials from its collections on its Web site. Users can search the Library's online catalog, as well as online versions of many of their publications and other special features.

## Louisiana State University Libraries' U.S. Federal Government Agencies
http://www.lib.lsu.edu/gov/fedgov.html

Here's a quick, hierarchical directory of all the Federal government agencies that have a presence on the Internet. The listings are arranged by Department.

## SEC Support Page
http://www.arc.com/sec/sec.html

This non-government site from the Advanced Research Corporation includes online text versions of the complete library of SEC brochures, from the SEC Docket and the SEC Digest. All publications are in text form, and are searchable from the site.

## Social Security Administration
http://www.ssa.gov

If you're wondering how much you can count on from Social Security when you retire, drop by this site and fill out their online form to request your own Personal Earnings and Benefit Estimate Statement to be sent to you by mail. You can also review FAQs about the Administration and its services and download common forms in Acrobat or Postscript format.

## STAT-USA
http://www.stat-usa.gov

The U.S. Department of Commerce offers this subscription service to provide access to trade data, economic bulletins, and other government information resources. The site produces, distributes, and assists other government agencies in producing information for the business community.

## THOMAS: Legislative Information on the Internet
http://thomas.loc.gov

THOMAS (named after our third president) provides complete databases of information related to the activities of the U.S. Congress, including the full text of bills introduced in Congress, committee reports, historical documents, and information about the legislative process in general.

## U.S. Bureau of the Census
http://www.census.gov

If it's statistics you're after, this site's for you. Over 1,000 Census Bureau publications are online in

Acrobat format, with statistical information on such topics as the nation's population, housing, business and manufacturing activity, international trade, farming, and state and local governments. In addition, surfers can check the current economic indicators updated regularly.

## U.S. Bureau of the Public Debt
http://www.publicdebt.treas.gov

Here is the definitive resource for information on U.S. Savings Bonds and Treasury Bonds. Get your questions answered on just about any topic, from purchasing Savings Bonds, to the Treasury Direct program, to State and Local Government Series securities. The Bureau also provides the Savings Bond Wizard, a free Windows program that calculates current redemption value and earned interest and generates inventory reports.

## U.S. Business Advisor
http://www.business.gov

This project of the Small Business Administration and National Performance Review provides businesses with one-stop access to federal government information. The site provides expert tools, step-by-step guides, answers to common questions, and plentiful links to other online government resources.

## U.S. Department of Commerce
http://www.doc.gov

The Department of Commerce promotes American business and trade, and the site provides speeches, press releases, publications, and information about its mission and operations. You can also connect to the Web sites of the individual agencies that make up the Department.

Charles A. Ponzi defrauded hundreds of investors in the 1920s and left as a legacy his namesake "Ponzi Scheme." Amazingly enough, Ponzi schemes and pyramid schemes are still being operated today, even on the Internet. If you're approached with any investment offer that sounds too good to be true, it probably is too good to be true.

## U.S. Department of Treasury
http://www.ustreas.gov

The Treasury's responsibilities include overseeing fiscal and tax policies, as well as manufacturing money (the only surefire way to "make money"). The site includes information about all of the Department's agencies and their activities.

## U.S. Government Printing Office
http://www.access.gpo.gov

The Government Printing Office (GPO) is the government's printer, with about 20,000 publications currently in print. Many databases are available for searching online, as well as the Office's catalog of publications.

## U.S. House of Representatives Internet Law Library U.S. Code
http://law.house.gov/usc.htm

The United States Code is the text of current public laws enacted by Congress, searchable in a variety of ways. If you need to know if it's legal, this is the place to check.

### U.S. International Trade Commission

http://www.usitc.gov

The U.S. International Trade Commission (USITC) is an independent, quasi-judicial federal agency that oversees fair trade practices and the impact of imports. The site includes reports on U.S. industries and the global trends prepared by the Commission's analysts and economists.

### U.S. Patent and Trademark Office

http://www.uspto.gov

The Patent and Trademark Office provides information about the process of applying for and receiving a patent or trademark, as well as a searchable database of bibliographic data dating from 1976. Application and order forms can be downloaded.

### U.S. Securities and Exchange Commission

http://www.sec.gov

The SEC administers federal securities laws and provides investors with information on investing wisely and avoiding securities fraud. Their Web site includes copies of many of their publications, daily news of Commission actions and rulings, press releases, and speeches. This is also the home of the EDGAR Database of Corporate Information (but more on that later). Don't miss the brochures provided online by their Office of Investor Education and Assistance.

### U.S. Tax Code

http://www.tns.lcs.mit.edu/uscode

While this version of the tax code is no longer actively maintained, it may still be useful. Provided in hypertext form, the code is completely searchable.

### White House

http://www.whitehouse.gov

Besides information about the presidency, the White House Web site offers links to frequently requested federal services and the Interactive Citizens' Handbook, a complete guide to the federal government.

## EDGAR

EDGAR is an acronym for the Electronic Data Gathering, Analysis, and Retrieval system, constructed by the SEC in the 1980s. The system was built to automate the collection of submissions by companies who are required to make certain regular reports to the U.S. SEC. Companies now make these filings electronically to the SEC's computers, and they are freely available within 24 hours from the SEC site.

That 24-hour delay provides a window of opportunity for other vendors to provide value-added services for a fee. These companies pay a hefty fee to the SEC for the privilege of getting instant access to all filings. Then, the companies will offer services for a fee to individual investors or professionals, such as e-mail notification, expanded search capabilities, and instant access to new filings.

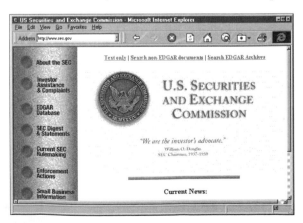

## EDGAR Online

**http://www.edgar-online.com**

This subscription-based service from Cybernet Data Systems, Inc. provides up-to-the-minute SEC EDGAR corporate filings, and an alert feature to notify subscribers when filings of specified companies are registered. All SEC EDGAR documents going back to 1994 are available, and visitors can get a free listing of EDGAR filings and a free copy of the last document filed. Also available are all initial public offerings (IPOs) as soon as they are filed.

## EDGAR Access

**http://edgar.disclosure.com**

Disclosure, Inc. offers this service, providing value-added delivery of EDGAR filings for subscribers. Personalized alerts notify you via e-mail instantly when companies you are following file with the SEC. Subscribers can also access one-page company reports on more than 5,000 U.S. companies, with annual financial statement information, a listing of company officers, top ownership data, earnings estimates, and a list of recent SEC filings.

## R.R. Donnelley Financial's EDGAR Resource Center

**http://www.rrdfin.com/edcenter.htm**

Targeted at corporate executives who manage their company's EDGAR filings, this site nonetheless offers individual investors a quick behind-the-scenes look that may help you understand EDGAR a bit better.

## Investorade

**http://www.dfw.net/~rajivroy**

Private investor Rajiv J. Roy built this handy online utility to quickly display the balance sheet and income statement summary from reports filed with

 Here are some of the filings you'll be able to find on EDGAR.

- S-1: Registration statement for initial public offerings.

- DEF 14A: Definitive proxy statement.

- 8-K: Report on recent events that might materially affect a company's business.

- 10-K: Annual report.

- 10-K/A: Amendment to a previously filed 10-K.

- NT 10-K: Notification that form 10-K will be submitted late.

- 10-K/A: Amendment to a previously filed 10-K.

- 10-Q: quarterly report.

- 10-Q/A: Amendment to a previously filed 10-Q.

- NT 10-Q: Notification that form type 10-Q will be submitted late.

- 11-K: Annual report of employee stock purchase, savings, and similar plans.

- SC 13D: Filing that reports beneficial ownership of shares of common stock in a public company.

- SC 13D/A: Amendment to an SC 13D filing.

- SC 13G: A statement of beneficial ownership of common stock.

- 497: Mutual fund prospectus.

- N-30D: Annual and semi-annual reports for mutual fund shareholders.

- N-30B-2: Interim reports for mutual fund shareholders.

### ask doug!

**Q:** Do all companies file electronically with EDGAR? Are all SEC documents available online? How many years of historical data is available?

**A:** As of May 1996, all publicly traded companies were required to file electronically with EDGAR. However, companies may apply for a hardship waiver from the SEC. These companies are allowed to file on paper, and their filings would not be available from EDGAR. Further, there are several SEC forms that do not have to be filed electronically. Some companies or individuals may choose to voluntarily make these filings electronically, and so some of these documents will appear in the EDGAR database. Filings may be available for some companies going back to January 1994. Electronic company filings were phased in between 1994 and 1996, so the availability of past forms depends on when a particular company began filing electronically.

the SEC's EDGAR. Enter a company name, click on a report, and get a summary of the information contained in the filing.

### LIVEDGAR
**http://www.gsionline.com**
Global Securities Information offers a subscription service for easy access to EDGAR filings. LIVEDGAR uses their own software program (or the World Wide Web) to connect to GSI's online database, providing comprehensive search capabilities and nicely formatted output.

### NYU EDGAR
**http://edgar.stern.nyu.edu**
From the Stern School of Business comes this free site, offering enhanced capabilities to access EDGAR filings. They provide a variety of search tools and capabilities, as well as a Java applet interface to the server and other experimental functions.

### SEC EDGAR
**http://www.sec.gov/edgarhp.htm**
In one of the best uses of your tax dollars (at least if you're an investor) is the SEC's free EDGAR database of filings from public companies. Documents are available for downloading 24 hours after receipt by the SEC. Enter a company name and a list of all available filings is returned. Click on a link, and you'll have the company's Form 10-K annual report or proxy statement at your fingertips. The document itself isn't pretty. It's a preformatted text document, and it includes some special tags that make it a little hard to read. But with a little practice, you'll get used to it. You can browse the provided Form Definitions to help understand each of the available forms.

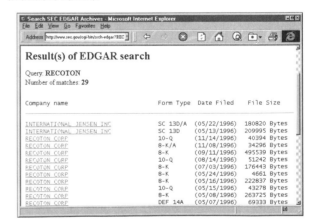

While "raw" EDGAR documents can be difficult to read, the SEC EDGAR site offers a freeware utility to translate an EDGAR text file into WordPerfect format. Most word processing software can import WordPerfect files, so this can be a quick fix to the problem. Another solution is a free Windows program provided by Chas. P. Young Co. that converts an EDGAR file to a plain ASCII document.

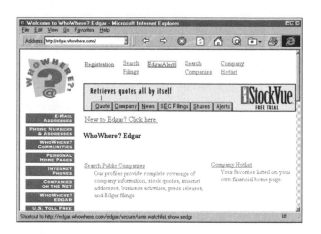

## SEC Live
http://www.seclive.com

SEC Live's services are provided on an annual subscription basis, with no per document or hourly charges. You can also set up an alert list of up to 15 companies or mutual funds, and the service will notify you when they file with the SEC. Users can sign up for a free trial on the site.

## Smart EDGAR
http://www.smart-edgar.com

Smart EDGAR provides nearly instantaneous access to SEC EDGAR filings for subscribers. A number of subscription plans are available, designed for individual investors. Users can establish a Watch List and be notified when filings are available.

## WhoWhere? EDGAR
http://edgar.whowhere.com

Register free on this site and the EdgarAlert! service will notify you by e-mail whenever one of your chosen companies makes an SEC filing. You can also keep a Company Hotlist on the companies you're following; you get a company profile, access to quotes and news, and a list of all SEC filings. Search for EDGAR filings directly from the site, too.

## WorthNet's SEC Zipped
http://worthnet.com/www/seczip

This free service allows users to search for SEC EDGAR documents, browse them in text, and then have them delivered by e-mail or downloaded as much smaller zipped files. This is the perfect solution if you have a slow connection to the Internet. WorthNet also provides a search mechanism to find filings made by some of the most successful money managers.

## Chas. P. Young Co. Electronic Publishing
http://www.cpy.com

This Houston firm specializes in Internet and EDGAR related services. Their EDGAR Utilities software program converts SEC EDGAR filings into commonly used word processing or spreadsheet formats. Though relatively expensive, the site does provide a freeware version of the software that converts an EDGAR file into ASCII text, creating a document that's much easier to read.

## FEDERAL RESERVE SYSTEM

The Federal Reserve System, known as "The Fed," is made up of 12 reserve banks located around the country and a board of governors. The Fed has three main functions: monetary policy, bank supervision, and regulation and the operation of a nationwide payments system.

The sites of the individual federal reserve banks provide economic data on their region, as well as educational materials and publications. Nearly all of them, in fine banking tradition, proudly display a photo of their building, each a solidly contructed edifice suitable to contain the vaults hidden within.

### Board of Governors of the Federal Reserve
http://www.bog.frb.fed.us

The Federal Reserve Board and its purpose is described in detail on this site. Also provided are statistical releases and working papers, press releases, and the complete edition of "The Beige Book," the Fed's *Summary of Commentary on Current Economic Conditions* published eight times a year. Learn how the Federal Open Market Committee operates and sets interest rates. Order "It's Your Money," a videotape on saving and investing, or copies of federal reserve publications. Online versions of many federal reserve brochures are available, too, mostly focused on

consumers and banking. If you'd like to begin to understand how our country's monetary policies work, this is the place to begin.

### Federal Reserve Bank of Atlanta
http://www.frbatlanta.org

The Atlanta Fed introduces users to its publications and programs, including their Monetary Museum. The site provides regular updates on the Atlanta Fed Dollar Index.

### Federal Reserve Bank of Boston
http://www.bos.frb.org

The Boston Fed provides monthly updates of New England Economic Indicators, as well as data files pertaining to banking, construction, labor market statistics, and other economic measures. Many economic publications, working papers, and current and back issues of most publications are available online.

### Federal Reserve Bank of Chicago
http://www.frbchi.org

The Chicago Fed offers economic and financial markets data for the region in ASCII format for foreign exchange rates, selected interest rates, and money markets.

### Federal Reserve Bank of Cleveland
http://www.clev.frb.org

Users can download monthly median Consumer Price Index data dating back to 1967 from The Federal Reserve Bank of Cleveland's Web site. They also offer analysis and information relating to banking, bank regulation, economics, and monetary policy.

## Federal Reserve Bank of Dallas
http://www.dallasfed.org

The Dallas Fed's Web site describes the Federal Reserve and its role in the economy, with reprints of articles and publications. Users can access economic data, interest rate series, and other research.

## Federal Reserve Bank of Kansas City
http://www.kc.frb.org

Besides regional economic information (both current and historic), the Kansas City Fed provides general information and publications, and a range of data from the bank's departments.

## Federal Reserve Bank of Minneapolis
http://woodrow.mpls.frb.fed.us

The Minneapolis Fed's Woodrow Web site offers consumer news, including information on mutual funds, treasury securities, and community development, and a searchable archive of the bank's research papers. Data available online includes regional information such as economic forecasts, agricultural credit conditions, and data by industry, as well as interest and exchange rate charts and discount rate information.

---

### the swami speaks

Now it's time for a few tips from the Swami for those of you who haven't yet ventured online. Basically, you have two options for connecting to the Internet. The first is a commercial online service, such as CompuServe, Prodigy, or America OnLine. These services provide their own proprietary content areas and databases in addition to Internet access. The second is a local or national Internet Service Provider (ISP). These companies typically provide no content of their own, they merely connect you to the Internet and provide you with an e-mail account. Each has advantages. Some of the commercial services have valuable information for investors that makes them worth the premium price they typically charge. And the commercial services usually have access points around the world, so if you travel, you can almost always connect to your e-mail with a local telephone call. The commercial services are very user-friendly, so if you've never been online before, they can provide a terrific introduction.

Local ISPs may be shoestring affairs, or they may be professionally run enterprises with a large corporate clientele. They are usually at the lower end of the price range, but their support and equipment may not be as flashy as their larger competitors.

National ISPs provide local access numbers all over the country, a plus for travelers, but their customer service may be a bit impersonal. The Swami's advice when making a decision: try out several options and see what works best for you. Many offer free trial accounts so you can see how well it works. Ask friends and colleagues about their Internet providers and see what they have to say.

Don't sign up for a service and immediately give everyone you know your e-mail address. If you find out a week later that you can only dial up your provider between the hours of 3:00 a.m. and 6:00 a.m., you'll be sorry when you have to send out change of address notifications with your address at a new provider.

### Federal Reserve Bank of New York
http://www.ny.frb.org

Besides fulfilling the duties the New York Fed shares in common with the other reserve banks, the New York Fed has several unique responsibilities, including the implementation of monetary policy. Their site includes detailed information on Savings Bonds and the Treasury Direct program, as well as downloadable versions of staff and research reports. An education area provides helpful resources for anyone who wants to learn more about how the Fed operates. Current and historical data is also provided.

### Federal Reserve Bank of Philadelphia
http://www.phil.frb.org

In addition to information about the Philadelphia Fed, its publications, and the economy of its region, this site offers the Cash Quiz to test your knowledge about U.S. currency. Their Financial Marketplace provides information on buying Treasury Securities, as well.

### Federal Reserve Bank of Richmond
http://www.rich.frb.org

A little slow out of the gate, the Richmond Fed is still constructing its Web site.

If you invest in bonds, you should check out the Treasury Direct program offered by the Department of the Treasury. Treasury Direct allows users to invest in T-Bills, T-Bonds and T-Notes without commissions. Contact the Treasury Department or your local Federal Reserve Bank for more information.

### Federal Reserve Bank of San Francisco
http://www.frbsf.org

The San Francisco Fed provides a step-by-step guide on how to invest in U.S. Treasury Securities. Investors can download purchase forms, view auction results and upcoming auction information, or request their free copy of "A Guide to Buying Treasury Securities." You can also get economic information about the region and a wealth of educational materials.

### Federal Reserve Bank of St. Louis
http://www.stls.frb.org

The St. Louis Fed is home to FRED, the Federal Reserve Economic Data database. FRED contains historical data series of financial and economic information, including daily U.S. interest rates, monetary and business indicators, exchange rates, and regional economic data.

# MARKETS AND EXCHANGES

Each year, trillions of dollars change hands in the stock markets of the United States, as investors and traders buy and sell shares of corporate America. The Web sites of the stock exchanges provide information about their operations and data on their listed companies.

## ask doug!

**Q:** Why do some companies list on more than one exchange?

**A:** The regional exchanges (like the Philadelphia Stock Exchange, the Pacific Stock Exchange, and the Chicago Stock Exchange) mostly trade in options and stocks of local companies, but they do trade in some national stocks as well. The national companies that list stocks on multiple exchanges do so for added flexibility in pricing. Occidental Petroleum, for instance, in listed on the Pacific Stock Exchange and the New York Stock Exchange. Usually, though, the stock's price follows the action on the dominant exchange, so Occidental's stock price is pretty much set by what the specialists do on the NYSE. The Chicago Stock Exchange provides a market for many of the top NASDAQ stocks, letting traders enter limit orders to buy on the bid and sell on the offer. By trading in the auction market, investors get added liquidity and fair executions at the best possible price.

## American Stock Exchange
http://www.amex.com

On the AMEX site, investors can find daily market summary, a directory of all AMEX-listed companies and complete information about equity options and derivative products. Don't miss their Dictionary of Financial Risk Management, a complete lexicon and textbook on managing risk in the markets.

## Arizona Stock Exchange
http://www.azx.com

The Arizona Stock Exchange is the only *open screen call market* for equity trading. This single-price auction system is designed to allow anonymous participants to trade at the truest market prices with the lowest possible transaction costs. All NYSE, AMEX, and NASDAQ NMS stocks can be traded on this exchange. Because of its low trading volume, the exchange is exempt from SEC regulation.

## Chicago Partnership Board, Inc
http://www.cpboard.com

If you're looking for something more adventurous than stocks, this site provides extensive information about the current market for limited partnerships, limited liability companies, non-listed real estate investment trusts, and other direct investments. These are all common vehicles for investing in real estate, venture capital, equipment leasing, cable TV, and oil and gas ventures. Most of these securities are not listed on stock exchanges, but you can buy or sell an interest in these issues in the secondary market. The Chicago Partnership Board provides an auction market for these securities, with a searchable database of actual listings for sale, auction schedules, access to financial statements, a directory of limited partnerships, and a glossary.

## Chicago Stock Exchange
http://www.chicagostockex.com

Over 3,800 issues are available for trading on the CHX, and the dollar value of shares traded on the exchange each year rank it as one of the largest U.S. exchanges. The CHX also trades many of the top NASDAQ issues under exchange trading rules. The site provides history and background on the Chicago Stock Exchange, as well as a directory of all listed companies, with quotes and contact information.

### NASDAQ

**http://www.nasdaq.com**

NASDAQ provides constantly updated, intra-day market summaries on the main page of its site, for the NASDAQ Composite and NASDAQ 100 Indexes. Deeper within the site are updates and lists of companies in all of NASDAQ's sector indexes, along with most active lists. Users can also access quotes and company addresses for all NASDAQ-traded stocks. A glossary of investment terms, daily market news, and a list of FAQs are also available.

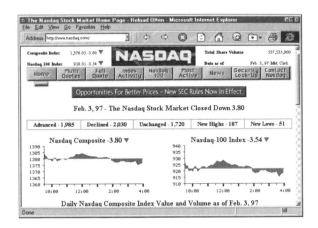

NASDAQ stocks have four or five characters in their ticker symbols. If the ticker symbol has five letters, the fifth letter has a special meaning, as outlined below:

- A Class A.
- B Class B.
- C Exempt from Nasdaq listing requirements for a limited period of time.
- D A new issue of an existing stock. (This is often the result of a reverse split.)
- E Delinquent in required filings with the SEC as determined by the NASD.
- F Foreign.
- G First Convertible Bond.
- H Second Convertible Bond, same company.
- I Third Convertible Bond, same company.
- J Voting.
- K Non-voting.
- L Miscellaneous situations such as foreign preferred, preferred when-issued, a second class of units, a third class of warrants, or a sixth class of preferred stock.

- M Fourth preferred, same company.
- N Third preferred, same company.
- O Second preferred, same company.
- P First preferred.
- Q In bankruptcy proceedings.
- R Rights.
- S Shares of beneficial interest.
- T With warrants or with rights.
- U Units.
- V When-issued and when-distributed.
- W Warrants.
- X Mutual Fund.
- Y ADR (American Depositary Receipts).
- Z Miscellaneous situations such as a second class of warrants, a fifth class of preferred stock, a stub, a foreign preferred when-issued, or any unit, receipt, or certificate representing a limited partnership interest.

## New York Stock Exchange

http://www.nyse.com

The Web site of The Big Board provides daily market summary statistics, a glossary of financial terms, a directory of links to Web sites of listed companies, a catalog of their publications (including books, directories, research papers and pamphlets), and downloadable data.

## Philadelphia Stock Exchange

http://www.phlx.com

The PHLX is the oldest exchange in the United States (founded in 1790) and the nation's first securities exchange on the World Wide Web. The PHLX's Semiconductor Sector (SOX) Index Option is the most actively traded sector index option offered by any exchange, and the exchange trades stocks, equity options, and currency options as well as index options. The site includes market news and commentary, daily settlement values for customized currency options, point and figure charts of equity options, and weekly charts of sector index options.

# GLOSSARY

BULLETIN BOARD STOCK—A stock that does not qualify for trading on the Nasdaq markets or other exchange. The OTC Bulletin Board is run by the National Association of Securities Dealers and is an unregulated market. Stocks that list on the OTC Bulletin Board do not have to file financial statements in the SEC EDGAR database and do not have to meet any listing requirements other than having someone make a market in the stock. OTC Bulletin Board stocks are generally very risky.

EDGAR—Acronym for Electronic Data Gathering, Analysis, and Retrieval. The SEC's electronic system is used by all publicly traded companies to transmit required filings to the SEC. The SEC provides a free EDGAR; other companies provide their own EDGAR services that include additional information and search capabilities.

EXCHANGE—An exchange is a market where securities, commodities, options, and futures are traded.

FORM 8-K—A filing required by the SEC to report unexpected material events or corporate changes that might affect a company's business. Such changes might include acquisition, bankruptcy, resignation of directors, or a change in the fiscal year.

FORM 10-K—An annual report filed with the SEC by a public company to provide a comprehensive overview of the company's activities in the past year. The report includes a profile of the company, management discussion and analysis (including events that might affect future sales and earnings), income statement and balance sheet, information on any lawsuits, and other pertinent financial information. A company must file its Form 10-K within 90 days after the close of the company's fiscal year.

FORM 10-Q—A public company's quarterly report filed with the SEC that provides a view of a company's financial position for the quarter, including a cash flow statement, income statement, and balance sheet. The filing is due 45 days after the end of each of the first three fiscal quarters, but no filing is due for the fourth quarter.

FORM DEF 14A—A company's Definitive Proxy Statement, filed with the SEC, providing official notification to shareholders of matters to be considered at an upcoming shareholders meeting, as well as summaries of executive salaries, incentives and benefits. This form is commonly known as a *proxy*.

LISTED STOCK—Any stock that sells on a stock exchange.

MARKET MAKER—On the NASDAQ system, a broker-dealer willing to accept the risk of holding a particular number of shares of a particular security in order to facilitate trading in that security. Over 500 firms act as NASDAQ market makers, displaying buy and sell quotations for a guaranteed number of shares.

NASD—The National Association of Securities Dealers, Inc., the self-regulatory organization of the securities industry. It is responsible for the operation and regulation of the NASDAQ stock market and over-the-counter markets.

NASDAQ—The National Association of Securities Dealers Automated Quotation System. A nationwide computerized quotation system for current bid and asked quotations on over 5,500 over-the-counter stocks.

OVER-THE-COUNTER—Used to describe a security traded through broker/dealers on telephone and computer networks (such as NASDAQ) rather than through an auction exchange. Abbreviated OTC.

PROXY—A formal document signed by a shareholder to authorize another shareholder, or commonly the company's management, to vote the holder's shares at the annual meeting. The *proxy statement* discloses important information about issues to be discussed at an annual meeting, as well as information about closely-held shares.

SPREAD—The difference between the price at which a market maker is willing to buy a security and the price at which the firm is willing to sell it (the difference between the bid and ask for a given security). Since each market maker can either buy or sell a stock at any given time, the spread is how a market maker makes a profit on each trade.

# Chapter 8
# Investment Talk

"Rule number one is: Stop listening to professionals! Twenty years in this business convinces me that any normal person using the customary three percent of the brain can pick stocks just as well, if not better, than the average Wall Street expert."

**—Peter Lynch**

**Critics of the Internet** often blast it for being too impersonal. But in countless corners of cyberspace there have emerged virtual communities where people have come together to share ideas. This kind of information sharing can be vastly more profitable than crunching numbers or scrutinizing research reports. Human interaction still tends to bring the most enjoyment and enhancement, even across optical fiber cables.

Of course, you wouldn't expect the Usenet newsgroups to resemble small-town America. The Usenet is more like New York City, with pockets of calm and civility amongst the general clammering of daily life. But there are mailing lists where communities of people meet each day to talk about investments and, as in a geographic neighborhood, the members of this community come to know and trust each other—and learn who not to trust! The language spoken is unique to each community. You can expect the day traders to be as abrupt as their trading style and the long-term investors as patient as tortoises, and the advice given is usually genuine. The end result is productive, educational, and profitable.

You can't just walk into one of these communities and instantly expect to command the trust and respect of all the other members; that has to be earned. So learn how to be a good online citizen, and remember to listen.

# USENET NEWSGROUPS

The Usenet is a large collection of newsgroups (over 15,000, in fact) that are delivered via a loose network of news servers run by universities, Internet Service Providers (ISPs), and corporations. There is no Usenet authority; Usenet is a true cooperative venture of all the participants in the network. Usenet newsgroups are broken down into families and sub-

families and sub-sub-families, getting more and more specific as the tree expands. In most of the newsgroups, you won't find "news," at least not the same kind you'll get from your daily newspaper. Newsgroups are like enormous bulletin boards, where users post comments, called *articles,* and others are free to respond. Finance and investing are always hot topics in the newsgroups devoted specifically to talking about stocks, funds, options, futures, and related subjects.

## alt.invest.penny-stocks
### alt.invest.penny-stocks

Penny stock investors are the daredevils of the stock market, risking life and limb (or at least their assets) just to make a few bucks on nickel and dime stocks. But despite the risks of investing in *emerging companies,* and the overall noise level on most newsgroups, alt.invest.penny-stocks almost (and that's a big caveat) seems like a civilized place. Perhaps it's because this newsgroup is relatively lightly travelled; the regulars know by now who's on the level, and a newcomer with a hot tip is glaringly obvious. If you can't shake the urge to get in on the micro-cap action, soak up the atmosphere here.

## alt.invest.technical-analysis.omega
### alt.invest.technical-analysis.omega

This group is devoted to the technical analysis software made by Omega Research, including Trade-Station and SuperCharts. There's not much traffic here.

## aus.invest
### aus.invest

Here's a lively forum for investors interested in the Australian markets. It's mainly populated with traders from Down Under.

If you've never visited a newsgroup before, try to read the FAQ or charter first and then lurk for a while without posting any messages. You want to try to get a feel for the group, how it operates and what topics are appropriate for discussion. If you make an unsuitable comment, you're bound to get a mailbox full of angry e-mail messages from other users.

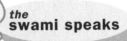

### the swami speaks

The Swami humbly offers for your news-reading pleasure a company called ClariNet. It provides newsgroups by subscription only to companies, universities, and ISPs. If you're lucky to have access to a ClariNet feed, you can read news briefs and headlines from the major wire services throughout the day.

## clari.biz.briefs

**clari.biz.briefs**

The day's top business stories are summarized in this newsgroup.

## clari.biz.currencies

**clari.biz.currencies**

This newsgroup features detailed daily analysis on the currency markets, as well as closing currency and commodity prices.

## clari.biz.economy

**clari.biz.economy**

If you like to track the status of our economy, this newsgroup provides daily reports on home sales, interest rates, consumer price index, and trade figures.

## clari.biz.industry

**clari.biz.industry**

Here's where you can get the full text of the day's top stories about leading public companies, including earnings reports and other market-moving news.

## clari.biz.market.commodities

**clari.biz.market.commodities**

Futures traders can get complete closing reports, as well as market recaps, from all the major commodities exchanges in this newsgroup.

## clari.biz.stocks

**clari.biz.stocks**

Each day, investors can get a wrap-up of stock market action from clari.biz.stocks.

## comp.os.ms-windows.apps.financial

**comp.os.ms-windows.apps.financial**

If you can't seem to get your Windows financial software to cooperate with your way of thinking, you can drop by and commiserate with the other users in comp.os.ms-windows.apps.financial. This group is populated with users who can find a bug in Quicken before they even get the shrink-wrap off the package. You can probably get a few helpful tips, too, if you hang around long enough.

### Deja News
**http://www.dejanews.com**

Deja News aims to harness the vast, sprawling Usenet and use its forces for good, not evil. They've largely succeeded. Start with an archive of every single message in every one of more than 15,000 newsgroups (accounting for over 500MB of text per day) going back to 1995. Then add search capabilities, allowing users to find messages in a particular newsgroup or family, or from a particular user, or on a particular topic, or containing particular text, from current or old posts. Now add a newsgroup reader to let users browse and post messages, with a better interface than most newsgroup software programs, and you've got Deja News. While the server is occasionally slow, you can't really object since, after all, Deja News is managing over 120GB of data. Deja News is a good introduction to the newsgroups for *newbies*, and a valuable research tool for investors. Search for a stock, for instance, and you'll get a feel for what other investors think about that company, and perhaps even some good insight.

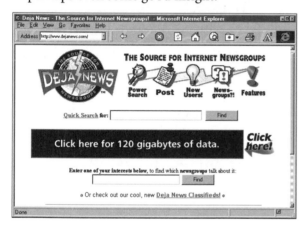

## microsoft.public.money
### microsoft.public.money

Microsoft provides this public newsgroup for support and discussion of their Microsoft Money program. Users can check out the discussions here for tips on connecting to Money's online banking partners, printing checks, or converting datafiles from another software program.

## misc.invest.canada
### misc.invest.canada

A bit of the wild West still lives on in the stock exchanges of Alberta and Vancouver, where resource companies and low-priced stocks abound. Canadian

 On Usenet, you should always cross-post with restraint. Cross-posting is sending the exact same message to a number of different newsgroups, usually (but not always) in the same family. Most of the time, cross-posting is unnecessary, so think carefully before you post.

investors and others looking for a bit of north-of-the-border excitement, can tune into misc.invest.canada to talk about any issues relating to Canadian investments, from funding retirement plans to particular stocks.

## misc.invest.financial-plan
### misc.invest.financial-plan

This relatively new newsgroup was established specifically for financial planners, to provide a forum for discussing the financial planning process. Frequent topics include the role of the financial planner, financial statements, taxes, insurance, retirement planning, estate planning, and other related issues. The group is moderated Newsgroup and is inhabited by both professionals and individual investors seeking advice.

## misc.invest.futures
### misc.invest.futures

Are orange juice futures about to break out? Or should you buy call options on March corn? Dive into misc.invest.futures and reap the harvest of its discussions on commodities. Frequent topics include members' outlooks on various components of the commodities markets, charting software, technical analysis, and trading systems.

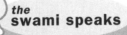

### the swami speaks

Newsgroups come in two basic varieties: moderated and unmoderated. Newsgroups are unmoderated unless their names specifically say that they're moderated. All posts to a moderated newsgroup must first be approved by the group's moderater, one or more volunteers who ensure that all discussions are appropriate for the subject of that particular newsgroup. While anyone can read the contents of a moderated newsgroup, if you attempt to post a message that is not in keeping with the group's focus, it will be returned to you by the moderater. Moderaters usually post a copy of the group's *charter* on a regular basis, explaining the purpose of the newsgroup and the guidelines by which all subscribers must adhere.

Always use descriptive subjects in your message headers. Many users scan newsgroup headers and then just download the messages in which they're interested. A header like "Need help" can be a little too broad to generate much response. Try, instead, a subject like "In search of a reliable quotes service," which is certainly more descriptive and more likely to get your question answered.

hierarchy. Unfortunately, that means this group is often rather unfocused and filled with advertisements instead of meaningful content. Cautious surfers can occasionally pick up announcements of new and interesting Web sites and the rare civil and informative discourse on topics related to finance.

## misc.invest.marketplace
### misc.invest.marketplace

The misc.invest.marketplace was born of the effort to cut down on the number of advertisements and solicitations in the other newsgroups. Here is the place to go to be bombarded with offers to buy everything from fish processing plants to investing software to "ground floor opportunities in the next Microsoft." Sometimes, information on legitimate investment newsletters and products can be found here, too.

## misc.invest.misc
### misc.invest.misc

Formerly known as simply the misc.invest newsgroup, this group is set up for discussion of topics not covered elsewhere in the rest of the misc.invest

## misc.invest.mutual-funds
### misc.invest.mutual-funds

Funds, funds, nothing but funds. That's what you'll come to misc.invest.mutual-funds to discuss, and that's what you'll find. Pointers to newsletters and specific fund family Web sites, definitions of terms like *no-load* and *index funds* and advice on the overall market outlook are all part of the landscape in the Usenet's mutual funds newsgroup.

## misc.invest.options
### misc.invest.options

From covered calls to naked puts, misc.invest.options is the place for discussion of financial options strategies and systems. Perhaps because options are less popular, this newsgroup is usually covered by a group of traders who know their stuff, and aren't afraid to challenge the predictions and statements made by others. Once the claims and counterclaims start flying, the fun really starts.

## misc.invest.real-estate
### misc.invest.real-estate

misc.invest.real-estate is the home for investors interested in everything from rental properties and land development to real estate investment trusts (REITs) and limited partnerships. Offers of properties for sale all over the world are continuously posted to the newsgroup, along with questions about managing commercial or residential rentals and tips on sources of financing.

## misc.invest.stocks
### misc.invest.stocks

To chat about the hot stock you've just discovered, subscribe to misc.invest.stocks and post a message. You're liable to either get a quick response or a telling silence in return. Besides discussions of particular stocks, you can also learn about dividend reinvestment plans, analysis techniques, dealing with brokers, financial Web sites, and other issues related to stock investing. If you're diligent in your research, you might be able to find a worthwhile stock tip or two.

## misc.invest.technical
### misc.invest.technical

Here is where the real traders congregate. Practitioners of the science of technical analysis gather here to exchange tips on data sources, charting software, and trading systems, as well as interpretations of chart patterns and market predictions. Regular market commentary is provided by the resident pundits, along with pointers to Internet resources for technical analysts.

## misc.taxes
### misc.taxes

U.S. Tax Law is notoriously (and some say needlessly) complicated, so this newsgroup is always certain to be filled with lots of questions about practical issues and tax-saving strategies. Fortunately, there always seem to be a number of tax professionals on hand to offer advice. While you should probably not rely exclusively on any advice you receive online regarding something as important as your taxes, most posters to the group always include their qualifications and point to a specific IRS Form and Section you can refer to for more information. That makes this a reasonable resource for most individuals.

## misc.taxes.moderated
### misc.taxes.moderated

Though it averages about half the traffic of its unmoderated parent, misc.taxes.moderated is still a formidable forum for discussions of taxing issues. Most of the posts are from individuals with a question about a particular problem: how to calculate the tax basis of stock purchased at a discount, the disadvantages and advantages of married couples filing separately, the deductibility of child care expenses. The discourse that follows is primarily provided by CPAs, enrolled agents, and tax preparers, and though they don't always share the same opinions, the resulting advice can be very helpful.

## realtynet.invest
### realtynet.invest

This group provides a forum for listings of real estate investment opportunities from all across the country. Few discussions happen in this newsgroup.

Keep your signature line brief when posting to an e-mail list or newsgroup. Most e-mail programs and newsgroup readers allow you to create a SIG that is appended to every message, to include your name, e-mail address, home page URL, and other salient information. However, some users get carried away, creating elaborate SIGs of ASCII art, quotes of wisdom, pithy epithets, and other non-essentials, raising the ire of other subscribers in the process. A SIG of four and no more than six lines will usually suffice.

### sci.econ

**sci.econ**

For a dose of hard core economic theory, check out this newsgroup in the science family. You'll be sure to find vigorous denouncements and defenses of Alan Greenspan each time the Federal Open Market Committee meets to consider interest rates, and sometimes the arguing gets a little loud. But most of the posts are reasoned discourses on the economy and the capital markets, primarily by academicians and econ majors.

### sci.econ.research

**sci.econ.research**

While this newsgroup is devoted to discussions of research, it's rarely used. Most of the activity seems to happen in its parent, sci.econ.research.

### uk.finance

**uk.finance**

For a spot of British financial advice and chitchat, tune in to uk.finance. You can even expect to find some of the same pleasantries you'd find in the British Isles, but in equal doses as the usual hyperbole prevalent elsewhere in Usenet. The few messages found here typically deal with specific issues of U.K. investing and retirement plans.

## FAQS

FAQs are Frequently Asked Questions. Collections of FAQs began to be assembled in many newsgroups when too many new users each asked the same questions when they subscribed to a group. It was easier for the old hands in the group to simply shoot off succinct recommendations to newbies to "Read the FAQ," rather than answer the same questions over and over again. Of course, they weren't always so polite in the way they made the recommendation, and so, in time, FAQs became not just recommended, but required, reading. Before you jump feet first into a newsgroup, read these files. Even if you don't ever plan on venturing into the wilds of Usenet, they are still informative, so take the time to review them during your online travels.

### Futures FAQ

**http://www.ilhawaii.net/~heinsite/FAQs/ futuresfaq.html**

What are commodities and futures? That's the first question answered in the Futures FAQ. If you're unsure, click to this site and soak up some of the wisdom you'll find here. The Futures FAQ provides a decent introduction to futures and commodities trading, from placing an order to understanding margin policies, to futures contract deliveries. It also delves into some technical analysis techniques and provides links to related sites.

## Investment FAQ Home Page
http://www.cs.umd.edu/users/cml/invest-faq/

Investment FAQ maintainer Christopher Lott has taken the art of the FAQ to a new level at this site. Completely converted into hypertext format, the Investment FAQ offers an easily navigable source of information on nearly every topic related to finance and investing. The FAQ is neatly divided by subject matter, including Exchanges, Regulation, Retirement Plans, Analysis, Bonds, Insurance, Stocks, Mutual Funds, Software, and Trivia. Want to know the origin of "bulls and bears" or why the market trades in sixteenths? The Investment FAQ can tell you.

## Investment FAQ (Alternate)
http://www.cis.ohio-state.edu/hypertext/faq/bngusenet/misc/invest/top.html

This is an alternate archive of the misc.invest FAQ, hosted by Ohio State University. It is usually not as current as the official version.

## Mutual Funds FAQ
http://www.moneypages.com/syndicate/faq/

From the basics like "What is a mutual fund?" to more specific questions like "What are the various forms of mutual fund account registration?," the Mutual Funds FAQ provides the scoop. The FAQ describes terms like *prospectus*, *statement of additional information*, *signature guarantee*, *dividend distributions*, and *capital gain distributions*. It also outlines disadvantages to investing in funds.

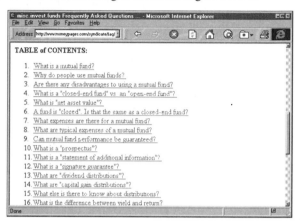

## Taxes FAQ
http://www.cis.ohio-state.edu/hypertext/faq/usenet-faqs/bygroup/misc/taxes/top.html

For answers to your most taxing questions, turn to the Taxes FAQ from the misc.taxes newsgroup. Though brief, you'll find here advice on topics ranging from Internet tax resources to information returns. Learn about estate taxes and gift taxes, and the basics of "basis."

## Technical Analysis FAQ
http://www.wiwi.uni-frankfurt.de/AG/JWGI/FAQS/tech-faq.htm

Though not actively maintained, this FAQ covers the basic framework of technical analysis (TA). You can get a brief overview of TA techniques and strategies such as McClellan Oscillators, Stochastics, Relative Strength Indicators, and the Elliot Wave Theory. The FAQ also describes the basics of charting and some of the more common patterns and formations.

# MAILING LISTS

A mailing list is a group of people who exchange e-mail about a particular subject. The list itself is usually run by a software program (the more popular list servers are Listserv, Listproc, and Majordomo), without human intervention. Users subscribe to the list free, and then can post messages and receive posts from other subscribers. Some lists have an option for users to receive the list in a digest format that collects each day's messages and sends them in one long e-mail message.

Some of the investment-related mailing lists provide the best examples of communities on the Internet. If you can find a group that fits with your personal investing philosophy, you'll be able to share your own insights with others as well as learn from the collective experience of the group.

## CANSLIM

CANSLIM is the stock picking system devised by William O'Neal, publisher of the *Investor's Business Daily* newspaper and author of *How To Make Money In Stocks*. This list provides a forum for discussing CANSLIM's philosophy of screening, purchasing, and selling common stocks. To subscribe, send a message to majordomo@xmission.com with the command:

    subscribe canslim

in the first line of the message.

## DayTrades

**http://pobox.com/~gsp**

From the GreatStocks Project comes this fast-paced list for short-term traders and technical analysts. DayTrades hopes to be a forum to give traders an extra edge in the speculative, high-risk, fast-paced, win/lose, zero-sum game of short-term trading. Traders can subscribe from the GreatStocks Web site.

## eINVEST

eINVEST is one of the oldest and most popular mailing lists devoted to discussions of online investment strategies and research methods. The list is maintained by Joseph Friedman, Professor of Economics and Finance at Temple University. To subscribe to eINVEST, send mail to listserv@vm.temple.edu and type the following in the first line of text (filling in your own name, of course):

    SUB E_INVEST yourfirstname yourlastname

## GreatStocks

**http://pobox.com/~gsp**

GreatStocks Project founder Doug Blair provides three mailing list discussion groups for individual investors: GreatStocks, MarketWise, and DayTrades. The GreatStocks list is a forum for members to share specific research and fundamental information on stocks. The companion Web site is filled with helpful articles, links, and reviews of Internet resources for investors. Instructions for subscribing to any of the lists are provided on the GreatStocks Web site.

Never, ever send a message to a group asking how to unsubscribe. When you subscribe to a list, you'll usually get back instructions telling you how to later remove yourself from the list. Save them, and when you decide to leave the list, refer to the instructions to learn how to issue the software command to remove yourself.

## Investment Club Mailing List

http://www.better-investing.org/computer/maillist.html

This list may be one of the best-kept secrets for investors online. The National Association of Investors Corp. (NAIC) Computer Group hosts this mailing list for discussions of all kinds of investing topics, not just investment club operations as its name suggests (although this is the best place to go online to meet with other club members from around the world). List members trade tips on growth stock investing, portfolio management, financial software, and other subjects related to NAIC's methodology of investing. Each month, one of the list's leaders runs a week-long study of a featured growth stock, providing an educational workshop for beginners and advanced investors alike.

## Investment Real Estate Mailing List

http://www.property.com

The host of this list, Dealmakers, is a real estate service for professional developers, investors, brokers, and management companies. The mailing list is for posting sales notices of investment property such as hotels, apartment buildings, mobile home parks, residential real estate developments, and residential income property, as well as providing a chance to network with others in the industry. Subscriptions are on the site.

## Investment-Talk

http://www.mission-a.com/ml/maillist.html

Hosted by Mission Advise, a financial services consulting company, Investment-Talk provides a forum for discussing topics related to the financial markets. Discussions on the list run the gamut of the investment spectrum, including bonds, commodities, equities, futures, foreign exchange, funds, and money markets.

## Kids Money

http://pages.prodigy.com/kidsmoney

Sponsored by Prodigy, this list is really for parents to discuss matters revolving around kids and money. Everything from allowances, extra jobs, gift giving, investing, and saving is covered by the members of this list. Join other parents and share your experiences and opinions on helping kids learn money management and financial responsibility.

## MarketWise

http://pobox.com/~gsp

Another list sponsored by the GreatStocks Project, MarketWise is devoted to discussions of analysis techniques, the overall market, investing strategies, tools, books, newsletters, brokers, and other broad topics of interest to investors. MarketWise is a companion to the GreatStocks list, so discussion of individual securities is not appropriate on MarketWise. Instructions for joining the list are on the GreatStocks Project Web site.

## Persfin-Digest

http://www.tiac.net/users/ikrakow

Ira Krakow's popular personal finance e-mail digest covers finance topics such as retirement planning, insurance, credit cards, mortgages, taxes, and investing. The list is moderated by Krakow, a computer consultant who adds his two cents wherever appropriate. Many financial professionals are subscribers and frequent contributors, and the moderated format makes for level-headed discussions of personal finance topics.

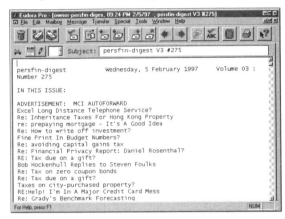

### RealTraders

**http://www.realtraders.com**

RealTraders is a discussion list populated by serious traders, and serious traders only. In fact, if you're not a truly gung-ho trader who can make a significant contribution to the RealTraders community, you won't even be allowed to join. That's right, membership is restricted to maximize bandwidth and make this list an unparalleled resource on the Internet for traders of options, commodities, stocks, and funds. If you think you qualify, sign up on the RealTraders Web site.

### Service-Talk

**http://www.mission-a.com/ml/maillist.html**

This list is provided for professional traders to give them the chance to talk about trading room systems and how best to use them. Subscribers can learn new tips and tricks for using service providers such as Quotron, Bloomberg, Reuters, Telerate, DBC Signal, and others. The list is maintained by Mission Advise, a consulting firm that services the field.

### MSTAR

**http://web.idirect.com/~bjasmine/lists/**

MSTAR is a moderated discussion list about financial astrology. Subscribers should be serious students of astrology who have a special interest in the stock market, finance and career counselling, and related topics.

# WEB BULLETIN BOARDS, CHAT AREAS, AND INTERNET RELAY CHAT

One of the more innovative uses of the World Wide Web is the ability to provide bulletin boards for user discussions. While these discussion boards are generally not as robust as a Usenet newsgroup or a forum on a commercial online service like CompuServe or America Online, they do offer a chance for investors to communicate with each other. Since these boards are built for the Web, no additional software is required, though some sites require users to register and log on before use.

A newer innovation on the Web is the use of Java applets to provide real-time chat capabilities. Users type their comments into a window in their browser. These are then broadcast immediately to all others who are connected to the chat area, like an enormous conference call or party line.

Internet Relay Chat (IRC) allows users on different systems at different locations to come together on any of hundreds of "channels" and discuss a specific topic. IRC is a real-time, text-based network, and though the current generation of IRC client software makes it easier than ever to connect to an IRC server, it still takes some practice to get used to using IRC.

## Avid Traders Chat

http://www.avidinfo.com

This site (for avid traders, of course) provides a 24-hour chat room for users to share ideas, opinions, and information. Avid Trading often hosts high profile traders and technicians for specially scheduled discussions. Registration is free, and topics tend to center around each day's trading activity.

## Closed-End Funds Discussion Forum

http://www.icefi.com

Sponsored by the Internet Closed-End Fund Investor, this Web board is open to all. It provides a resource for talking about closed-end funds. The group is fairly active, and topics range from technical analysis of closed-end funds to specific country funds.

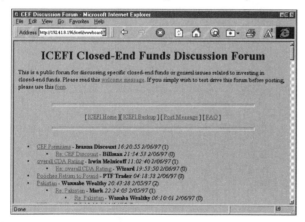

## #commodity IRC Channel

#commodity

You can find this channel on Undernet during trading hours, where commodity traders meet to pitch tips and news.

## Creative Real Estate Interactive News Group

http://www.real-estate-online.com

Creative Real Estate On-Line is a publisher of educational information about real estate, with material contributed by leaders in the real estate, legal, accounting, financial, and related professions. Their News Group is a forum for discussion of real estate, mortgages, and notes.

## #daytraders IRC Channel

http://www.geocities.com/WallStreet/3811/irc-day.html

#daytraders is an Undernet IRC channel for short-term traders and speculators. Each day during market hours, the channel becomes filled with stock tips, market news, rumors, and other information contributed by professional traders and brokers. Absolute beginners to the markets are not invited to participate.

## Excite Talk! Money & Investing

http://www.excite.com

Excite, a major Internet search engine, provides a number of discussion boards, including one devoted to financial and investing topics. Unfortunately, discussions tend to ramble, and the organization of the boards makes it hard to follow conversations. Worse, touts abound, raising the level of noise to an almost unbearable level. Still, given Excite's array of related resources (including some excellent tours of financial sites on the Web), these groups have potential.

## Financial Risk Management Discussion Group

http://www.contingencyanalysis.com

Contingency Analysis, a risk management consultant, is the host of this forum. They provide three

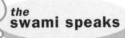

### the swami speaks

The Swami admonishes you to remember that intellectual property rights are still valid online. That means you should not plagiarize someone else's writings or violate another person's or company's copyrights, just as you wouldn't offline. Plagiarism is theft, pure and simple, so you should never present another person's work as your own to a mailing list or newsgroup. And just because a document doesn't have a copyright symbol doesn't mean it can be freely distributed. Unless you have specific rights to post an article from a Web site, wire service, newsgroup, or mailing list, it's not only dishonorable but downright illegal to post or re-publish that work. Most of the time, you can simply present the URL where others can find the article for themselves.

message sections for discussions: General, Theory, or Risk Selection. Users can read the latest news or swap ideas with risk management professionals from around the world. Topics include the risk-taking process, trading, portfolio management, option pricing theory, value at risk, Modern Portfolio Theory, and credit exposure estimation.

### The Financial Times
http://www.usa.ft.com

Set up as a local newsgroup on *The Financial Times* server, the Your Views discussion group encourages debate on the issues raised by this British newspaper. You can read messages posted about articles in the *Times* and on the site, add your own comments and rejoinders, or start new discussions.

### Fortitude Funds Newsgroup
http://www.fortitude.com/wwwboard

Fortitude Funds, a group of managed futures funds, sponsors a number of Web-based discussion boards on these topics: Hedge Funds, Stocks, Metals, and Currencies. Directed more at financial professionals are discussion groups for Commodity Trading Advisors (CTAs), Marketing Offshore Funds, and Who's Who In The Financial Industry.

### *Fortune Magazine* Forums
http://www.fortune.com

*Fortune Magazine* provides three separate Web discussion boards for readers. Personal Finance and Investing is the place for investors to share insights on the best mutual funds, the most promising industries, or stocks and the market. Smart Managing is for discussions of corporate governance and management, such as economic value added. The Economy and Politics takes a larger view of the dismal science of economics, from Reagonomics to Clintonomics, flat taxes to the Fed.

### #futures IRC Channel
#futures

This channel on Undernet is open during trading days for traders to discuss commodities and futures, trading systems, and price trends.

### H$H Investment Forum
http://www.hh-club.com

The H$H Investment Forum is devoted to low-priced stock analysis, and subscribers have access to their BBS-style conference board. Members can ask questions, post their favorite stocks picks, or chat about mutual funds and different investment strategies.

## *Individual Investor* Interactive Forums
http://www.individualinvestor.com

The companion Web site for *Individual Investor* magazine provides discussion centers for each company in their Magic 25 featured list of stocks. Users can discuss the magazine's analysis and provide their own critiques and predictions of each stock's performance.

## #invest IRC Channel
#invest

Each Sunday evening from 9-10 p.m., #invest is active on Undernet for discussions of the upcoming week. Investors can chat about their best picks for the week, their expectations, and their strategies.

## INVESTools
http://www.investools.com

INVESTools, the financial newsletter and research center, offers users several free forums for discussion. Separate bulletin boards are available for chats about mutual funds, stocks, newsletters, internet resources, and general investment topics.

## Market Talk
http://www.markettalk.com

This site uses boxing metaphors to delineate its discussion groups, including "The Purse" (Stocks), "Weighing In" (Industries), and "Below the Belt" (Gossip). Despite the odd design consideration, the site is neatly organized and exists, it seems, solely to provide a forum for market talk. Some moderators and special guests add some value to the discussions.

## *Money Magazine* Bulletin Board
http://www.money.com

Whatever financial topic is on your mind, the bulletin boards of the *Money Magazine* Web site can provide an outlet. With the traffic this site gets,

topics fill up fast, with plenty of insights, opinions, and tips. Discussions on this board can span nearly every imaginable financial topic, including individual stocks, dividend reinvestment plans, options trading, mortgage financing, and tax-sheltered annuities. The bulletin board has a *sysop* (system operator) on hand to monitor posts and keep participants honest and civil. Lurkers can benefit from the expansive array of topics here, just a few clicks from the rest of *Money Magazine*'s excellent Web resources.

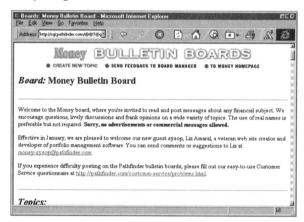

## Mutual Funds Moderated Newsgroup
http://www.brill.com/wwwboard

The Mutual Funds Interactive mega-site sponsors this discussion board focused exclusively on mutual fund investing. It is advertised as the Web's only moderated forum dedicated to mutual funds. And it seems to be popular with lots of Web investors, judging from the number of messages posted on the board each month. Users chat about specific funds, strategies, portfolio management and asset allocation, sector trading, expense ratios and variable annuities, and related topics.

## *New York Times* Forums
http://www.nytimes.com

The Web site of the *Times* features a number of forums for users to discuss news, sports, the arts, and related topics. One forum is set aside for discussions about the stock market. The talk here tends to be general in nature, with many posts about the prospects of the overall market. Occasionally, you can spot a reasoned analysis of a particular stock or fund.

### On-Finances
**http://www.crestar.com/cbmm_onfmenu.html**
Crestar Bank sponsors the Money Talks boards so users can chat with other individuals about any personal finance topic. Subgroups are available on Banking, Small Business Finances, Borrowing Money, Insurance, and Investing. It doesn't look like many users have jumped at the chance to participate, however.

### Real Traders
**http://www.realtraders.com**
RealTraders is an effort to build a virtual community on the Internet, made up of traders who pool their knowledge in an effort to learn from each other. On their site, they offer a threaded bulletin board discussion group, the Blue Jay Cafe II, and a live Java Conference Room. RealTraders monitors the board to keep out commercials and errant posts, raising the overall level of discussion. Traders of stocks, commodities, or financial options are welcome to participate.

### The Silicon Investor
**http://www.techstocks.com**
Over 100,000 members of The Silicon Investor visit the site's StockTalk bulletin boards for discussion of technology stocks. Many of these members are employees of high-tech companies or experienced tech investors, so the insights you'll get here are among the best you'll find on the Internet. Sure, there will be disagreements, and mudslinging, and

flame wars, but it's all part of the fun. Search for a company profile on any of the more than 500 technology or 200 bio-tech companies in their database, and then jump to the latest discussions on the stock, too. You can create a custom group of stocks that you follow, and then quickly access information on those companies. Charts and quotes are also provided, and you can follow the progress of the TechStocks120 Index on the site, as well.

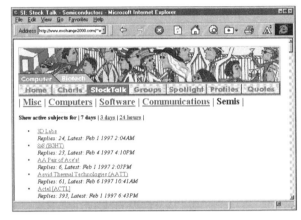

### The Stock Club
**http://www.stockclub.com**
The Stock Club is an online discussion forum for any publicly traded stock. Stock Club members can read and post responses in hundreds of forums devoted to individual stocks. Stock Club forums can also be used like a mailing list—you can subscribe to forums or to specific threads and be notified by e-mail immediately when new comments are added. Each stock's folder includes topics like fundamental analysis, news, and Internet resources, to help keep discussions organized. If a stock you're following doesn't have a forum devoted to it, then create one yourself! In addition, the Stock Club has built bulletin boards for over a dozen different topics, such as fundamental analysis, day trading, options strategies, investment software, and online

brokerages. The Stock Club is an easy-to-use environment for networking with other investors.

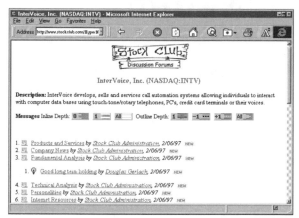

## Thomson MarketEdge
### http://www.marketedge.com

MarketEdge, a subscription-based service for investors on the Web, offers bulletin boards for discussions of stocks and mutual funds. Another board offers subscribers the chance to chat with Bob Gabele, the industry's leading expert on insider trading activity.

## TradeNet Stock Chat
### http://www.halcyon.com/tcorner

TradeNet offers four forums for investors: Fundamental Analysis, Technical Analysis, the Rumor Mill, and the Nirvana Omnitrader Forum (for users of Omnitrader software). Users can post comments and participate in occasional live chats. While the format can be a little tough to get used to, there seems to be an active community in residence here, primarily composed of traders.

## Winstar Government Securities Co.
### http://www.winstarsecurities.com/windiscuss

If you have questions about U.S. government securities, this bond dealer can help, with their online discussion group.

# INTERNET RADIO

Some users may find it ironic to make a multi-thousand dollar computer do the work of a $19.95 radio, but Internet audio is gaining popularity as a method of disseminating news online. Indeed, there are a number of virtual radio stations that now broadcast news and commentary over the Internet using technologies such as RealAudio, TrueSpeech, or Streamworks. Often these broadcasts are live, providing instantaneous access to market updates.

To take advantage of these sites, you'll need to download and install an audio player, but each site will provide a link and instructions for setting up your system to take advantage of their broadcasts.

## Atlantic Broadcasting System
### http://www.abslive.com

Atlantic Broadcasting System (ABS) produces live commentary on the U.S. stock markets in RealAudio format each day from 8:20 a.m. until 4:20 p.m. ABS monitors the markets for significant movements and issues alerts at the sign of major market advances or declines. Regularly scheduled programs review major U.S. market averages, winners and losers on the NYSE and NASDAQ, overseas stock and currency markets, technology stocks, and sector roundups. Links are provided to live broadcasts from

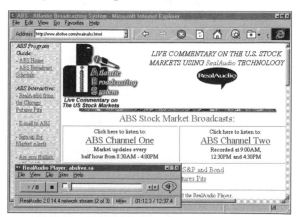

the S&P and Bond Futures Pits in Chicago. ABS also gives users a chance to talk with other traders in an interactive Java chat room.

### The KRLD Internet Report
**http://www.krld.com/ireport2.htm**

This AM station from Dallas/Fort Worth produces "The Internet Report," hosted by John Rody, that looks at online trends and news. The KRLD Web site features RealAudio transcripts of the programs. In particular, look for the December 21, 1996 program on Internet investing. You can hear Rody's interviews with such Internet investing celebrities as Ira Krakow, publisher of the *Persfin Digest*; Bill Rini of The Syndicate; and Motley Fool Tom Gardner.

### NetRadio Finance & Business
**http://www.netradio.net**

This leading Internet broadcasting site features RealAudio broadcasts of business news each day, interviews, industry reviews, and commentary from the NetRadio staff and special guests.

### Talk America
**http://www.talkamerica.com**

Talk America offers live talk programming 24 hours a day, seven days a week, using Xing Streamworks. The financial programs include Bob Hardcastle's weekly "Money Talk" program that looks back on each week's financial news, with commentary and discussion. Also, Bruce A. Lefavi, author of the book *Bullet Proof Your Financial Future*, helps listeners plan their financial future.

**ask doug!**

**Q:** What is the *Business Cycle*?

**A:** Our country's economy generally moves in cycles of about five years: three or so years of expansion followed by one or two years of contraction (also known as recession). It's important to understand this because many industries follow these cycles closely. For instance, food companies tend to be unaffected by recessions because everyone has to eat. But you don't have to eat in a restaurant. In hard times, people stay home more often. Therefore, the restaurant industry is cyclical.

Other cyclical industries include automobile manufacturing, entertainment, house construction, household appliances, and oil and industrial companies, particularly the steel industry. During a recession, companies and individuals alike postpone non-essential purchases.

Besides food companies, other non-cyclical industries include drugs, household products, tobacco companies, breweries, utilities, and soft drinks. These are all products that people cannot (or choose not) to do without during a recession.

It can be tough to predict how long any of the cycles will last, but it's important to know if a stock you own is in a cyclical industry group.

# GLOSSARY

ACCUMULATION—Buying additional shares of stock, usually done by institutions and usually in large quantities.

BETA—A measurement of the volatility of a stock or other investment. The market is assumed to have a beta of 1.0, and a stock with a beta of 1.2 is expected to rise 1.2 points for every 1.0 point the market rises. Conversely, that stock will fall 1.2 points for every 1.0 point drop in the overall market. A beta of less than 1.0, such as 0.8, implies that stock will rise only 0.8 points for every 1.0 climb in the market. A negative beta suggests that the stock will move in the opposite direction of the market as a whole.

CAPITALIZATION—Also known as market capitalization or market cap. Calculated by multiplying the number of shares outstanding by the share price, ostensibly to determine the value of an entire company.

CONSUMER PRICE INDEX—Abbreviated CPI. The U.S. Department of Commerce collects monthly statistics on the change in prices of goods and services and calculates this indicator, thereby measuring the pace of inflation.

DOW JONES INDUSTRIAL AVERAGE—Known as the Dow or the Dow 30, and abbreviated DJIA. The DJIA is an average (not an index) of 30 very large industrial companies and is commonly seen as representative of the market as a whole.

ECONOMETRICS—Within the field of economics, this is the application of statistical and mathematical methods to test economic theories and solve economic problems.

EFFICIENT MARKET THEORY—This theory states that all available knowledge is already reflected in any particular stock price, so that price represents its actual value. Therefore, no stock selection method is likely to produce a better return than the market itself over time.

FINANCIAL OPTIONS—Futures such as stock and bond indexes, currencies, and interest rates, as opposed to raw material commodities.

FLOAT—The number of shares of a security that are outstanding and available for trading by the general public.

IRC—Internet Relay Chat, a network for real-time chat on the Internet.

MAILING LIST—A discussion group delivered via e-mail.

NEWSGROUP—A particular Usenet channel devoted to a specific topic.

USENET—An international network of news servers connected via the Internet that carries thousands of newsgroups.

# Chapter 9
# International Investing

"When prosperity comes, do not use all of it."
—Confucius

**If you thought** the U.S. stock market was the only game on the planet, consider this: the U.S. financial markets only comprise one-third of the world market capitalization. The remainder are foreign securities, traded in markets all around the world.

The allure of international investing is understandable. As many countries around the world emerge from economic torpor, their stock markets are growing at stupendous rates. Influxes of Western capital into the countries of the former Soviet Union have created new opportunities. Pundits recommend that individual investors maintain anywhere from 10 percent to 60 percent of their portfolios in international equities in order to diversify and increase returns.

Of course, these increased returns can bring increased risk, as well. Some of these high-flying markets carry a high degree of volatility. The task of balancing risk and reward, as with any portfolio, becomes even more important when dealing in foreign equities.

Traditionally, international markets have been exceptionally difficult for individual investors to enter, largely because of the problems in getting accurate information from countries far-flung on the globe. The World Wide Web is particularly helpful in overcoming part of this obstacle. With a few mouse clicks, investors can be on the Web site of a foreign government agency to read economic reports, or visit a stock exchange to get information on listed companies, or sample the research of a brokerage firm that's half a world away.

# GLOBAL INVESTING SITES

For a global perspective of the world's financial markets, or for information on international investing in general, investors can check these Web sites. You'll find quotes, news, analysis, and other information covering a wide spectrum of global investing.

## BCA Emerging Markets Analyst
http://www.bcapub.com/ema

This monthly publication offers performance and return analysis on selected equity and debt assets in the emerging markets. Included on the site is performance data for equities and Brady Bonds, plus an occasional feature article.

## Data Broadcasting Corp
http://www.dbc.com

When you need a quote for a stock on the Karachi Stock Exchange, where are you going to turn? Or if you want the exchange rate for the Bahraini Dinar? Just jump to Data Broadcasting Corp. (DBC) on the Web and you'll get the information you need. They offer market quotes for stocks that trade on at least 27 stock exchanges outside North America, as well as market indexes from around the world and quotes for American Depository Receipts (ADRs) listed on U.S. exchanges.

## Data Broadcasting Corp. Signal/Europe
http://www.dbceuro.com

Besides Europe, DBC's U.K.-based operation offers real-time and delayed data on markets in the Middle East, North Africa, and Russia. The Signal satellite service is available by subscription, and provides quotes, news, mutual fund, and money market fund data and portfolio management.

## Dow Jones Telerate—Europe, Middle East, Africa
http://emea.telerate.com

This division of Dow Jones Telerate provides real-time financial information and news for investors interested in European, African, and Middle East markets. Their Web site includes samples of their services, including prices on stocks, commodities and currencies, news, and analysis.

**the swami speaks**

The Swami, of course, is a polyglot, so he has no problem understanding the many languages of the world. However, he knows you may not be so linguistically gifted. Fortunately, many Web site hosts understand that English is a leading tongue of international business. Many foreign firms provide alternate versions of their sites in English, in addition to the language of their own countries. If you arrive at a site and find that it's in a foreign language, look for a text link to an English version on the page. Sometimes, particularly on European and Asian sites, the link will be indicated by a small graphic of a British flag. Click and you'll arrive in a more familiar environ.

## Emerging Markets Companion
**http://www.emgmkts.com**

Investors interested in the world's emerging markets can check in with the EMC Web site for news, prices, and fundamental research from Latin America, Eastern Europe, Asia, Africa, Mexico, Brazil, Argentina, Chile, Venezuela, Russia, Hungary, Poland, Singapore, Taiwan, the Philippines, China, India, and Turkey.

## Financial Information Network
**http://www.finetwork.com**

The Network offers free global market commentary on interest rates, currencies, the treasury market, equities, and international markets in London, Tokyo, Mexico, and Moscow. Users can also retrieve fact sheets on new issues, or access the institutional LDC Bond Watch.

## Global Exchange News
**http://www.ino.com/gen**

INO Global Markets has built a searchable directory of all the major exchanges in the world that trade futures and options. The exchanges are listed alphabetically by country or can be reached by clicking on a world map.

## International Business Network
**http://www1.usa1.com/~ibnet**

The International Business Network (IBN) is dedicated to the exchange of business information and the facilitation of international trade. The site provides links to resources related to international finance.

## International Finance & Commodities Institute
**http://finance.wat.ch/IFCI**

The Institute's objective is to promote global understanding of commodity trading and financial futures and options. Their site offers feature articles, educational and training materials, and details of the organization.

## International Financial Encyclopaedia
**http://www.euro.net/innovation/Finance_Base/Fin_encyc.html**

The Encyclopaedia is an interactive guide to terms, phrases, organizations, and related financial topics, with descriptions and illustrations.

## International Trade Administration
**http://www.ita.doc.gov**

The International Trade Administration (ITA) is an agency of the U.S. Department of Commerce dedicated to helping U.S. businesses compete in the global marketplace. The site includes world trade statistics and current economic analysis, as well as links related to other information about trade policy and regulations.

## Internet Securities, Inc. Emerging Markets

**http://www.securities.com**

Internet Securities, Inc. (ISI) Emerging Markets is an online subscription-based service that offers information on business and financial markets in the emerging markets of the Baltic States, Czech Republic, Poland, Ukraine, Bulgaria, Hungary, Russia, China, India, and Colombia. On this site investors can find daily news in several languages along with English translations, company profiles, weekly market reviews, country and industry reports, complete financial data in Excel format for downloading, historical stock quotes, and graphs and macroeconomic data.

## Organization for Economic Co-operation and Development

**http://www.oecd.org**

The Organization for Economic Co-operation and Development (OECD), based in Paris, France, is a forum for governments of industrialized democracies to formulate economic and social policies. The group publishes hundreds of publications and newsletters each year, providing samples of some on their site.

## Overseas Private Investment Corporation

**http://www.opic.gov**

This is an independent U.S. government agency that supports American private investment in over 140 emerging economies around the world. The agency sells financial services, such as long-term political risk insurance and limited recourse project financing, to American companies.

 Investors with a socially responsible bent may be hesitant to invest overseas, particularly in countries where there are concerns that human rights violations may be taking place. Others may argue that the infusion of American capital into emerging markets benefits the citizens of these countries by helping to raise the standard of living. There are complex moral and philosophical arguments to be made on both sides, and it's your responsibility as an investor to understand your own position.

## Pangaea Partners, Ltd

**http://www.pangaeapartners.com**

Pangaea Partners provides investment banking and financial consulting services in emerging markets, such as those in the former Soviet Union, Africa, the Middle East, and the Caribbean. The site includes general business information, privatization reports, and market overviews in Kyrgyzstan, Tunisia, Madagascar, Georgia, and Zambia.

## PC Quote Europe

**http://www.pcquote-europe.co.uk**

The European division of PC Quote offers delayed, end-of-day, and real-time quotes from 57 world exchanges. They cover the stock, futures, and Forex markets, as well as world market indices. Their Investor's Emporium also offers books and software related to investing.

## Polyconomics, Inc.

**http://www.polyconomics.com**

Polyconomics is a research firm that makes political and economic assessments of global developments. The site includes archives of past research bulletins and in-depth analysis of events and policy changes that have a significant impact on American, Asian, and Latin American capital markets.

### Qualisteam Banking & Finance
http://www.qualisteam.com/aindex.html

Qualisteam is a French consulting firm specializing in information technology for financial companies. Their site is a comprehensive collection of classified links to international sources, including over 1,000 bank Web sites, stock exchanges from 65 countries, and sites related to bonds, mutual funds, stocks, futures, financial journals. The site is in English and French.

### WEBS on the Web
http://websontheweb.com

World Equity Benchmark Shares (WEBS) is a relatively new approach to international investing. Each WEBS share represents an underlying portfolio of publicly traded stocks in a selected country, but which trade as a single security on the American Stock Exchange. This site provides a prospectus and detailed information on WEBS.

### The World Bank
http://www.worldbank.org

The World Bank's goal is to reduce poverty and improve living standards by promoting sustainable growth and investments in people, through loans, technical assistance, and policy guidance to developing countries. The site includes some detailed research on developing economies and other activities of the bank.

### World Federation of Investors Corporation
http://www.wfic.org

World Federation of Investors Corporation (WFIC) is an international group with member chapters in 16 countries around the world. The organization's goal is to introduce individuals to investing, via investment clubs and educational programs. The page includes links to its member organizations, with information on each group and their activities. Every other year, the Federation sponsors a World Congress for investors to come together for education and advancement. For individuals who are looking to learn about investing in the stock market, the members of the World Federation stand ready to help.

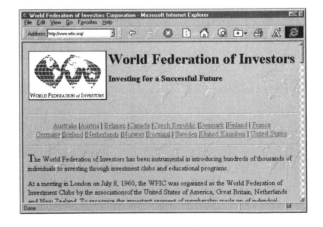

## World's Stock Exchanges and Chambers of Trade
http://www.geocities.com/WallStreet/3347/ing.htm

Brazilian Érico Hack has put together a directory, in English and Portuguese, of the major stock exchanges of the world.

# AFRICA AND THE MIDDLE EAST

The emerging economies of Africa offer opportunities for investors to participate in the early stages of growth of many financial markets on the continent. On the other hand, the Israeli markets are long-established and are home to many internationally known companies, including numerous high-tech and financial corporations. In between these two extremes, adventuresome investors can discover still other possibilities of potential interest.

## AFRICA

### ABSA Group
http://www.absa.co.za

ABSA is Africa's largest banking and financial services group, the parent of a number of retail banks. The site is filled with personal finance resources, news, account application forms, and details of their trust products.

### The African Stock Exchange Guide
http://africa.com/pages/jse/

Virtual Africa provides this directory of companies listed on stock exchanges in Africa. The guide is searchable and lists companies by industry group,

 A big advantage to investing globally is that the economies of other countries are driven by much different factors than the U.S. economy. Adding international equities to your portfolio, whether individual stocks or a mutual fund, can provide an added measure of diversification. If the U.S. markets slump, chances are that many of the world markets may not be adversely affected.

exchange, or alphabetically. A brief profile is available for each company, as well.

### Bureau for Financial Analysis Network
http://www.bfanet.com

The Bureau provides a comprehensive financial database about companies listed on the Johannesburg Stock Exchange. Financial reports, news, market summaries, and a customized portfolio service are provided.

### Johannesburg Stock Exchange
http://www.jse.co.za

The Johannesburg Stock Exchange (JSE) is over 100 years old. This site includes a guide to listed companies, market statistics, daily market updates, news, and quotes.

### Rand Merchant Bank
http://www.rmb.co.za/fin.html

Rand Merchant Bank, based in Johannesburg, is one of South Africa's largest investment banks. The firm offers economic and market reports about the South African financial market, as well as educational articles about investing in the South African equities, bond, and futures markets.

### South African Futures Exchange
**http://www.safex.co.za**

SAFEX offers both financial and agricultural contracts for trading. The site offers historical data and current statistics, background on the Exchange, listed futures, contract specifications, and advice on futures trading.

### Sharenet
**http://www.sharenet.co.za/sharenet**

Sharenet offers closing prices on the Johannesburg Stock Exchange, South African Futures Exchange (SAFEX), Gilts, Unit Trusts, and numerous other indicators. Subscribers can download daily data files, and delayed quotes are available free during the day. Analysis, news, and commentary are also available.

# MIDDLE EAST

### Israel's Business Arena—by *Globes*
**http://www.globes.co.il**

*Globes* is Israel's business newspaper, and this attractive and feature-filled site offers news and data, including daily headlines and articles. Their Stock Market section provides a comprehensive look at Israeli markets, with daily quotes, reports on technology and communications stocks, and plenty of commentary. In English or Hebrew.

### Israel's Infomedia
**http://www.ibc.co.il**

Infomedia is an online guide to Israeli industry and business. It includes a searchable directory of businesses in many sectors.

### *Middle East Business Review* Home Page
**http://sun.rhbnc.ac.uk/mgt/mbr.html**

The University of London publishes this journal, which focuses on cross-cultural and management issues in the Middle East. The site provides a summary of the *Review* and its annual Middle East Business Conference, but no other content.

### Standard & Poor's Israeli Public Companies
**http://www.standardpoor.co.il**

This Israeli site provides online S&P reports of Israeli public companies and financial institutions. Each report includes a business summary and financial data. Israeli companies trading on U.S. exchanges are also included.

### Stock Management And Forecast Software
**http://www.trendline.co.il/cos**

This program combines a trading system with portfolio management tools for investors trading stocks on the Israeli Stock Exchange. Technical specifications and ordering information are provided.

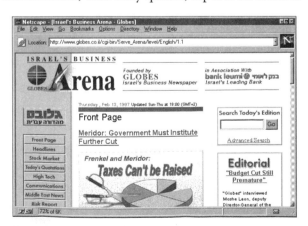

# ASIA AND THE PACIFIC

Many Asian countries are global economic leaders, and the persistent growth of the region has created many interesting opportunities for investment. China, even with its difficult environment for foreign investment, excites many investors when they consider the enormous potential customer basis in the world's largest country. The turnover of Hong Kong to China has increased uncertainty about the future of that country's markets and whether the Chinese will stifle the enormous industrial output of the island. In addition to the established markets of Japan, Taiwan, Singapore, and Maylasia, other countries are undergoing massive expansion.

## *Asia Inc.* Online
http://www.asia-inc.com

*Asia Inc.* is a leading business magazine centered on the region. Their companion Web site includes such features as "Who's Who in Asia," conference rooms, an online reference library to Asian data and resources, and "Russian Business News." A financial section offers stock market closings, an Asian IPO watch, and Hong Kong market commentary.

## Asian Development Bank
http://www.asiandevbank.org

Asian Development Bank (ADB) provides lending, co-financing, and technical assistance for companies doing business in Asia. The bank provides research, publications, descriptions of projects, and other services on their Web site.

**ask doug!**

**Q:** What are WEBS?

**A:** WEBS are World Equity Benchmark Shares, an index fund made up of 17 index series. Each series represents one of 17 countries and tracks the appropriate Morgan Stanley Capital International (MSCI) Index for that country. Since they are passive index funds, WEBS have low annual operating expenses and management fees and no sales load. WEBS shares trade on the American Stock Exchange and provide a way for investors to target a specific country for investment without worrying about identifying particular foreign stocks or dealing with foreign currencies. For more information, see WEBS on the Web (http://www.websontheweb.com)

## Asian Studies WWW Virtual Library
http://coombs.anu.edu.au/WWWVL-AsianStudies.html

Dr. T. Matthew Ciolek of the Australian National University provides this exhaustive series of links to Web sites related to Asia. Links are organized by topic and region.

## Barton's Asian Stock Charts
http://www.inet.co.th/cyberclub/barton

This free weekly service offers charts and forecasts of ten Asian stock market indexes: Hong Kong, India, Indonesia, Japan, Korea, Malaysia, the Philippines, Singapore, Taiwan, and Thailand.

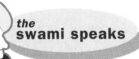

**the swami speaks**

Where the Swami comes from, date formats are different than those used in the U.S. While it's common in this country to abbreviate dates MM/DD/YY (month/day/year), foreign countries use the format DD/MM/YY or YY/DD/MM. When you see the date 10/02/97 on a foreign site, it means February 10, 1997, not October 2, 1997. Also, some countries use a period (.) instead of a dash or slash when writing dates, so you may come across 10.2.1997 in use, too.

## Indonesia NET Exchange
http://www.indoexchange.com

This site is a comprehensive resource for the Indonesian capital markets, with an Asian news wire service, live stock quotes, market updates, industry reports, economic research, company profiles, and information about mutual funds.

# CHINA, HONG KONG, AND TAIWAN

## AsiaInfo Services, Inc.
http://usai.asiainfo.com

AsiaInfo is a U.S. firm that provides services related to business opportunities in China, including their Daily China News Wire Service sent via e-mail, industry reports, publications, and databases.

## China Business Net
http://www.business-china.com

This site acts as a central clearing house for Chinese business opportunities and resources and includes

stock, futures, and exchange rates; listings of Chinese investment projects; and a virtual trade show featuring Chinese companies and products.

## China Economic Information Network
http://www.cei.go.cn/indexe.html

This official site provides economic and business information about China. Their "Guide to China Investment" offers details of the laws, regulations, and policies surrounding foreign investment in the country. The Guide also includes a database of opportunities throughout the country.

## Core Pacific Financial Group
http://www.cps.com.tw

Core Pacific is the parent of several financial and consulting companies headquartered in Tapei. Their site publishes a daily market roundup and stock prices from the Taiwan Stock Exchange Market. In English and Chinese.

## InTechTra's Hong Kong Stock Reports
http://www.asiawind.com/pub/hksr/

InTechTra's subscription service sends a daily closing report on the Hong Kong stock market via e-mail. Each report includes a market summary, top ten best and worst performers of the day, analyzed data, charts, news, portfolio management, stock alert, market watch, warrant report, forum, historical data, and other information. Subscribers can also establish their own portfolio and get customized alerts and company reports. Visitors can access free charts and other information on the Hong Kong markets.

## National Investment Trust Co. Ltd.
http://www.nitc.com.tw

This Taiwan-based investment trust company issues and manages unit trust funds. The site provides daily

NAVs, quarterly reports, and other details of their family of funds.

# INDIA

## Bee Management Consultancy Pvt. Ltd.
http://www.angelfire.com/biz/Rajiv

This Bombay, India firm specializes in providing liaison facilities, representation, and advice for business people and investors.

## Economic Times
http://www.economictimes.com

India's leading business newspaper provides daily coverage of Indian stock markets, with both news and analysis. A special Investor's Guide features a database of 200 mutual funds, technical analysis of equities, and industry commentary.

## India Business Update
http://allindia.com/bizindia/

Check in here for daily updates on the Indian Stock Market, including main news stories of the state of the Indian economy, stock indexes, Forex rates, and gold and silver quotes.

## Invest-India
http://quark.kode.net/india/

Invest-India offers financial news and information, including closing stock prices from the Bombay Stock Exchange.

## MakroIndia
http://www.makroindia.com

MakroIndia provides investment advisory and capital market services on the Indian capital markets. Users

Few financial markets around the world are as highly regulated as the United States. Accounting standards, securities laws, and exchange regulations vary from country to country. These variations are often substantial, even so far as to render a simple concept as profits subject to differing interpretations.

can receive free end-of-day quotes from the Mumbai Stock Exchange and National Stock Exchange, on the site or via e-mailed portfolio updates. The site also offers short-term trading advice for some stocks on the Mumbai Stock Exchange, a bulletin board for discussion, lists of Indian initial public offerings, weekly mutual fund updates, and Java stock charting.

## National Stock Exchange of India
http://www.nseindia.com

Investors can get daily quotes on companies listed on the National Stock Exchange (NSE) or access directories of listed companies, debentures, and warrants. Information on the NSE-50 Index is also provided, along with a history of the exchange.

## Parag Parikh Financial Advisory Services Ltd.
http://www.allindia.com/parag

This financial advisor publishes a weekly and monthly review of India's financial markets, looking at economic trends, capital markets, government finance, inflation and money supply, as well as select companies.

Many foreign countries use commas in place of decimals in their number systems. When you come across $80,00, it's not eighty thousand dollars missing a digit, but eighty dollars.

# JAPAN

## Nagoya Stock Exchange
**http://www.iijnet.or.jp/nse-jp/index-e.htm**
This Japanese exchange offers market summaries and quotations for the 576 companies listed there. In English or Japanese.

## Okasan Economic Research Institute
**http://www.iijnet.or.jp/ORI/english/index.htm**
The Institute publishes research reports, economic outlooks, and corporate earnings forecasts for the Japanese markets, and all are available on the Web site. The organization is a division of Okasan Securities, Ltd.

## Tokyo Stock Exchange
**http://www.tse.or.jp/eindex.html**
For investors interested in the Japanese markets, the Tokyo Stock Exchange provides information on the exchange, links to listed companies, regular updates of the TOPIX index, and market updates.

# MALAYSIA

## Kuala Lumpur Stock Exchange
**http://www.klse.com.my**
The Kuala Lumpur Stock Exchange Web site provides a directory of listed companies and other information about the exchange.

## Securities Commission in Malaysia
**http://www.at-asia.com/sc**
The Commission regulates the Kuala Lumpur Stock Exchange and other markets in Malaysia.

## *The Star* Online
**http://thestar.com.my**
This Malaysian newspaper provides daily data and reports from the Kuala Lumpur Stock Exchange, along with business headlines and news.

# RUSSIA

## AK&M
**http://www.fe.msk.ru/infomarket/akm/welcome.html**
AK&M, a Russian consulting company, maintains a database of companies listed on the Russian stock markets, along with analyses of their businesses, shareholder news, and company ratings.

## Alfa Capital
**http://www.alfa.rosmail.com**
Alfa Capital is a Russian investment bank offering a full schedule of brokerage, merchant, and investment banking services. The site includes their research on market sectors, individual companies, and weekly market overviews.

## BISNIS On-Line

http://www.itaiep.doc.gov/bisnis/bisnis.html

This is the home page of the Department of Commerce's Business Information Service for the Newly Independent States, dubbed BISNIS. The site intends to be a one-stop shop for those interested in doing business in Russia and the other states of the former Soviet Union.

## Emerging Markets Navigator

http://www.emn.ru

Focused on the Russian markets, this site offers rankings of Moscow banks and discussions of default risks, along with business news and links to related sites.

## Federal Commission for the Securities Market

http://feast.fe.msk.ru/infomarket/fedcom/emarkt.html

This agency of the Russian Federation is responsible for the supervision of the country's capital markets. The Commission hosts REDGAR, the Russian Electronic Data Gathering And Retrieval system (really), which is only available in Russian. It also has some related English documents describing laws and regulations.

## Friends and Partners

http://www.friends-partners.org/friends

Friends and Partners is a general information source for Russia developed by citizens of the U.S. and Russia in order to promote better understanding between the two countries. The site includes various databases and links related to business and economics topics.

U.S. citizens must report all income on their Federal income tax returns, no matter where that income was earned. Earning income outside the United States does not exempt you from your responsibility for filing tax returns and reporting your earnings, including that from foreign investments.

## InfoMarket

http://www.fe.msk.ru/infomarket/ewelcome.html

InfoMarket offers information on the securities and capital markets of Russia, sponsored by the Institute of Commercial Engineering with data provided by the Russian Ministry of Finance and Central Bank and other Russian agencies and businesses. Investors can access news, quotes, indexes, and historical data. InfoMarket also hosts the Web sites of a number of other finance-related Russian firms.

## Investing in Russia

http://www.nvst.com/rsrc/russia.htm

This series of articles by Dr. Pyotr Johannevich van de Waal-Palms outlines how privatization of Russian business has produced an opportunity for acquisitions, investments, and joint ventures. Topics covered include how to approach deals in Russia, Russia's place in the global economy, and valuation of Russian corporations.

## Open Media Research Institute

http://www.omri.cz

Open Media Research Institute provides a news service devoted to Russian and Central and Eastern European countries. Their Web site offers a daily digest, Russian Regional Report, and analytical briefs of breaking news.

### Palms' Portal to Eastern Europe & the C.I.S.

**http://www.aa.net/~russia/pindex .html**

Palms & Company, Inc. Investment Bankers has compiled a sprawling site focused on doing business or investing in Eastern Europe or Russia. The firm is a specialist in mergers, acquisitions, U.S. government investment guarantees, tax abatements, economic policies, and regulations, as well as the traps and pitfalls of dealing in the Russian markets. As an expert on these emerging markets, Dr. Pyotr Johannevich van de Waal-Palms has written an array of articles and commentary on the subject that are also available.

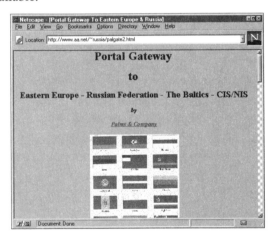

### *Passport* International

**http://www.maestro.com/ing/zig/rol.htm**

Based in Moscow, Passport International is the largest Russian publishing company, producing *Passport*, the business magazine of Russia and the Commonwealth of Independent States (C.I.S.). This bimonthly English-language magazine looks at business, politics, and culture of the region. Each month's table of contents and cover is published on the Web site.

### REESWeb: Russian and East European Studies

**http://www.pitt.edu/~cjp/rees.html**

REESWeb, from the University of Pittsburgh's University Center for Russian and East European Studies, is a comprehensive index of Internet resources on the region. Sites are listed by discipline (such as Business, Economics and Law, Government Affairs) or by type.

### RINACO Plus

**http://www.fe.msk.ru/infomarket/rinacoplus/**

This Moscow-based brokerage house provides securities pricing, research reports, newsletters, industry reports, and other information about the Russian equities and debt markets.

### Russia Commercial Guide

**http://www.friends-partners.org/oldfriends/ economics/comm.guide.tables/ ru.comm.guide.index.html**

Published by the U.S. Embassy in Moscow, the Russia Country Commercial Guide presents the state of the current commercial environment with economic, political, and market analysis. The Guide is a good overview of the many factors that influence business and investment in the country.

### Russia Portfolio

**http://world.std.com/~rusport**

*Russia Portfolio* is a newsletter with information about investment opportunities in Russia. The site includes highlights from recent and past issues and a downloadable sample in Acrobat format.

## Russian-American Exchange

http://www.cris.com/~Rusamex

Russian-American Exchange (RUSAMEX) is an import/export firm dealing with transactions to and from Russia and other CIS countries. Their specialty is exporting foodstuffs to the former USSR.

## Russian Legal Server

http://solar.rtd.utk.edu/~nikforov/main.html

The Russian Legal Server's goal is to provide access to legal and related information concerning the Russian Federation, to promote understanding as well as facilitate international business. The site includes tutorials on Russian legal research, news, and texts of various publications.

## Russian National Commercial Bank

http://www.rncb.ru

This Moscow-based investment bank is host to information on foreign investment in Russian equities, foreign currency exchange rates, and share prices for stocks on the Russian trading system.

## The St. Petersburg Press

http://www.spb.su/times

*The St. Petersburg Press* is an English-language newspaper that covers events in Russia and St. Petersburg. The Web site carries articles from the business section about financial and economic developments.

## Skate

http://www.skate.ru

Skate advertises itself as "Your Key To The Russian Financial Markets," and this site plainly lives up to its hype. Investors can access their Corporate Action Watch, with reports on the Russian stock market and its inner workings and intra-day and

closing prices of the *Moscow Times* market index. In-depth coverage of over 150 publicly traded Russian companies (called the Skate blue chips) is also available for a relatively expensive fee. And there is a subscription newsletter on the Russian capital markets.

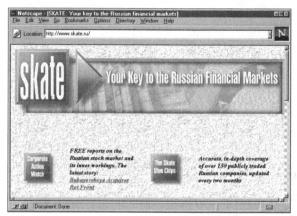

## TEAMinfo

http://www.econ.ag.gov/TEAMinfo/

Transition Economies: Agricultural Market (TEAM) is a clearinghouse for information on agricultural commodities markets in the former centrally planned economies of Central and Eastern Europe and the former Soviet Union. Though sponsored by the USDA Economic Research Service, most of the reports are hopelessly outdated.

## Tovarichestvo Palmsa Inc.

http://sungraph.jinr.dubna.su/palms

This site from investment bankers Palms & Company, Inc. focuses on Russian investment opportunities, with an extensive collection of articles by Dr. Pyotr Johannevich van de Waal-Palms, the leading expert on Russian-American trade.

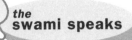

### the swami speaks

Warning: Expect Delays Ahead. That's the Swami's best advice if you're surfing across the oceans. The Internet is built so that there are many potential pathways that a packet of data may take en route from one server to another. Think of the Internet as a map of the Interstate highway system in the U.S. You can drive a fairly direct route from New York City to Los Angeles, and that might be the fastest way to get from one coast to the other. But if traffic is very heavy, say, between Kansas City and Denver, your trip might be shorter if you take a detour via Oklahoma City, even though the actual distance you drive may be longer. The Internet works in much the same way, in that packets of data seek out the best route to get from one point to another.

When those packets of data need to travel overseas, however, things begin to slow down because there aren't as many data pipelines crossing the oceans. The telecommunications infrastructure in many countries may not be as robust as it is in the U.S., either. And you might be using the Internet during an hour off-peak for you, but it could be prime time halfway around the world. These factors can all slow down the transmission of data to your own computer.

## SINGAPORE

### AsiaOne
**http://www.asia1.com.sg**
AsiaOne is a project of Singapore Press Holdings, a leading publishing and printing group in Southeast Asia. The site includes an expansive array of news and business information, including real-time share prices from the Stock Exchange of Singapore and the Kuala Lumpur Stock Exchange, market reports, company research, global analysis, and news and quotes for commodities and funds. The site also includes online editions of business and trade journals.

### Financial Interactive Services Hub
**http://www.infront.com.sg**
Financial Interactive Services Hub (FISH) is a comprehensive financial resource for investors interested in the growing Singapore stock markets. The site provides an array of quotes, data, and news on stocks, futures, options, currencies, bonds, and funds.

### MediaCity Investment Centre
**http://www.mediacity.com.sg/ic/investor/pick.htm**
MediaCity offers a free stock portfolio watch service for companies listed on the Singapore Stock Exchange, plus Asian-Pacific and world financial news updates.

### Singapore Company Research
**http://www.asia1.com.sg/company**
For a fee, this service provides detailed research reports on Singapore-listed companies. Each report contains financial information, a company history, capital structure, management information, and company news.

### Stock Exchange of Singapore
**http://www.ses.com.sg**
The Stock Exchange of Singapore is a leading Asian stock market, with a searchable list of the 200 Singapore companies and 50 foreign firms who are listed

on the exchange. Details of IPOs, market wrap-ups, and an overview of the exchange are also provided.

## Singapore International Monetary Exchange

http://www.simex.com

Singapore International Monetary Exchange (SIMEX) provides its history, product updates, market commentaries, and charts and statistics on futures and options that trade on the exchange.

## Overseas Union Bank Ltd.

http://www.oub.com.sg

Overseas Union Bank offers a weekly financial review of the markets in Singapore, Malaysia, and Thailand, plus information on their banking and investment services.

# OTHER COUNTRIES

## Asian Securities Limited

http://www.hway.net/asian

This Pakistani stock broker is a corporate member of the Karachi Stock Exchange. They offer daily stock quotes, weekly market analysis, and detailed company reports.

## Datascope Online

http://www.planet.com.tr/datascope

Datascope provides information on a wide spectrum ranging from stocks exchanged over the Istanbul Stock Exchange to exchange rates, government bonds, foreign trade figures, and sector reports.

Income, capital gains, or dividends earned on foreign investments may be subject to taxes in the country in which they are paid. However, you may be eligible for a foreign tax credit when you file your tax returns with the IRS, thus avoiding double taxation.

## Istanbul Stock Exchange

http://www.ise.org

Learn about companies that trade on the Istanbul Stock Exchange, with both current and historic data, or browse the directory of other issues that trade here: bonds and bills, repos, real estate certificates, international markets, and derivatives. The site also offers updates on stock market indices and their Government Debt Securities Indices.

## Phillipine Stock Watch

http://is.eunet.ch/astarte/pbo/stock/mainstck.html

What was the world's best performing stock market in 1993? This site proudly proclaims that the Phillipines' Makati Stock Exchange is the holder of that distinction. The site provides background on the exchange, company listings, and daily market information.

## Sri Lanka Daily News

http://www.lanka.net/lakehouse

Here, investors can get daily stock market updates on the Colombo Stock Exchange, provided by Sri Lanka's largest English-language newspaper. Also, local prices for coconuts and coconut products are listed, along with Sri Lanka economic indicators and business news stories.

### The Stock Exchange of Thailand

http://www.set.or.th

Thailand's stock exchange incorporates real-time market information and background information on listed companies on this site, along with general information, market summaries, news, and economic statistics.

# AUSTRALIA AND NEW ZEALAND

Australia may be known as "the land down under," but the Australian stock market is above ground and thriving. Many banks, investment companies, brokers, and stock exchanges are on the Web, from Australia and its neighbor, New Zealand.

### AMP

http://www.amp.com.au

AMP is a financial services company offering life insurance, financial planning services, and mutual funds management. Their site contains a range of information on the company, as well as tools and calculators to help individuals analyze their investment and insurance needs. AMP also offers weekly opinion on the Australian financial markets.

### Australian Stock Exchange Quote WebLink

http://www.weblink.com.au/webinvestor

This investment center offers live ASX share prices, real-time business and financial news, and other services for subscribers. Visitors can read educational articles or browse their Investor Glossary.

### Australian Bureau of Statistics

http://www.statistics.gov.au

This site provides a look at Australia by the numbers, from the official statistician of the Commonwealth of Australia. Regular reports of current key economic and social indicators are published here, along with other statistics about Australia and its territories.

### Australian Financial Review

http://www.afr.com.au

This financial publication provides a look at news from Australia and the world, along with coverage of the investment, banking, and real estate markets. Daily market reports and feature articles provide a good inside look at Australian finance. They also provide a dictionary of financial terms, as well as archives of past articles.

### Australian Financial Services Directory

http://www.afsd.com.au

This guide to Australia's financial resources lists hundreds of sources of investment information and advice, both online and off. The catalog includes categories such as Financial Publications, Financial Data and Software, Trading Systems, Market Commentary, Stock Brokers, and Commodities and Futures. Also included are articles contributed by a

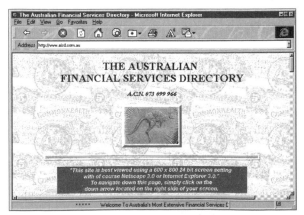

number of financial professionals and academicians on related topics.

## Australian Industry Educational Resource Centre

**http://www.ozemail.com.au/~kline/**

This site is a comprehensive catalogue of educational resources developed by Australia's leading companies, industry associations, and government agencies. Their goal is to assist students and teachers in quickly finding accurate and up-to-date information on Australian industry, environmental and social issues, career, and employment opportunities.

## The Australian Sharemarket Investor

**http://www.aer.com.au**

Australia's leading independent research firm publishes a newsletter with comprehensive information about the people and events that impact upon the country's financial markets. They provide a sample of their newsletter, as well as a directory of public Australian firms on the World Wide Web.

## Australian Stock Exchange ShareNet

**http://www.asx.com.au**

The Australian Stock Exchange ShareNet is a complete center for information about the Australian

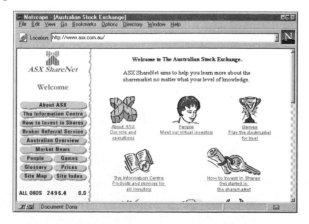

equities and derivatives markets. Some highlights of the site include a Broker Referral Service, daily share prices, market news, and plenty of educational material designed to help investors get started in the sharemarket. A detailed glossary explains all the terms you need to know to get started in the Australian market. For a bit of fun, test your investing skill and expertise in a sharemarket game.

## Beyond The Black Stump Shares & Money Page

**http://werple.net.au/~lions/stocks.htm**

"Beyond The Black Stump" is an Australian expression that means "in the middle of nowhere," says the site's publisher, Peter Garriga. This carefully organized Web catalog includes both Australian and global links, and the database is searchable. The financial page is a good starting point for surfing the Web.

## BT Funds Management

**http://www.btfunds.com.au**

The Bankers Trust Australia Group offers funds management and services for institutions, companies, and individuals. They offer an Easy Investment Planner on their site, a Java applet savings calculator, as well as unit prices for BT funds and other information for individual investors.

## Burdett, Buckridge and Young, Ltd.

**http://www.bby.com.au**

Burdett, Buckridge and Young is a leading Australian investment banking and stock brokerage, providing investors with a range of services. Clients can access the company's equities research on their Web site, and others can download a daily market report in Acrobat format.

### Business Review Weekly

**http://www.brw.com.au**

Australia's leading business magazine provides a well-organized Web site, with feature stories, columns, and commentary from the printed edition. The *Review* covers the stock markets, the economy, industry trends, real estate, and business management topics. Archives are available for searching or browsing.

### Cochrane Investment Services

**http://www.cochrane.net.au**

This independent investment research firm is headed by George Cochrane, a former journalist and well-known investment advisor. Cochrane advertises his *Gold Stocks '96* publication for sale on this page, along with snippets of his technical look at gold stocks on the Australian market.

### County NatWest Investment Management

**http://www.county.com.au**

This leading Australian financial company offers a series of managed funds, including the County Direct Investment Trust for which investors can download an electronic prospectus. The site also includes a collection of articles dealing with principles of investment funds management, economic trends, and industry issues, as well as the Internet edition of the Australian Financial Review Dictionary of Investment Terms.

### Deutsche Morgan Grenfell Securities Australia

**http://www.bain.com.au**

The Australian division of the global investment bank offers equity research on its site for clients, but nothing else for other investors.

**ask doug!**

**Q:** What's an ADR?

**A:** ADRs are American Depositary Receipts, securities that trade on a U.S. exchange in dollars but represent the stock of a foreign company. The underlying shares of stock are held (deposited) in a bank. Each ADR can represent one share, a fraction of a share, or several shares of the underlying stock. ADRs allow individual investors to buy shares of stock in some of the world's leading companies without the obstacles of dealing with a foreign stock exchange.

### Dicksons Ltd.

**http://www.opennet.net.au/dicksons**

Dicksons can trace its heritage as an Australian stockbroker back to 1860, but they've moved comfortably into the 1990s with a Web site filled with research, corporate profiles, stock news, and a daily snapshot of overnight trading activity. Check out their "Top Stock List for the Serious Investor," and the "Chartist Corner," with highlights of technical analysis from the past week.

### Farmboy's Financial Pages

**http://www.iap.net.au/~farmboy**

Farmboy (whoever he is) assembles several data files users can download free from this Web site, such as Australia's top 100 dividend paying stocks, leading ASX indexes, U.S. and Australian economic data, and international indices that are deemed relevant to the Australian stock market. Graphs are also available on a weekly and daily basis for a number of securities.

## Global Register Australia

http://www.globalregister.com.au

This site offers closing prices on Australian Stock Exchange issues and a directory of Australian companies.

## Global Register New Zealand

http://www.globalregister.co.nz

The Global Register provides information on New Zealand public companies, trusts, mutual funds, securities, financial data, investments, stock prices, and bonds. The site also offers a free personal news monitor sent via e-mail with news about your selected companies.

## Greenchip Funds Management

http://www.greenchip.com.au

Greenchip provides performance results, strategies, and background on their family of funds.

## HotCopper

http://www.hotcopper.com.au

Ron Gully was one of the first in Australia to build a Web site revolving around the stock markets, and HotCopper is the outgrowth of his initial hobby. HotCopper now offers an historical Australian stock market database and guides like *The Register of Australian Mining 1996-1997*. HotTips is the site's forum for discussing Australian stocks on the move.

## Andrew Kelly's Financial Markets Page

http://www.cs.monash.edu.au/~kelly/finance/

Investor Andrew Kelly has compiled a home page packed with links to information on Australian and overseas shares and companies, world stock exchanges, world futures markets, Australian stockbrokers, investment tips, financial information, and finance papers.

## Macquarie Bank

http://www.macquarie.com.au

Macquarie provides investment banking, stockbroking, and funds management services to individuals and institutions. Investors can access unit price updates, money market rates, weekly economic reports, daily equities reports, as well as information on Macquarie's funds and services.

## Mercantile Mutual

http://www.mercantilemutual.com.au

One of Australia's leading financial services groups, Mercantile Mutual provides a broad range of financial services including: life, property, motor, and health insurance; investment products, managed funds, superannuation and annuities; home and investment loans; and call and term deposits through ING Mercantile Mutual Bank. The site includes information on the products and their monthly market review.

## Netquote Information Services

http://www.netquote.interpro.net.au

Netquote offers live stock quotes from the Australian Stock Exchange options, by subscription. Subscribers can also manage their portfolios, read news and research, and receive the latest announcements from the Sydney Futures Exchange (SFE) and the Australian Stock Exchange. Visitors can get free delayed quotes and a selection of broker research. A Java-enabled browser is required to access the site.

Mutual funds that invest internationally tend to have higher expenses than domestic funds. These expenses reflect transaction costs, exchange fees, custodial fees, taxes, brokerage costs, and other costs that are often higher when conducting transactions in other countries.

## New Zealand Investment Center

http://www.charm.net/~lordhill

Shareholders can learn about companies listed on the New Zealand Stock Exchange on this site, with daily share prices, advice and opinion, well-constructed company profiles, dividend yields and earnings ratios, and economic and government data related to the markets.

## Norwich Union Financial Services Group

http://www.norwich.com.au

Norwich Union is one of the world's oldest insurance and investment organizations offering life insurance, investment management and financial planning services. Their site offers daily market commentary, monthly economic views, and information on the Norwich funds.

## Option Brokers International

http://www.tne.net.au/obiaust

From Adelaide, Australia comes this futures broker, with a Web site full of option recommendations, data delivery via e-mail, and computer support for traders.

## Gerry Pauley's Australian Stocks and Shares

http://www.wantree.com.au/~tpauleyg/shares.html

Pauley's site features graphs on a selection of stocks listed on the Australian Stock Exchange using his free graphics software. Subscribers can download weekly data on some 400 Australian stocks and indices. Links to other resources are also provided.

## Peace Shield Ethical Investments Pty. Ltd.

http://www.iinet.net.au/~pshield/

This group offers articles on information on ethical investing for those who want to contribute towards creating a better world in a practical way.

## Personal Investment Magazine

http://www.personalinvestment.com.au

Australia's money magazine offers a Web site filled with informative commentary on the markets, profiles of individual stocks, articles on financial planning strategies, and regular columns on economic topics. The magazine's archives are searchable online, and a subscribers-only area provides live share prices, portfolio tracking, mortgage and interest rate information, and financial calculators.

## Phillips Henderson Ward Ltd.

http://www.phw.com.au

This stockbroker publishes earnings and dividend estimates for over 120 Australian listed companies on their Web site and also offers regularly updated research reports, trading ideas, and articles about investing in Australia. The site also provides a Stock of the Day section, which they promise to update at least once a week.

## Pont Securities
http://www.pont.com.au

Pont is a discount stockbroker that offers e-mail trading, with a 10 percent discount. Their site provides delayed share quotes, as well as information specifically for overseas clients and the tax ramifications of holding an account with them.

## The Privateer
http://www.the-privateer.com

This newsletter, delivered via e-mail, is directed at "Individual Capitalists." More than a market letter, *The Privateer* is concerned with economic, political, and financial principles, as well as money and markets. From a global review of the U.S., European, and Asian markets, to a recommended portfolio of stocks from the Australian markets, the newsletter always analyzes the global financial and economic situation before reaching a specific conclusion. The site includes charts of stocks, market indices, bonds, currencies, and precious metals. It also has a sample issue of *The Privateer* and current articles.

## Research Technology
http://www.researchtech.com.au

For real-time quotes and news, as well as market analysis software, turn to Research Technology. The company is dedicated to providing reliable data for analysis. The site offers a selection of articles from their newsletter, downloadable software demos, and catalogs of the company's books, videos, and seminars.

## Rivkin Croll Smith
http://www.intersol.com.au/rivkin.html

Rivkin Croll Smith is a discount stockbroker and insurance agent. The site provides details of their services.

## *Shares Magazine* Online
http://www.shares.aust.com

*Shares Magazine* Online allows subscribers to check their stock prices via the Internet, create personal portfolios, and get the price updates e-mailed daily, weekly, or monthly. Live share prices are available on the site, along with independent commentary by Australian financial experts.

## Sydney Futures Exchange
http://www.sfe.com.au

Attractive and informative, the Web site of the Sydney Futures Exchange (SFE) provides traders with plenty of information, including contract specifications, news, data files, and history and descriptions of the exchange and its operations.

## Ultradata Australia
http://www.ultradata.com.au

Geared for companies in the financial industry, Ultradata provides software and computer services, including online solutions.

## Vinton Smith, Dougall Ltd.
http://www.sofcom.com.au/VintonSmith

This full-service brokerage firm in Melbourne describes their firm on this page, along with some stock market news—from 1995.

## Wilson HTM Ltd.
http://www.wilsonhtm.com.au

Wilson HTM is an Australian stock broker, offering market research, quotes, and information about their services.

Many investors find the best way to increase the international exposure in their portfolios is by investing in American companies that have large international operations. Many U.S. companies are global leaders in their industries, and derive much, if not most, of their sales from foreign sources. Coca-Cola and Motorola are two good examples of American firms who are international leaders. By investing in stocks such as these, an individual can participate in the growth of the global economy without the risks of owning foreign stocks directly.

# CANADA

From the wild and woolly markets of western Canada, where emerging natural resources companies keep the Alberta and Vancouver exchanges packed with action, to the more subdued metropolitan exchanges of Montreal and Toronto, investors can find much financial information about our northern neighbor on the Web.

## AAA Personal Financial Management
http://www.io.org/~nobid

Jeff Parent's personal financial planning site is designed for Canadians. Topics covered include the full range of estate and tax planning. A special download area has a number of useful spreadsheets, including a mutual fund database and a simple compound annual return calculator. A risk tolerance questionnaire helps you design a suitable investment portfolio.

## AGF Trust Company
http://www.agf.com/agftrust

AGF Trust Company offers an integrated suite of investment products, including wrap programs, discretionary money management, off-shore trusts, trust services, Guaranteed Investment Certificates (GICs), Registered Retirement Income Funds (RRIFs), Individual Pension Plans (IPPs), Registered Retirement Savings Plans (RRSPs), and personal cash management services. The company works with both individuals and financial professionals.

## Alberta Stock Exchange Guide to Listed Companies
http://www.cadvision.com/stuartdr/ASEinfo/ase.htm

This service, available for a fee, offers corporate filings made by Canadian companies listed on the Alberta Stock Exchange.

## Bidding on Bay Street
http://www.eucanect.com/investments/bayst.html

This online newsletter features junior stocks listed on Canadian exchanges. Each monthly issue profiles one or two new stocks, with updates on past recommendations. Back issues are archived, and free e-mail updates are also available.

## Canaccord Capital Corporation
http://www.canaccord.com

Canaccord is a Canadian investment firm, with expertise in the resource sector, including the oil, gold, and metals markets. They publish a daily letter on their site. There are also research reports for registered users only.

## Canada Net Financial Pages

http://www.visions.com/stocksbonds/

The stocks and bonds department of this Canadian Web guide features end-of-day stock quotes from the Toronto, Vancouver, Alberta, and Montreal stock exchanges. Also available is a searchable database of all Canadian mutual funds and a selection of financial articles.

## Canada Stockwatch

http://www.canada-stockwatch.com

Canada Stockwatch is a complete source of news and real-time quotes from the Vancouver, Alberta, Toronto, and Montreal stock exchanges. They have over half a million press releases from all Canadian public companies in their database. Subscribers can also receive real-time quotes and track their complete portfolio, or receive e-mailed news and other market statistics. Many of the services on the site are available free.

## Canadian Association of Petroleum Producers

http://www.capp.ca

The Canadian Association of Petroleum Producers (CAPP) members represent 95 percent of the crude oil and natural gas produced in Canada each year. The site includes links to member companies, industry reports, and links to related sites.

## Canadian Corporate News NewsNet

http://www.cdn-news.com

Canadian Corporate News NewsNet is an Internet newswire providing real-time access to news releases, powerful search/filtering tools, and automated e-mail delivery of releases related to Canadian firms. The service is free.

## Canadian Derivatives Clearing Corporation

http://www.cdcc.ca

Canadian Derivatives Clearing Corporation acts as the issuer, clearinghouse, and guarantor of all derivative products trading on the Montreal, Toronto, and Vancouver stock exchanges. The site presents brochures and publications in Acrobat format, in French and English, including the "List of Option Eligible Equity Issues" and "Risk Management."

## Canadian Financial Network, Inc.

http://www.canadianfinance.com

This guide to Web financial resources includes a section of links specifically related to Canadian investing.

## Canadian NewsWire Ltd.

http://www.newswire.ca

Canadian NewsWire distributes news releases for over 5,000 organizations, and their Web site provides their database. Users can search for news by organization, stock symbol, keyword, date, subject, or industry. An e-mail service is also available to deliver custom news to an investor's mailbox.

## Canadian Oil & Gas Financial Database

http://www.mossr.com

This site provides information on 200 actively traded companies in the Canadian oil and gas industry, with links, charts, statistics, and industry reports.

## The Canadian Speculator

http://www.specstock.com

Each week, The Canadian Speculator seeks out junior Canadian companies with the potential to rise by 100 percent to 200 percent in the next three months, providing detailed analysis to subscribers. Back issues are available on the site.

### The Canadian Stock Market Reporter
http://www.canstock.com

Available by subscription, The Canadian Stock Market Reporter is a full-featured investing Web site, with real-time and delayed quotes; charts from 30 days to 36 months; portfolio trackers; market updates, including volume and price leaders; and news releases. A free trial is available.

### Carlson On-Line Services
http://www.fin-info.com

Carlson is a comprehensive source of research on Canadian public companies. Investors find stock quotes, press releases, and charts on any company listed on the Toronto, Montreal, Alberta, and Vancouver stock exchanges or quoted on the Canadian Dealing Network. The site also provides links to Canadian corporations' home pages.

### CMA Leduc Securities NetBroker
http://www.netaxis.qc.ca/cma

This full-service broker offers interest rate commentary and recommended lists of mutual funds and emerging growth stocks, along with information on opening an account.

### CT Securities
http://www.ctsecurities.com

This division of Canada Trust is the home of Easyline Brokerage. It offers free stock quotes and a portfolio service for up to 20 stocks for guests. Customers can access their CT accounts via EasyWeb, an online banking service.

### DeThomas Financial Corp.
http://www.oak.net/erwin

Financial advisor Gerald F. Erwin offers information on his Canadian No Load Mutual Fund Club, which allows investors to buy shares in a handful of funds with no commissions. He also has information on his retirement planning services.

### Digital Ink
http://giant.mindlink.net/financial

Digital Ink publishes financial information on public companies traded on the Vancouver Stock Exchange. Company profiles can be browsed alphabetically or by industry group. Charts, news, quotes, and contact information are available for many companies.

### The Fund Library
http://www.fundlib.com

This interactive site features over 3,000 pages of information on Canadian mutual funds. Some of the highlights of the site include an active discussion forum, daily NAVs for many Canadian funds, and RealAudio commentary from fund managers. Personalized pages for frequent visitors and news releases make this site a must for Canadian mutual fund investors.

## Independent Financial & Insurance Services

http://www.geocities.com/WallStreet/4682

David Philip Gladstone is a leading independent broker of financial and insurance services in Montreal. Here he describes his services and programs.

## Industry Canada Online

http://strategis.ic.gc.ca/engdoc/main.html

This site offers information on Canadian businesses, including reports on Canadian industries. The Canadian Industry Statistics provide detailed reports on industry structure, international trade, and sector performance. They also offer detailed information on structure and performance by size of enterprise, country of ownership, and profit-based measures.

Investors can use their online Benchmarking Tool, which compares any company to its industry averages. The reports are prepared by the Canadian federal government and focus on manufacturing firms.

## Markets West

http://www.markets-west.com/info-data/

Markets West is an information service and database that specializes in providing complete market information on the Vancouver and Alberta stock exchanges. The site provides company profiles and links to an extensive selection of commentary on western Canadian stock markets.

## Montreal Exchange

http://www.me.org

The Montreal Exchange offers access to information such as regular updates of the Canadian Market Portfolio Index (XXM index); quotes for listed companies and derivative products; and market summaries of stock, options, and futures activity. Also

Some countries place significant restrictions on foreign investments, allowing non-citizens to own only certain classes of shares or not permitting a withdrawal of capital for a certain period. Make sure you understand a foreign market as completely as possible before investing directly one of its security.

provided is a glossary, a description of how indexes are calculated, and other background and educational resources. The site is in English or French.

## Quantitative Markets

http://sms.business.uwo.ca/~jschmitz/qm.html

This monthly newsletter reports the publisher's computer-generated market forecasts for the Toronto Stock Exchange. The sophisticated quantitative models and their performance results are updated each month.

## RRIFmetic

http://www.fimetrics.com

This Canadian retirement planning software balances your assets with your lifestyle to generate an investment schedule to provide a smooth future net income. The program uses estimates of future assets (such as salary, capital gain, and Canadian Pension Plan (CPP) payments) and includes the Seniors Benefit entitlement.

## Klaus D. Roertsch, Chartered Accountant

**http://web.idirect.com/~roetsch**

Roertsch heads an accounting firm serving the greater Toronto area. His expertise is in personal and corporate taxes.

## Tef@, The Electronic Filing Agency

**http://www.tefa.com**

Tef@ has been set up to provide public companies with a complete range of services from the Canadian System for Electronic Document Analysis and Retrieval (SEDAR). Investors can search their database of filings and press releases from Canadian companies.

## Scudder Funds of Canada

**http://www.scudder.ca**

The Canadian arm of this global mutual leader provides portfolio managers with a quarterly review and market highlights on the markets in Canada, the U.S., Europe, the Pacific Rim, and global emerging markets. Scudder also gives profiles of no-load funds, their performance, and daily NAVs.

## SEDAR

**http://www.sedar.cds.ca**

SEDAR is the System for Electronic Document Analysis and Retrieval from the Canadian Securities Administration (CSA) and the Canadian Depository for Securities. Similar to EDGAR in the U.S., SEDAR is the program whereby all Canadian firms make required filings electronically with the CSA. No filings are available on this site, however—only information about the system.

## Telenium

**http://www.telenium.ca**

Telenium is an online financial information service for Canadian investors, providing subscription-based news and quotes packages using their proprietary software. Free quotes are provided on their Web site for the Montreal, Toronto, Alberta, Vancouver, and Winnipeg commodity exchanges.

## TeleQuote Web

**http://www.telequote.com**

TeleQuote offers investors an easy way to monitor stocks, options, indices, and more, from 40 exchanges, including all the Canadian and U.S. exchanges. Fundamental data and news is also provided, and data can be downloaded for use offline or viewed via the Web site. Two separate subscription packages are available.

## Vancouver Stock Exchange

**http://www.vse.com**

The Vancouver Stock Exchange (VSE) is home to over 1,500 stocks, and information on all companies is provided on this site, including contact details and trading background. The VSE also offers a weekly statistical overview of the Vancouver marketplace, with trading totals and lists of most active stocks, largest gainers and largest losers.

## Virtual Investor Guide

http://web.canlink.com/virtual

This online newsletter features financial and investment links to help the average investor locate resources on the Internet. Some editorial content is also provided.

## Wolverton Securities, Ltd.

http://www.wolverton.com/wolverton

This full-service broker is one of Canada's oldest brokerage houses. They provide current recommendations and research reports on their site.

# EUROPE

The European markets are facing strong forces from diverse directions. Many new Eastern European countries are still grappling with the forces of capitalism in their fragile economies, while Western Europe deals with the ramifications of the impending European Union and a common currency.

Some European stock markets are among the oldest in the world. The Amsterdam stock market is generally recognized as the first, established in the 1600s. The World Wide Web has ushered in a new era, and individuals can find plenty of information geared for overseas investors, too.

## European Association of Securities Dealers Automated Quotation

http://www.easdaq.be

The European Association of Securities Dealers Automated Quotation (EASDAQ) is a pan-European, multi-national stock market for high-growth, inter-

nationally oriented companies. EASDAQ uses a multiple market-making system similar to NASDAQ's in the U.S, with price quotations taking place within a computerized trading platform. The site includes an overview of this new market.

## European Derivative Investments and Funds Association

http://www.emfa.org

The European Derivative Investments and Funds Association (EMFA) is a trade association promoting the understanding and use of derivative instruments and alternative techniques in fund management, including managed futures, hedge funds, currencies, and Forex. The site includes some articles from their newsletter, as well as relevant links to other Web resources.

# AUSTRIA

## Vienna Stock Exchange

http://www.vienna-stock-exchange.at

Most of the pricing and news available from the Vienna Stock Exchange (VSX) is in German, though some press releases and background about the exchange is available in English.

## Vienna Stock Exchange Prices

http://apollo.wu-wien.ac.at/cgi-bin/boerse1.pl

This site at the University of Economics in Vienna provides prices for shares and indices from the Wiener Börse. Also provided is an updated graph of the Austrian Traded Index and other data.

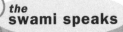

**the swami speaks**

Mirror, mirror on the Web, intones the Swami....Generally speaking, and with all other things being equal, a Web server that is closer to you will be a bit faster than sites that are far away. Many sites that are popular with a widespread audience use a trick called *mirroring* to bring their sites closer to users. Actually, there's little magic involved. A mirror is simply a second Web server set up in a remote location with an identical set of files as the original server. The mirrored server is regularly updated (often during times of low usage) so it always provides the exact same content as the original. If you see a link on a popular site to a mirror that's closer to you, you'll certainly be better off surfing the mirror rather than the original site, and you won't be missing any features or content.

## CENTRAL AND EASTERN EUROPE

### Central and Eastern Europe Business Information Center

http://www.itaiep.doc.gov/eebic/ceebic.html

Going by the moniker CEEBICnet, this site serves as a clearinghouse for information to facilitate trade and investment between the United States and Central and Eastern Europe. It includes detailed profiles of the countries of the region, descriptions of publications and events, and U.S. Embassy cables with news from each country.

### Ljubljana Stock Exchange

http://www.ljse.si

The Ljubljana Stock Exchange (LSE) is the marketplace for stocks and bonds in Slovenia. The Web site includes information about the exchange and listed companies.

### Zagreb Stock Exchange

http://ksaver208.zse.com.hr

The official site of the Zagreb Stock Exchange includes information about the Croatian markets, listed securities on the exchange, daily updated reports, news flashes, and basic information on foreign investment in Croatia.

## THE CZECH REPUBLIC

### Czech Capital Market

http://stock.eunet.cz/index_e.html

This site provides daily updates, charts, and quotes for stocks on the Prague Stock Exchange, as well as documents and regulations for trading on the exchange. In English and Czech.

### Komero Brokerage House, Ltd

http://www.anet.cz/komero/komero.htm

Komero is a regional brokerage specializing in the Czech capital markets. Their site offers tables of risks and returns for selected Czech shares, bond research, and charts and figures of market indexes.

# FRANCE

## Finacor Group

http://www.finacor.fr

The Paris-based futures and arbitrage firm provides data, quotes, and research, including coverage of emerging markets. Market indexes are updated regularly, and news summaries are provided, too.

## Paris Stock Exchange

http://www.bourse-de-paris.fr

The official site of La SBF-Bourse de Paris lets investors search for companies, get stock quotations (updated several times a day), or review statistics and graphs. In French and English.

# GERMANY

## Deutsche Börse Group

http://www.exchange.de/index.html

The Group is the holding company of the German Stock Exchange, and the site describes the exchange and its market indexes. Corporate profiles of listed companies, articles, and educational materials are also available. In German and English.

## DWS Group

http://www.dws.de/index.en.htm

This German mutual fund companies provides information about their offered funds, daily prices, and current performance figures. DWS also provides advice about investment planning and a glossary. Acrobat versions of their brochures can also be downloaded.

Closed-end funds are another way to invest internationally. There are several types of closed-end funds that invest in securities outside the U.S.: single-country funds that focus on the securities of a single country; regional funds that invest in specific areas of the world such as Latin America or the Pacific Rim; emerging markets funds; and global funds. Since closed-end funds have limited capitalization, they can often invest in markets that are harder for their open-ended cousins to enter.

## Deutsche Bank

http://www.deutsche-bank.de/index_e.htm

Besides providing information about Deutsche Bank and their online banking, the site offers current share prices for selected shares on the German exchanges, banknote exchange rates, and foreign exchange rates.

## Infos

http://www.infos.com/english/index.html

Infos is a resource for German mutual funds and foreign funds that are publicly traded in Germany. The site provides quotes and charts, as well as a customized portfolio service.

# ITALY

## Heard In Rome

http://www.italnet.it/links

"Heard In Rome" is a weekly report looking at Italian politics and Italian financial markets. Visitors can search the site's database for news from the Italian political scene or evaluate some sample issues.

### Italian Stock Exchange Charts

http://www.linknet.it/borsa/borsa_en.htm

This site prepares charts of many Italian stocks that can be downloaded or viewed online.

### Tex.NET Financial Page

http://robot1.texnet.it/finanza

Tex.NET provides current and historical quotes and data from stocks and funds trading on the Milan Stock Exchange.

### Invest In Italy

http://www.agora.stm.it/invest_ital/invest.html

Sponsored by the Italian Ministry of Foreign Trade, this site is home to business and financial information about Italy. The site includes lots of compelling economic reasons to invest in the country. In Italian and English.

## THE NETHERLANDS

### Amsterdam Stock Exchange

http://www.financeweb.ase.nl

Visitors to the Amsterdam Stock Exchange site can access quotes of stocks and bonds that trade here, real-time updates of the Amsterdam EOE-index and summaries of activities of listed companies. In English and Dutch.

### IMG Holland NV

http://www.prconsult.nl/img/eng/indxeng.htm

IMG Holland is an independent brokerage and financial advisory firm in Amsterdam, serving individual and institutional investors. Daily market reports are provided in Dutch.

**ask doug!**

**Q:** What's the difference between global funds and international funds?

**A:** There's just one small difference between global and international funds. Global funds can invest anywhere in the world, including the United States. International funds invest only in foreign securities. That small distinction, however, can make a big difference for investors looking for international exposure. If you bought a global fund, you might be surprised to learn that half of that fund's assets are invested in U.S. stocks. As always, be sure to read the prospectus to understand a fund's objectives and guidelines.

### Radobank International

http://rabobank.info.nl/engels/default.htm

The first Dutch bank on the Internet, Radobank publishes a good deal of information about Dutch financial markets, such as a bi-weekly study of the Dutch economy or social-economic reports of Dutch regions. Other information about the firm is included.

## PORTUGAL

### Lisbon Stock Exchange

http://www.bvl.pt/english

The Lisbon exchange provides investors with current and historical data, news, a listing of associated companies, and intra-day updates of the current top ten shares and bonds. In English and Portuguese.

## SCANDINAVIA

### Finnish Finance Network
http://www.shh.fi/ffn

Finnish Finance Network is a comprehensive Finnish financial resource, with hundreds of links of relevance to the Finnish markets. The site includes Finnish companies with Web pages, financial research, and other links to Scandinavian and international resources.

### Invest in Denmark
http://www.investindk.com

This site provides an introduction to the Danish business environment, from Denmark's Ministry of Business and Industry. Provided are facts and figures, news, and other information.

### Invest in Sweden Agency
http://www.isa.se

Invest in Sweden Agency (SWA) is a service for foreign investors in Sweden, offering advice, facts, and commentary to encourage cooperation. Overall, the site provides a good introduction to Sweden and its financial climate.

### Oslo Stock Exchange
http://nettvik.no/finansen/oslobors/engelsk/ose_eng.html

The Oslo Stock Exchange's home on the Web provides directories of brokers, listed companies, and bond issuers, along with daily quotes and statistics. In Norwegian and English.

 Foreign markets represent about two-thirds of the world's capitalization. Many of those markets are in the developing stages, with economies growing much faster than that of the U.S., and with resulting potential for larger returns than domestic stocks (though with added risk).

### Stockholm Stock Exchange
http://www.xsse.se/eng/index.html

Northern Europe's leading exchange offers online pricing of equities and indexes, a Web directory of listed companies, and a history of the exchange. In English or Swedish.

## SPAIN

### Madrid Stock Exchange
http://www.bolsamadrid.es

The official site of the Bolsa de Madrid (and the only Spanish site done in English that I know of) provides the usual charts, quotes, and market snapshots, with most of the information (but not all) available in English.

## SWITZERLAND

### Investment Forum Ltd. of Switzerland
http://www.access.ch/investmentforum/

Directed at the overseas investor, this site offers information about "interesting and advantageous" investment opportunities available in Switzerland. The site describes the services that the Investment Forum can provide, and their newsletters and publications. Samples and excerpts are provided.

## the swami speaks

**Q:** Can I open a numbered account at a Swiss bank?

**A:** Swiss law protects the privacy of individuals, including the relationship between banks and their clients. This level of secrecy is attractive to some investors and applies to both numbered and non-numbered accounts.

If you're looking to evade U.S. taxes, however, you may find that not even a Swiss bank account can help you. The Internal Revenue Service requires that individuals report any overseas accounts you own if the sum of those accounts is greater than $10,000. Further, you still owe capital gains and other taxes on income earned abroad, and there are severe penalties for non-compliance. Despite the privacy that Swiss banks afford customers, they may still cooperate with U.S. officials if criminal activity is suspected.

Many private Swiss banks require an introduction and do not encourage walk-in clients at either their U.S. offices or Swiss headquarters. You'll need a reference from your own bank, as well as $100,000 to $250,000 to open the account.

Finally, some foreign countries and institutions do not recognize U.S. wills and trusts, so you need to consult an attorney who specializes in this area if you have assets on deposit overseas.

## Surge Trading S.A.
http://www.surgetrd.com

Surge Trading is a Geneva-based broker specializing in Forex, futures, options, and stocks. Each day, the firm's analysts provide free reports on the Forex,

corn, wheat, sugar, cocoa, and coffee markets. The site is available in English, French, German, Spanish, or Russian.

## Swiss Commodities Futures and Options Association
http://finance.wat.ch/scfoa

Swiss Commodities Futures and Options Association (SCFOA) is a non-profit professional association focused on the use of derivative financial instruments, particularly standard futures and options contracts on financial instruments and commodities. The Assocation publishes some informative articles on their site, along with information about membership.

## Swiss Exchange
http://www.bourse.ch

This site offers daily stock market updates of Swiss and foreign shares, bonds, and derivatives. Commentary is provided in French each day. Other news and announcements about the exchange are posted on the site, too.

## JML Swiss Investment Marketplace
http://www.jml.ch/jml/

If you're looking to learn the ins and outs of foreign investing, this site is a good start. A special How-To section describes strategies for structuring a portfolio using offshore trusts, Swiss annuities, gold, or mutual funds. Topics such as financial havens, privacy, and liability protection are also discussed in relative detail.

# UNITED KINGDOM

Though, ostensibly, our British cousins speak the same language, their financial terminology is markedly different. Terms such as *ordinary shares, Investment Trust Personal Equity Plan,* and *gilts* are common. Investors in the UK can find a wealth of financial planning information on these sites, and other investors can learn more about the British markets.

## AAA Investment Guide
**http://www.wisebuy.co.uk**

This online guide offers comprehensive information on savings, investments, and tax avoidance for UK residents and expatriates. The Guide is in two parts, with the first explaining investment and savings strategies, and the second listing over 100 types of investments.

## The Association of Investment Trust Companies
**http://www.iii.co.uk/aitc**

The Association of Investment Trust Companies (AITC) seeks to educate investors about investment trusts. The site profiles several hundred investment trust companies, with details on the size of their holdings, contact information, dividend payment dates, and more. A glossary is available, and users can download Touchbase 3, an interactive software guide to investment trusts.

## The Association of Unit Trust and Investment Funds
**http://www.iii.co.uk/autif**

The Association of Unit Trust and Investment Funds (AUTIF) is an industry trade group. Their site

Want to know what's probably the single easiest way to invest internationally? Buy a mutual fund. This is one area in which a fund's professional management skills can be particularly necessary. International funds have staffs of analysts who have specific expertise and knowledge of a country's or region's economy, markets, politics, history, and traditions. They can travel abroad to visit foreign companies directly and may even have representatives or consultants in foreign countries. It's next to impossible for an individual investor to match this kind of research capability.

publishes contact details and profiles of more than 120 Unit Trust management companies.

## Biz/ed
**http://www.bizednet.bris.ac.uk**

This British site is dedicated to business and economics information, especially for students, teachers, and lecturers. The site has corporate profiles and other data, along with suggested courses of study to learn how to analyze stocks.

## Durlacher Stockbrokers
**http://www.durlacher.co.uk**

This full service London-based stockbroker specializes in high-tech stocks. Their Web site features research reports on intranet technology, the Internet, the computer and video game industry, and the British film industry, along with information about the firm's services.

### Electronic Share Information Ltd.
http://www.esi.co.uk

Electronic Share Information (ESI) is an independent subscription service that aims to provide professional-quality financial information to private investors. Besides share and trust quotes from the London Stock Exchange, the service offers personal portfolio valuation, five-year price histories, headlines, news stories, and stock charts. Real-time prices are also available, depending on the subscription plan.

### The Financial Times
http://www.usa.ft.com

London's internationally recognized newspaper provides excellent coverage of the markets, with company snapshots of key financial and fundamental information for more than 11,000 companies; closing spot rates in London for 38 currencies; daily closing prices of 3,000 equities on the London Stock Exchange; and fund and index prices. Daily news and discussion forums are also available.

### Gartmore Investment Management
http://www.iii.co.uk/gartmore

Gartmore is the manager of investment trusts, unit trusts, and investment products, all of which are profiled here on the site. Gartmore is also an advisor of U.S. mutual funds in partnership with NationsBank.

### Global Asset Management
http://www.ukinfo.gam.com

Global Asset Management (GAM) is leading manager of globally focused investment trusts and unit trusts. Each fund is profiled here, with asset allocation, performance details, and fund manager commentary.

### interactive investor
http://www.iii.co.uk

Updated daily, this site is a comprehensive resource for investment information about the UK and offshore markets. The site integrates information from many financial product providers, as well as fund performance, news, investment company profiles, financial advisor profiles, dictionaries, and a directory of personal finance sites on the Web. Registered users can monitor their customized portfolios on the site, or ask a team of industry experts any personal finance-related question.

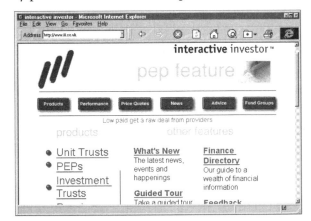

### London International Financial Futures and Options Exchange
http://www.liffe.com

One of the largest futures and options markets in the world is the London International Financial Futures and Options Exchange (LIFFE). The site offers contract statistics and a description of the operation of the Exchange, as well as press releases, details of educational courses, information on LIFFE's publications, charts, prices, and historical data.

## London Stock Exchange—AIM
http://www.stockex.co.uk/aim

AIM is the London Stock Exchange's market designed for small, young, and growing companies. The site contains profiles of traded companies and details of the market's regulations and policies.

## M&G Group
http://www.iii.co.uk/m_g/

One of the largest investment houses in the UK, the M&G Group offers unit trusts, investment trusts, Personal Equity Plans (PEPs), and other services. Daily prices are published on the site.

## Micropal
http://www.globalinvestor.co.uk/micropal

Micropal's site is a resource for fund investors, with a directory of fund managers; market commentary from industry experts, journalists, and fund managers; and performance tables illustrating short- and long-term comparative returns and ranking within industry groups. Registration is required, which may (or may not) grant you access to any of the information.

## Micropal Performance History Service
http://www.iii.co.uk/micropal

Using this comprehensive site, you can browse performance information on every unit trust, investment trust, PEP, and offshore fund that trades in the UK. View the top performing funds over one, three, or five years, or subscribe for more detailed information.

## MoneyWorld—The UK's Personal Finance Website
http://www.moneyworld.co.uk

If you're a UK investor and haven't yet been to MoneyWorld, drop everything right now and check out this expansive site! The site's table of contents is practically endless with daily news; regular features and columns; the UK Personal Finance Directory of Web sites; rates and performance of unit and investment trusts, mortgages, savings accounts; a "Find a Stockbroker" service; and a glossary of investing terms. Don't miss their guides, a series of informative mini-manuals on a variety of topics.

## Prolific Asset Management
http://www.iii.co.uk/prolific

One of the Britain's leading fund management groups (with over £ 6bn under management) allows the financial professional or private investor to obtain market analyses, fund objectives, strategy, and portfolios.

## Save & Prosper Group Limited
http://www.prosper.co.uk

This investment house, with its apt name, offers low-cost funds, pension plans, credit cards, and savings accounts. On their site, they have arranged daily prices of unit trusts, a UK report, an international report, and other information for customers.

There are major risks involved in international investing. Among them are currency risks, or unexpected changes in the exchange rate that can adversely affect your investment. Another is political risk, the chance that upheavals within a government or regime can disrupt the economy or markets. Third is economic risk, such as a natural disaster that destroys a crop that is the mainstay of an agrarian economy, thus disrupting the entire country and the markets. Finally, there are information risks, the difficulty in getting timely or accurate information about a foreign company and its performance.

## Charles Stanley & Co.

**http://www.charles-stanley.co.uk**

Charles Stanley & Co. offers a full array of brokerage services. Clients and registered users can access pricing and other information on the site.

## OTHER COUNTRIES

### Cyprus Financial Mirror

**http://www.cfm.cy.net**

This Cyprus newspaper provides information and news about the Cyprus Stock Exchange, including tips, and a Market Talk page with behind-the-scenes examinations of business life on this island nation.

## MEXICO

A single Mexican company may be responsible for many investors' interest in global investing. Telefonos de Mexico, S.A. was a popular holding of individuals interested in the exceptional growth opportunities of Mexico's national phone system. With the low per capita ratio of phones to population in that country, and the need for a telecommunications system to serve the other needs of an emerging economy, many investors saw the stock as a terrific growth opportunity.

Unfortunately, the subsequent devaluation of the peso to the dollar in December 1994 led to a major drop in the price of the stock, solely due to the currency devaluation. The stock fell from a high of $67 that past August to a low of $25 the following March. The incident is a sobering reminder of the risks of investing outside the U.S.

There are a few sites that provide information on the investing climate in Mexico, which to some is nearly as hot as the temperature.

### Infosel Financiero

**http://if.infosel.com.mx/infosel/if/ingles/ingles.htm**

InfoSel Financiero is a leading source of Mexican financial, economic, corporate, and political information. Their site offers investors delayed quotes of publicly traded corporations on the Mexican Stock Exchange, Mexican ADRs in New York, peso/dollar rates, money market rates, and the relevant news. A real-time service is available for professionals.

### Mexican Commentary

**http://ourworld.compuserve.com/homepages/mexcom**

*Mexican Commentary* is an online newsletter that analyzes Mexican companies. The site includes a comprehensive collection of links and reports, including company news, quotes, economic news, archives of past newsletters, current charts, and more. Subscribers receive the newsletter via e-mail.

# CENTRAL AND SOUTH AMERICA

## Aldesa Valores
http://www.aldesa.fi.cr
This Costa Rican brokerage firm provides a guide to investing in that country, as well as information on the Costa Rican markets. The firm also offers a family of mutual funds.

## Argentina: Your Smartest Choice
http://www.overnet.com.ar/Users/carminatti3.html
An essay from a Buenos Aires economist Hernán Carminatti offering an economic overview for investors. Carminatti works for Banco Privado Group, a local investment bank in Argentina.

## Brazil Financial
http://darkwing.uoregon.edu/~sergiok/brfinancial.html
Sergio Koreisha has built an extensive series of links covering all aspects of commerce in Brazil. From the country's economy to its financial markets, this directory lists hundreds of sites that can teach you all about Brazil and its place in the world's markets.

## Business TIPS on Cuba
http://www.tips.cu/tips.html
This online business magazine is published by the National Office of Technological Information Promotion System (TIPS) in Cuba. Each monthly edition is available in Spanish, English, French, Portuguese, German, Italian, and Russian, and examines the legislative and business aspects of foreign investment in Cuba.

## Center for Latin American Capital Markets Research
http://netrus.net/users/gmorles
The Center publishes original research for academics, investors, and professionals interested in Latin American capital markets. The site provides links to major exchanges and sources of general economic data, news, and quotes.

## COINVERTIR
http://www.coinvertir.org.co
COINVERTIR is the Invest in Colombia Corporation, a non-profit organization that provides business and economic information about the country. Their Web site is a repository for publications, in Acrobat format, that outline Colombia's economy and investment opportunities.

## The Commodities & Futures Exchange
http://www.bmf.com.br/english/index.htm
The Exchange, in Sao Paulo, Brazil, offers a daily report on trading, downloadable data files, and history and information about the exchange. Coffee, live cattle, and cotton are among the leading commodities traded on this exchange. In English and Portuguese.

## Ministry of Economy and Public Works and Services of Argentina
http://www.mecon.ar/default.htm
This official site from the government of Argentina offers detailed information about the country's economic climate and opportunities. Reports, databases, news, and charts are all provided.

Just because a foreign stock trades in the U.S. as an ADR, don't assume that its financial reporting is on par with U.S. standards. ADRs that trade on the New York or American stock exchange or NASDAQ do file financial statements that meet generally accepted accounting principles, but these ADRs only represent about one-quarter of all the ADRs available to American investors. The remaining 75 percent trade over the counter on pink sheets and are only required to file an English translation of their annual report at year end.

### Rio de Janeiro Stock Exchange
http://www.bvrj.com.br/bving/menu.htm

The English edition of this exchange offers some background on the Brazilian markets and its own history, and little else.

### São Paulo Stock Exchange
http://www.bovespa.com.br/indexi.htm

BOVESPA, as this exchange is known, is home to over 500 companies. BOVESPA publishes a Daily Information Bulletin of each day's transactions that can be downloaded; a summary version is posted on the Web. In English and Portuguese.

### Santiago Stock Exchange
http://www.bolsantiago.cl/ingles

This site is home to information about the Chilean market, with a daily market summary of all traded stocks, a complete list of Chilean brokers, shares listed on the Exchange, and Chilean companies that are listed as ADRs on foreign exchanges. In English and Spanish.

### Summit Analytical Associates
http://www.s2a.com

Summit Analytical Associates are specialists in political risk assessment, focusing on Latin America. Their site publishes reports such as "Political Risk Report: Latin America" and "The Mexican Market: The Political Dimension." Other reports are available by subscription. Summit aims to assist personal investors in minimizing their political risk exposure in the emerging markets of the region.

# GLOSSARY

**ADR**—American Depository Receipt. An ADR is a security that trades on a U.S. stock exchange but represents shares of a particular foreign security.

**CURRENCY RISK**—Or Exchange Rate Risk. When investing in foreign markets, the chance that fluctuations in the exchange rate will have an adverse impact on the investment.

**ECONOMIC RISK**—When investing in foreign markets, the chance that instability in that country's economic climate will adversely affect the investment.

**EMERGING MARKET**—The stock market of a developing country.

**EU**—European Union, established in 1995 by the Maastricht Treaty, which strives to create a single currency and economic integration for member countries.

**EUROBOND**—A bond issued and traded in a foreign country but denominated in another currency, such as dollars.

**EURODOLLARS**—U.S. dollars on deposit with a foreign bank and outside the jurisdiction of the United States.

**EXCHANGE RATE**—The price of one currency in terms of another.

**GLOBAL FUND**—A mutual fund that invests in securities anywhere in the world, including the U.S.

**INTERNATIONAL FUND**—A mutual fund that invests only in securities outside the U.S.

**POLITICAL RISK**—When investing in foreign markets, the potential that turmoil within the country's government or political realm will adversely affect the investment.

**WEBS**—World Equity Benchmark Shares, a series of index funds, each focused on a particular country and trading on the American Stock Exchange.

# Chapter 10

# Personal Finance

"Put not your trust in money, but put your money in trust."

—Oliver Wendell Holmes

# BANKING

Online banking aims to change the way customers conduct business with their banks. Users can simply log on to the Internet, connect to their bank's Web site with a secure browser, and pay bills electronically, or handle nearly any banking need.

Inveterate Web investors may be interested to know that it's now possible to open a bank account on the Internet without journeying to a branch office. Whether you're shopping for the best interest rates or looking for a new bank in your neighborhood, there are sites that can provide pointers and tips. You can also get the scoop on new Internet payment schemes, like Ecash and CyberCash, which preserve your privacy while online but still enable you to make purchases from online vendors.

### Bank Rate Monitor
**http://www.bankrate.com**

Looking for the best rates on Certificates of Deposit in the country or the best deal on savings accounts? Bank Rate Monitor collects data on consumer bank rates for mortgages, credit cards, home equity loans, auto loans, personal loans, CDs, and bank fees. Finding the best options for your financial needs can be as easy as searching their database. They add a mix of daily banking news and personal

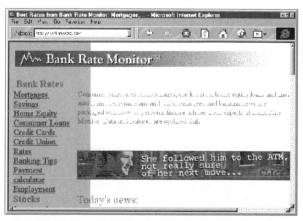

finance articles, as well as special services such as free e-mail interest rate alerts.

### Banking.com
**http://www.banking.com**

Banking.com is a pointer site for resources related to online banking provided by nFront, a consultant involved in bringing banks online. The site includes links to their clients, a glossary of banking terms, and related publications.

### BanxQuote
**http://www.banx.com**

BanxQuote is a leading provider of information technology for financial institutions. Their site includes regularly updated deposit and loan rates and other market data, quoted by leading providers in each market. It also features state-by-state, regional, and national composite benchmarks, as well as useful links and snapshot profiles of financial institutions. Users can check out interest rates on savings accounts, money markets, and certificates of deposit from banks all over the country.

### Credit Union On-line, Organizational Link
**http://www.creditunions.com**

COOL is a professional group of credit unions across the country. Their Web site offers a directory of credit unions on the Web, credit union news, and details of their e-mail discussion group devoted entirely to credit unions. If you're looking for an alternative to increasingly expensive bank services, a credit union is a great option.

The arrival of Internet banking means you're no longer beholden to the banks in your community. Many online banks will accept accounts from customers anywhere in the country. While the personal touch can sometimes be helpful at a local branch office, more people are skipping the teller and doing much of their banking by ATM machine, mail, telephone, or by computer. The fact that the bank holding your certificate of deposit is located several states away is probably not that important, especially if they are offering a significantly higher interest rate.

### Mark Bernkopf's Central Banking Resource Center

**http://adams.patriot.net/~bernkopf**

Bernkopf, a consultant and former White House researcher, has built a directory of Internet sites of central banks and ministries of finance, economy, and treasury. It includes links to banking institutes and associations, national mints, banknote printers, and currency museums, as well.

### NETBanker

**http://www.netbanker.com**

NETBanker is the Internet companion to the *Online Banking Report*, a financial services industry newsletter for those involved in the home banking business. The site includes directories of banks offering online products and the Web sites of the 100 largest banks.

### Online Banking Association

**http://www.obanet.org**

Online Banking Association (OBA) is a professional organization for financial institutions that provide

services online. Directed at those in the industry, the site does provide a good listing of related Web links and an excellent search engine for news about electronic banking.

### Qualisteam

**http://www.qualisteam.com/aindex.html**

Qualisteam is a French financial consultant. Their banking and finance site provides bountiful links to banks, financial companies, stock exchanges, and other investing sites. Over 1,000 banks from all around the globe are linked from the Qualisteam pages.

## ONLINE BANKS

Online banking certainly has its advantages. Forget about writing a check and mailing it to pay your monthly bills—now you can connect to your bank online, enter a payment, and the bank does the rest. Forget about balancing your checkbook. Your bank can give you instant access to all your cleared transactions throughout the month. Debit cards, credit cards, home loans, certificates of deposit, checking accounts, and savings accounts are among the products that you will find accessible at these online banks. In many cases, you can even open an account electronically, without ever stepping foot in a branch office.

Some banks only offer online access to users of a personal finance program such as Quicken or Microsoft Money. Many other banks are now Web-based so you can access account information with just a secure browser. Fees vary, especially for electronic bill payment services, but many of these banks are offering some of the highest interest rates in the country for savings products. Depending on your needs, an online bank might be a less expensive alternative than its brick-and-mortar cousins.

## Apollo Trust Company

**http://bankswith.apollotrust.com**

This bank, in Apollo, PA, offers account holders access to statements via their Web site. More online services are promised.

## Atlanta Internet Bank

**http://www.atlantabank.com**

Carolina First Bank of Greenville, SC provides a full slate of banking services on their Atlanta Internet Bank site. Customers can pay bills, transfer funds, or access account statements at any time.

## Bank of America

**http://www.bankamerica.com**

Bank of America's HomeBanking enables customer to check current balances on accounts any time, on the Internet, on America Online, by direct connection to the bank with Managing Your Money, or by phone. The service allows pre-scheduled bill payments and downloading of account data as well.

## Britton and Koontz First National Bank

**http://www.bkbank.com**

This Natchez, MS bank has an online branch office that offers customers access to account information, balances, check re-ordering, account transfers, and other services.

## Busey Bank

**http://www.busey.com**

Busey Bank of Champaign/Urbana, IL offers Anytime Banking via the Internet, with electronic transaction accounts, VISA Check Cards, ATM cards, and bill payment service.

---

### the swami speaks

Sometimes your screen just isn't big enough to display enough of a Web page. Here are a few of the Swami's favorite tips for making room in your browser. In Netscape Navigator, you can display text, graphics, or both on the Toolbar buttons. Once you know your way around, you can just display the graphics. Or, text buttons take up even less space. You can remove those directory buttons, too, to free up more space. On the Options menu, there are options to Show Toolbar and Show Directory Buttons that can be disabled. To change the face of the buttons, select Options, General Preferences, Appearance, and choose the appropriate option.

In Internet Explorer, select Options from the View menu to change the face of the toolbar buttons. Or deselect View Toolbar, or View Status Bar to remove them from the screen altogether.

---

## Chase Manhattan Bank

**http://www.chase.com**

Chase offers online banking, though not over the Internet, using Microsoft Money, or Quicken. You can reconcile your checkbook, print an account statement anytime, transfer funds between accounts, and even pay bills electronically.

## CheckFree

**http://www.checkfree.com**

CheckFree has been offering its online bill payment services to individuals for years. Customers allow CheckFree to withdraw funds from their personal bank account and transfer those funds electronically to the other party's bank. If an electronic transfer

One of the biggest financial planning mistakes most people make is carrying too much credit card debt. Shop around for a card with a lower rate, or, better yet, move that debt to the top of the list when you pay your bills each month. That's the same thing as getting a risk-free double-digit return on your money.

isn't possible, CheckFree sends a check drawn on your account. Customers can sign up for the service directly through their own bank, or by using personal finance software like Quicken. Or they can use Web BillPay, paying bills online from the Web BillPay Web site. Web BillPay requires no additional software, just a secure Web browser. The basic service is about $10 a month, but you'd save about half that amount in postage stamps alone.

## Citizens Bank Online
http://www.citizensonline.com

Citizens Bank offers Internet users the chance to open a HomeBanking account online, offering checking, savings, certificates of deposit, and credit cards. The bank has branch offices in Illinois, Indiana, and Kentucky.

## European Union Bank
http://www.eubank.ag

From the islands of Antigua and Barbados comes the first offshore bank to offer Internet accounts. The bank offers numbered accounts, multicurrency accounts, international wire transfers, online checking, trusts, and investment services.

## First National Bank and Trust (Florida)
http://www.fnbt.com

First National's online banking provides loan, checking, and savings account information for customers, including current bank statements, individual check inquiries, and balance information. Users can download any of their checking or savings account transactions into Quicken or Microsoft Money.

## First National Bank and Trust (Minnesota)
http://www.banking.com/fnbpipe/

First National Bank and Trust Online proclaims itself to be "Your drive-through on the Information Superhighway," and its opening page presents an image of a drive-through bank. The bank offers individual and joint checking accounts, but no lollipops for the kids.

## First Union
http://www.firstunion.com

First Union Cyberbanking allows customers to access their checking, savings, consumer loans, asset management, and credit card accounts via the World Wide Web. Individuals can apply online to open some of these account types, but others require a visit to a branch office.

## First USA
http://www.firstusa.com

FirstAccess Online Banking allows First USA customers the chance to review First USA credit card, checking, savings, and loan statements online. Another service, FirstAccess BillPay, lets users pay bills and automatic recurring payments by computer on the Internet or via a dial-up connection.

## Huntington Banks
http://www.huntington.com

Huntington Banks's online service provides access to account balances, along with bill paying and transaction tracking. Customized reports can be generated online or data exported for use in Quicken, Microsoft Money, or another personal finance program.

## nBank
http://www.banking.com/nbank

Surfers can apply online for one of nBank's online checking accounts, CDs, mortgages, or debit cards. The online bank is a division of First National Bank of Commerce, GA.

## Salem Five Cents Savings Bank
http://www.salemfive.com

Salem Five, headquartered in Salem, Massachusetts, is a billion dollar, full-service financial services company. Their "VirtualBanking" and "InternetBanking" packages offer customers home banking with no balance requirements, no monthly fee, and no ATM fees, either via a direct modem connection or on the World Wide Web.

## Security First Network Bank
http://www.sfnb.com

Security First Network Bank can lay claim to being the first Internet bank. In fact, Security First set up their Internet branch office before opening a "real" branch in Atlanta! The bank offers no-fee checking, 23 free electronic payments a month, online statements, check registers, and no minimum balance requirements. Instead of getting a package of canceled checks each month, account holders access images of cleared checks online. Security First also offers credit cards, money market accounts, and

certificates of deposit. Separate investing services are also available.

## Signet Bank
http://www.signet.com

Signet's online banking services provide 24-hour access to accounts, including recent activity, past statements, and the ability to transfer funds between accounts. If you'd like to be warned when your account balances drop below a certain level, you can even arrange to have an e-mail or fax message sent to you.

## Sandy Spring National Bank
http://www.ssnb.com

This Maryland bank offers online banking on the Web, giving you the ability to check your balance, get snapshot statements, transfer funds between accounts, and pay bills electronically.

## State National Bank
http://www.statenb.com

This bank in Big Spring, Texas offers Internet banking, but provides no details on their site of the particular services that are included.

### U.S. Bancorp

**http://www.usbank.com**

With UBank On-Line Express, customers have free access to U.S. bank accounts to check account balances, transfer funds between accounts, and review statements and individual transactions. The service can be used with Microsoft Money, Quicken, or America Online to check balances, download account details, and pay bills.

### Wells Fargo

**http://www.wellsfargo.com**

San Francisco-based Wells Fargo has been a leader in providing online access for its banking customers, and it now offers free direct access to accounts through the Internet. Their Bill Pay service allows you to make unlimited payments to anyone in the U.S. You can view current balances on checking, savings, and credit card accounts or transfer funds between your accounts. Account information can be downloaded to your financial software, as well.

### Wilber National Bank

**http://www.wilberbank.com**

Wilber Online, from this upstate New York bank, lets account holders pay bills, transfer funds between accounts or banks, review account statements, or apply for loans, and other bank products.

## ELECTRONIC CASH

Call it cyber money, digital cash, electronic payment, or what you will—there's no doubt the cashless society is about to become even less dependent on paper money and coins as online transactions become more popular.

There are a number of products available that facilitate online transactions with merchants, whether you're buying a shirt or downloading a set of data. These systems allow you to be completely anonymous, if you choose. They also make payments of as little as a quarter feasible. While users today are accustomed to cruising the Web for free, some visionaries foresee a time when users will ante up a dime or quarter to view specific pages or files online, a dollar for a special article, or five dollars for access to a monthly magazine on the Web.

Though the specifics vary from vendor to vendor, here's how the new digital money works. First, you set up an account with one of the companies listed below. You provide them with a stash of cash or your credit card number. When you make a purchase from an online store, instead of providing your credit card number, you pay with the cyber dollars you have in your account. The merchant collects the cyber dollars that subsequently are converted back to cash in the merchant's account.

Nowhere in this system is any personal information about the user available to the merchant, unless the user chooses to provide it. Of course, in order to have a product shipped, the user would have to provide a name and address. But if the product purchased was a software program downloaded from the Internet, the user might choose not to reveal any personal information.

### CyberCash

**http://www.cybercash.com**

CyberCash is a secure Internet payment system that allows users to shop online, pay with credit cards, and maintain financial privacy. Using their CyberCash Wallet software, you can spend small amounts of cash (from $0.25-$10.00) for instantaneous purchases online or use one of your existing credit cards for larger purchases. CyberCash encrypts all transactions with "industrial strength" security. The Wallet software is free for downloading from the site.

## DigiCash

**http://www.digicash.com**

DigiCash is the developer of Ecash, an electronic payment scheme. The site includes links to providers of Ecash, as well as an extensive directory of merchants who accept Ecash.

## First Virtual

**http://www.fv.com**

First Virtual provides its customers with a VirtualPIN (Personal Identification Number), which serves as an alias for your credit card. When you make a purchase from a participating vendor, you provide just your VirtualPIN. First Virtual then sends you an e-mail message asking you to confirm or cancel the sale. If confirmed, the transaction is completed by First Virtual, off the Internet. There is a $2 annual fee for the service and you can apply on-line. Links are provided to First Virtual merchants so you can start shopping right away.

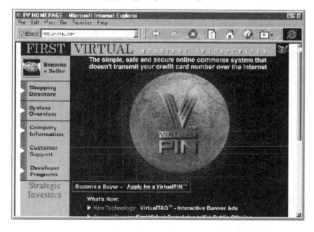

## Mark Twain Banks

**http://www.marktwain.com/ecash.html**

Ecash is a software solution that allows you to pay real money for online purchases, without your credit card. Ecash is private and works on all major platforms. Users can sign up online and download free Ecash software from the site.

## NetCash

**http://www.netbank.com/~netcash**

NetCash is a system that provides for electronic transactions via e-mail by the use of "coupons" protected by unique serial numbers. Users convert dollars to NetCash and then can use these coupons to make online purchases.

# FINANCIAL PLANNING AND INSURANCE

The Internet has quickly become a convenient and quick source of information on financial planning, retirement planning, and insurance, including auto, home, or life insurance products, and annuities. Individuals can get price quotes and compare insurance policies on the Web or calculate their retirement needs with the help of interactive tools. Whether you're still trying to figure out the difference between whole life and term life, or you're looking for information on the options in your pension plan, or you're shopping for insurance bargains, these sites can help.

## AccuQuote

**http://www.accuquote.com**

AccuQuote allows individuals to compare the prices and features of over 800 top-rated life insurance products, by filling out an online form. The company will then provide comparisons over the phone. AccuQuote also provides a "Life Insurance Needs Calculator" and information about different types of insurance, as well as a list of FAQs about life insurance.

There's no time like the present to review your will to make sure it fits your current situation. And if you don't have a will, invest a couple of hundred dollars to have an attorney draw one up for you. At the least, you can buy a low-cost software program that will help you prepare your own will. Don't procrastinate any longer.

## America Assured
**http://www.america-assured.com**

America Assured provides information about insurance and annuities, including a "Premier Instant Online" term life insurance quoting service. The company provides users with a comparison of 11 of the lowest guaranteed premiums for policies of differing lengths, taken from their database of 175 companies and over 550 policies. America Assured also provides an Annuity Spreadsheet that users can download for free, updated each day.

## Annuities OnLine
**http://www.annuity.com**

Annuities Online distributes no-load life insurance products, single premium annuities, indexed annuities, tax-sheltered annuities, tax-sheltered life insurance, and individual retirement plans. Their site provides complete information about annuities and how to make them a part of your savings, investment, and retirement programs. Product kits and applications are available for downloading from the site.

## The Cedar Group
**http://www.cdrgrp.com/cdrgrp**

The Cedar Group offers active management of your 401(k), 403(b), or 457 account with a statistical analysis specific to your company retirement plan. Each week, the firm will send you updated fund rankings and investment recommendations specific to your goals and needs.

## Robert Clofine's Estate Planning Page
**http://home.prolog.net/~clofine**

Pennsylvania attorney Clofine addresses estate planning, wills, trusts, taxes, and related financial planning matters in an extensive series of articles.

## CPAdvisor
**http://www.cpadvisor.com**

CPAdvisor is your door to dozens of tools and over a thousand pages of timely accounting, business, tax, and financial information. Articles on topics such as asset protection, business planning, charitable planning, estate planning, home purchasing/refinancing, individual income taxes, insurance, legal issues, marriage, divorce, private foundations, retirement planning, and wills are all available here. Links to interactive online tools and calculators can help you refinance your mortgage or fund a retirement plan. Your telephone area code is required to enter the site, giving you access to a CPA near you.

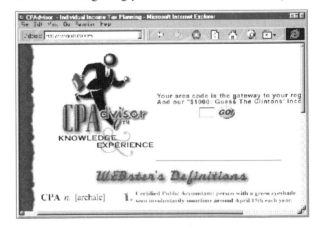

## CyberAccountant

http://www.cyber-cpa.com

The CyberAccountant provides information on taxes, accounting, and financial planning for businesses as well as individuals, through their network of qualified financial professionals.

## DT Online

http://www.dtonline.com

Big Six accounting firm Deloitte & Touche has adopted the motto, "Better living through financial planning," and has designed this site to meet that goal. Focusing on the nuts and bolts of financial planning, the site presents extensive information about investing, insurance, retirement planning, education planning, and taxes. Both individuals and small business owners can find helpful and knowledgeable advice in these pages.

## *Financial Planning* Online

http://www.fponline.com

The online edition of *Financial Planning* magazine is an interactive information resource for professional financial planners and investment advisors.

## Financial Online

http://www.financialonline.com

This financial and estate planning site offers a limited directory of resources.

## Financial Privacy News

http://apollo.co.uk/a/Offshore/Privacy/

*Financial Privacy News* is a printed monthly newsletter focusing on a variety of subjects regarding privacy. Its goal is to show subscribers how to preserve assets and develop tax-free income opportunities. Surfers can request a free issue from this page.

**the swami speaks**

Many users come to the Swami seeking advice on printing Web pages. It seems that the combination of graphics and text on many Web pages throws some printers for a loop, particularly for users who are unaccustomed to printing complex documents. Remember that each table border, each hard rule, and each graphic puts an additional strain on your printer. If your printer balks at a particular page, you can try setting a lower dpi (dots per inch) print resolution in the printer Control Panel. Make sure you're using an up-to-date Web browser, since older browsers can't handle many of the newer HTML attributes. Finally, if your printer is older than a few years, you may try upgrading its memory. You can buy add-in memory chips to expand your printer's memory, enabling it to print more complicated pages.

## FinanCenter

http://www.financenter.com

FinanCenter provides interactive calculators for home and auto buying, credit card planning, budgeting, reaching savings, investment goals, and other financial needs. The stocks calculators help answer questions such as "What future return makes selling now worthwhile?" or "Which are better: growth, or income stocks?" Enter data at the prompts and the programs do the rest.

## Financiers' Colloquium

http://www.connix.com/~yankdndy/

This site aims to explain why real and paper asset prices move up and down in cycles. Articles, graphs, and forecasts are provided.

## Fine Ants

http://www.prismnet.com/~andrew

This subscription-based weekly e-mail magazine is directed at those who wish to improve their lifestyle. It offers hundreds of financial ideas offered each year.

## FINWeb

http://riskWeb.bus.utexas.edu/finWeb.html

FINWeb, from the University of Texas, provides links and resources concerning economics and finance-related topics. Much of the site is academic in nature.

## The Insurance News Network

http://www.insure.com

The Insurance News Network is a complete reference guide to auto, home, and life insurance, and to annuities. The site provides free ratings of insurance companies provided by Standard & Poor's and Duff and Phelps Credit Rating Co., as well as a searchable database of Morningstar infor-

mation, rankings on thousands of variable annuity policies, and investment-fund subaccounts. An Insurance Glossary, state-by-state guide to insurance, and array of insurance news help make this a great resource for anyone who has insurance needs.

## Larson's TIAA-CREF Performance Watch

http://larsons.com/cref.html

This site tracks the investment performance of variable funds available through the retirement programs in the Teachers Insurance and Annuity Association-College Retirement Equities Fund (TIAA-CREF). The cumulative total return is updated weekly in tables showing short- and long-term changes in investment value. A discussion forum provides a place where TIAA-CREF participants may share ideas, information, and strategies.

## LawTalk From Indiana University

http://www.law.indiana.edu/law/lawtalk.html

The faculty at the Indiana University School of Law has prepared this collection of RealAudio files. A section addresses business and personal finance law topics with very short segments.

## Liberty Financial Companies

http://www.lib.com

Liberty Financial is an insurance and financial services company, and their Web site offers a library of articles on mutual funds, retirement plans, annuities, and institutional investment management.

## LifeNet

http://lifenet.com

LifeNet is an Internet resource for life insurance, estate planning, and financial service information. The site includes interactive calculators to help guide you through the process of buying a home, buying low-cost life insurance, accumulating wealth, retirement planning, and estate planning.

## Making Sense Out Of Dollars

http://www.zelacom.com/dollars/
welcome.html

This monthly newsletter is published on the Internet, designed for individuals with little or no knowledge of the financial world. It contains down-to-earth, easy-to-apply financial advice that can help you build a secure and comfortable financial future.

## National Financial Services Network

http://www.nfsn.com

National Financial Services Network is a comprehensive online network for financial services, featuring banking, insurance, and investment products from leading institutions and financial service providers. Individuals can search for loans (mortgages, home equity, auto, boat, RV, airplane, consumer, and student), leases, CDs, credit cards, insurance, investments, electronic banking, and software.

## The New England

http://www.tne.com

This provider of insurance and financial services offers help to individuals on life insurance, disability income insurance, education funding, retirement planning, estate planning, business insurance, group life insurance, health insurance, and mutual fund investing. Articles as well as financial calculators help users learn exactly where they stand and how to better plan their future.

## Personal Finance Network

http://www.wwbroadcast.com/pfn

This Web broadcasting site offers RealAudio commentary and analysis on financial topics such as mutual funds, pensions, and investing.

## Private Investments, Ltd.

http://www.privateinvestments.com

Private Investments, Ltd. provides financial consulting services and gold sales. Their site offers information on Swiss annuities, offshore investments, and gold, reflecting an investment philosophy that values privacy and preservation of wealth.

## The Prudential Insurance Company of America

http://www.prudential.com

Besides insurance, The Prudential provides a wide array of financial services, from retirement planning to real estate, investing to estate planning. The site includes information on life, auto, home owner's policies, retirement planning calculators, a college cost calculator, health care checklist, real estate locator, banking services, and information on wills, trusts, and strategies you can use to minimize estate taxes.

## Quicken InsureMarket

http://www.insuremarket.com

This personal insurance service provides real-time insurance quotes, referrals to agents, and quotes comparisons from the nation's leading insurance companies. The site also offers information on the basics of insurance and interactive planning tools, including a risk evaluator that shows you how to reduce life's risks and make smarter insurance decisions. Life insurance services are currently provided, with auto and home policies promised in the future.

## QuoteSmith Corporation
**http://www.quotesmith.com**

QuoteSmith's insurance price comparison service lets users view premium rates and coverages of 200 leading life insurance companies. Individuals can even apply for the coverage of their choice online. All quotes are accompanied by ratings from A.M. Best, Duff and Phelps, Moody's, Standard & Poor's, and Weiss Research, Inc. The company's tax-deferred annuity and Medicare supplement insurance price comparison services are in development.

## Research Press, Inc. Financial Solutions
**http://www.rpifs.com**

Vernon K. Jacobs, CPA, has established this site to offer legal strategies for saving taxes, protecting assets, and achieving greater privacy. Articles and a free e-mail newsletter are offered.

## RISKWeb
**http://www.riskWeb.com**

RISKWeb is an e-mail discussion forum for academics and professionals in the fields of risk management and insurance. The site includes a solid collection of links to other resources and articles on related topics.

## The SCREAMING Capitalist
**http://www.cadvision.com/screaming**

Kevin Cork is a Canadian financial planner who offers advice on investing, life insurance, and the basics of financial planning, with a twist. The site is

---

 **ask doug!**

**Q:** What is a variable annuity, and is it a good investment?

**A:** A variable annuity is an insurance product that allows you invest in mutual funds, deferring taxes until you withdraw funds from the annuity (generally at retirement). The insurance feature generally is a guarantee that if the annuitant dies before beginning withdrawals, then his or her heirs receive at least as much as was originally invested in the annuity. Variable annuities usually let you transfer funds between subaccounts, much as you would in a family of mutual funds. But they do have their drawbacks. Fees are usually much higher in annuities than mutual funds, and there are often steep penalties if you want to withdraw funds before retirement. Worse, money withdrawn from annuities is taxable as ordinary income, instead of at the capital gains tax rate, so individuals in high tax brackets will find this a real disadvantage. If the capital gains tax rate were cut, this pitfall would be even more significant. Another problem is that if you die with money in an annuity, the IRS taxes your heirs on the income built up in the annuity over the years. If you had simply bought similar securities outright, your heirs would not have owed any taxes. Finally, you should never hold an annuity in a retirement plan such as a 401(k), 403(b), or IRA. Holding a tax-deferred annuity inside a tax-deferred retirement account doesn't make sense, especially when you consider the higher expenses of annuities in general. Most experts suggest that you should only consider a variable annuity if you have maximized out all other retirement plans available to you, fully funding a 401(k) plan, deductible or non-deductible IRA, and any other tax-advantaged plans first. As always, a consultation with a good financial planner may be the best way to figure out the place of an annuity in your particular situation.

offbeat and irreverent, but the information he provides is solid.

## Sensible Investment Strategies
**http://www.seninvest.com**

Jack L. Piazza is a financial planner who offers a low-cost way to customize an investment strategy. Investors can consult online with Piazza and receive a detailed plan for investing in highly rated, no-load mutual funds, for just one low fee.

## TIAA-CREF
**http://www.tiaa-cref.org**

TIAA-CREF provides annuities and pension plans primarily for employees of educational institutions. Their site provides updated performance information, retirement planning resources, free retirement planning software for downloading, a dictionary of terms, articles, and calculators.

## TIAA-CREF Information
**http://www.hamline.edu/~jharriga**

John J. Harrigan is the author of "Getting More Out of TIAA-CREF" and the publisher of "College Retirement Finance," a market timing system for TIAA-CREF accounts. His Web site offers TIAA-CREF unit updates compared to market index benchmarks, news on TIAA-CREF, and information on his book.

## Understanding and Controlling Your Finances
**http://www.iftech.com/centers/finance/finance0.htm**

This online book is a complete guide for beginners that aims to help them get a handle on their personal finances. It includes a variety of interactive calcula-

tors to help users understand the concepts under discussion.

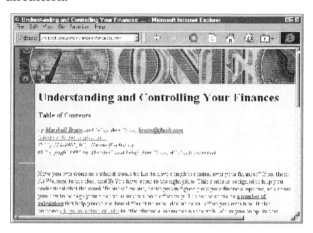

## WebSaver Annuity
**http://www.Websaver.com**

The WebSaver Annuity is the first retirement product designed exclusively for the Internet, offered by Independence Life, Annuity Company, a subsidiary of Liberty Financial Companies. The WebSaver Annuity is a guaranteed return annuity, retirement savings plan that allows customers to order a policy online. The site also includes an interactive tax deferral calculator, questions and answers about annuities, and other information about the product.

# TAXES

The complexity of the U.S. tax code has provided a steady stream of business for book and software publishers, as well as tax preparers and accountants. The World Wide Web has its share of informational resources related to taxes, including news and downloadable tax forms. There are sites that will help file your taxes electronically and software programs that you can download and use immediately. You'll also find a number of experts who offer their own advice and commentary about reducing your tax burden.

**ask doug!**

**Q:** What is a wash sale?

**A:** A wash sale occurs when you sell an asset in order to take a tax loss, and then repurchase the same asset within 30 days of the sale. Wash sales are illegal. If you have a loss from a wash sale, it is used to figure the basis of the new purchase, and if you have a gain, it is taxable. If you sell a security in order to take a tax loss, you have to wait until after the 30-day period to purchase the same or substantially identical security.

## 1040.com
http://www.1040.com

Drake Software, a provider of solutions for tax preparation professionals, has built this handy resource for individuals to find tax-related information. Users can download federal and state tax forms, instructions, and IRS publications. The site also includes many helpful articles, news, and links to other Web resources. A database of tax preparers is also available so you can find help in your area, and you can file your 1040A or 1040 EZ returns online with their service.

## Deloitte & Touche Tax News and Views
http://www.dtonline.com/tnv/tnv.htm

Tax News and Views is designed to bring you the latest tax news from Washington. Deloitte & Touche keeps an eye on what Congress and the President are doing with your money. Updated regularly, this site posts news on developments in tax policy from Capitol Hill and the IRS. It also includes tax-planning guides for consumers and guides to changes in the tax laws.

## Ernst & Young Tax Tips
http://www.ey.com/us/tax/eyustax.htm

Every day, while millions surf the Web, the tax professionals at Ernst & Young are busy tracking the IRS, the tax code, the courts, and the Congress. This site follows news developments and planning opportunities for taxpayers ranging from corporations to small businesses to individual filers. Features of the site include a Nanny Tax flowchart, and articles such as "How To Analyze A Mutual Fund's Tax Efficiency" and "Beware The Tax Consequences When Lending Money To Friends And Family." Plenty of other tips, hints, tax tools, forms, and publications are available.

## Interactive Nest Egg Tax Center
http://nestegg.iddis.com/nestegg/articles/taxctr.html

This section of the personal finance site, Interactive Nest Egg, is devoted to taxes. It includes forms and schedules for small business owners and personal investors, in Acrobat format, and links to Nest Egg's tax-related articles.

## Internal Revenue Service
http://www.irs.ustreas.gov

The IRS Web site is a surprisingly efficient way of getting tax information. Users can search for particular forms and instructions, which can be downloaded in Adobe Acrobat format. You can also consult the IRS "plain language" regulations for answers to your questions. The site includes lists of FAQs for both individuals and small business owners.

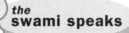

**the swami speaks**

The Swami has perfectly organized bookmarks, but chances are your bookmarks could benefit from some of the Swami's advice. (Internet Explorer calls its bookmarks Favorites.) Both Explorer and Navigator allow you to create folders in which you can store different categories of bookmarks. Try creating one called Investing to keep your favorite investing sites. You might create a Personal folder or a Business folder, whatever makes sense for the way you work.

Don't throw out all those security purchase confirmations and account statements. You need to be able to determine the cost basis of all of your stocks, bonds, and funds, which can only be done with those statements. Even if you carefully track all your transactions in a portfolio management or personal finance software program, you may still need those records as backup if you are audited by the IRS.

## Jackson Hewitt Tax Service
http://www.infi.net/~jhewitt

Jackson Hewitt is the second largest tax preparation firm in America with over 1,300 offices in 44 states. Their site offers a Tax Tip of the Day, an online edition of their *Tax Lines Magazine*, and articles such as "What to Bring to Your Tax Interview" and "Fifty of the Most Overlooked Tax Savings."

## Kiplinger TaxCut
http://www.conductor.com

Kiplinger TaxCut is a leading tax preparation software. The Conductor site offers individuals the chance to learn about the software or purchase it online and download a copy right away.

## Kiplinger Tax Letter
http://kiplinger.com/newsletter/tax.html

Published since the 1920s, the *Kiplinger Tax Letter* is the nation's most widely read tax advisory service. A recent sample issue is available on the site, along with links to Kiplinger's other extensive Web resources.

## J.K. Lasser's Your Income Tax
http://www.mcp.com/mgr/lasser

For 60 years, J.K. Lasser has published *Your Income Tax* to help taxpayers save money at tax time. Now, the complete guide is available on the Web free. The online edition provides expert advice, practical examples, money-saving tips, and long-term planning strategies. Each chapter is available in Adobe Acrobat format.

## National Association of Computerized Tax Processors
http://www.nactp.org

The National Association of Computerized Tax Processors NACTP is an organization of tax preparation software companies, electronic filing processors, tax form publishers, and tax processing service bureaus. Their site provides links to the IRS and state sites that have tax forms available for downloading.

## National Association of Enrolled Agents
http://www.cais.com/naea/naeamain.html

The National Association of Enrolled Agents (NAEA) is a professional organization, but their site includes links and news helpful to individual taxpayers. Their journal is also available online in Adobe

Acrobat format, along with tax FAQs and a directory of enrolled agents across the country.

### National Association of Tax Practitioners
**http://www.natptax.com**

This site includes information about the services of the National Association of Tax Practitioners (NATP), a group of professionals involved in the tax preparation industry. Most of the information is for the benefit of their members and not outsiders.

### Personal Tax Edge
**http://www.parsonstech.com**

Parsons Technology is the developer of Personal Tax Edge, an income tax preparation program that can be purchased and downloaded from the site. They also offer electronic filing, a tax reference library, downloadable forms, and tax tips.

### Rotfleisch and Samulovitch
**http://www.pathcom.com/~davidr**

Rotfleisch and Samulovitch are Canadian tax and business lawyers, providing articles and information about taxes, including Tuesday's Tax Tidbit and the Top Ten Tax Tidbits.

### SecureTax
**http://www.securetax.com**

SecureTax offers a free online tax preparation program. Users can prepare their federal and state tax returns online, with no additional software. Enter the basic data and SecureTax handles the calculations, with access to 85 federal forms and forms for 45 states. There is an additional charge for printing, electronically filing your returns, or running

your results through their AuditAlert function. You can practice using the forms, as well.

### Tax and Accounting Sites
**http://www.uni.edu/schmidt/bookmark.html**

This directory of Internet resources on tax and accounting topics is meant for educators, students, and professionals, but any individual can benefit from the hundreds of resources linked here, in dozens of categories.

### Tax Analysts Home Page
**http://www.tax.org**

Tax Analysts is a nonprofit organization dedicated to serving tax professionals. It publishes *Tax Notes* magazine. They offer online databases of tax resources, as well as tax news, feature stories, and discussion groups.

### The Tax Prophet
**http://www.taxprophet.com**

Robert L. Sommers is a tax attorney and columnist for the *San Francisco Examiner*. His articles are archived on this site. There are also lists of Frequently Asked Questions, copies of his firm's newsletter, interactive tax applications, and a tax fairy tale, "The Slaying of the Tax Dragon," based on a true story.

## Tax Talk-Plain and Simple
**http://village.ios.com/~taxtalk**

*Tax Talk* is a monthly newsletter written in plain language that tells individuals, investors, and small business owners about hundreds of legal tax loopholes. Users can request a free issue on the site.

## Tax Tips and Facts
**http://www.rak-1.com**

Roger A. Kahan, a Certified Public Accountant and business consultant from Massachusetts, publishes a handful of tips each month on his site dealing with tax and business issues.

## TaxSites
**http://www.best.com/~ftmexpat/html/tindex.html**

Frank McNeil publishes this comprehensive list of Web sites dealing with income taxes. The lists are categorized and feature occasional annotations by McNeil.

If you file your tax returns using Form 1040, 1040A, or 1040EZ, you can get your tax refund much more quickly by requesting that it be directly deposited to your bank account. You can make the request right on those forms; no other special form is required.

## TaxWeb
**http://www.taxWeb.com/index.html**

TaxWeb is a consumer-oriented resource for federal, state, and local tax-related developments. On the site, surfers can find answers to general tax questions, links to current federal and state-sponsored tax sites, a discussion group, and downloadable tax forms.

## TurboTax Online
**http://www.turbotax.com**

Intuit provides product information about their tax preparation software, along with details of their electronic filing option, tax guides for individuals and small businesses, and a tax calendar. Users of the program can get support from the site as well.

# GLOSSARY

AGENT—A representative of an insurance company, licensed by the state, who sells insurance contracts and provides services to the policyholder.

ANNUITY—An insurance or retirement program that provides an equal stream of income to the recipient for a specific number of years or for the recipient's lifetime.

BENEFIT—The amount payable by the insurance company to a beneficiary or claimant under the terms of an insurance policy.

BINDER—A written or oral contract that holds insurance in force until a new policy is issued, or an existing policy is endorsed.

CASH SURRENDER VALUE—The amount available to an insurance policyholder if the policy is voluntarily terminated prior to maturity.

CERTIFIED FINANCIAL PLANNER (CFP)—Professional designation conferred by the College of Financial Planning upon those who pass a series of exams demonstrating their competency in financial planning.

CERTIFIED INSURANCE COUNSELOR (CIC)—Professional designation conferred by the Society of Certified Insurance Counselors upon those who pass a series of exams demonstrating their knowledge of property and liability insurance.

CHARTERED FINANCIAL CONSULTANT (ChFC)—An advanced professional designation conferred by The American College upon individuals who exhibit expertise in the fields of financial planning, investments, and life and health insurance.

CHARTERED LIFE UNDERWRITER (CLU)—An advanced professional designation conferred by The American College upon individuals who exhibit expertise in the fields of life and health insurance.

CHARTERED PROPERTY and CASUALTY UNDERWRITER (CPCU)—Advanced professional designation conferred by the American Institute for Property and Liability Underwriters upon individuals who exhibit expertise in property and liability insurance.

CLAIM—A request for payment under the terms of an insurance policy.

DEDUCTIBLE—The amount a policyholder pays per claim toward the total cost of a covered loss.

DEFERRED COMPENSATION—A plan to delay compensation to employees until a future date.

DEFINED BENEFIT PLAN—A pension plan in which the benefits to be paid to recipients are specified.

DEFINED CONTRIBUTION PLAN—A pension plan in which the contributions are paid in at a particular fixed level. The benefits eventually paid out to each employee vary.

EMPLOYMENT STOCK OWNERSHIP PLAN (ESOP)—A defined contribution pension plan in which employees invest in the stock of their employer.

ENROLLED AGENT—An individual who has technical competence in the field of taxation and is licensed by the government. Enrolled agents can represent taxpayers at administrative levels of the Internal Revenue Service.

FIXED ANNUITY—An annuity that pays a regular payment at a guaranteed fixed amount.

INDIVIDUAL RETIREMENT ACCOUNT (IRA)—An account to which an individual makes annual contributions. Subject to coverage by another pension plan and income limits, the contributions may be tax-deductible.

INHERITANCE TAX—A tax on property received by an heir.

IRREVOCABLE TRUST—A trust in which the creator can not re-acquire the property placed into the trust.

JOINT TENANTS—A form of property ownership in which a survivor or survivors automatically take ownership of the share of a co-owner upon his or her death.

PENSION PLAN—A plan maintained by an employer or union to provide for the payment of benefits to employees upon retirement.

QUALIFIED PLAN—A tax-advantaged retirement plan meeting certain requirements of the Internal Revenue Service.

STRAIGHT LIFE INSURANCE—Whole life insurance on which premiums are payable for life.

TERM INSURANCE—Life insurance that is payable in a specified amount to a beneficiary if an insured dies during the period of coverage. Term insurance expires without value if the insured survives the coverage period and is usually the least expensive form of life insurance.

UNIVERSAL LIFE INSURANCE—A combination of term insurance and tax-deferred savings plan, under which the policyholder can change the death benefit and vary the amount of premium payments.

VARIABLE ANNUITY—An annuity that pays a varying amount to the annuitant, depending upon the success of a separate investment account underlying the annuity.

VARIABLE LIFE INSURANCE—Life insurance under which benefits vary according to the value of a separate investment account underlying the policy.

WHOLE LIFE INSURANCE—Also known as cash-value life insurance. Insurance in which part of the premiums are used to provide death benefits and the remainder earns interest.

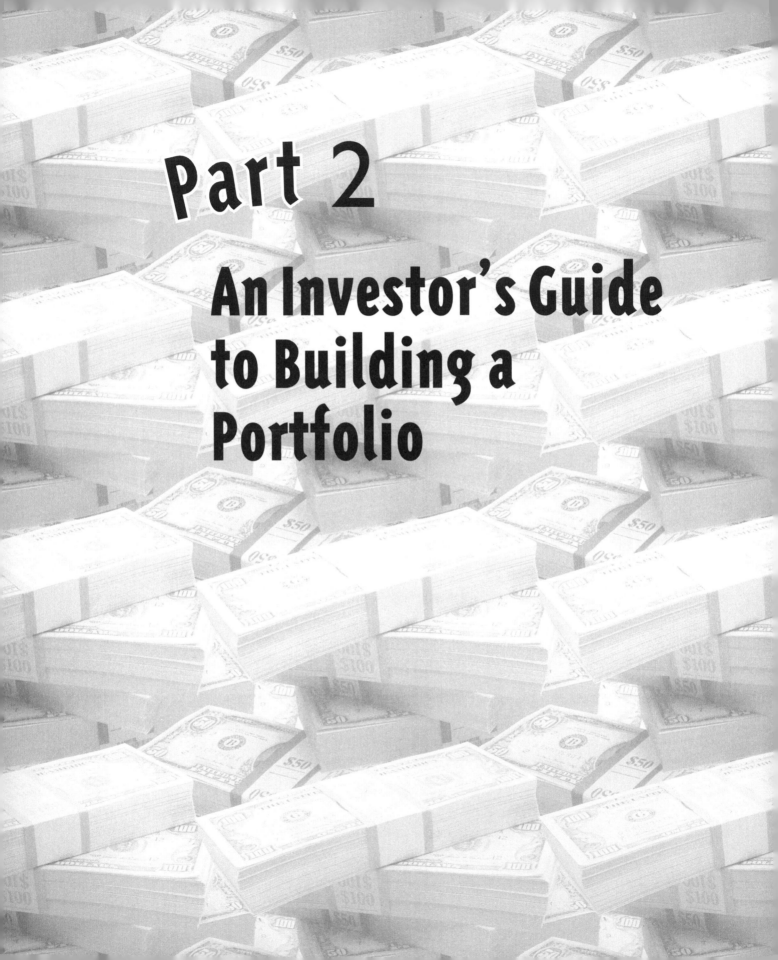

# Part 2

# An Investor's Guide to Building a Portfolio

# Chapter 11

# Your First Steps In Investing

*"No good man ever grew rich all at once."*

**—Publius Syrus**

**Now that you've seen** the array of resources for investors available on the Internet, let's put them to work. Part 2 of this book will help you implement an investing strategy using the Internet and your personal computer as the main tools in your financial toolbox. Step by step, you'll see how to build and manage a portfolio of common stocks.

# RISK AND RETURN

First, you need to understand a single inalienable truth about investing: **Over the long term, common stocks outperform most other assets.**

In the history of the U.S. stock markets, common stocks have had an average annual return of about 11 percent. Over the past 15 years that figure has been closer to 15 percent. Of course, there have been some rocky patches along the way, years in which the market has dropped 20 percent or even more. While that certainly can be a bit painful, it's important to realize that the stock market has recovered from each downturn and soared to even greater heights.

Compare those results with the 4-9 percent returns typically provided by Treasury bonds, certificates of deposit, corporate bonds, money market funds, or savings accounts. You'll see why so many investors are turning to stocks to help them meet their financial goals, whether for retirement planning, to pay for education needs, or to help reach other long-term goals.

The Capital PC User Group Investment Special Interest Group (http://cpcug.org/user/invest) offers long-term performance charts of major market indexes, like the semi-logarithmic graph of the Dow Jones Industrial Average from 1897, shown in Figure 11.1.

The increased returns provided by the stock market bring increased risks, however. Risk is inevitable in any effort to protect or invest your money. Stuff-

ing wads of dollar bills under your mattress puts that money at risk of robbery or a fire. Keeping your money in the bank, however, also carries the risk that the bank could fail. That risk is minimized, though, by the regulations imposed by the government on banking operations and the mandatory coverage that the bank provides customers from the Federal Deposit Insurance Corporation (FDIC).

U.S. Treasury bonds, bills, and notes carry the risk that the federal government could default on its obligations. That is an assuredly minimal risk. Likewise, there is a risk that a corporation could go bankrupt. If that happens, the owners of its common stock will likely end up owning shares that are worthless. The issuer of a corporate or municipal bond could default on its promises to repay interest or principal, leaving the bondholder with nothing.

There are other risks involved in investing. Individuals who keep most of their money tucked away in savings accounts may be surprised to learn that while they're trying to protect their principal, they may actually be losing ground because of inflation (the rising costs of good and services). Historically, inflation has grown at an average rate of over 4 per-

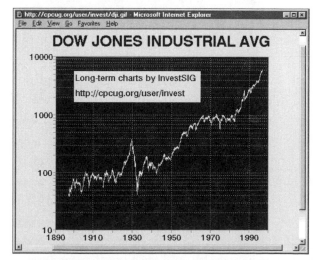

**Figure 11.1**
Dow Jones Industrial Average from 1897

### ask doug!

**Q:** What happens to stockholders when a corporation goes bankrupt?

**A:** Holders of common stock are at the bottom of the list when a company goes belly-up. Only if there are any assets left in the business after all other creditors and preferred stockholders are paid would common stockholders receive any payment. Since stockholders are owners of a business, they accept this risk for the nearly limitless upside potential for their shares.

One of the biggest risks you face is simply ignoring the need to plan for your long-term financial goals. If you don't put your financial house in order, who will?

cent each year. If funds are invested in an account that pays an interest rate less than the rate of inflation, that investment will have less purchasing power when the cash is eventually withdrawn. Inflation is a risk that can whittle away at your nest egg.

The most common type of risk associated with investing is *market risk.* This is the potential that your investments will fluctuate in value over time. You may buy a stock and then see its share price drop significantly from your purchase price.

Different kinds of stocks carry different levels of risks. *Blue chip stocks* are companies that have a long history of increasing earnings and paying dividends. Blue chip stocks are about six times more volatile than Treasury bills and other short-term income investments, but they are less volatile than stocks in general, making them generally safer investments than others. Stocks of technology companies, on the other hand, can grow very rapidly and their share prices can be subject to sharp adjustments (that is, increased market risk). Small-cap stocks usually carry higher risk, as well, and are more than ten times as unstable as short-term government bonds. Bonds are also subject to fluctuating prices or interest rates,

and the interest rate that a bank pays on a savings account may also change from month to month. Even if you invest in a long-term fixed-rate vehicle, such as a certificate of deposit, you can still be exposed to market risk if overall interest rates rise above the rate paid on your CD.

Risk is an unavoidable component of investing. It is necessary to accept a certain amount of risk in order to generate a reasonable return on your investment. The more risk you are willing to assume, the greater the potential return your investments can provide. The amount of risk you should assume is dependent on two primary factors: your personal tolerance and your investing time frame.

It's very important to understand how much risk you can accept in your own investing. It's not a good sign if you are constantly worried about your investment portfolio and fearful of what will happen if share prices fall. You should be comfortable with the risk level of the assets you own, whether you are investing on your own or following the advice of a financial planner or full-service broker.

A good rule of thumb is if you can pass the "sleep" test. If you stare at the ceiling from your bed each night, thinking of how you'll cope if the market crashes, taking your portfolio along with it, then you're probably invested in assets that are too risky for your personal comfort. You should reduce your risk exposure until you own a portfolio that allows you to sleep at night.

Your investing time frame, the second factor affecting your risk tolerance, hearkens back to our understanding that over time, the stock market can provide superior returns. Stocks are a terrific long-term investment, but in the short term they can fluctuate widely. If you have a time-specific goal in mind, such as paying for your child's college education or funding a retirement plan, you need to consider the length of time until you need access to those funds before you can assess how much risk you can reasonably assume. If you have 30 years before your retirement, you can invest comfortably in aggressive growth stocks. If you have three years until you'll start paying college tuition, those equities might not be appropriate. Your personal definition of what constitutes too much risk may change over time.

Investors can manage the risk in their portfolios in several ways. You can reduce the risks of a particular asset by carefully choosing the securities you own. For instance, credit agencies such as Standard & Poor's, Moody's, and Duff & Phelps routinely rate bond issuers, assigning a grade that indicates the financial strength of the corporation or government agency issuing the bond. By choosing high-grade bonds, you reduce the risk of default. If you invest in stocks, you can purchase only those companies who meet your standards of excellence in criteria such as quality of management and persistence of historical growth.

You can also reduce the risk and increase returns in your portfolio through diversification. A diversified portfolio helps reduce risk because different investments rise and fall according to different external and internal impulses. If you owned one security and its value declined 30 percent, then the value of your entire portfolio declines by 30 percent. If you owned equal amounts of ten separate securities, and the same issue declined 30 percent, then your entire portfolio only drops in value by three percent.

Spreading out your portfolio among different types of assets is another way of reducing risk. Again, a factor that may negatively impact the stock market

---

**the swami speaks**

Though much of the Web appears to be little more than a swirling mass of random colors, the Swami would like to point out the color coding used to represent hypertext links on a Web page. There are two types of links: visited and unvisited. Each type is represented by a different color, and the color of links changes after you visit a site. This helps you to know where you've been and where you may still travel. By default, Netscape Navigator and Internet Explorer use purple to indicate visited links and blue to represent unvisited links. However, Web site designers can customize the scheme on their pages, so you'll come across a world of colors to represent both kinds of links. Navigator recognizes a third kind of link: *activated*. If you use Navigator, you may see a brief flash of color at the precise moment you click a link. That's not a quirk in your video driver; it's the activated link color.

---

may not have an effect on bond prices. If you held an even mix of bonds, cash, and stocks, and all of your stocks declined 20 percent in a market correction, the overall impact on your portfolio would be a loss of just 6.7 percent.

Likewise, it is possible to build a diversified portfolio of common stocks, including companies of different sizes (small-cap, mid-cap, and large-cap stocks) or from different industry groups (utilities, technology, consumer goods, energy, or industrials, for instance). If an industry-wide problem affects a particular sector, other companies are less likely to be affected.

# INVESTING STRATEGIES

The stock market is where millions of investors are investing their hard-earned dollars in order to meet their future financial needs. There are several different approaches to investing in stocks that investors employ, each designed to reduce the risks in investing while increasing returns. Each has advantages and disadvantages, and different individuals may find different approaches best suited to their own styles, abilities, and personal preferences.

## TECHNICAL ANALYSIS

Technical analysis is an attempt to find relationships in charts of historical price and volume information about a particular security in order to predict future price movements (see Figure 11.2). The method doesn't look at any outside factors, such as the company's fundamentals or the economic outlook. It's strictly by the charts. Market technicians believe that the market price of a security reflects all known information about that security.

Investors who use technical analysis rely upon their computers and, increasingly, the Internet, to

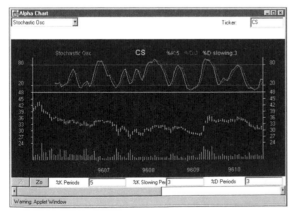

**Figure 11.2**
AlphaChart <http://www.alphachart.com> is a source of free technical analysis charts on the Web.

Once you select or build your own investing style, stick with it. If you try to mix approaches, you'll just end up diluting the effectiveness of your chosen strategy, thereby diminishing your returns.

collect an extensive array of price and volume data about securities. They import that data into any of dozens of available charting programs and attempt to discern patterns in the graphs, each with distinctive names such as *head and shoulders, cup and saucer, double bottom, dome,* and *descending tops.* Each of these patterns and trend lines indicates a likely future direction for the security under study.

Technical analysis also employs the use of indicators, which are signals generated by the relationships between different pieces of data. The method can be used with stocks, commodities, indexes, or options. It's also very, well, technical. Technical analysis requires careful study to learn to identify and interpret the various patterns on the charts. Although there are some excellent software programs specifically for technical analysis, the learning curve just to get started using its techniques can be formidable.

### Equity Analytics, Ltd.
**http://www.e-analytics.com**
Charles J. Kaplan, President of Equity Analytics, Ltd., has written several articles on technical analysis, including "10 Points For Beginning Technical Traders" and a tutorial on technical indicators. He also recommends several books on the subject and provides a glossary of technical analysis terms.

Another disadvantage of technical analysis is that it requires an investor to make a daily or at least weekly commitment to follow the charts, both on current holdings and on potential purchases. Even with charting software, this can mean being glued to your computer screen for hours at a session, and require an ample serving of number-crunching skills. Technicians also need a never-ending supply of current price and volume data.

Finally, there are those who claim it is unlikely that there is any cause-and-effect relationship between a stock's past price performance and its future performance. They say relying on chart patterns is a bit like expecting it to rain on June 21st if June 10th is sunny, just because that's what happened last year.

 Market timing systems often claim a certain rate of return based upon backtesting on historical data. However, the actual buy and sell signals generated by the system are much more efficient than the real world. Actual orders placed in the marketplace at the levels indicated by the signals may or may not have been executed at those prices. Some systems build in an allowance for these inefficiencies, as well as for commission costs. You should always check to make sure a model accounts for these two factors.

## MARKET TIMING

One component of technical analysis is that there is a time to buy and a time to sell. This is known as *market timing*. This approach is an attempt to minimize risk by determining when to buy or sell a particular security or to get in or out of the market in general.

Market timers typically devise a system based upon rigorous testing of reams of data to find out what economic or financial signals may have indicated the beginning of past market downturns. Once these models have been constructed, they are then *backtested*, verifying that the signals are successful when applied to historical data.

Some systems generate very few signals in the course of a year, while others are switching in and out of the market dozens of times throughout the year. Frequent trading has its downside, as commissions can swallow your profits whole. That's one reason many models are built around mutual funds that can be traded commission-free.

Like technical analysis, market timing can require a time commitment that many investors find overwhelming. Market timing models must be followed

precisely in order to be effective. While many market timers offer subscription services, sending you their signals via e-mail or fax, other services provide you with the data and software that enables you to generate your own signals according to their model.

### Market Timing in a Spreadsheet
**http://www.halcyon.com/rhagan**

Roger Hagan has produced a videotape documenting his approach to market timing using any spreadsheet software. His Web site includes loads of graphs, observations, and background on Hagan's system of mutual fund timing. If you're set on market timing, this is the place on the Web to go.

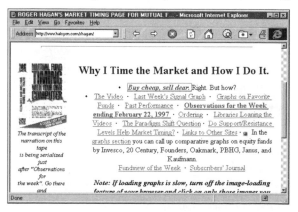

While many stock market timers aim to avoid bear markets, that can be easier said than done. According to one study of the 1,276 trading days during the bull market of 1982 to 1987, the Standard & Poor's 500 Index returned a total annual return of 26.3 percent. If an investor missed just the ten days with the biggest gains during this period, his or her return dropped to 18.3 percent. If the investor missed the 40 biggest days (out of 1,276 days), the total annual return fell all the way to 4.3 percent. The risks of being wrong in efforts to time the market are substantial (see Figure 11.3).

Still, some investors think they can use a slightly different tactic to time the market: they think they can improve their returns by selling before the market falls. Short of gazing into a crystal ball, there is no reliable way of knowing when the market will turn in any direction, at least in the short term. In the market correction of 1987, only a very few of the entire population of well-paid, well-educated, well-informed experts on Wall Street were able to predict the impending downturn.

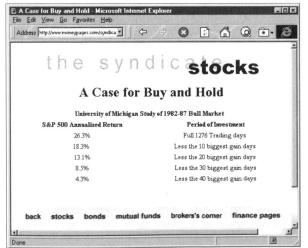

**Figure 11.3**
The disadvantage of trying to time the market.
(http://www.moneypages.com/syndicate/stocks/buyhold.html)

On the other hand, the stock market has shown a consistent, long-term, upward trend over its entire history.

## INDEX FUNDS

Armed with the knowledge that stocks provide one of the best long-term investments, investors have flocked in recent years to an easy, low-maintenance method of participating in the stock market's gains. As if following the exhortation, "If you can't beat 'em, join 'em," these investors have bought an *index fund.*

An index fund is a mutual fund that simply mimics the holdings of a particular market index. The most popular index funds are built upon the Standard & Poor's 500 Index, providing investors the same level of risk and reward offered by overall market.

There are hundreds of market indexes. Some of the better known are managed by Standard & Poor's, such as the S&P 500, S&P 100, SmallCap 600, and MidCap 400 indexes. There are indexes to track every sector of the market, and indexes for small-cap, mid-cap, and large-cap stocks. There are foreign country indexes and global indexes. There are commodities and metals indexes, in addition to stock indexes.

Dow Jones calculates indexes for three regions, 29 countries, nine market sectors, and 121 industry groups. In the technology sector, you can find the NASDAQ High Technology Index, AMEX High Technology Index, PSE High Technology Index, Morgan Stanley High Tech Index, and the Semiconductor Index. If you're interested in the Internet, Hambrecht & Quist has created the Hambrecht & Quist Internet Index. All market indexes have ticker symbols so that you can check their performance on an Internet quote service, though the symbols often vary from provider to provider.

### Dow Jones Industrial Average Centennial
http://djia100.dowjones.com

This special site established by Dow Jones & Company commemorates the 100th anniversary of the Dow Jones Industrial Average. It offers the history of the average, answers to frequently asked questions, and other information.

### Dow Jones Global Indexes
http://www.dowjones.com/indexes

This division of Dow Jones tracks the world equity markets with indexes that follow three regions, 29 countries, nine market sectors, and 121 industry groups.

### Standard & Poor's Indexes
http://www.stockinfo.
standardpoor.com/idxinfo.htm

Standard & Poor's (S&P) offers lists of component companies of their market indexes, current statistics, and news about additions and deletions.

The Dow Jones Industrial Average (commonly known as "the Dow," DJIA, or "the Dow 30") and its sibling Transportation and Utility averages are other popular market barometers, although they are technically not indexes but averages. Most indexes weight the stocks they track by market capitalization, but the Dow Jones averages are unweighted.

Mutual funds are managed portfolios of stocks and other securities, and that means someone has to manage them. Investors pay for that management, whether through a *load* (a commission-like fee paid upon buying or selling a fund) or as part of the fund's regular expenses.

Index funds, on the other hand, don't require as much management since the potential pool of in-

The biggest disadvantage of investing in index funds is also the biggest advantage. You're guaranteed to never underperform the general market when you buy an index fund, but you're also guaranteed to never beat the market.

vestments is set by the underlying index. The manager of an index fund still makes buy and sell decisions and must manage inflows and outflows of cash.

A popular misconception about index funds is that they own all of the stocks in the index they track. Particularly in very large indexes, an index fund may only own a representative sample of the securities in the index. The goal of the index fund is to match the returns of the specified market benchmark, not necessarily to hold all of the stocks in the index or in the same proportion.

### The Vanguard Group
http://www.vanguard.com

The most popular index fund is the Vanguard Index Trust 500, holding the stocks in the S&P 500. Vanguard is a leader in the funds industry in keeping mutual fund costs low, so its index funds offer returns very close to those of the underlying

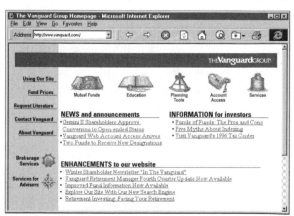

averages. In fact, so many investors turned to index funds in 1996 that the Vanguard Index Trust 500 is the second largest mutual fund in the country.

This *passive management* approach (as compared to *active management* techniques of picking stocks) translates into savings for fundholders. Index funds usually have very low expense ratios, since advisory fees, distribution charges, and operating expenses are much lower than in the average equity mutual fund. Transaction costs, such as brokerage fees, are also reduced.

That isn't to say that there aren't any expenses that an index fund incurs—there are still the costs of printing and mailing statements to account holders, office supplies, rent, salaries, and so on. Index funds are able to provide a savings for the index fund investor in the form of increased return because they don't need to pay for high-priced research analysts and other expenses of actively managed funds.

## THE DOGS OF THE DOW

Also known as the Dow Dividend Strategy, the Dogs of the Dow is a technique developed by Michael O'Higgins and presented in his book, *Beating the Dow*. This approach is easy to implement and has generated an average annual return of 17.7 percent since 1973, compared to a return of 11.9 percent for the Dow Jones Industrial Average in the same period.

The Dogs of the Dow method works like this:

1  Determine the ten stocks with the highest dividend yields in the Dow Jones Industrial Average.

2  Buy equal amounts of each.

3  Wait one year, then repeat.

That's all there is to it!

**Dogs of the Dow**
**http://www.dogsofthedow.com**
Here's a home page that's part doghouse. Investor Pete Grosz has set up this page to provide information on the Dogs approach, as well as track the performance of the strategy throughout the year. Instructions to implement the strategy are provided, along with answers to frequently asked questions.

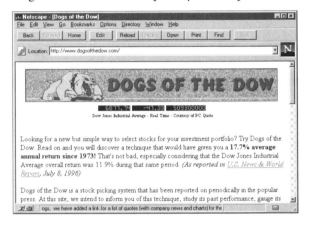

The companies that are paying the highest dividend yields in the Dow 30 are likely to be those stocks that are facing temporary problems. However, since the Dow 30 companies are theoretically among the best and most stable companies in the U.S., these stocks are quite likely to rebound. When they do, their share prices will climb.

There are additional variations on the Dogs theory that provide the chance of slightly increased return. One method is to invest in the five Dogs with the lowest stock prices. This is called the "Flying Five," "Puppies of the Dow", or "Small Dogs of the Dow," and it provides a slightly better return with a bit more risk.

The Motley Fools (http://www.fool.com) follow an additional variant on the Dow strategy, which they call the "Foolish Four." The cheapest stock of the Dogs is usually a company in real trouble, and this stock tends to drag down the performance of

**the swami speaks**

Clicked a link by mistake? The Swami says press the escape key on purpose to instantly stop the page from loading. It's usually easier and faster than clicking the stop button with your mouse.

the entire strategy. The second cheapest stock in the group, on the other hand, generally doesn't have the same kind of problems. As a result, it has plenty of upside potential. Historically, this stock has been the best performer of all the Dogs. To take advantage of this characteristic, the Foolish Four doubles up on the second cheapest stock and eliminates the cheapest stock altogether. The returns generated by this deviation surpass both the Flying Five and original Dogs of the Dow approachs.

These strategies all provide a way to limit risks by investing in some of America's best established corporations and promises better-than-average returns. No management is required by the investor, with the exception of the annual review. The disadvantages of the Dogs of the Dow system lie in its annual turnover, with commission costs and tax liabilities reducing returns.

## FUNDAMENTAL ANALYSIS

When you go shopping for a new car, don't you try to buy the best car you can for the best price? You want a vehicle that will run for a long time without breaking down, at least as long as you need. You don't want to have to think about whether or not you'll make it work each morning—you just want your car to get you there. You want a car that will re-

quire as little maintenance as possible, not one that needs a tune-up every few thousand miles. You don't want to pay too much for your new car—if you can get a well-made car that fits all your needs for a price that's a bargain, you'll be one happy car owner.

Investing in common stocks isn't much different. You can buy the stock of a high-quality company at a bargain price, put it away in your portfolio, and not worry about it except during your quarterly portfolio checkup. Over the long term, that company will grow, its stock price will appreciate as well, and your portfolio will become all the richer.

The Value Point Analysis Financial Forum (http://www.eduvest.com/) allows users to input and calculate the value of a particular stock, using fundamental analysis (see Figure 11.4).

Just like shopping for a car, however, you need to do your homework first to make sure you're getting a good deal on a good company. By investing in quality companies at reasonable prices, you can limit your risks and increase your returns.

This method of analysis is called *fundamental analysis*, which can be described as the study and purchase of companies, rather than stocks. Factors such as a

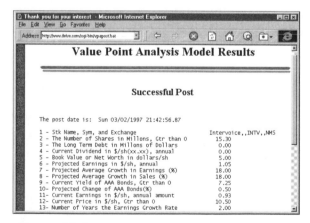

**Figure 11.4**
The Value Point Analysis Financial Forum

## ask doug!

**Q:** Where did the terms *bull market* and *bear market* come from?

**A:** A bear market is a decline of 15 percent or more in the overall market and lasting for an extended period. The term is thought to come from the bear skin jobbers of long ago, who sold bear skins that had not yet been caught. Speculators who sold shares they did not own, then bought the shares after a price drop and delivered them to the purchaser, became known as bears. At the time, bear baiting and bull baiting were still popular sports, and bulls were understood to be the opposite of bears—those who bought on the expectation that prices would rise.

company's growth rates, balance sheet, and quality of management are analyzed to determine the true value of a security. Fundamentalists aren't concerned with price patterns on a chart, but with indicators of a company's underlying financial strength.

Sounds like a reasonable approach to investing in the stock market, right? You wouldn't buy a car based on a chart of all the prices of cars at all the dealers in town, with no identification of what make or model each was. So why buy stocks for your portfolio that way?

Part of the reason behind investors' flight to index funds is that only one in five mutual funds is able to beat the market average each year. That's right—80 percent of all mutual funds in the U.S. underperform the S&P 500 each year. These are funds with professional money managers, complete research staffs, and an array of analytical tools and data at their fingertips, but they still can't beat the market.

You might be thinking, "If those folks can't do it, why should I even try to beat the market?" Here's why: there are individuals across the country just like you, who had little experience when they started investing in the market, who began by investing just $20 to $100 a month in the stock market, and who are now outperforming the market on a regular basis. These individuals—grandmothers and housewives, doctors and lawyers, farmers and truck drivers, people from all walks of life, from all strata of society—have all found investing success by being part of an *investment club* and using fundamental analysis to pick long-term growth stocks for their portfolios.

According to the National Association of Investors Corp. (NAIC), a total of 42.9 percent of its member clubs beat the S&P 500 in 1996. That means twice as many investment clubs (made up of individuals just like you) beat the market than did professionally managed mutual funds. In fact, the average investment club has a 19.1 percent annual return over its lifetime. Interestingly, all-female clubs have an even higher average annual return of 21.3 percent.

## NAIC Online
### http://www.better-investing.org/

NAIC is a not-for-profit organization begun in 1951 and dedicated to investment education. They have developed an approach to investing in

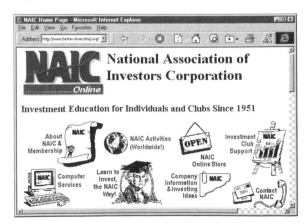

common stock based upon fundamental analysis of long-term growth companies, used by both individual investors and investment clubs. They provide a full range of educational materials, manuals, and software to investors and investment clubs.

You don't have to be a member of an investment club in order to put NAIC's principles of fundamental analysis to work. You only need a few hours each month to start building a portfolio of common stocks. Once your portfolio is solidly established, you need only spend a few hours each quarter evaluating the performance of the companies you own.

There are many reasons that long-term-growth stock investing works so well for individual investors.

1   You won't need to make an enormous time commitment. It will take some time for you to learn how to invest, but you won't need more than a couple of hours each month to study and manage your portfolio.

2   You don't need to be a number cruncher. While you will need to do some basic calculations and understand some mathematical ratios, there isn't any complicated numerical analysis involved.

3   You can harness the time value of money. Since you'll be investing for the long term, you can use the tendency of the market and individual stocks to grow over time, fattening your portfolio. Table 11.1 shows the return on an initial investment of $1,000 invested at different rates over a number of years.

4   You can increase your portfolio substantially by investing regularly. By adding to your holdings over time, you can build a significant portfolio with small amounts of money invested over a period of years. Table 11.2 demonstrates the power of investing regularly, beginning with a $1,000 investment and adding $1,000 each year.

5   You can reduce risk by buying quality growth companies at good prices. You can probably identify many of America's best companies by name: McDonald's, Pepsico, Colgate-Palmolive, Coca-Cola, Microsoft. It shouldn't be surprising that over the years these companies have made bundles for their shareholders.

## Table 11.1

Return on an initial investment of $1,000 at different rates of return

| Years Invested | 11 Percent Return | 7 Percent Return | 3 Percent Return |
| --- | --- | --- | --- |
| 10 years | $2,558 | $1,838 | $1,305 |
| 20 years | $7,263 | $3,617 | $1,754 |
| 30 years | $20,624 | $7,114 | $2,357 |
| 40 years | $58,559 | $13,995 | $3,167 |
| 50 years | $166,275 | $27,530 | $4,256 |

**Table 11.2**

Return on an initial investment of $1,000 at different rates, with an additional $1,000 investment at the beginning of each year

| Years Invested | 11 Percent Return | 7 Percent Return | 3 Percent Return |
|---|---|---|---|
| 10 years | $16,722 | $13,816 | $11,464 |
| 20 years | $64,203 | $40,995 | $26,870 |
| 30 years | $199,021 | $94,461 | $47,575 |
| 40 years | $581,826 | $199,635 | $75,401 |
| 50 years | $1,668,771 | $406,529 | $112,797 |

# GLOSSARY

DOW JONES INDUSTRIAL AVERAGE (DJIA)—An average of 30 industrial companies that trade on the New York Stock Exchange and are intended to be representative of the market as a whole.

FUNDAMENTAL ANALYSIS—A method of evaluating stocks based on fundamental factors, such as revenues, earnings, future growth, return on equity, and profit margins, in order to determine a company's underlying value and potential for future growth.

INFLATION—The rising cost of goods and services.

MARKET INDEX—A collection of securities tracked together and intended to represent the performance of the market as a whole or for a particular sector.

MARKET TIMING—An attempt to sell a stock or portfolio when a market is at a high and buy at a low. Generally an exercise in futility.

RETURN—The percentage of profit returned on an investment.

RISK—A measure of the volatility and possibility of loss in an investment.

STANDARD & POOR'S 500 INDEX—A market average of 500 companies intended to be representative of the market as a whole.

TECHNICAL ANALYSIS—A method of evaluating securities by analyzing price and volume data of a stock's market activity, using charts to identify patterns that can suggest future activity.

# Chapter 12
# Choosing a Broker

*"There is no such thing as an innocent purchaser of stocks."*

**—Louis D. Brandeis**

**At some point** in your investing, you'll probably need to deal with a broker if you want to buy stocks. However, there are ways to bypass brokers altogether and still invest in stocks, such as dividend reinvestment plans (DRIPs) and direct purchase stocks, which allow you to buy stock directly from the public companies who sponsor them. The Internet is also making possible a whole new online marketplace for securities.

Brokers come in two varieties: full-service and discounters, and each has advantages and disadvantages. We will discuss both of them so that you can make an educated decision on which kind you want to use.

Since full-service brokers work on commission, they get paid for each trade in an account, not by how well the portfolio performs, which puts them in the same category as salespeople. Unscrupulous brokers have been known to trade excessively in clients' accounts for the sole purpose of generating commissions–a practice known as *churning*. The vast majority of brokers are honest, and the industry is highly regulated, but the practice of rewarding brokers by the number of transactions they produce still can put them at philosophical odds with the interests of a client's portfolio. This makes it all the more important to find a broker you can trust.

# FULL-SERVICE BROKERS

Traditionally, full-service brokers have provided entree to the stock market to individual investors. The names of the largest full-service brokerage firms are familiar to most people: PaineWebber, Merrill Lynch, Dean Witter, and Smith Barney.

When you open an account with one of these firms, you will deal with a particular representative each time you call or visit your own broker. Your broker is charged with the task of understanding your investing needs, tolerances, and goals. In fact, your broker is required by law to know these things about you. He or she can get into hot water with the Securities and Exchange Commission for recommending an inappropriate investment.

Your broker can be given complete, limited, or no authorization to actually execute trades in your account for you. That means you can go on vacation to enjoy the beaches of Anguilla and not worry about watching your portfolio. On the other hand, turning your portfolio over to someone you don't trust is probably not such a good idea.

Full-service brokers offer advice, research, and other information to their account holders. These companies have staffs of analysts who are experts in particular industries and who issue the research reports constantly quoted in the financial news rating stocks. Clients usually have the inside track on receiving word of these upgrades and downgrades before the general public.

The PaineWebbers and Merrill Lynches of the industry have comprehensive product lines to service all your financial needs, including retirement accounts, annuities, municipal bonds, Treasury bills, life insurance, options, precious metals, as well as stocks and mutual funds. Full-service brokers can help you create financial plans for college funds, retirement, or tax-saving strategies.

If you're interested in getting in on the ground floor of initial public offerings, a full-service broker is likely to be the only way you'll have any chance of buying at the opening price. Most full-service brokers also serve as investment banks to the corporate community and thus are the underwriters of public offerings.

Full-service brokers charge significant commissions for trading securities, as well as annual maintenance fees. So, all these benefits come at a price. These costs can be cheap compared to the levels of service provided, or you may end up paying a premium for the privilege of merely doing business with a prestigious firm.

## NATIONAL FULL-SERVICE BROKERS

The national full-service brokerage firms have established Web sites that provide a central resource for current account holders as well as potential clients. They typically provide research, commentary, complete information about their product lines, educational material and, of course, referrals to retail brokers in your area. Some are adding online access to account information for their clients, as well. The following are a few of them:

### A.G. Edwards

**http://www.agedwards.com**

Like most of the full-service brokers, A.G. Edwards wants you to know that they've been around for a while—since 1887, in fact, as is prominently displayed on their site. The site offers market news and commentary, but not much in the way of nitty gritty research (that's saved for clients). Otherwise, you can find information about A.G. Edwards's services for businesses and executives, and a section called Planning for a Secure Future that covers asset allocation, saving for a child's education, and retirement and estate planning. A bit of educational material is thrown in as well, but for any more than that, you'll need to talk to an A.G. Edwards representative in person.

### Edward Jones

**http://www.edwardjones.com**

Edward Jones's Web site takes an old-fashioned approach to its presentation—the site looks like a spiral ring notebook filled with handwriting. However, the

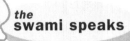

**the swami speaks**

How'd you like to run with the Swami? If you use Windows 95, you can type a URL into the Run program on your Start menu, and Internet Explorer will automatically launch and go to that page.

site is slim on research and other tools and heavy on marketing hype. It's very clear what kind of clientele the firm seeks: they don't offer options, commodities, or penny stocks, just "predictable, low-risk investments that perform well over time," including certificates of deposit, bonds, mutual funds, stocks, and life insurance.

### Merrill Lynch

**http://www.ml.com**

Merrill Lynch wants to take Web browsers on a "Journey to Financial Success." That's the theme of their Web home. The site's excellent Learning Center is joined by the Personal Finance Center, the Business Planning Center, and the Financial News & Research Center. You can search for a Merrill Lynch office near you or just search their site for information on a particular topic. Clients can view their accounts online, too.

### PaineWebber

**http://www.painewebber.com**

PaineWebber's Web site is their Intelligence Center, and it will test your investing prowess (if you'll let it) via an interactive "Test Your Investment Intelligence" quiz. Find the PaineWebber branch office nearest you or get Research & News from the firm's acclaimed Investment Strategy Group. PaineWebber's EDGE service provides clients with access to account information, as well as customized news and quotes.

## Prudential Securities

**http://www.prusec.com**

Prudential's Virtual Financial Advisor takes Web surfers on a tour of their services and products. You can find information about events in your area, get investment research directly from their analysts and economists, view your Prudential Securities accounts, and explore an array of information about stocks, bonds, funds, and investment strategies. "Life's Financial Concerns" is an interesting area that addresses some of the topics that investors are most worried about: college education for the kids, retirement planning, taking care of elderly parents, health and insurance needs, and business financial planning.

## Smith Barney

**http://www.smithbarney.com**

Account access is the focus of Smith Barney on the Web, with customized news, charts, and research available for a client's portfolio. An online newspaper offers daily research, market rates, and articles on investing and market strategies. All surfers

can access headlines from the prior day's commentary from Smith Barney's Equity Research Department, with links to other Web sites, charts, and summary financial data.

## HOW TO SELECT A FULL-SERVICE BROKER

If you've decided that a full-service broker is your best option, you'll now have to find one. The key to developing a successful relationship with a full-service broker is just that—it has to be a relationship. Both you and the broker have to be honest. As a client, you have to be forthright about your needs, desires, and fears. You have to be able to put your trust in your broker.

Finding the broker that's right for you can take some energy. Ideally, your broker will have an office somewhere near you so that you can meet in person with him or her, at least occasionally. Get referrals from your friends and coworkers, pick out names from the phone book, and then visit or call several of these prospects. You may find a full-service broker who advertises in a local newspaper. All of the national full-service brokerage houses that are on the Web can refer you to one of their branch offices and a representative near you.

And if you end up with a broker who doesn't seem to be filling your needs, you should take your business elsewhere. There's nothing stopping you from using more than one broker, either.

It's perfectly appropriate to meet with several brokers at different firms to try to find the person who can serve you and your needs best. Consider each meeting to be an interview for someone to fill the position of your personal financial representative—because that's what he or she really is.

Don't be shy in your meetings with potential brokers—you won't be the first person they've met with about opening an account. Some brokers may have a mini-presentation they will show you. Here are some questions you should ask:

- "What is your professional background? Where did you go to college?" These questions are part of the getting-to-know-you phase.

- "What is your investment experience? What is your approach to the market? What is your performance record for your clients?" Try to find out if the broker does his own research or if he relies on his firm's research. Some brokers like to do their own analysis to supplement their firm's work.

- "How do you get paid?" Brokerage firms generally pay their brokers based on the amount invested by customers and the number of transactions in their accounts. Some firms have their own mutual funds and other products, and brokers may receive bonuses for selling those products. Make sure you get a copy of the firm's commission

---

### ask doug!

**Q:** The stocks in my portfolio are constantly being upgraded and downgraded by various analysts, but how can I tell what their ratings mean? For instance, what does *outperform* mean, and how does it compare to a *buy* recommendation?

**A:** Every investment firm has its own definitions of its ratings. For instance, Wertheim Schroder's Stock Rating System is based on how well a stock is expected to perform against the market as a whole:

1  Outperform Significantly
2  Outperform
3  Perform In Line
4  Underperform
5  Underperform Significantly

While these rankings don't tell you what the ratings mean in absolute terms, the ranking gives you an idea of how Wertheim Schroder rates stocks' suitability for purchase for their clients.

Most firms' ratings can be whittled down to *Buy*, *Hold*, and *Sell*. *Outperform*, *Neutral*, and *Underperform* mean essentially the same thing, respectively, although sometimes they don't.

Some other examples: Smith Barney downgrades a stock to Outperform from Buy, and upgrades a stock to Outperform from Neutral.

Goldman Sachs has a *priority list*, which are stocks they think are better buys than those on their *recommended list*.

PaineWebber calls their similar list their *focus list*.

Prudential Securities offers a *select list*, as well as a *Single Best Idea*, too.

Merrill Lynch uses ratings like *near term neutral*, *accumulate*, *near term accumulate*, *long term buy*, *long term accumulate*, *average*, *above average*, and a couple of other variations. They also have their list of *Focus 1* stocks.

Oppenheimer rates stocks *market perform*, *neutral*, *short-term positive*, or *buy*, among other flavors.

Confused? Most of these firms are in the retail brokerage business and have representatives who are happy to interpret the results for clients. Usually, though, brokers have plenty of time to act when their own firm issues an updated research report before that report hits the mainstream news media. You may notice that while firms have plenty of ways to recommend buying stocks, they have far fewer terms in their lexicon for selling a stock.

schedule and that you understand what fees or charges may apply when opening, closing, or transferring an account.

- "How do you usually work with clients? What kind of services could I expect from you if I were your client?" Some full-service brokerage firms can provide financial planning services, such as insurance and retirement planning, in addition to brokerage services. Also, discuss how this broker would feel about sending you research reports and S&P tear sheets if you request them.

- "Do you require discretionary powers?" Some brokers want full authority to trade on your behalf. This is called *establishing a discretionary account*. If a broker pushes you to sign over trading authority to him or her, it should probably be interpreted as a bad sign.

- "Have you ever had any disciplinary problems with NASD or the SEC?" Granted, this is not a question you can slip into a casual conversation, but it's important to ask. You might mention that you were planning to call NASD and check the records of the brokers you were interviewing and give the broker a chance to explain any incidents that might be on file.

After you've met with a few brokers, you'll probably have a much better idea of how brokers in general operate. After you've made your choice, the process of opening an account is really no different than opening a bank account. There will be forms to fill out, and the firm will check your credit history.

Your new broker will then meet with you to determine your level of sophistication about the markets, your risk tolerance, your financial goals, your investing history, and other details of your personal finances. Brokers are prohibited from making inappropriate recommendations to their clients. In order

There are some brokers who realize that by helping their clients to learn about investing, they both can benefit. Others think that the less you know, the better for them. If you can find a broker who's willing to spend just a little extra effort on explaining what he or she has planned for your account, or who recommends that you join an organization like NAIC or AAII to increase your knowledge, you may have the best deal of all.

to know what is suitable and what is not, your broker needs to have the details of your situation. Don't hold back; be forthright in providing this information. If you do resist, you will not allow the broker to do his or her best job on your behalf.

The following sites will help you get started selecting a broker:

## AAII Brokers Guide
http://www.aaii.org/brokers/
The American Association of Individual Investors offers a variety of articles on finding and using brokers.

## How To Select a Broker
http://www.nasd.com/it4a.html
The National Association of Securities Dealers, Inc. (NASD) offers this brief guide to choosing a broker.

## "Opening an Account with a Broker" by David Gardner (The Motley Fool)
http://www.fool.com/invstng/if004.htm
As usual, the Motley Fools have some choice words on the selection of a broker, and the disadvantages of full-service firms.

OPTI 5 1/4    NYTEL 96 3/4    GTE 100    SBO 38 1/4

## HOW TO TELL IF A BROKER IS LEGITIMATE

The securities industry is highly regulated, both at the state and national level. Typically, brokerage firms and individual brokers are members of the NASD and are registered with the Securities and Exchange Commission (SEC). NASD requires that firms meet certain stringent net capital, bonding, and other requirements, and that all personnel be appropriately registered with NASD.

Individual NASD registration consists of passing an examination, the most common of which qualifies an individual to be employed as a stockbroker. He or she must pass the Series 7 General Securities Exam and can then be known as a registered representative. Individual brokers who advise clients regarding options, commodities, and other securities must pass specific NASD exams in those areas.

Individual brokers and brokerage firms must also be licensed to do business in each state, usually by the state's securities commission.

The following sites provide directories of state securities regulatory agencies:

### AAII Information Guide
http://www.aaii.org/iigii.html

### NASD Regulation Directory of State Securities Regulators
http://www.nasdr.com/2340.htm

### NCII State Securities Agencies Web Sites
http://www.ncii.org/ncii/states.html

### SEC Directory of State Securities Regulators
http://www.sec.gov/consumer/state.htm

NASD requires that all member firms carry coverage for their clients from the U.S. Securities Investor

**ask doug!**

**Q:** What is a *registered investment advisor?*

**A:** A registered investment advisor provides securities advice in return for compensation and must register with the SEC to use the title. However, there are no educational or professional qualifications required to register with the SEC and no examination to pass, either. NASD registered brokers are specifically exempt from SEC registration. Practically anyone, upon filing an application and paying a fee, can become a registered investment advisor, so the title itself doesn't mean that a person has any particular expertise in providing investment advice.

Protection Corporation (SIPC) of up to $500,000 per account. SIPC is a federally chartered private corporation, similar to the FDIC, which protects individuals in the event that a firm should go bankrupt. Most firms provide additional protection as well from a major insurance carrier. This coverage protects customers from having their assets disappear if the firm should fail, but it doesn't protect from losses on investments.

In order to check on the disciplinary history of a firm or a particular individual, you can contact NASD Regulation, a subsidiary of NASD. Their public disclosure program maintains a database of pending and final disciplinary actions taken by NASD or federal or state securities agencies against individual brokers or firms. It also includes civil judgments and arbitration decisions and criminal convictions and indictments against NASD member firms and their associated persons. You can call NASD Regulation at

800-289-9999, or visit their Web site (see High Yield Links) for more information.

If there is any question about the integrity of a broker or firm, you should also check with your state's securities regulatory agency. Also, see the following to check on the integrity of a broker:

### NASD Regulation, Inc.
http://www.nasdr.com

NASD Regulation is responsible for registration, education, testing, and examination of NASD member firms and their employees. Their public disclosure program gives investors access to information on NASD member firms and representatives. The Web site includes complete information on the program and how to file a complaint.

### SEC Enforcement Division
http://www.sec.gov/enforce.htm

The SEC provides investor alerts, records of enforcement actions and administrative proceedings, and how to contact the SEC if you suspect investment fraud.

# DISCOUNT BROKERS

In the 1970s, Charles Schwab led a revolution that turned the brokerage industry upside-down. His concept of a brokerage firm that offered cut-rate commissions to individual investors was unheard of at the time.

Now, 20 years later, the discount brokerage industry is flourishing. Minimum commissions offered by discount brokers have fallen below $10 in some cases. And discount brokers have led the way onto the Internet for the rest of the financial industry.

Discount brokers differ from full-service brokers in four major ways. The first, of course, is cost. A

When selecting a discount broker, be extra careful to look at all the fees and minimums involved. Some require a minimum money market balance of, say, $1000 before they pay interest on the funds in your account. Others may charge a fee to issue certificates, which might be disadvantageous if you plan to invest in DRIPs and need shares registered in your name rather than a street name.

trade in a discount brokerage account can cost one-tenth the commission for the same trade at a full-service broker. Second, discount brokers cannot offer advice or recommendations to their clients. Third, discount brokers usually offer little in the way of research, news, or information, though they may offer certain reports for a charge. Finally, full-service brokers offer a much wider range of products and services than most discount firms.

True, some discount brokers do offer securities research and other information—some even have their own staff of analysts—but there is a direct relationship between commissions charged and services provided. The firms with the lowest commissions offer bare-bones services. Pay a bit more in commissions and you can get much more in the way of research.

## ONLINE TRADING

Though a few discount brokers have offered online trading for years, either via services like CompuServe, America Online, or Prodigy, the Internet has opened the door to a new era. Using the World Wide Web, investors can conduct all their brokerage business online, in an easy-to-use graphic format.

An added bonus of online trading is that many of these sites offer rather extensive research on their Web sites for clients. In addition to tracking the prices of securities in your portfolio, you can get news, charts, industry reports, and other information on stocks you own.

Each listing in this section indicates a firm's lowest minimum commission for equity trades executed online, or their flat-rate commission if applicable. This information is provided for comparison purposes only, and there may be limitations on number of shares per trade, which exchanges are available, or other surcharges. Check each firm's commission schedule for further details.

## Accutrade

**http://www.accutrade.com**

Accutrade offers institutional-quality research to clients on their Web site, including market news, daily earnings, price charts, top performers, industry reports, and mutual fund news and reports. Screening programs for stocks or funds allow you to target specific criteria. The stock and fund reports are in-depth and comprehensive. Minimum commission: $28 + 2 cents per share.

## American Express Financial Direct

**http://www.americanexpress.com/direct**

American Express offers a complete Internet trading network, with research tools, real-time access to breaking news, and financial data. There are two classes of service: InvestDirect and InvestDirect/PT. PT stands for Power Tools, and it adds a comprehensive array of news (from Comtex), corporate news (from MarketGuide, S&P MarketScope, and Zack's), search tools, check writing privileges, and cash access through your Amex Gold Card. PT Expert goes a step further and gives more complete information for a flat rate of $34.95 per month. Minimum commission: $26.95 + $.005 per share (InvestDirect); $34.95 per trade + $.005 per share (InvestDirect/pt).

### the swami speaks

The Swami says that when you download files using the latest versions of Netscape Navigator or Internet Explorer, a dialog box will pop up to give you the status of the download. When it does, you can navigate your Web browser to another site and let the download continue in the background. Another option is to open multiple windows at a time. You can also use this when you want to compare information on multiple sites.

## K. Aufhauser & Company

**http://www.aufhauser.com**

Aufhauser's WealthWEB was the first site to offer trading on the Internet. It has added free research reports from MarketGuide on publicly traded companies for their customers. Otherwise, their online services are straightforward: quotes and portfolio tracking for stocks, treasuries, corporate and municipal bonds, options, mutual funds, CDs, precious metals, and foreign securities. Minimum commission: $24.99 ($22.50 if placed online).

## Ceres Securities Online

**http://www.ceres.com**

Ceres Securities is a deep-discount broker offering $18.00 flat-rate trading, regardless of the number of shares. They provide little in the way of perks to their clients; the main attraction is the low commission. Financial writer Andrew Tobias does provides daily commentary on their Web site. Flat-rate commission: $18.00.

## CompuTEL Securities

**http://www.rapidtrade.com**

CompuTel offers clients free and discounted research services from a multitude of partners, ranging from Thomson MarketEdge to INVESTools to Zack's. Minimum commission: $19.75 (Internet trading).

## Datek Online

*HIGH YIELD $ Site*

**http://www.datek.com**

Datek is currently the online leader of the low commissions, $9.99 for up to 5,000 shares, though they currently only trade NASDAQ and NYSE stocks. Datek claims to enter more than 50 percent of all electronic orders in the NASDAQ stock market each day and guarantees execution of all marketable orders within 60 seconds or your trade is free. At these rates, expect no hand-holding and no other services, though. Minimum commission: $9.99.

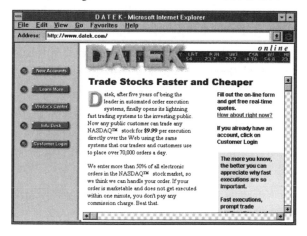

## E-Broker

**http://www.ebroker.com**

E-Broker is an Internet-only broker that features a flat-rate commission of $12 per stock trade for any number of shares ($35 minimum commission for option contracts). They have no 800 numbers and offer no research, just a cut-rate commission. Flat-rate commission: $12.00.

Fees, fees, fees—beware the fees of discount brokers! Discount brokers have done well for investors by offering very low commission rates, but many of them make up for it by charging for everything they can think of: issuing a physical certificate, opening your account, closing your account. There can be account inactivity fees, account maintenance fees, and so on. Some brokers' commissions increase if you don't use their online trading services and talk to a human instead. Make sure you understand all the fees your broker may charge you before you sign the application form.

## E*TRADE Securities, Inc.

**http://www.etrade.com**

E*TRADE was the first to develop electronic brokerage services for individual investors. Their Web site provides few frills, just stock and option trading at $14.95 or $19.95 for up to 5,000 shares. Account holders have free access to real-time news (from Reuters, PR Newswire, BusinessWire, and Newsbytes) and charts for stocks in their portfolio, and E*TRADE offers a money market fund. Minimum commission: $14.95.

## Lombard Brokerage

**http://www.lombard.com**

Lombard's Web site is called the Real-Time Trading and Research Information Center, and real-time quotes for stocks, options, and bonds are available for all customers. Other research services available include stock and fund reports from Thomson Financial that include analyst ratings, balance sheet information, and insider trading activity. Intra-day or historical graphs are also provided. Minimum commission: $14.95.

**the swami speaks**

If you think that text on the Web is too hard to read, perhaps it's time for your yearly eye exam, says the Swami. Barring that, you can always adjust the font size and style in your browser to make text easier to read. Internet Explorer lets you change font sizes on the fly just by clicking the Font Size button on the toolbar, a tip the Swami guarantees to come in handy when you reach a site put together by someone who must sit way too close to his or her computer monitor. In Navigator, you can change the text size and style for both the fixed and proportionate fonts from the Options menu, by choosing General Preferences and Fonts. In Internet Explorer, select View, Options, General, Font Settings.

### National Discount Brokers
**http://pawws.com/Ndb_phtml**

National Discount Brokers Online (NDB) offers online stock trading only as part of the Portfolio Accounting World Wide (PAWWS) from Security APL Financial Network. Account holders must register with PAWWS and then have free access to their comprehensive tax-lot, cost-basis portfolio service, including news, quotes, research, and charts. The advantage of this approach is that trading via NDB is then just a click away, consolidating research, portfolio management, and trading in one convenient location. Minimum commission: $20.

### The Net Investor
**http://netinvestor.com**

The online arm of Howe Barnes Investments, Inc., The Net Investor is another affiliate of the PAWWS Financial Network. They offer online trading of stocks, options, mutual funds and bonds; free real-time quotes; historical and intra-day price and volume graphs; plus financial news, company profiles, mutual fund reports, company research, price forecasts, and earnings analysis. Access to PAWWS's solid portfolio service is integrated into The Net Investor's online accounts. Minimum commission: $29.00 plus 1.5 cents per share.

### Pacific Brokerage Services
**http://www.tradepbs.com**

Despite the plain appearance of their site, Pacific Brokerage Services (PBS) has hidden away a nice little collection of services for online investors. Besides MarketGuide company snapshots, real-time market and index updates, quotations for stocks, options, and currencies, surfers can download a daily ASCII file of price and volume information for over 5,000 stocks. Users can also request a historical pricing file for most securities, with data beginning in September 1996. But the real attraction is Pacific's online trading via the Web, with a flat transaction charge of only $11 for up to 5,000 shares. Minimum commission: $11.00 (plus a $4 handling fee).

### PC Financial Network
**http://www.pcfn.com**

PC Financial Network (PCFN) is America's largest online brokerage network, and their Web site provides a cornucopia of tools for investors. Account holders receive free real-time quotations, news, customized portfolio alerts, model portfolios, and company reports from several sources. All surfers should check out PCFN's Research & Ideas for the free in-depth company reports on the firm's current recommendations. Investors on the cutting edge will also want to check out PCFN's browser plug-ins to provide charting, a stock ticker, and an easy-access company report menu. Minimum commission: $39.95.

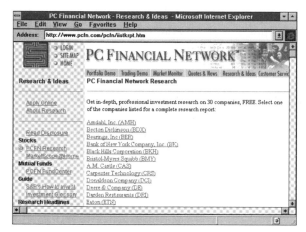

## Quick & Reilly

**http://www.quick-reilly.com**

QuickWay Net is this national discount brokerage firm's Web-based trading site, offering quotes, historical graphs, news, economic reports, portfolio tracking, and securities research for account holders, provided by Reuters Money Network. Even visitors have access to much of this information in return for registering on their site. Minimum commission: $26.75.

## Savoy Discount Brokerage

**http://www.savoystocks.com**

Savoy offers SmartNet Trading on the Web, as well as account access via their SmartTrade Software for Windows. The Savoy site has many educational articles, including a glossary of investment terms and a Short Selling Tutorial that are very helpful. Minimum commission: $25 flat rate for online trades.

There's no law that says once you choose a broker you're stuck with that firm for life. If you can find a better deal that meets all of your needs, it's no problem to transfer your account. The brokerage industry has standardized the transfer of accounts so it usually takes a day or so to accomplish (while brokers hate to see your account go away, they love to see new accounts being transferred to them, so they've joined together to make it as easy as possible for investors). Be sure to watch out for account closing fees that some discount brokers levy, however.

It's also not written anywhere that you may only use one broker at a time. Of course, it may be convenient to have all your accounts with the same company. But many investors do business with several different brokers.

Take Mr. Investor. He uses one broker for his IRA account, another for his "regular" account, and still another for a college savings account for his kids. He trades less frequently and in larger amounts in the IRA account, so he uses a more expensive discount broker, one that offers free research reports. His regular brokerage account is at a deep discount firm. This is where he does most of his buying and selling, so he wants to minimize his commissions. He has his college savings plan set up to deposit funds each month directly from his checking account, so each month that money is automatically invested in a long-term mutual fund at a broker that offers free automatic transactions and no-commission mutual fund trading. In this way, Mr. Investor has maximized the level of information he receives at minimum expense.

### ask doug!

**Q:** How do I know if a full-service or discount broker is for me?

**A:** The short answer is: If you don't know, then you probably should be using a full-service broker! Most investors who use discount brokers do so because they conduct their own research and make their own investment decisions. If you're not comfortable putting together your own portfolio, then a full-service broker may be for you. Depending on your investing strategy, it may benefit you to use the services of a full-service broker. If you invest in micro-cap stocks that require constant monitoring, or regional stocks, or you want to invest in IPOs, then a full-service broker is probably your better choice.

On the other hand, if you're making your own decisions about your investments, or you want to take advantage of online trading, then a discounter might be a good fit.

If you like to do your own research, but have no other access to research information (which, these days, usually means you don't have access to a computer, fax machine, online service, or the Internet), then a full-service broker might be a good choice. Perhaps you'd like to take advantage of the range of financial planning services and products that full-service brokers offer, such as annuities and customized asset allocation strategies.

Another solution is to use both a discounter and a traditional broker for different portfolios, or for different strategies. Just don't abuse your relationship with your full-service broker by hitting him up for advice and then only trading in your discount brokerage account.

### Charles Schwab
**http://www.schwab.com**

The king of the discount brokers offers a Byzantine Web site, where Schwab account holders can trade, get real-time quotes, check order status, balances, and positions on the Web. Schwab's online trading services are available through two stand-alone programs—StreetSmart and e.Schwab—as well as directly on the Web. Commissions and services vary significantly depending on which of the myriad options you select. The bottom line is a minimum commission of $29.95, or 20 percent off regular Schwab commissions, depending on which package you sign up for. Customers do receive free market news from Thomson MarketEdge, Briefing.com and MarketGuide, but research reports are an additional fee and are no particular bargain. Minimum commission: $29.95.

### Waterhouse Securities, Inc.
**http://www.waterhouse.com**

Waterhouse offers real-time quotes, personal portfolio tracking, charts, and news as part of their webBroker service. They also offer Windows software for clients to trade online via their private network. Minimum commission: $12.00 (through March 1998).

## BYPASSING THE BROKER

For the truly independent individual investor, there is another option, eliminating the need for a broker altogether. Individuals with as little as $10 to spare can buy shares of stock in companies like IBM, Sears Roebuck, Rubbermaid, Coca-Cola, AT&T, McDonalds, or Xerox. Over time, an individual investing on a regular basis can build a sizable portfolio—and never once pay a commission to a stockbroker.

How is this possible? By participating in a company's Dividend Reinvestment Plan (DRIP). DRIPs are run by publicly traded companies for their shareholders. Instead of sending dividend checks to DRIP account holders, the company reinvests those dividends by purchasing additional shares (or fractional shares) in the shareholder's name. Over 1,200 companies have dividend reinvestment plans for their shareholders.

These reinvested dividends are usually free of commissions and fees (though, increasingly, DRIP plans are beginning to tag on nominal fees). The best part of DRIPs is that they also allow shareholders to purchase additional shares at little or no commission.

In order to enroll in a DRIP, a person needs only to own the required number of shares. Most of the time, only a single share is needed to get started. In fact, there are now more than 200 companies who will sell you those first few shares directly and enroll you in their DRIP at the same time. These are known as *direct purchase stocks*.

**ask doug!**

**Q:** Why do companies have DRIPs? It seems like an awful lot of trouble.

**A:** Companies like DRIPs for several reasons. DRIPs provide a stable base of shareholders that are likely to have a long-term, *buy-and-hold* investment philosophy. Individuals, particularly those who are dollar cost averaging into their DRIPs, may see the drop in a stock's share price as a buying opportunity, as opposed to institutions and traders who move in and out of stocks with short-term goals in mind. This base of individual shareholders can help stabilize a company's share price. DRIPs can also help companies raise additional capital without making a public offering.

## Direct Stock Purchase Plans

http://www.natcorp.com/ir/direct.html

This page, provided by National Corporate Services, describes direct purchase plans and provides links and telephone numbers for companies with these programs.

## Directions: An Investor's Guide to North American Equities

http://aries.phys.yorku.ca/~rothery/
stocks.drips.html

Norman Rothery has compiled this guide to DRIPs and to their Canadian cousins, Share Purchase Plans (SPPs). Links are provided to charts and quotes for each company. Rothery also includes a list of U.S. direct purchase stocks.

## Directory of Dividend Re-Investment Programs

http://www.cs.cmu.edu/~jdg/drip.html

John Greiner has supplemented this directory with information about getting started with DRIPs, a bibliography and links to other online resources. The directory itself includes telephone numbers, discounts if offered, and other information.

## "Dividend Reinvestment Plans"

http://www.moneypages.com/syndicate/
stocks/cc-drips.html

This article by Charles Carlson, CFA, is an overview of DRIPs—how they work, how to get started, pitfalls to look out for. Carlson is the author of *Buying Stocks Without a Broker* and *No-Load Stocks*.

There are a few disadvantages to DRIPs. Accounting for a large number of small transactions can be time-consuming. DRIPs generate paperwork, since each DRIP you own will send its own statement. Additional purchases of stock are only made at specific dates, so you have no control of the purchase price. DRIPs have limits to how much you can invest per month or quarter. If you need to sell shares, you will have to wait until the next scheduled purchase date of the plan.

## DRP Club

**http://www.concentric.net/~drpclub**

The DRP Club is a subscription service that provides investors with strategies for creating financial independence using dividend reinvestment plans. The site provides information about their products and a listing of companies with DRIPs.

## First Trust

**http://www.drpira.com**

First Trust is the nation's largest independent trustee of retirement plans. They offer IRAs that allow individuals to invest in dividend reinvestment plans, including their Value Plus IRA.

## First Chicago Trust Company

**http://www.fctc.com/faq/index.html**

One of the leading bank transfer agents, First Chicago provides this list of Frequently Asked Questions about DRIPs.

## Monmouth Real Estate Investment Corporation

**http://www.mreic.com**

Eugene W. Landy, President of this New Jersey-based firm, offers a compelling essay on the "Benefits of Dividend Reinvestment Plans," and other information about the advantages of raising capital via DRIPs.

## The Moneypaper

**http://www.moneypaper.com**

The Moneypaper is a newsletter focusing on investing in dividend reinvestment plans. They also offer a service to sell subscribers the first share necessary to enroll in nearly any DRIP in the country.

## National Association of Investors Corporation

**http://www.better-investing.org**

NAIC's Low Cost Investment Plan allows NAIC members to buy a share in any of 145 companies with dividend reinvestment plans for the share price and just a $7 fee. Individuals are then automatically enrolled in that company's DRIP.

## NetStock Direct

**http://www.netstockdirect.com**

Focusing on direct purchase stocks, NetStock Direct is a smorgasbord of information about DRIPs in general, with directories of both DRIPs and direct purchase stocks, a weekly column by Charles Carlson, and guides to investing in direct purchase stocks. Their direct stock purchase plan clearinghouse lets investors request enrollment

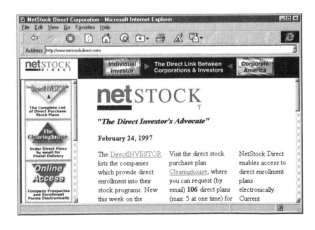

forms for any of 106 direct plans for postal delivery. A handful of companies even let investors enroll in their plans online.

## No-Load Stocks

**http://noload.base.org**

Mark Keller maintains this listing of generally available no-load and direct stock purchase plans. He includes plan details for many of the companies and an e-mail discussion list for those interested in talking with other investors about these stocks.

---

## GLOSSARY

AT THE OPENING—An order for execution at the best possible price at the next opening of the market.

AT THE CLOSE—An order to buy or sell a stock during the last 30 seconds of a day's trading.

DAY ORDER—An order good only for the day the order is placed, after which it is automatically canceled.

DISCOUNT BROKER—A brokerage firm that provides limited advice and services but savings of 50 percent or more compared to full-service firms.

DIRECT PURCHASE STOCK—Shares that are available for purchase directly from a publicly-traded corporation, instead of through a broker. Also known as *no-load* stocks.

DIVIDEND REINVESTMENT PLAN—Abbreviated DRIP or DRP. A program sponsored by a corporation whereby shareholders can elect to have dividends reinvested in purchases of additional shares. Most DRIPs also allow account holders to make additional purchases free of commissions.

G.T.C.—Good 'Til Canceled. An order that is to be carried from day to day until executed or canceled.

LIMIT ORDER—An order to be executed at a specified price, the *limit price.*

MARKET ORDER—An order to be executed at the best price possible immediately after placed with the broker.

REGISTERED INVESTMENT ADVISOR—A person who provides securities advice in return for compensation and is registered with the Securities and Exchange Commission.

STOP ORDER—An order to automatically sell when the market price of a security reaches a specified level below the current price, to protect the shareholder from sudden price declines. Stop orders are market orders once the stop is reached.

STOP-LIMIT ORDER—A combination of a stop order and limit order. Once the specified stop price is reached, the order becomes a limit order subject to the stop-limit price. (A regular stop order becomes a market order once the stop price is reached.)

# Chapter 13
# How to Study a Stock

"Have you noticed how many investment experts, or those who claim that designation, offer you sure-fire formulas? These so-called paths to prosperity require no judgement on your part, just blind fidelity. Would that investing were actually that simple! Everyone could become a millionaire without expending intellectual effort."

**—Thomas E. O'Hara and Helen J. McLane**

# THREE BENCHMARKS FOR INVESTING IN STOCK

The stock market has generally returned between 11 and 14 percent annually over time. As the members of the National Association of Investors Corporation (NAIC) have learned in the organization's 45-year history, individual investors can generate even better returns if they follow NAIC's methods.

What was once a tedious and time-consuming job of pencil scratching on paper forms, however, has become much easier with the introduction of several software programs. NAIC offers several programs that use its precepts to help investors build a portfolio of common stock. Among them are NAIC Investors Toolkit and STB Stock Analyst.

While the number-crunching chores of investing are simplified by the use of calculators and computers, investors still need to acquire the necessary background about any stock they are considering for purchase. The success of fundamental analysis depends upon having an understanding of the companies in an investor's portfolio. Fundamental analysts should think like a company's owners since they do, in fact, own a share of the corporation. Long-term growth stock investors buy companies, not stocks.

In order to understand a business and its operations, there are several resources, both online and offline, that you should use:

- Ask the company to send you a copy of its annual report, recent press releases, and other background information. Increasingly, you can find much of this information on the Web.

- Read the company's recent Form 10Q and Form 10K filings from EDGAR (http://www.sec.gov/edgarhp.htm). These are the quarterly and annual reports filed with the SEC.

- Read any research or analysts' reports that may be available, such as *The Value Line Investment Survey* or *Standard & Poor's Stock Reports.*

- Do a search of the Internet for items of interest about the company. For instance, you can go to The Silicon Investor (http://www.techstocks.com) or Deja News (http://www.dejanews.com) to see what other investors might have to say about a particular stock. Remember that their approach may differ from yours, however.

- Acquire five to ten years of fundamental data about the company. You'll need this much information in order to effectively analyze the company and its future potential. Chapter 2 lists many sources of fundamental data for investors.

WallSt.com (http://www.wallst.com) offers Standard & Poor's Stock Reports and other research that you can download in Acrobat format.

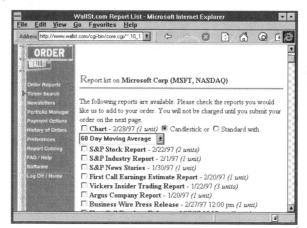

In order to meet your goal of doubling the value of your portfolio every five years, you need to find companies whose stocks will provide the necessary 15 percent average annual total return over the long term. You should look for companies that have outstanding attributes of growth, quality, and value. NAIC's Stock Selection Guide (SSG) is a good place to start.

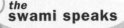

**the swami speaks**

In your quest for knowledge, intones the Swami, do not forget to use the many Internet search engines. There are several major sites on the Web that aim to index the knowledge of the Internet, including Alta Vista, Yahoo!, InfoSeek, Excite, and Lycos. They can help you find a needle in a haystack, at least by reducing the size of the haystack if nothing else. A bit of Boolean logic will help you even further. These are the logical operators that are used to limit a search, words such as AND, NOT, and OR. Each search engine can implement these operators in a different way. Some use symbols such as +, -, (, ), and | to represent the pieces of the equation. For instance, a search on MICROSOFT will return more pages that you could ever sort through. But limiting your search to: Microsoft Corp AND stock AND earnings only displays articles dealing with an investment in Microsoft stock. You should consult the help pages of your chosen search engine for tips on using their index most effectively.

Many data providers make adjustments to the historical figures to account for one-time charges and the effects of acquisitions and divestitures, so you may find that data from different sources may vary significantly. You can usually determine the reasons for adjustments that may have been made by reading footnotes. Make sure never to mix data from different sources-a data provider will make constant adjustments to all historical numbers, so stick with one source.

## GROWTH

When considering a company's growth, begin by looking at its sales or revenues growth first. In order to turn a profit, a company must first generate revenues: Revenues - Expenses = Profits. As is obvious from this equation, without revenues, there can be no profits. On a long-term basis, companies must always increase their revenues in order to increase their earnings. (Also, expenses must not increase too much or too fast, but more on that later.) A company that does not have adequate revenues growth should be eliminated right away from consideration.

How much revenue growth should you look for in a company? As a rule of thumb, expect larger companies to have slower revenue growth rates and smaller companies to have higher growth rates. As a company gets larger, it becomes progressively more difficult for a company to reach each new doubling of revenues. Consider that going to $1 from $2 represents a doubling of value. Now consider a company doubling its sales from $1 billion to $2 billion. Sheer economics dictates that finding another $1 billion in revenues is a formidable task for any business. That's also why it's impossible for a company to grow 50 percent or 60 percent or 70 percent a year over a long period of time.

It's unreasonable to expect a large-cap stock (companies with sales of several billion dollars) to have a sales growth rate higher than 10 percent. Small-cap stocks (with sales of several hundred million dollars) can grow at a rate of 20 percent or more. In between, you'll find mid-cap stocks. This generalization can help you as you consider how quickly a company can grow in the future, recognizing that growth is bound to slow as a company gets bigger.

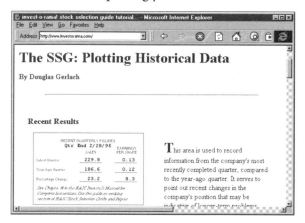

### Invest-O-Rama! Stock Selection Guide Tutorial
**http://www.investorama.com/ features/ssg_00.html**

For a structured method of evaluating long-term growth stocks, there's none better than NAIC's Stock Selection Guide (SSG). On Invest-O-Rama!, I've prepared a tutorial that can assist you in using this tool and interpreting your results.

## How Much Growth?

While sales growth is important, there is such a thing as too much growth, at least for long-term oriented investors. There are lots of opportunities for buying high-growth stocks in the market, but many of these stocks do not have the necessary track record of sustaining such rapid growth. A start-up corporation often grows very quickly, especially in the first five or so years of its life. The company's stock price will reflect this growth, as investors attempt to ride the crest of the company's ascension, hoping to be able to "jump out the top" and sell their shares at a profit. These traders know that inevitably this kind of growth will slow to a more sustainable level as the company matures. They just hope to be able to bail out in time.

Eventually, such a company's growth must slow to a more reasonable level. When it does, the company's stock price falls drastically. Since it's impossible to predict when this will happen, it's best to avoid stocks that don't have a minimum five-year track record of sustainable and reasonable growth, as well as stocks that are *high-fliers*.

NAIC Investors Toolkit is a computerized version of the SSG (see Figure 13.1), NAIC's primary tool for investing in common stock. The graph displays the growth of a company's past earnings, revenues, and pre-tax profits.

After determining that a company's past sales growth rate is acceptable, you can look at its earnings. As sales grow, earnings should increase at a similar rate. It is possible for a company to increase its earnings faster than revenues, but only temporarily. For instance, economies of scale can increase a company's profitability without a comparable increase in sales. This is not unlike buying a case of soda at a warehouse store that gives you a unit price lower than buying a six-pack of the same soda at the grocery store. The six-pack, in turn, is much cheaper per can than buying a single can of soda from a vending machine. You could probably get an even better price per can if you bought a truckload of soda

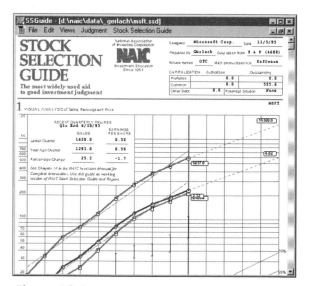

**Figure 13.1**
NAIC Investors Toolkit

The focus on your analysis of a company's past performance should be to identify the major trends in its history. However, if the company has an anomaly, a downturn in an otherwise consistent growth trend due to some unique event, you can eliminate that data from consideration as an *outlier*. You should determine that the point that lies outside the trend is just a one-time occurrence and, if so, ignore that particular data in your study.

at one time, but that introduces a whole new set of problems, including transportation and storage. In the same way, there are limits to the savings that companies can realize.

Companies can also increase their profits by cutting their work force or making each worker more productive, reducing the costs of their raw materials and supplies, or by raising the prices they charge for their products and services. Again, there are limits to how many workers can be laid off and how high prices can be raised. These are short-term fixes that can help long-term profitability, but it's impossible for a business to keep cutting expenses forever. That brings us back to the importance of revenues in the profit equation.

In general, a company can increase its sales at a fairly consistent rate. In comparison, earnings can fluctuate due to a one-time accounting charge against a company's profits and other factors the company may have little control over, such as increased raw materials costs. If a company's earnings are increasing faster than sales, that can indicate real problems in the way the company is managing its expenses. If the trend continues, the company will have no profits to show for all of its sales.

If a company can demonstrate the ability to grow its earnings and revenues over time, it then becomes

reasonable to expect a similar performance in the future. However, since you know that most companies experience a slowdown in growth as they get larger, it's prudent to expect the growth of even the best companies to also slow a bit.

STB Stock Analyst, available from NAIC, provides a tool for projecting future growth. Figure 13.2 demonstrates this.

To determine a company's past growth rates, NAIC's SSG provides a way to graph a ten-year history of sales and earnings growth and then to determine the historical growth rate trends. Software such as NAIC's Investors Toolkit or STB Stock Analyst can calculate these rates and generate the graphs automatically. Individual reports in the Value Line Investment Survey calculate each company's past five- and ten-year average growth rates. You can manually calculate the changes in growth from year to year and then average them to get an approximation of the company's past trends.

This is the first benchmark in your process of selecting a stock for purchase—Growth. If a company does not have a solid history of five years of revenue

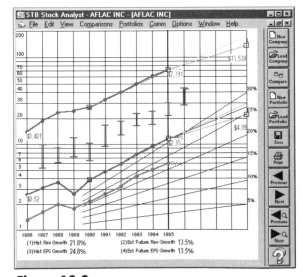

**Figure 13.2**
STB Stock Analyst

and earnings growth, it's not a candidate for investment, but a candidate for speculation. A company can be increasing its sales year after year, but unless the company can consistently demonstrate the ability to convert those revenues into profits, you have no idea of knowing if it's likely to ever figure out how to make a buck.

## Projecting Future Growth

Once you've decided that a company has grown its sales and earnings at acceptable rates, you need to determine if it can sustain that growth over the next five years. It helps if you can place where the company in its life cycle (see "Ask Doug") to determine if it can sustain future growth at a rate as high as it has in the past. When projecting future growth rates, you should keep in mind the following:

1   Rates of growth for any company typically decline over time.

2   Growth rates differ by industry and by size of company.

3   Earnings cannot grow faster than revenues over time.

Most companies are doing very well if they can increase sales and earnings at a rate of 15 percent over the long term.

**ask doug!**

**Q:** What is the life cycle of a company?

**A:** When a business begins, it requires an investment of capital to purchase supplies, equipment, and materials; to pay salaries, rent, and advertising charges; and to cover other expenses. As sales grow, those revenues are usually reinvested in purchasing more raw materials and buying more advertising, in an effort to fuel more growth. As a result, young companies often have rapid sales growth but little or no earnings. To investors, this is the speculative stage of a company's life cycle. Since the company has no proven track record, an investment made now is entirely a gamble on the company's prospects.

A company that is successful in these early days will eventually reach the break-even point, when the company begins to be profitable. If growth continues at the same rate, the company enters the explosive growth stage, the second phase in its life cycle. A company can continue to grow at a torrid rate for a number of years before its growth inevitably slows.

Next, a company enters the mature growth phase, and its growth rate settles to a figure the company can sustain over the long term. If it cannot, the company will likely enter a period of slow but steady decline. For long-term investors, the best opportunities lie in the explosive growth and mature growth stages of the company's history. Rapidly growing companies pose a problem to long-term investors, however, since they are often valued by the market on the basis of short-term trends and not long-term potential, leading to share prices that are subject to rapid drops once the company's explosive growth ends. It's important to recognize if a company is in an explosive growth stage so that you aren't overly optimistic in your future projections of that company's growth.

If the data source you're using only reports a company's Net Income After Taxes and Tax Rate, you can calculate the Pre-Tax Profit using this formula: Net Profit ÷ (1- Tax Rate) = Pre-Tax Profit.

Here are some questions you should ask about a company's past growth:

- What is the company's sales growth rate over the past five to ten years?

- What is the company's earnings growth rate over the past five to ten years?

- Have sales and earnings been increasing steadily?

- How do these growth rates compare with other companies of the same size and in the same industry group?

- Are there any years in which sales and/or earnings declined? If so, were they one-time problems, cyclical changes, or indications of potential fundamental changes in the company's business?

- Have earnings been increasing at about the same rate as sales, and not faster?

- Does the company have the potential of providing sufficient growth of both sales and earnings in the future to meet your goals?

- What is your assessment of future sales and earnings growth?

Once you have these answers, next you want to make sure that your portfolio is built upon a stable foundation.

## QUALITY

You want the companies in your portfolio to be well-managed enterprises. Besides being able to grow its sales, the company has to be able to generate sufficient profits from those sales. The company also has to be able to provide a sufficient return for its investors. Well-run companies that can consistently achieve these two goals will outperform their peers.

## Profit Margin

As discussed earlier, profits (also known as earnings or net income) are what's left after subtracting a company's expenses from its revenues. Expenses, including such items as materials, supplies, salaries, advertising, office rent, and taxes, are the costs of operating a business. One of the key measures of profitability is a company's profit margin, the percentage of each dollar of sales that's left after paying all these expenses: Profits ÷ Revenues = % Profit Margin.

As a way of evaluating a company's management expertise, this falls somewhat short, for the simple reason that a company has control of most of its expenses, with the notable exception of income taxes. The income tax rate corporations must pay on their earnings is subject to the whims and ways of politicians and is largely beyond control of the corporation itself.

Therefore, calculate the profit margin prior to taxes: Pre-Tax Profits ÷ Revenues = % Pre-Tax Profit Margin.

The Pre-Tax Profit Margin by itself doesn't tell you very much about the company. It is very important, however, as a comparative measure. You should compare a company's profit margins to others in the same industry and see which companies are most profitable. Businesses that can generate higher profits on the same amount of revenues are less susceptible to pressures from competition, the economy, or manufacturing costs. Companies with slimmer profit margins can suffer severely in the event of a price war within their industry, or if their suppliers raise the costs of the necessary raw materials. The skill of management plays a large role in a company's ability to generate higher profit margins than competitors. Ironically, very high profit margins relative to the industry norms are sometimes problematic. If a company is very profitable, it sends an invitation to other companies in its sector that there's probably plenty of room for competitive products in that company's market. Once the competition enters the fray, profit margins will likely decline. NAIC Investors Toolkit helps investors evaluate a company's pre-tax profit margins and return on equity (see Figure 13.3).

You should also evaluate a company's profitability by looking at its historical patterns over the past five to ten years. Stable, well-run companies can maintain a level of profitability over time. Declining profit margins are a warning signal that costs are rising faster than a company can pass them along in its product pricing. Obviously, if such a trend continues, the company will end up with no profits whatsoever.

It's rare for mature companies to be able to steadily increase their profit margins over time. It's hard enough to maintain margins, without trying to beat last year's numbers, so don't chalk it up as a negative because a company's pre-tax profit margins are flat. Stability is the most important factor.

Also, you will note that a company's profit margins are rarely the same from year to year. You can

Watch out for one-time charges on a company's financial statements. Some companies tend to write off losses as one-time charges in order to boost operating earnings. Extraordinary events should be just that—extraordinary. Some charges, such as those due to changes in accounting guidelines, are legitimate and unavoidable. If a company is recording such charges on a regular basis, though, it could be an indication that they are having some fundamental problems. At any rate, you should always try to understand the nature of any extraordinary income or expenses the company may report.

expect them to vary somewhat, particularly if the company is in an economically sensitive sector, but if they fluctuate widely, it may be a sign that the company's management is not doing the best job at building a stable business.

Here are some questions you should ask when evaluating a company's pre-tax profit margins:

- Has the pre-tax profit margin been stable over the past five to ten years, or is it trending downwards? Do the pre-tax profit margins fluctuate widely from year to year?

- How does the company's pre-tax profit compare with others in the industry? Is it above the industry average?

## Stockholders' Equity

The second factor in determining if a company meets your criteria for quality is whether it provides a stable rate of return on stockholders' equity.

*Stockholders' equity*, sometimes known as *owners' equity*, is the amount of capital the company has raised by issuing shares of stock. Each year a company

**Figure 13.3**
NAIC Investors Toolkit

### ask doug!

**Q:** What is a company's sustainable growth rate and how do I calculate it?

**A:** A company's sustainable growth rate (also known as the internal growth rate or implicit growth rate) is the rate of growth a company can fuel with its retained earnings without borrowing or issuing additional shares of stock to raise additional capital.

You can use a company's return on equity to calculate its sustainable growth rate like this: (Retained Earnings / Total Earnings) x % Return on Equity = % Sustainable Growth Rate.

If a company pays no dividends, reinvesting all its earnings, its retained earnings and total earnings will be exactly the same. In that case, the company's sustainable earnings growth rate will be the same as its return on equity.

As a rule of thumb, a company's sustainable growth rate is the potential limit to its future earnings growth. Over time, a company will find it difficult to increase earnings faster than it generates a return on invested capital.

earns a profit, it first pays dividends (if any), and the rest of its profits are kept and reinvested as additional capital in the business. These are known as *retained earnings* and are recorded on the company's balance sheet in the Stockholders' Equity section. The total of paid-in capital (the money raised by issuing stock) and retained earnings is total stockholders' equity, which is also known as *book value*. Book value is generally expressed on a per-share basis, calculated by dividing stockholders' equity by the number of shares outstanding.

Any investment requires a return on the original capital, and publicly traded corporations are no different. You can measure this return by dividing the amount of profits (earnings per share) the company generates each year by the equity owned by the stockholders (book value per share): Earnings Per Share ÷ Book Value Per Share = % Return on Equity.

Like the pre-tax profit margin, a company's return on equity (ROE) can vary by industry and over time. ROE is an indication of how well a company's management is using its capital to generate on the investment of its shareholders. An exceptionally well-run company will have a high, stable ROE.

Here are some questions to ask about a company's return on equity:

- Has the return on equity been stable over the past five to ten years, or is it trending downwards? Does the return on equity fluctuate widely from year to year?

- How does the company's return on equity compare with others in the industry? Is it above the industry average?

Together, the pre-tax profit margin and return on equity are two of the most important factors that should be considered when evaluating a company. Those corporations that exhibit superior results in these two areas are likely to meet your second benchmark, quality. By selecting companies that meet these criteria of quality, you can reduce risk in your portfolio.

## VALUE

The final benchmark in your quest to purchase suitable long-term stock is value. While you should aim to own a portfolio of well-run growth stocks, you have to be able to recognize when a stock is selling for a bargain price and when it's selling at a premium.

Unfortunately, stocks don't come with manufacturers' suggested retail prices, so you'll have to figure out for yourself when a stock is selling at a reasonable price and when it's too expensive.

## Determine Future Earnings Per Share

Now, you return to your estimates of how fast the company will grow in the future, with a goal of determining what the company's earnings per share will be in five years. As you study companies, you may notice that it is very common for a company to have stable revenues growth but less consistent earnings growth. There are many factors that can affect profits, but revenues are less susceptible to outside pressures.

As a result, it's a good idea to rely on your projection of a company's future sales growth and then analyze the various components that affect the bottom line to come up with an earnings estimate. This is known as *revenues-based earnings projection*, and it is the same method many analysts use when studying a company.

You can use the same technique to calculate your own earnings estimate. You'll need to define five variables for the equation, each looking five years into the future:

1  Revenues. What is your projection of the company's total revenues in five years?

2  Pre-Tax Profit Margin. Is the pre-tax profit margin stable? Is there a trend? Is there a reasonable median figure that you can select? You can use the average from the past five years or a more conservative choice, depending on the past trends.

3  Tax Rate. Taxes seem to always be increasing. Look at the tax rate for the past five years and estimate if taxes will be the same, higher, or lower in the future.

If you have a spreadsheet, you can calculate the future value of a number that's growing at a specific rate using this formula: Initial Value x [(1 + % Growth Rate) ^ Number of Years ] = Future Value. (The caret, or exponentiation sign, raises a number to the specified power.) For instance, if you wanted to know what an initial investment of $1,000 would be in five years if it grew at 15 percent annually, here's what you would do: $1,000 x (1.15 ^ 5) = $2,011.35.

4  Preferred Dividends. If the company has a class of preferred stock, the total amount of dividends that will be paid to these shareholders must be projected.

5  Number of Shares Outstanding. Has the company been issuing additional shares of stock? Or are they buying back shares, reducing the number outstanding?

Many of these variables are fairly constant over time for well-managed companies. *The Value Line Investment Survey* includes all of these figures projected five years into the future.

Now, plug all those variables into this series of equations: Revenues x Pre-Tax Profit Margin = Pre-Tax Profit. Then, Pre-Tax Profit x (1 - Tax Rate) = Net Profit. And finally (Net Profit - Preferred Dividends) ÷ Number of Shares Outstanding = Earnings Per Share.

For an example of a spreadsheet that can calculate future earnings based on projected revenues (ftp://better-investing.org/pub/bits-reprints/preferrd.xls), see Figure 13.4.

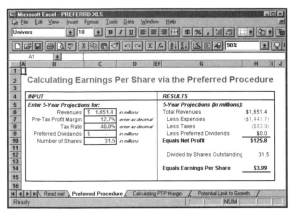

**Figure 13.4**
Calculating Earnings Per Share

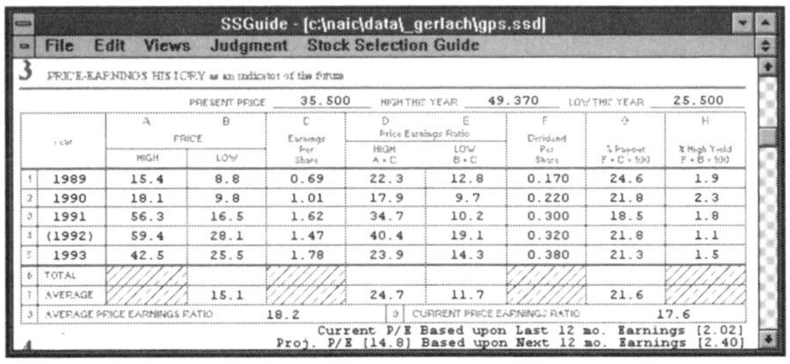

**Figure 13.5**
Price/earnings history

## Estimate Future High Price

To estimate the future high price of a stock, you need to understand *Price/Earnings Ratios*. The P/E ratio is a relative measure, comparing a stock's price to its earnings. It's often described as how much investors pay for each dollar of a company's earnings. P/E ratios can be used to compare a stock's current price with its historical prices to give you an indication of how the stock is valued today compared to the past. You can also compare the P/E ratio of a stock to other stocks in its industry, or to the market in general, or an industry average.

As you evaluate a company's history, you can see that prices vary throughout the year, and earnings have grown. You can determine how investors have valued the company and its growth by calculating high and low P/E ratios for each year, using the high and low prices and earnings per share for the year.

NAIC Investor's Toolkit lets users evaluate a company's price/earnings history for trends and indications of the stock's future potential (see Figure 13.5).

It may be helpful to think of the stock's P/E ratios as a proxy for its price, year by year. As the company's earnings grow, so, too, should its price, and

investor sentiment and the laws of supply and demand will cause the price to fluctuate.

Calculate the average of the high P/E ratios from the past five years—just add them together and divide by five. Examine any trends of the high P/E ratios from the recent past and compare them to the five-year average. Now, ask yourself: what is the highest P/E ratio the stock is likely to sell for in the next five years? Is it the average P/E ratio, or should this figure be adjusted?

Just as revenues and earnings growth slows with time, a stock's P/E ratio is likely to slow as well. Most companies would be hard-pressed to support a P/E ratio of between 20 and 25 over the long term, even with growth rates in excess of 15 percent. Be conservative in your judgment.

Now that you have determined the stock's likely high P/E ratio and earnings per share, multiply the two numbers. The result is a projected high price for the next five years.

## Determine Potential Low Earnings Per Share

In order to determine the down-side potential for your investment in the next five years, you need to figure out what the company's lowest possible earnings might be in five years. Of course, the company could earn nothing or even have a loss, but you don't need to concern yourself with predicting catastrophic events. If the company has been growing consistently in the past, it's probably a safe assumption that earnings will never drop below the earnings of the most recent year, or the most recent four quarters. If you're feeling conservative, you should designate the latest annual earnings per share as the potential low earnings per share of the next five years.

NAIC Investor's Toolkit helps project future high and low prices for a stock, as well as compare the potential risk and reward of the investment (see Figure 13.6).

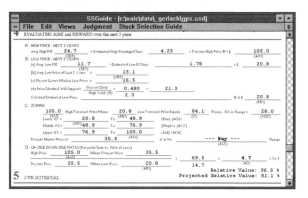

**Figure 13.6**
Evaluated risk and reward

## Estimate Potential Low Price

Estimating a potential low price for the next five years can be done in the same manner as calculating the future high price, by multiplying the estimated low EPS by the average low P/E ratio that the stock has sold for in the past. Again, you may need to adjust the average low P/E ratio to account for any variations in the past and the overall tendency for a company's growth to slow.

NAIC's SSG provides several additional choices for future low price, though the technique described above works well in most cases. Since you are predicting the potential down-side of your investment, you should check that your future low price is somewhere between 10 and 30 percent below the current price. The stock's past price volatility and current growth rate should be considered in making your low price decision.

## Is the Stock a Good Value?

There are two tests that can help you decide if a stock is a good value.

The first is determining if there is enough reward to justify purchasing this stock at its current price.

With your future high and low prices in hand, subtract the low price from the high price and divide the difference by three. Then, add this number to the low price to create the buy zone. If the estimated future low price is $20 and the estimated future high price is $80, then the zoning would look like this:

$80 - $20 = $60 range

$60 ÷ 3 = $20 1/3 of range

Buy zone: $20 to $40

Maybe zone: $40 to $60

Sell zone: $60 to $80

If the current price falls within this zone, the stock meets the first criterion of having three times more up-side potential than down-side potential. In this example, if the current price is $30, there is the potential down-side risk of the stock falling to $20, a $10 loss, but the potential gain of $50 if the stock reaches $80.

The second test is determining if the current P/E ratio is reasonable in light of the historical P/E ratios of the stock. Add together your average high and low P/E ratios and then divide them by 2 to calculate the average P/E ratio of the past five years. Now, divide the current P/E ratio by the average P/E ratio. The resulting figure, usually displayed as a percentage, is the stock's relative value. If the relative value is less than 100 percent (that is, the stock's current P/E ratio is below the historical average) then the stock meets your second test of value.

It is acceptable in some cases to purchase a stock with a relative value of up to 115 percent. If a stock's relative value is any higher, the stock is overvalued by the market.

## Is the Stock a Good Investment?

For dividend-paying stocks, the dividend can provide an extra boost to your investment return and should also be considered.

One of the biggest advantages of using your computer in your investment analysis is that software programs make short work of complicated calculations such as total return (see Figure 13.7). NAIC Investors Toolkit determines the annual return that an investment will provide based on your choice of a future high price and the expected dividend yield. A 15 percent annual return will allow you to reach your goal of doubling your investment every five years.

Before you make your final decision to purchase a stock, here are some key questions to ask about its value:

- Are your estimated future high and low prices reasonable and conservative? Have you adjusted the average high and low P/E ratios to reflect lowered expectations in the future?

- Does this stock provide a likely up-side that is three times the potential down-side?

- Is the stock's relative value less than 110 percent?

- Will the stock provide an average annual total return of 15 percent over the next five years? Can you expect the stock price to double in that time?

By following the three benchmarks of growth, quality, and value, you can successfully invest in common stocks and watch your portfolio grow. As you become more experienced, you can learn more about a company by reading its financial statements, and apply these principles to the information you discover in those documents.

**Figure 13.7**
NAIC Investors Toolkit calculates total return.

## GLOSSARY

DATA—Current or historical numerical information about a company. Data can be obtained from financial statements or from other research sources.

EARNINGS PER SHARE—The amount of a company's profits divided by the number of outstanding shares.

INCOME—A company's earnings. Can be expressed as net income or net income before taxes.

OUTLIER—A point that falls outside a trend and is considered irrelevant.

PRE-TAX PROFIT—The amount of a company's income after all expenses have been paid but before taxes.

RELATIVE VALUE—The measure of a stock's current P/E ratio divided by its historical average P/E ratio.

REVENUES—Also known as sales. The total amount received by a company in return for goods or services sold.

STOCKHOLDERS' EQUITY—The capital originally invested by shareholders in a company, plus all earnings reinvested in the business.

TOTAL RETURN—The amount earned on an investment from all sources, including dividends and price appreciation.

# Chapter 14

# Understanding Financial Statements and Annual Reports

*"The way to stop financial joy-riding is to arrest the chauffeur, not the automobile."*

**-Woodrow Wilson**

**Individuals are often** frightened away from investing at the thought of trying to understand financial statements. In order to become a truly successful investor, however, you will need to learn to navigate the basics of financial statements, annual reports, and some other "official" documents you'll encounter along the way. It's really not so difficult to understand some of the most fundamental concepts and ratios that can be used in your analysis of a publicly traded company.

# ANNUAL REPORTS

The annual report is usually the most substantial information shareholders receive each year from a company. These reports are prepared in order to give shareholders and others who have an interest in the firm an accounting of the company's operations and results in the past year. Current shareholders receive the company's annual report as a matter of practice, and others can request a copy by contacting the company, by phone, fax, e-mail, or by letter.

Reviewing a company's annual report is an essential part of the process of researching a company as a potential investment. Annual reports are created with the general public in mind, so they generally provide a good overview of the company's business, products, and services. This is especially helpful if a company is involved in a sector such as technology or industrial manufacturing, where you can't evaluate their products firsthand by taking a trip to the shopping mall or grocery store.

Annual reports have several components. They usually begin with a letter to shareholders from the corporation's management, from its president, chief executive officer, or chairman of the board. Here, the company's top executives have a chance to summarize the highlights of the firm's performance in the past year, bragging about their accomplishments

> *the*
> **swami speaks**
>
> More and more companies now publish editions of their annual reports on their Web sites, in Acrobat or HTML format. The Swami says this can be a quick and convenient way to get a copy of an annual report, so be sure to check the company's Web site to see if they make theirs available. At the very least, most corporations provide a link to e-mail their Investor Relations staff to request a copy of the annual report.

all the while. A forthright company will also address the low points of the year, if any, and tell shareholders what's being done to correct or improve any problems encountered in the year.

Next, the report will provide a review of the company's operations. In most annual reports, this section may look at a company by product lines or corporate divisions and will look at the company's performance in a bit more detail. The company will describe new products launched during the year, outline new plans and goals, and discuss their strategies for success. Companies often provide graphs, pie charts, and other illustrations of financial operations, and this section may make up the largest part of an annual report.

The third part of an annual report is the financial review. Often, this section is printed in small type on less expensive paper than the rest of the report, but the information provided here is usually the most important feature of an annual report.

The financial section includes a report from the company's independent auditors. Publicly traded companies hire an outside auditor to verify that the company has followed accepted accounting

Annual reports are usually a product of a company's public relations machine, so they are elegantly designed, printed in glorious color on glossy paper, and lavishly illustrated with graphs and photographs. The purpose of many annual reports is to reassure shareholders and potential shareholders that the company is a stable and worthwhile investment—not necessarily to clearly present a company's financial position.

 Want a copy of a company's annual report? All you have to do is ask for it. Corporations print enormous quantities of their annual reports for shareholders and prospective shareholders, and reports are sent automatically to all stockholders. If you're considering the purchase of a company's stock, a telephone call to the company's Investor Relations office is all it takes to get your own copy.

principles and procedures. If the auditor's letter is longer than two or three paragraphs, it could be an indication that the company's practices are in question. Read this letter carefully and note any qualifications made by the auditors.

Annual reports are also required to include management's discussion and analysis of the financial statements. These narratives describe the significant financial developments of the year, offering broad explanations and comparisons with prior years. Here a company can explain why their sales or earnings were less than impressive or how a new acquisition is affecting a company's profitability. Management's discussion and analysis statements are often dense reading, but they provide very important information for investors. You can gloss over the photos and pretty charts in the beginning of an annual report, but slow down when you get to this statement and read it thoroughly.

### Public Register's Annual Report Service
**http://www.prars.com**

Public Register's Annual Report Service (PRARS) is an annual report service that can provide you with annual reports, prospectuses, or 10Ks on over 3,200

public companies, at no charge. Simply select your choice of reports from their Web site, and PRARS promises to ship your reports within 24 hours.

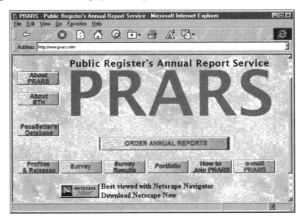

Annual reports also provide a section of investor information, such as the company's address and telephone numbers, corporate investor relations contacts, exchanges on which the company's stock is listed, dividend payment schedule, dividend reinvestment plan information if the company offers one, time and location of the next annual meeting, and the names and affiliations of the company's board of directors.

Many annual reports also include a multiyear financial summary that can be very helpful to the

You may notice lots of graphs in annual reports with arrows and trend lines pointing in an upward direction, designed to indicate at a glance how admirably the company has performed. Before you become too impressed, however, consider that companies seldom (if ever) include graphs of the opposite nature, with downward arrows and declining trends. Companies want to highlight the positive qualities and de-emphasize the negative aspects of their operations, particularly in their annual reports.

long-term investor. These summaries often present ten years of data: sales, expenses, taxes, earnings, dividends, stock prices, and more.

The real "meat" of an annual report, however, is in the financial statement itself. Reports include several different financial statements, each providing a different snapshot of the company:

- Income Statement

- Balance Sheet

- Cash Flow Statement

While reading and understanding financial statements can be a daunting task at first, you don't need to be an MBA to be able to interpret them. Also accompanying the financial statements are a number of explanatory notes that are often very illuminating.

In this next section, we'll take a closer look at some of the more important information you can glean from financial statements.

# FINANCIAL STATEMENTS

If you want the truth about a subject, you should always go directly to the source. The financial statements of a publicly traded corporation are the source of most of the undeniable truths about that company and its business.

Unfortunately, for most investors financial statements might as well be written in Sanskrit. This aversion to financial statements is somewhat ironic, considering how much emphasis investors place on a few financial figures and ratios, such as a stock's price, earnings per share, and price/earnings ratios.

Imagine if you woke up one morning and the newspapers had replaced the price/earnings ratio in their stock tables with debt/capital ratios or return on equity. It might take a short while to adjust to the change, but soon enough everyone would be looking at companies and their valuations in new ways.

Don't ignore financial statements. Take the time to read them and learn a few key ratios, and you'll eventually learn to identify and appreciate well-managed corporations. That can only lead to better returns in your portfolio.

## INCOME STATEMENT

Every company is in operation for one reason—to make a profit. The Income Statement reports the company's profits (or losses) for a period and outlines how they were attained.

The equation for determining a company's profits is easy: Revenues - expenses = profits. The Income Statement expands upon this equation by providing some additional details of expenses and income. Table 14.1 shows how most income statements are laid out.

**Table 14.1**
Income statement for year ended December 31 (In $ millions, except earnings per share)

|  | 1994 | 1995 | 1996 |
| --- | --- | --- | --- |
| Revenues | $4,649 | $5,737 | $8,471 |
| Operating Expenses: |  |  |  |
| Cost of Goods Sold | 759 | 802 | 1,125 |
| Research and Development | 612 | 787 | 1,364 |
| Sales and Marketing | 1,386 | 1,835 | 2,579 |
| General and Administrative | 166 | 275 | 325 |
| Total Operating Expenses | 2,923 | 3,899 | 5,593 |
| Operating Income | 1,726 | 2,028 | 3,058 |
| Interest Income | 50 | 201 | 340 |
| Nonrecurring Items | (38) | (50) | 0 |
| Other Expenses | (16) | (12) | (19) |
| Income Before Income Taxes | 1,722 | 2,167 | 3,379 |
| Provision for Income Taxes | 612 | 722 | 1,218 |
| Net Income Available: for Shareholders | $1,110 | $1,445 | $2,161 |
| Weighted Average Shares Outstanding | 1,312 | 1,284 | 1,292 |
| Earnings Per Share | $0.85 | $1.13 | $1.67 |

Here's an explanation of the items in the table.

- Revenues: The Company reports its total revenues, or sales, from the operation of its business.

- Operating expenses: The company reports its expenses. First, the company reports the Cost of Goods Sold (the actual expenses related to manufacturing the products that the company sold). Some statements subtract the Cost of Goods Sold from Revenues, thereby calculating the Gross Margin (or Gross Profit).

- Next, some other expenses are summarized, such as Sales and Marketing expenses; Research and Development expenses; and General and Administrative expenses. Sometimes the last three of these expense categories are combined into a single Selling, General and Administrative expense line. These are the costs of doing business.

- Operating Income: Subtract all of the company's Operating Expenses from its Revenues to determine its Operating Income.

- Non-Operating Items: Corporations typically have other sources of income and expenses that are reported next. Interest expense and income is most common, but there could be other nonrecurring income or expenses that are included here. Usually these figures are relatively minor.

- Income Before Income Taxes: After adding and subtracting the non-operating items, the income statement reports Income Before Income Taxes.

- Income Taxes: Sometimes a company will report a Provision for Income Taxes, the money they have designated for the payment of corporate taxes but may or may not have actually paid yet.

- Net Income: Subtract Income Taxes from Income Before Income Taxes to determine the company's Net Income. This is the company's total profits for the period.

- Preferred Dividends: If a company has a class of preferred stock, it may pay Preferred Dividends. This expense is listed next.

- Net Income Available for Common Stockholders: If a company doesn't pay Preferred Dividends, this figure will be the same as the Net Income reported above.

- Average Shares Outstanding: The company reports the average number of shares of common stock that were outstanding during the period.

- Net Income Per Share: Divide the Net Income by the number of Average Shares Outstanding, and the resulting figure is the company's Net Income Per Share, more commonly known as Earnings Per Share (EPS). This is the amount of profit relative to each share of stock that the company has issued and is outstanding.

There can be other entries on the Income Statement, such as one-time adjustments for accounting changes or restructuring charges. Also, companies in different industries, particularly financial companies such as banks, insurance companies, and real estate investment trusts, often include other specific items of information on their statements.

As you can see, by stepping through the Income Statement, you can get a good idea of how and where a company is making money. But in and of themselves, the numbers on the Income Statement mean very little. Fortunately, Income Statements are typically presented with two or three years of results to help you make short-term comparisons. If a company's earnings per share have been flat compared to the prior year, you can look at a number of items on the Income Statement to see if you can figure out the problem. Have Revenues increased, or were they flat

**ask doug!**

**Q:** What's *dilution?*

**A:** Some companies issue convertible securities, such as warrants, that give the owners rights to convert those securities into shares of common stock in the company after a particular period of time or under specific circumstances. Many companies issue stock options to employees and directors, which also can be converted into shares of stock depending on pre-set criteria.

A company's Earnings Per Share is determined by the number of shares of stock that are currently outstanding, representing each stockholder's share of the company's profits. These are often referred to as primary earnings per share. A problem arises, however, if the owners of all of the options or warrants exercised their rights and converted those securities into shares of stock. Suddenly, there are that many more stockholders, but the same amount of profits to be spread around. That means the Earnings Per Share figure would be reduced, or *diluted.*

To represent the dilution that might occur with the addition of these shares, companies report a separate line on their Income Statement: Net Income Per Common Share—Fully Diluted, which will be a few pennies less than Net Income Per Common Share—Primary.

Watch out for the impact of dilution, since it's a quick way to reduce your ownership stake in a public company. It's more conservative and probably best to use diluted Earnings Per Share in your stock analysis.

The phrase *the bottom line* comes from the income statement. The bottom line is a business's profits, the net income figure on the last line of the income statement.

Financial statements for publicly traded companies are presented in accordance with Generally Accepted Accounting Principles (GAAP), guidelines that try to ensure that a company's financial position is presented clearly and fairly. Even so, the terminology and layout of financial statements from different companies can be strikingly different. It can take some practice to understand financial statements and learn to understand the concepts behind the numbers.

as well? Slowing sales can be a serious problem, since, in the long run, you have to be able to increase sales in order to increase profits.

Did any of the Operating Expenses or Costs of Goods Sold increase significantly? Increased raw material costs could have impacted profits, which might have long-term implications. The roll out of a new product could have led to increased sales and marketing expenses, potentially just a short-term situation.

Was there a one-time expense or adjustment due to an accounting change? Chances are this might not be indicative of any fundamental problem with the company.

## BALANCE SHEET

The Balance Sheet contains three parts: a statement of a company's Assets, a statement of a company's Liabilities, and a statement of Stockholders' Equity.

The Balance Sheet provides indications that a company is in good financial health. There are a number of tests and comparisons you can make in order to determine how strong a company is. The basic equation outlined on the Balance Sheet is this: Assets = Liabilities + Stockholders' Equity. That's why the statement is called a Balance Sheet—the total of liabilities and stockholders' equity "balances" the value of the company's assets.

Let's take a look at how a Balance Sheet is organized. Balance sheets are organized so the most liquid items are listed first. Subsequently, items are listed in order of decreasing liquidity. See Table 14.2 for a balance sheet example.

## Assets

A company's Assets are detailed first, beginning with Current Assets. Current Assets include cash and other assets that are expected to be available as cash within one year. These include, with the most liquid assets listed first:

1   Cash and Cash Equivalents: Most of us have no trouble understanding what cash is. Cash equivalents are securities, such as Treasury Bills, that can be quickly and conveniently converted to cash.

2   Accounts Receivable: These are funds that are owed by customers as of the end of the period.

3   Inventories: These are usually broken out into Finished Goods, Work in Progress, and Raw Materials, the various stages in the manufacturing process of a product. At any point in time, a company will have warehouses and factories filled with these goods and materials.

4   Other Current Assets: This item can include prepaid expenses and other assets of relatively small value.

5   Total Current Assets: This is the sum of all of the above assets.

**Table 14.2**

Balance sheet for year ended December 31 (In $ millions)

|  |  | 1995 | 1996 |
|---|---|---:|---:|
| **Assets** |  |  |  |
|  | Current Assets: |  |  |
|  | Cash and Cash Equivalents | $4,250 | $6,620 |
|  | Accounts Receivable | 581 | 639 |
|  | Inventories | 289 | 260 |
|  | Other Current Assets | 200 | 320 |
|  | Total Current Assets | 5,520 | 7,839 |
|  | Property, Plant, and Equipment | 972 | 1,021 |
|  | Accumulated Depreciation | 320 | 405 |
|  | Other Assets | 398 | 828 |
| Total Assets |  | $7,210 | $10,093 |
| **Liabilities and Stockholders' Equity** |  |  |  |
|  | Current Liabilities: |  |  |
|  | Accounts Payable | $563 | $808 |
|  | Income Taxes Payable | 410 | 484 |
|  | Current Portion of Long-Term Debt | 82 | 113 |
|  | Accrued Compensation | 130 | 202 |
|  | Unearned Revenues | 54 | 560 |
|  | Other Current Liabilities | 108 | 258 |
| Total Current Liabilities |  | 1,347 | 2,425 |
|  | Long-Term Debt | 300 | 220 |
|  | Minority Interest | 230 | 540 |
| Total Liabilities |  | 1,877 | 3,185 |
| **Stockholders' Equity** |  |  |  |
|  | Common Stock and Paid-in Capital—Shares Authorized 3,000; Shares Issued and Outstanding, 1,176 and 1,194 | 2,005 | 2,924 |
|  | Retained Earnings | 3,328 | 3,984 |
| Total Stockholders' Equity |  | 5,333 | 6,908 |
| Total Liabilities and Stockholders' Equity |  | $7,210 | $10,093 |

Financial statements can vary significantly from industry to industry. Accounting practices used in managing a real estate investment trust will be very different from a semiconductor manufacturer's. When studying financial statements, you should try to compare the figures with those of companies in the same industry group.

The next section of the Balance Sheet is called Property, Plant, and Equipment. It summarizes the value of a firm's fixed assets, those physical assets that are not likely to be converted to cash:

- Property, Plant, and Equipment, at Cost: Sometimes subtotals will be reported for Land, Buildings and Machinery, and Equipment. *At cost* means that the value of these items is determined by the prices that were paid to purchase them originally.

- Accumulated Depreciation: Fixed assets like those listed above wear out in time. Manufacturing machinery eventually becomes obsolete; delivery trucks break down and become prohibitively expensive to repair; office equipment becomes cantankerous and needs to be replaced. To reflect this change in value of fixed assets over time, companies use depreciation. If a piece of machinery has a useful life of ten years, then one-tenth of the cost of that equipment is added to the accumulated depreciation account each year. Depreciation is a non-cash expense, since no actual funds are involved in the transaction, but the depreciation account allows the determination of something approximating the *real* value of the fixed assets. There are accounting rules that govern deprecia-

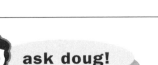

**ask doug!**

**Q:** What is *goodwill?*

**A:** Goodwill appears on financial statements as an asset when a company acquires another business for a price greater than its *book value* (the value of all its assets less liabilities). It is the difference between the acquisition price and the value of all the company's assets.

As an example, if you wanted to buy the entire Coca-Cola Company, you could figure out the value of all of their assets—the land, buildings, and equipment they own; the raw materials and inventory in the warehouses; the cash they have in the bank; and so on. Then subtract all their liabilities to determine the book value of the company. But another important asset of the Coca-Cola Company is its brand name itself. You would have to pay a premium well in excess of the value of the physical assets in order to acquire the Coca-Cola name. The premium you pay would then go on your books as an asset, known as Goodwill.

tion, and companies can use the *straight-line* method (described above) or an accelerated method, where greater amounts are deducted in earlier years.

- Other Assets: The company may include a line for Other Assets or separate lines for Goodwill and other items.

- Total Assets: The sum of all the above lines is the company's Total Assets.

## Liabilities

Next, the company lists its Liabilities. These are debts owed, funds still to be paid to suppliers, and other obligations of the corporation. Current Liabilities are listed first, those expenses that are expected to be paid within the year. You can expect to see items such as these included in the company's accounting of Current Liabilities:

- Accounts Payable: These are moneys owed to others for supplies, materials, and services.

- Income Taxes Payable: These are taxes owed but not yet paid for the past year.

- Current Portion of Long-Term Debt: This is the amount of a company's long-term debt that must be paid within a year.

- Accrued Compensation, Interest, and Expenses: Accrual is an accounting method that recognizes expenses and income when incurred or earned, rather than when actually received or disbursed. If the company owes wages to employees for work completed in the past year, it is listed here. Likewise, interest owed to the bank for short-term loans or to bondholders is included in this item.

- Dividends Payable: If the company has declared a dividend but not yet paid it to shareholders, the amount to be paid would be itemized here.

- Other Current Liabilities: The company may summarize other minor short-term liabilities here, if any.

- Total Current Liabilities: The above liabilities are added together to determine the total of the company's current obligations.

The next item to appear on the Balance Sheet is Long-Term Debt. This is money the company has borrowed but is not due to be repaid within the year. The company may also list Debentures (debts se-

Even though generally accepted accounting principles provide guidelines for the preparation of financial statements, there are still many areas subject to interpretation. Fortunately, accountants tend to be conservative when preparing statements, understating assets and income while overstating liabilities and expenses. That way, any surprises in the books will likely to turn out to be pleasant ones.

cured by the company's general credit), Non-callable Notes, and other long-term borrowings.

If a company owns less than 100 percent of any subsidiary, the outsider's share of that subsidiary will be included on the balance sheet as a liability, labeled Minority Interest. There may also be other items such as Deferred Income Taxes that are included on the Liabilities statement at this point.

The total of Long-Term Debt, Current Liabilities, and Other Liabilities is the company's Total Liabilities.

## Stockholders' Equity

Now, the company reports the equity its shareholders have invested in the corporation. This is a summary of all the funding that the company has raised by issuing stock, either preferred shares or common stock or both, as well as the profits that the company has not paid out as dividends to shareholders but has reinvested in the company's growth over the years. The Stockholders' Equity section looks something like this:

- Preferred Stock: If a company has a class of preferred stock, the value of those shares is listed first. It is determined by multiplying the number of shares outstanding by the par value of each preferred share.

**Q:** What is Par Value?

**A:** Par value is the stated face value of a security, an arbitrary figure assigned by the company. The par value of preferred stock is used to determine the annual dividend paid to preferred shareholders. Common stock typically has a par value of a few cents per share, and the par value of issued shares of common stock is used to determine the value of that stock in the company ledgers. However, the par value of common stock has little relevance for shareholders. In fact, most new companies today do not even assign a par value to their shares.

**Q:** What is Treasury Stock?

**A:** Treasury Stock is shares of the company's own stock that have been repurchased by the company. When a company initiates a stock buyback program, it buys shares on the open market, and those shares become Treasury Stock, which may be held by the company, eventually reissued, or retired. Treasury Stock is not considered when calculating the number of shares outstanding, so a stock buyback can increase a company's earnings per share. However, because the company's cash is used to reacquire its own shares, Treasury Stock reduces stockholders' equity.

- Common Stock: The company next lists the number of shares of common stock that are authorized and the number of shares that are outstanding, as well as the par value of the shares. By multiplying the par value of the shares by the number of shares outstanding, the company determines the value of those shares on its books.

- Paid-In Capital: Whenever a company issues shares of common stock to the public, as in an initial public offering, the proceeds from those sales make up the company's Paid-In Capital. Following a public offering, the value of those shares of stock as they trade in the secondary market is irrelevant to the Balance Sheet; the company has already received its influx of capital. This figure may sometimes be known as Capital Surplus, though that's not an indication that the company has too much capital!

- Retained Earnings: These are the total of all earnings the corporation has not paid to shareholders over the years but has instead reinvested in the company. Each year, as the company makes a profit, those profits rightfully belong to shareholders. Some of those profits may actually be distributed to shareholders as dividends. The bulk of the profits, however, will be retained by the company in the hopes that the company's management will reinvest the earnings to generate greater profits in the future.

- Other Items: Occasionally, the Statement of Stockholders' Equity will include items such as Foreign Currency Translation, adjustments for the exchange of foreign currencies into U.S. dollars, or the cost to acquire Treasury Stock.

The total of all of these items is Total Stockholders' Equity. Add Total Liabilities to these figures and you'll get the corporation's Total Liabilities and Total Stockholders' Equity. On every Balance Sheet, this figure exactly equals Total Assets.

## CASH FLOW STATEMENT

The third component found in a company's financial statements is the Cash Flow Statement (see Table 14.3). Sometimes known as the Statement of Changes in Financial Condition, this statement outlines the sources and uses of the company's working capital.

**Table 14.3**

Cash flow statement for year ended December 31 (In $ millions)

|  |  | 1994 | 1995 | 1996 |
|---|---|---|---|---|
| **Cash Flows from Operations** | | | | |
| | Net Income | $1,110 | $1,445 | $2,161 |
| | Depreciation and Amortization | 245 | 271 | 481 |
| | Current Liabilities | 358 | 417 | 1,088 |
| | Accounts Receivable | (149) | (94) | (75) |
| | Other Current Assets | (6) | (60) | 26 |
| | Net Cash from Operations | 1,558 | 1,979 | 3,681 |
| **Cash Flows Used for Financing** | | | | |
| | Common Stock Issued | 274 | 328 | 501 |
| | Common Stock Repurchased | (357) | (654) | (1,268) |
| | Stock Option Income Tax Benefits | 167 | 187 | 351 |
| | Net Cash From Financing | 84 | (139) | (416) |
| **Cash Flows Used for Investments** | | | | |
| | Additions to Property, Plant, and Equipment | (281) | (494) | (496) |
| | Other Assets | (68) | (233) | (627) |
| | Short-Term Investments | (867) | (653) | (1,552) |
| | Net Cash Used or Investments | (1,216) | (1,380) | (2,675) |
| Net Change in Cash and Equivalents | | 426 | 460 | 590 |
| Effect of Exchange Rates on Cash | | (10) | 9 | (5) |
| Cash and Equivalents, Beginning of Year | | 1,013 | 1,429 | 1,898 |
| Cash and Equivalents, End of Year | | 1,429 | 1,898 | 2,483 |
| Short-Term Investments | | 2,137 | 2,788 | 4,339 |
| Cash and Short-Term Investments | | $3,566 | $4,686 | $6,822 |

The Cash Flow Statement is based on cash transactions, instead of the accrual method of accounting used on the Income Statement and Balance Sheet. Cash accounting means that sales and expenses are included when they are received or disbursed, and not when they were incurred.

There are three sections to the Cash Flow Statement:

1  Operating Activities: The items in this section are the actual dollars the company received and paid during the period related to the operation of its businesses. The first item on the Cash Flow Statement is Net Income, taken directly from the Income Statement. Then, non-cash expenses or deductions such as depreciation and amortization are added back to Net Income. Remember, this is a Cash Flow Statement, so accounting items that do not represent the movement of cash on the income statement and balance sheet, such as depreciation and amortization, need to be reconciled.

All changes in assets and liabilities since the beginning of the year are also recorded here. Increases or decreases in the company's inventories, accounts receivable, accounts payable, and other assets and liabilities, to reach the total Net Cash From Operating Activities.

2  Financing activities: If the company has issued or repurchased common or preferred stock, or borrowed or repaid any debt, those amounts are recorded here. Again, this is cash flowing into the company (issuances of stock or borrowing money) or flowing out of the company (purchases of stock on the market or repaying debts).

3  Investing activities: If the company has made any acquisitions or sales of property or equipment or bought or sold any investments in the year, those amounts are recorded here. Purchases of equipment or investments represent funds moving out of the company; sales of property or investments is a cash inflow.

All of the entries on the Cash Flow Statement are now added up to determine the changes in the company's cash position during the year.

1  Increase (Decrease) during the year.

2  Cash at start of year.

3  Cash at end of year.

Cash Flow Statements typically have three years of results for comparison purposes. You should look to see if cash has been increasing or decreasing over the years.

You should also scan the statement for items that seem out of line. These can be indications that the company is experiencing problems, or that it is laying the groundwork for future growth. If the company has been buying back its stock or has invested in new equipment or property, the amount of its available cash may decline.

## UNDERSTANDING FINANCIAL STATEMENTS

The following are definitions of some key financial ratios to use when analyzing a company's financial statements. Most of these ratios are more valuable when compared to the company's historical figures, or to other companies in the same industry.

• Acid Test Ratio: (Current Assets-Current Inventory) ÷ Current Liabilities = ACID TEST RATIO. This ratio is sometimes known as the *Quick Assets Ratio* or *Quick Ratio*. Is there enough cash to meet the company's current debts? Or are too much of the company's assets tied up in inventory? This

**ask doug!**

**Q:** What is amortization?

**A:** Similar to depreciation, amortization is a non-cash expense. Businesses use amortization to account for the purchase of an intangible asset, such as a patent. Rather than showing the entire expense of a major purchase on the books in a single year, a company will write off a portion of the expense against operating income each year during the useful life of the asset.

figure should be greater than 1:1, which means more assets than liabilities. The greater the assets the better, since it means that the company has a relatively liquid position.

- Bond Ratio: Face Value of Bonds ÷ (Total Value of Bonds, Preferred & Common + Surplus + Retained Earnings) = BOND RATIO. In general, the Bond Ratio should be no greater than 25 percent. In addition, the Bond Ratio and Preferred Stock Ratio should, combined, constitute no more than half of the company's capital structure.

- Book Value: Value of Common Stock + Retained Earnings + Cash Surplus = BOOK VALUE. In and of itself, a company's book value can't tell you much. Over time, you should look to see that a company's book value is increasing. Divide this figure by the number of shares of stock outstanding to determine book value per share.

- Common Stock Ratio: (Stated Value of Common Stock + Surplus) ÷ Total Capitalization = COMMON STOCK RATIO. This is the portion of a company's capitalization represented by owners' equity. The Common Stock Ratio should be greater than 50 percent. A conservatively financed company will have a higher common stock ratio.

- Current Ratio: Current Assets ÷ Current Liabilities = CURRENT RATIO. A ratio of less than 2:1 is a danger sign, meaning the company could run short of working capital. A ratio too much in excess of 2:1 may indicate the company has too much cash and is not employing its cash to the best income-producing advantage.

- Debt/Equity Ratio: Long-Term Debt ÷ Shareholders' Equity = DEBT/EQUITY RATIO. Companies that are conservatively financed have little debt and thus a low debt/equity ratio, indicating lower risk and somewhat lower potential for large losses or large gains. A company with a high debt/equity ratio can be indicative of large losses in the past or an aggressive financing strategy. A good rule of thumb is that the debt/equity ratio should not exceed 50 percent (the company has twice as much equity as debt). Utilities can support higher debt loads because their future revenue stream is more predictable.

- Inventory Turnover: Cost of Goods Sold ÷ Average Inventory at Cost = INVENTORY TURNOVER. The higher a company's inventory turnover the better. This calculation gives you an idea how many times a company's inventory is sold and replaced in a given period. Companies with a high inventory turnover are selling products, always a good sign, and are probably producing quality merchandise and the proper pricing for their customers. A company with a low inventory turnover may be ineffectively managing its inventory, by carrying too much inventory or carrying outdated goods.

- Plant Turnover: Sales ÷ (Property, Plant & Equipment) = PLANT TURNOVER. A higher Plant Turnover figure is more favorable. Ideally, Plant

Turnover should increase over time. If the company increases its plant without a corresponding increase in sales, there may be a problem with the way that management is utilizing assets.

- Pre-Tax Profit Margin: Profit Before Taxes ÷ Net Sales = PRE-TAX PROFIT MARGIN. You should compare the company's profit margins over several years to see if there is a trend of rising or declining profitability. Profit margins vary widely by industry.

- Preferred Stock Ratio: Stated Value of Preferred Stock ÷ (Total Value of Bonds, Preferred & Common + Surplus + Retained Earnings) = PREFERRED STOCK RATIO. The Bond Ratio and Preferred Stock Ratio together should not be greater than 50 percent.

- Return on Equity: Net Income ÷ Book Value = % RETURN ON EQUITY. A company's Return on Equity should be consistent over time and higher than the return generated by others in the same industry. A company with a higher Return on Equity is likely to be led by capable management.

- Working Capital: Current Assets-Current Liabilities = WORKING CAPITAL. Is this a sufficient reserve to offset financial difficulties if business falls off? Does it allow for the company to take advantage of opportunities requiring cash? Has this figure been declining over the years?

## THE FINE PRINT

The final words on financial statements are the final words—that is, the notes that accompany the tables of numbers. No financial statement is complete without sometimes lengthy notes that provide supplementary details about the financial figures. Notes can explain how certain calculations or adjustments were made, breakdowns of revenues by region or country, and details of employee stock ownership plans.

**ask doug!**

**Q:** What is *Safe Harbor?*

**A:** The Safe Harbor for Forward-Looking Information is a regulation that protects company management and allows them to discuss a company's financial prospects and projections without fear of litigation, as long as the discussions are held in good faith. Companies invoke this act when making projections to remind investors that the information presented is just a projection.

The "Management's Discussion and Analysis" (MDA) section is a company's chance to review its operations, particularly with concern to profits; demonstrate that its debt and capital resources are sufficient; and prove that the company has enough cash flow and working capital to meet its short-term obligations.

The "Notes to Financial Statements" are every bit as important as the numbers themselves. Even though they may be printed in tiny, illegible type, you should make it a practice to always consult the notes when reviewing the financial tables.

Both the MDA and the Notes can be tedious reading, but if you discover a discrepancy in the financial statements, it may be discussed in further detail here.

## FORM 10K AND FORM 10Q

A company's annual report includes all the financial statements discussed above, but you can also retrieve the same statements from a company's Form 10K filed each year with the Securities and Exchange

Commission. Form 10K contains the company's financial statements, management's discussion and analysis, and other information about the company the SEC requires to be disclosed to shareholders.

Form 10Q is the quarterly report that companies must file. It also contains the same financial statements as the Form 10K, representing the company's position throughout the year. Companies file three Form 10Q reports each year; the final quarter is replaced by the Form 10K annual report.

The SEC's EDGAR project (http://www.sec.gov/edgarhp.htm) makes both the Form 10K and Form 10Q available for free to investors 24 hours after being received by the Commission. There are a number of other filings that companies make regularly with the IRS, such as their annual Proxy Statements, as well.

### Investorade

### http://www.dallas.net/~rajivr

If you can't stand wading through Form 10Qs and Form 10Ks to get to the bottom of the financial statements, investor Rajiv Roy has a smart utility for you. His Investorade site searches EDGAR

```
.../0000950134-96-005380.txt+INTERVOICE_INC+10-Q - Microsoft Intern...  _ □ ×
File  Edit  View  Go  Favorites  Help
Address  http://www.dfw.net/cgiwrap/rajivroy/read_rdata?764244/0000950134-96-005380.   ⇦   e

            INTERVOICE INC FORM 10-Q


                   BALANCE SHEET


PERIOD-TYPE                  6-MOS
FISCAL-YEAR-END                        FEB-28-1997
PERIOD-START                           MAR-01-1996
PERIOD-END                             AUG-31-1996
CASH                                    24,138,198
SECURITIES                                       0
RECEIVABLES                             27,615,137
ALLOWANCES                                 653,586
INVENTORY                               16,061,453
CURRENT-ASSETS                          70,123,214
PP&E                                    32,888,384
DEPRECIATION                            11,339,093
TOTAL-ASSETS                            98,372,331
CURRENT-LIABILITIES                     17,750,906
BONDS                                            0
PREFERRED-MANDATORY                              0
PREFERRED                                        0
COMMON                                       9,588
OTHER-SE                                79,898,763
TOTAL-LIABILITY-AND-EQUITY              98,372,331
```

for Form 10K and Form 10Q filings and then displays just a brief summary of the balance sheet and income statement information contained in those filings. Just enter in a company name, and the program does the rest.

The SEC requires that companies file Form 10Q within 45 days after the end of their quarter. Form 10K reports must be received by the SEC within 90 days after the end of their fiscal year. As a rule, most companies take just about that long to make their filings.

A company will send you their Form 10K and Form 10Q reports upon request, although it is certainly faster to download them from EDGAR.

## PROXY STATEMENTS

There's nothing quite like a Proxy Statement to remind you that when you own stock, you are actually one of the owners of a corporation. Once a year, a corporation's management sends a copy of their Annual Report to shareholders and a notice of the corporation's Annual Meeting. The Board of Directors also sends a request that shareholders allow the Board to vote on that shareholder's behalf at

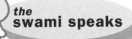

*the* **swami speaks**

The Swami says you don't have to be a shareholder to profit from Proxy Statements. Proxy Statements are among the required forms companies file electronically with the SEC's EDGAR, so they are available to every online investor from the SEC's Web site at http://www.sec.gov/edgarhp.htm.

When you search EDGAR for a company's proxy statement, look for Form Type DEF 14A, the *Definitive Proxy Statement*. This is the usual proxy statement filed by a company's management.

There are other proxy statements that are filed with the SEC, most relating to mergers and acquisitions and solicitations by those other than a company's management for control of stockholders' proxies (as in a proxy fight).

the annual meeting. As a shareholder, no matter how small your stake, your vote counts.

The SEC requires that the solicitation of a proxy by a Board of Directors be accompanied by a Proxy Statement, which outlines important information about the matters under consideration at the annual meeting. These might include the election of directors, approval of the company's independent auditors, and approval of other resolutions such as changes in the company's common or preferred stock and employee bonus plans.

In addition to summarizing the items that will be on the ballot at the annual meeting, the Proxy Statement provides additional insight into a company's management and operations. A company's Proxy Statement can be very helpful when researching a potential investment. Here are a few key questions

you should ask as you review a company's Proxy Statement.

1. How many of the directors who serve on the company's Board are outsiders? Outsiders are individuals who are unaffiliated with the company. The Board should not be weighted with current employees, professionals such as attorneys and investment bankers who receive fees from the company, or retired employees of the company.

2. What are the ages, genders, backgrounds, and length of service of the directors? What are their other Board affiliations? The Board of Directors should be balanced with individuals who bring many different skills to the boardroom. Be sure to look at the other boards on which directors sit—you may be surprised how often an invitation to sit on a board is reciprocated. Unfortunately, this may be a sign of an old boys' network at work, and that shareholders' interests may not be the first priority.

3. Do the directors and corporate officers own stock in the company? The Proxy Statement provides a summary of each director's stock ownership. Ideally, each director and corporate officer should own shares in the company—this helps to ensure that shareholders' interests are aligned with the company's management. Some investors even make it a practice to vote against any director who is not a shareholder. Not every director is in a financial position to own a significant share of stock, and new directors may need some time to accumulate a stake in the company.

4. Are the company's executives compensated too generously? The Proxy Statement outlines the compensation, including salary, bonuses, stock options, retirement plans, and other perquisites that executives receive. Executives should be

paid fairly and in proportion to other companies in the same industry or of the same size. Companies often reward their employees with bonuses when the company does well; if a company rewards employees when the company's performance is mediocre, something may be amiss. Many companies offer stock options to executives to encourage them to think like owners and not employees. A warning sign to watch out for are certain agreements that may have been made with members of senior management; sometimes these loans and deals may be a little too cozy.

5   How much and in what manner are the directors compensated? Directors receive compensation for attending Board and committee meetings, and these payments are disclosed in the Proxy Statement. Occasionally, directors receive fees that are a bit too lavish for the work involved. A new trend that many shareholders applaud is the payment of directors in company stock rather than cash. When the stock does well, the directors benefit directly.

6   How has the company's stock performed in the past five years compared to its peers? Each Proxy Statement contains a Comparison of Five Year Cumulative Total Return, a graph that compares the stock's past performance to its peer group and to a stock index such as the S&P 500. This chart will give you a good picture of the company's performance and how other similar companies have done during the period.

# GLOSSARY

ANNUAL REPORT—A corporation's annual statement of financial operations, typically a glossy, colorful publication. Annual reports include a balance sheet, income statement, auditor's report, and description of a company's operations. The Securities and Exchange Commission requires that publicly traded companies file an annual report, called a Form 10-K, with the Commission. The 10-K contains more detailed financial information than many annual reports.

BALANCE SHEET—A company's financial statement that reports its assets, liabilities, and net worth at a specific time. Liabilities always equal assets, hence the name "balance sheet."

BOARD OF DIRECTORS—A corporation's Board is elected by stockholders to oversee the management of a company.

BOOK VALUE—Usually Book Value Per Share. Calculated by dividing the Net Worth of a Company (common stock plus retained earnings) by the number of shares outstanding. This is the accounting value of a share of stock, the value of the company's assets a shareholder would theoretically receive if the company were liquidated.

CASH AND CASH EQUIVALENTS—A section of a company's balance sheet reports the value of Cash and Cash Equivalents. These are assets that are cash or can be converted into cash immediately, such as bank accounts, marketable securities and Treasury Bills.

CASH FLOW—The amount of cash a company generates during a period, calculated by adding noncash charges (such as depreciation) to net income after taxes. Cash Flow Per Share is calculated by dividing the Cash Flow by the number of outstanding shares, and is sometimes used in lieu of Earnings Per Share in analyzing a company. Cash Flow can be used as an indication of a company's financial strength.

CURRENT ASSETS—Appears on a company's balance sheet, representing cash, accounts receivable, inventory, marketable securities, prepaid expenses and other assets that can be converted to cash within one year.

CURRENT LIABILITIES—Appears on a company's balance sheet, representing amounts owed for interest, accounts payable, short-term loans, expenses incurred but unpaid, and other debts due within one year.

CURRENT RATIO—Indicator of a company's ability to pay short-term obligations, calculated by dividing current assets by current liabilities. Used to compare companies within a single industry: the higher the ratio, the more liquid the company.

DEBT FINANCING—A company can raise working capital by issuing bonds or notes to individuals or institutions, along with a promise to pay interest as well as to repay the principal. The other major way of raising capital is to issue shares of stock in a public offering.

DEBT SERVICE—The repayment of interest and principal of a debt.

DEBT/EQUITY RATIO—A measure of a company's financial leverage, calculated by dividing long-term debt by shareholders' equity. A higher debt/equity ratio generally means that a company has been aggressive in financing its growth with debt, which can result in volatile earnings as a result of the additional interest expense.

DEPRECIATION—An expense recorded regularly on a company's books to reduce the value of a long-term tangible asset. Since it is a non-cash expense, it increases free cash flow while decreasing the amount of a company's reported earnings.

DILUTION—Dilution is the effect on a company's earnings per share caused by the conversion of convertible securities or the issuance of additional shares of stock. Dilution reduces earnings per share by increasing the number of shares potentially outstanding.

EQUITY—On the balance sheet, the value of the funds contributed by the owners (the stockholders) plus the retained earnings (or losses). The balance sheet may list Owners' Equity or Shareholders' Equity.

INCOME STATEMENT—A company's financial statement summarizing revenues and expenses in a specific period, also known as a profit and loss statement.

INVENTORY—Included on a company's balance sheet. Inventory can be raw materials, items already available for sale or in the process of being manufactured.

INVENTORY TURNOVER—The ratio of annual sales to inventory. Low turnover may indicate excess inventory or poor sale—not a good sign.

LIABILITY—The legal obligation to pay a debt. Current liabilities are debts payable within twelve months; long-term liabilities are debts payable over a period of more than twelve months.

LONG-TERM ASSETS—On the balance sheet, the value of a company's property, equipment, and other capital assets, less depreciation. These are usually recorded "at cost" and so do not necessarily reflect the market value of the assets.

LONG-TERM DEBT—Loans with obligations of over one year on which interest is paid.

LONG-TERM DEBT/CAPITALIZATION—A ratio that indicates a company's financial leverage. It is calculated by dividing long-term debt by the capital available to the company (the sum of long-term debt, preferred stock and stockholders' equity).

LONG-TERM LIABILITIES—A company's liabilities for leases, bond repayments, and other items due in more than one year.

NET INCOME—The company's total earnings, reflecting revenues adjusted for costs of doing business, depreciation, interest, taxes, and other expenses.

OPERATING EXPENSES—The day-to-day costs of running a business.

OPERATING INCOME—The profit realized from a business's operations.

OTHER CURRENT ASSETS—A balance sheet item. The value of non-cash assets, such as prepaid expenses and accounts receivable, due within one year.

OTHER LONG-TERM LIABILITIES—A balance sheet item. Value of leases, future employee benefits, deferred taxes and other obligations not requiring interest payments that must be paid over a period of more than one year.

PAR VALUE—A dollar amount assigned to a security when first issued. For stocks, par is usually a small dollar amount that bears no relationship to the security's market price.

PREFERRED STOCK—A class of ownership in a corporation with a stated dividend that must be paid before dividends to common stockholders. Preferred shareholders have a claim, prior to common stockholders, on earnings and assets in the event of liquidation. Preferred stock does not usually have voting rights.

PRICE-TO-CASH-FLOW RATIO—Calculated by dividing a stock's Price per share by its Cash Flow per share, to determine the market's expectation of a company's financial liquidity.

PRICE-TO-SALES RATIO—Calculated by dividing a stock's current Price by its Revenues per share. Another technique for finding a stock's valuation relative to its own past performance, other companies or the market itself.

PROSPECTUS—A formal written statement that discloses the terms of a public offering of a security or a mutual fund. The prospectus is required to divulge particular essential information to investors about the proposed offering.

PROXY—A formal document signed by a shareholder to authorize another shareholder, or commonly the company's management, to vote the holder's shares at the annual meeting. The Proxy Statement discloses important information about issues to be discussed at an annual meeting, as well as information about closely held shares.

QUICK RATIO—Calculated by subtracting inventories from current assets, then dividing by current liabilities. The Quick Ratio is an indicator of a company's financial strength. Also known as the Acid Test.

RETAINED EARNINGS—Earnings not paid out in dividends but retained by the company to be reinvested in its core business or to pay debt.

RETURN ON ASSETS—Abbreviated ROA. Calculated by dividing a company's annual earnings by its total assets, displayed as a percentage. Useful to indicate how profitable a company is relative to its total assets.

RETURN ON EQUITY—Abbreviated ROE. Calculated by dividing a company's annual income by its Book Value (or its earnings per share by book value per share), displayed as a percentage. A measure of a company's profitability.

TOTAL DEBT TO TOTAL ASSETS—Calculated by adding short-term and long-term debt, then dividing by a company's total assets. Used to measure a company's financial risk, determining how much of the company's assets have been financed by debt.

# Chapter 15

# Finding Stocks to Study

*"Any player unaware of the fool in the market probably is the fool in the market."*

**-Warren Buffett**

**With over 8,000** publicly traded stocks in the United States, finding the right stocks for your portfolio can be a daunting task. But now that know something about what to look for, how do you find stocks that will help you meet your goals? There are dozens of ways you can get ideas for investing.

## IDEAS FROM THE MEDIA

Entire television networks, such as CNBC and CN-Nfn, are devoted to covering the world of finance. Newspapers like *The Wall Street Journal, Barron's,* and *Investor's Business Daily* provide in-depth news and analysis of stocks, mutual funds, and bonds, as well as the people and companies behind the scene.

### Investment Wizard
### http://www.ozsoft.com

Investment Wizard is a subscription service that tracks stock recommendations made in the media and by Wall Street analysts. Each day, their database is updated with hundreds of fresh opinions and new recommendations about stocks and mutual funds. Just enter a company's ticker symbol in the database and you can access their complete digest of Wall Street opinions for that stock. The service is just $5 a month, a reasonable alternative to reading dozens of periodicals and publications yourself each month.

Newsstands are filled with business, personal finance and investment magazines, including *Money, Individual Investor, Worth, Kiplinger's Personal Finance, Your Money, Fortune, BusinessWeek,* and *Forbes.* All of these publications cover the markets and can be a good source of ideas. NAIC's monthly magazine, *Better Investing,* and their Computer Group's journal, *Better Investing BITS,* are also excellent places to find long-term growth stocks to study.

All these resources have Web sites you can explore, too.

## IDEAS FROM PERSONAL OBSERVATION

Peter Lynch, in his book *Beating the Street,* advocates using what you already know to become a better investor. As you shop for groceries, what new products are flying off the shelves or offer a big improvement over their competitors? What stores or restaurants in your town always have a full parking lot? With a little research, you can find out if any of these companies are publicly owned and if their stocks are worth studying.

## FROM AN ADVISORY SERVICE OR NEWSLETTER

There are hundreds of publishers of stock and mutual fund newsletters who will gladly sell you a subscription to their daily, weekly, or monthly tomes. Many of these services focus on a specific sector of the market, such as low-cost stocks, tech stocks, "special situations," growth stocks, value stock, a particular mutual fund family, or options. Often these newsletters maintain a constantly updated portfolio of recommendations that they expect subscribers to follow exactly, and others present just present stock picks and commentary from which readers pick and choose.

*The Value Line Investment Survey* is a popular source of data for many investors, but their recommended portfolios are the core of their approach

**ask doug!**

**Q:** Is *The Value Line Investment Survey* available on the Internet anywhere?

**A:** Unfortunately, *Value Line* is not available anywhere on the World Wide Web. It is, however, available on CompuServe in the Publications Online area (if you have a CompuServe account, you can GO PUBONLINE to reach this area). Individual *Value Line* company reports are available for downloading in Adobe Acrobat format for $5 apiece.

and advice. These newsletters often sell for a premium price, since they are intended to eliminate the need for subscribers to do their research and simply invest in the stocks or portfolios as they are recommended. The Internet has been a hotbed for the growth of these kinds of services and newsletters, and many advisories are now distributed exclusively online.

## IDEAS FROM FRIENDS, RELATIVES, AND COWORKERS

This doesn't mean you have to buy every stock that your brother-in-law tells you is going to go through the roof. If you have friends who are interested in the stock market and you understand the approach they use in investing, it can't hurt to do some research on their suggestions. This is one of the advantages of investment clubs. A dozen people meet once a month, bringing together their collective observations and ideas to shared with their fellow club members.

## STOCK SCREENING

Another more methodical technique for finding stocks for study is through screening. Screening is the process of sifting through the universe of stocks, eliminating those that do not fit the user's pre-defined criteria. The goal is to create a manageable group of stocks for further study.

Screening is made possible only by the use of a computer, since it would be very difficult to manually sort through the data on thousands of stocks to find those that fit a particular set of criteria.

One of the simplest screens that can be built is a list of companies in a particular industry or sector. To build a listing of all companies who make semiconductor chips, you'd begin with a list of all stocks, and then eliminate all companies who don't make chips.

The next step might be to take this list of chip manufacturers and eliminate all those who didn't make a profit last year. Then you could scratch off companies who have too much debt, and so on, until you ended up with a list of 10 or 15 stocks that you can research more fully.

There are a number of software programs available for stock screening. Besides the program itself, all require an additional data set in order to be used. The Internet also is home to a few screening programs, as well as to sources of data that are often more frequently updated than data delivered on disk or CD-ROM.

The process of screening a database can be broken down into two steps:

1  Identify your goals. What kinds of stocks are you looking for? Are you looking for undervalued stocks, growth stocks, income stocks? You should also determine what is unacceptable. For instance, you may wish to avoid stocks that have too much debt or are too small.

One thing to remember about screening is that its end result is not a list of stocks to buy. Screening simply reduces the universe of stocks to a more manageable number. Often, stocks will meet your criteria but will still not be suitable candidates for investing for other reasons.

 Avoid choosing criteria for your screens that have the effect of canceling out each other. For instance, if you are screening for growth stocks, you shouldn't require a high dividend yield. Companies that are growing rapidly often use cash for expansion and don't pay high dividends.

**2**  Select your criteria. Once you know your goals, you can begin the process of determining the exact criteria upon which you can build your screen. Do this step by step, pausing along the way if possible. If you pre-screen after defining each criterion, you'll ensure that you don't build a screen that returns zero results, forcing you to debug a list of seven or eight variables. Begin with your most definite specifications and move on to those items that are more flexible.

There are screening programs available on the Web and for your personal computer that enable you to screen for stocks that meet a particular set of fundamentals.

## RESEARCH: MAGAZINE'S INVESTORNET

For free rudimentary stock and fund screening, check out *Research:* magazine's InvestorNet's Web site at (http://www.researchmag.com/investor.htm). They offer 11 basic criteria on which investors can build a screen. When results are displayed, you can access more information about those companies, as well. The *Research:* site requires users to register, and some reports are only available by subscription, but stock and a separate funds screening program is free.

Using some of the criteria we've outlined in earlier chapters about stock selection, we can walk through the process of screening using *Research:* magazine's service.

The first criterion available is Current Price. You can select variables between $0 and $100 as the minimum and maximum share prices of the stocks in the screen. For the most part, a stock's price in itself is not relevant to its value. However, low-priced stocks (penny stocks) generally do not have the five-year operating histories that demonstrate if the company can successfully maintain growth over the long term. Also, penny stocks are among the most volatile investments and don't fit our long-term buy-and-hold strategy. Therefore, you can eliminate stocks selling for less than $5 a share from the screen, setting the maximum price to be greater than $100: **Current Price between $5 and >$100**.

The second criterion that *Research:* provides is Price/Earnings Ratio. By itself, the P/E Ratio tells us only a little about a stock. The market itself, as measured by both the Dow Jones Industrial Average and the S&P 500 Index, currently has a P/E Ratio of around 20.

Stocks with a P/E Ratio greater than this average are likely to be companies that are growing much faster than the market in general. Since these companies will probably not be able to sustain that growth over the long term, their P/E Ratios are likely to decline towards the market's average.

Our goal is to find stocks that are undervalued by the market, so we can expect these stocks to have lower P/E Ratios. However, we must recognize that a technology stock with a P/E Ratio of 25 might be undervalued, while a bank stock with the same P/E might be overvalued. A stock's P/E Ratio must be compared to the others in its industry group. As a general rule of thumb, then, we'll limit our universe to stocks with a P/E Ratio of between 10 and 25: **Price/Earnings (P/E) Ratio from 10 to 25**.

*Research:* then provides a choice to screen companies by Current Dividend Yield. If we were looking for income stocks, we could set a goal for our desired rate of return. Since we're not concerned with income stocks, and we see dividends as a nice bonus but not essential to our portfolio, we'll exclude this option.

Market Capitalization is the next field available to us. Market Cap is used to measure a company's size as determined by the market. It is figured by multiplying the number of shares outstanding times the share price. By eliminating stocks that sell for less than $5 from our criteria, we have already excluded many of the very small companies that probably aren't suitable for our goals. We might also exclude companies with Market Caps less than, say, $50 million from our screen, since these companies are also less likely to have long-term track records. For the maximum Market Cap, we can plug in some enormous number such as $50 billion since most large caps have a proven operating history (good or bad): **Market Capitalization that is between ($mil) 50 and 50000**.

The next option is to screen companies by Return on Equity. If you recall, Return on Equity is a measure of how well the company has provided a return on the capital invested in the business, both the shareholders' original capital and its retained earnings. It is most useful when compared among companies in the same industry group, so we'll ignore the option for now.

An item called Average Analyst Opinion is next on the list. This is a measure of the Buy/Hold/Sell consensus opinions of Wall Street analysts who follow the stock. *Research:* uses a method they call Average Qualitative Opinion (AQO) to assign a numerical rating to consensus estimates.

For our purposes, companies that have weak analyst support may have problems serious enough to warrant staying away. On Wall Street, a Hold rating is often a euphemism for Sell, since analysts are hesitant to put out a completely negative rating. We can be sure that most of the analysts who follow a company are positive about its prospects: **Average Analyst Opinion (AQO) from Buy/Hold to Strong Buy**.

The next item on the *Research:* list has to do with the price appreciation of the stock in the past five years. Since our goal is to double our money every five years, it's reasonable to expect that stocks we purchase have proved to provide this return in the past: **(Where) $10K invested five years ago is now worth at least ($000) 20**.

Having set our growth criteria, we can add some other measures. *Research:* allows us to screen companies based on their institutional ownership. We will eliminate companies with "too much" institutional ownership, as well as companies with too little: **Institutional Ownership less than or equal to 50 percent and greater than or equal to 15 percent**.

Finally, we'll add a criterion to make sure that the companies we're looking at are financially sound. One of the key balance sheet ratios we can use for this test is the Debt to Equity Ratio. While we don't mind if companies borrow money to fund their expansion needs, we want to make sure they don't have too much debt. Too much debt can be a drag on a company's earnings, and we'd like to see companies with a Debt to Equity Ratio of less than 50 percent (see Figure 15.1): **Debt/Equity Ratio between 0 percent and 50 percent (range low 10 to 100 high)**.

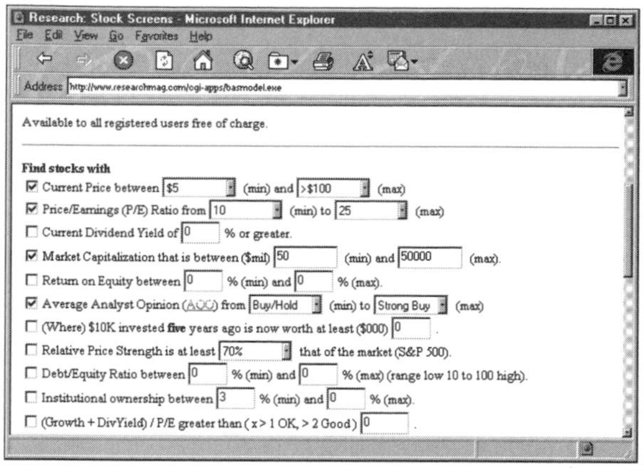

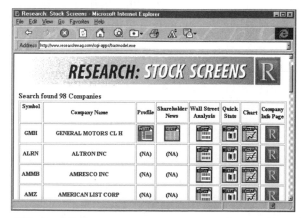

**Figure 15.1**
*Research:* screening criteria

The last two items on the criteria list, Relative Price Strength and (Growth + DivYield) / P/E, are of less importance to our initial goal, so we'll leave them for now. If our initial search returns too many companies, we can always fine tune our criteria with some of these options, reducing our pool of stocks to a more manageable number.

Submitting these criteria resulted in 98 companies being screened (see Figure 15.2). From the results, we can click to get a price chart, quick stats, and other reports.

## MARKETGUIDE STOCKQUEST

MarketGuide is a provider of data on the Web (http://www.marketguide.com). They also provide a screening program for Windows called StockQuest that can be downloaded free from their Web site. The software is a lite version of their full-powered MarketGuide for Windows software used by financial professionals.

StockQuest works with data files that can be purchased and downloaded from MarketGuide's site. Data for over 8,000 companies is included in the StockQuest database, and the program can screen these companies on 50 separate, pre-defined variables. Results can be displayed on screen or exported to a spreadsheet format.

We can start by entering some of the same parameters as we used in our *Research:* screen:

- Price greater than or equal to $5.

- P/E Ratio between 10 and 25.

As criteria are entered in the program (see Figure 15.3), the software displays the number of matches in the right column, giving us an indication of how quickly we're whittling down the universe of stocks.

Next, instead of using Market Capitalization, however, we'll use Total Annual Sales. Since Market

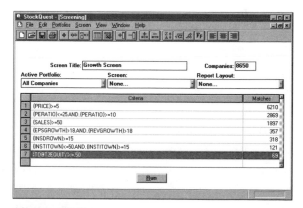

**Figure 15.2**
*Research:* screening results

**Figure 15.3**
StockQuest screening criteria

> **ask doug!**
>
> **Q:** I've been warned to watch out if institutions own too much of a stock. But how much institutional ownership is too much?
>
> **A:** It's a good sign when institutions such as mutual funds and large pension plans own shares of stock in a company. Institutional ownership generally means that there are analysts who cover the stock and that the stock will be on the radar screen of Wall Street. This awareness generally helps the stock to be noticed by other investors. On the other hand, too much institutional ownership is not necessarily a good thing. Institutions buy and sell in large blocks, and they are notorious for dumping a stock at the first sign of trouble, regardless of the size or scope of the problem. This can drive the price down drastically.
>
> The answer to your question varies from investor to investor. Some use rigid guidelines and others say, "I can't tell you how much is too much, but I know it when I see it." Companies should have a healthy mix of owners, including institutions, insiders, and individuals. As a very general rule of thumb, if institutions own more than 50 percent or 60 percent of the outstanding shares of stock in a company, it might be a warning sign.

Cap is dependent on a company's stock price and the overall market's perception of the stock's future performance, it can be an unreliable indicator of a company's size. If investors are overly optimistic about a small company's potential, they may bid up the price, giving the stock a Market Cap out of proportion to its real size. A better indicator of a company's size is Annual Sales, so we'll use that as our criterion:

- Sales greater than $50 million.

Next, since growth is our main objective, we'll set criteria for Revenues and Earnings Per Share growth. StockQuest provides a three-year historical growth rate for Revenues and EPS, and we'll set both to eliminate companies that haven't grown 18 percent annually during that time frame. This is a little above our goal of a 15 percent return.

- Revenues Growth and EPS Growth greater than 18 percent.

We can use the same criterion for institutional ownership that we used on the *Research:* site:

- Institutional Ownership less than or equal to 50 percent and greater than or equal to 15 percent.

We can also learn from insiders who own stock in their companies. It's a positive indicator when a company's management, officers, directors, and employees own shares of their stock. This ensures that the people running the company have shareholders' interests in mind, since they themselves are shareholders. We'll set the criterion to require a certain level of insider ownership:

- Insider Ownership is greater than or equal to 15 percent.

Since we still have over 100 companies that have passed our screen so far, we need to keep working. As with *Research:*, we can use the Debt/Equity Ratio to narrow the field:

- Total Debt/Equity Ratio less than or equal to .5.

Finally, we've narrowed the field to 69 companies. While we probably can't study all the companies individually, we can run further screens on this group or browse the results and see what looks most interesting to study. StockQuest allows the results to be displayed and sorted according to customized criteria (see Figure 15.4).

## STB PROSPECTOR

STB Prospector is a screening program for Windows (see Figure 15.5) sold by the NAIC (http://www.better-investing.org). The NAIC database includes 3,500 companies, all with five-year operating histories. Prospector is a way of panning for gold in this data set. The program allows screening on 60 preset variables.

We can begin by using the same basic criteria used in StockQuest:

- Price greater than or equal to $5.

- P/E Ratio between 10 and 25.

- Sales greater than $50 million.

Prospector allows us to screen on both five- and ten-year historical earnings per share and revenues growth rates, so we'll make sure that companies can support a long-term growth rate of 15 percent or better for both their sales and earnings.

- Five-year and ten-year revenues growth greater than 18 percent.

One of the most important aspects of screening is the timeliness of the data. Screening a database that's several months old is unlikely to give you any current insights, except to tell you what you should have bought a long time ago. In this regard, the online data sources may have an advantage, assuming their database is updated regularly.

- Five-year and ten-year earnings per share growth greater than 18 percent.

Another field unique to Prospector is Relative Value. This is the current P/E Ratio divided by the average P/E Ratio of the past five years. Ideally, stocks we purchase should have a Relative Value of less than 100 percent, indicating they are on the low side of their historical range:

- Relative Value less than 100 percent.

Finally, we'll narrow the field by only including companies with relatively low debt:

- Debt/Equity Ratio less than 50 percent.

We have eliminated all but 73 companies, which can now be displayed (Figure 15.6). Prospector also allows the results to be sorted by any of the criteria,

| TICKER | NAME | Current Price | P/E Excluding Xord Items | TTM Sales $ | 3 Yr. EPS Growth Rate% | 3 Yr. Sales Growth Rate% | Insider Ownership Percent | Institutional Percent Held | Qt Tot. De Tot. E. |
|--------|------|---------------|--------------------------|-------------|------------------------|--------------------------|---------------------------|----------------------------|--------------------|
| HLD | Harolds Stores Inc. | 14.125 | 24.27 | 100.792 | 31.14 | 24.14 | 77.91 | 26.34 | |
| HELX | Helix Technology Corp. | 27.750 | 11.13 | 139.909 | 90.78 | 34.50 | 33.01 | 37.06 | |
| HUMCF | Hummingbird Communicatio | 31.375 | 19.75 | 69.948 | 306.94 | 113.41 | 46.98 | 44.57 | |
| IECE | IEC Electronics Corp. | 7.000 | 20.17 | 172.792 | 189.22 | 43.52 | 25.59 | 45.35 | |
| INVX | Innovex Inc. | 28.375 | 15.67 | 69.570 | 103.19 | 41.50 | 25.46 | 36.38 | |
| IDTI | Integrated Device Tech. | 8.813 | 13.54 | 611.822 | 152.22 | 42.21 | 24.01 | 29.10 | |
| LIBHA | Liberty Homes, Inc. | 13.375 | 10.60 | 170.130 | 69.74 | 35.09 | 48.84 | 25.54 | |
| MAXS | Maxwell Shoe Company In | 7.500 | 11.18 | 108.001 | 68.40 | 26.48 | 48.51 | 40.59 | |
| MU | Micron Technology, Inc. | 31.250 | 11.38 | 3,653.800 | 74.55 | 64.00 | 40.00 | 21.53 | |
| MODI | Modine Manufacturing Co. | 24.250 | 12.13 | 999.723 | 21.81 | 20.17 | 43.06 | 35.94 | |
| MOOV | Moovies Inc. | 5.625 | 18.50 | 74.826 | 63.59 | 99.34 | 35.21 | 28.84 | |
| MPAA | Motorcar Parts & Access. | 14.000 | 14.30 | 55.230 | 47.77 | 36.92 | 30.34 | 28.11 | |
| NATR | Nature's Sunshine Prod. | 19.625 | 24.44 | 240.941 | 25.40 | 26.71 | 37.94 | 37.53 | |

**Figure 15.4**
StockQuest screening results

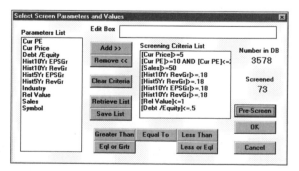

**Figure 15.5**
STB Prospector screening criteria

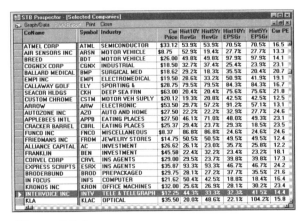

**Figure 15.6**
STB Prospector screening results

or you can create a customized weighted sort of the results.

Another nice feature of Prospector is the summary report and graph that the program displays whenever you click on a company name in the results screen (Figure 15.7). To continue with your analysis, the data files used by STB Prospector can be used with any NAIC software program, including Investor's Toolkit and STB Stock Analyst.

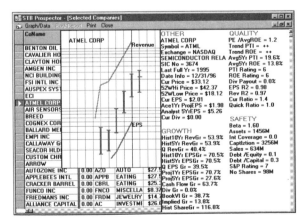

**Figure 15.7**
STB Prospector company report

# OTHER SCREENING SOFTWARE

There are other fundamental screening programs available for use both online and off. Check out the following sites.

## The American Association of Individual Investors (AAII)

### http://www.aaii.org

AAII has developed a program called Stock Investor, for Windows or DOS. Updated each quarter, the program comes with 300 predetermined variables and allows customized variables. It works with the AAII database of 6,800 stocks.

## Investors Alliance

### http://www.freequote.com

This non-profit organization offers a program called Power Investor for Windows, which can screen the Alliance's database of 11,500 stocks and 5,000 mutual funds. With your Investors Alliance membership, you can update the data daily through their online service.

## Thomson MarketEdge

### http://www.marketedge.com

This subscription-based service for investors provides company screening to subscribers. MarketEdge allows screening of 8,000 companies on variables in seven categories. Results are linked to their comprehensive company reports.

# GLOSSARY

ANALYSTS CONSENSUS ESTIMATE—Abbreviated ACE. The median estimates of a company's earnings per share growth made by approximately 2,000 Wall Street analysts from more than 150 contributing firms.

SCREENING—To search a database in an attempt to eliminate those securities that do not meet an investor's criteria.

INSIDER OWNERSHIP—Shares owned by corporate officers, directors, key employees, and others who have access to sensitive information about a company.

INSIDER SENTIMENT—Indicates whether insiders are buying or selling the company's stock.

INSTITUTIONAL OWNERSHIP—Shares owned by large non-individual investors such as insurance companies, pension funds, or mutual funds, and who can have a large impact on the market price of a security.

MARKET CAPITALIZATION—Total shares outstanding at the end of the most recent quarter multiplied by the previous week's closing price.

RELATIVE VALUE—A comparison of a stock's current Price/Earnings Ratio to its average Price/Earnings Ratio. It is a positive sign when a stock is selling for less than its historical average P/E Ratio.

# Chapter 16

# Building a Portfolio

"We seem to be on firm ground in repeating the
old aphorisms that in speculation **when** to buy
and sell is more important than **what** to buy, and
also that almost by mathematical law more
speculators must lose than can profit."

**—Benjamin Graham and David Dodd**

**Once you develop** your skills at picking individual stocks, you need to begin building your portfolio. Simply buying lots of stocks isn't enough—you need to lay out your portfolio so it provides the maximum rewards at minimal risks. There are a few guidelines you should follow in creating a balanced, diversified, and profitable portfolio of common stocks.

> There are intangible benefits in becoming a successful independent investor. Not to sound like a self-help guru, but isn't there value in taking control of your own financial future beyond the dollar returns in your portfolio? Don't you become enriched by proving to yourself that you can keep up with the pros on Wall Street, or sharing the gift of your successful investing with your friends and family members? If you apply the principles of investing to other parts of your life, you may reap rewards far beyond a profitable portfolio.

## DON'T TRY TO MAKE MONEY FAST

Of all the qualities you need to be a successful investor, one of the most important is *patience.* If you invest with a five-to-ten-year horizon, you may not see significant returns in your portfolio for several years. You must be prepared to invest in the market and then sit patiently while your returns compound.

NAIC's Portfolio Evaluation Review Technique (PERT), implemented in their Investors Toolkit, helps users track the progress of their holdings (see Figure 16.1). You can use this to monitor your investments, patiently.

Don't be discouraged if at first your stocks don't seem to increase in price quickly. You may recall the discussion of buy-and-hold investing in Chapter 1: most of the returns made in a five-year bull market were largely due to gains earned in just 40 trading days. Stock prices tend to move in bursts, so you need to be patient while your selected stocks sit at or around the price at which you purchased them. In time, you'll see these stock prices grow.

On the flip side of the coin, one of the biggest mistakes many investors make is *trying to make money fast.* Greed and impatience are the biggest enemies of long-term investing. If you are blinded by the prospect of "making a quick buck" in the stock market, you probably will end up like most market timers—buying high and selling low.

Investing in common stock is best suited to help you meet long-term goals. If your child is just entering high school, it's a little too late to start investing in the stock market and hope to make enough to pay tuition costs. The time to worry about college tuition is when your child is starting to walk. If you invest regularly for fifteen or more years, chances are you'll have enough equity built up in your portfolio to pay for the costs of college.

| Div. | Company | % Yld | Est EPS | EPS Qtr. End | EPS $ | EPS % Chg | Sales Mill. $ | Sales % Chg | Pre-Tax Profit Mill. $ | Pre-Tax Profit % Sales | Pre-Tax Profit % Chg | Trailing 12 Months EPS $ | Trailing 12 Months EPS % Chg | Curr. P/E | Price | RV | 5 Yr. Avg P/E Ratio Hi | Avg. | Low |
|---|---|---|---|---|---|---|---|---|---|---|---|---|---|---|---|---|---|---|---|
| 0.96 | ConAgra, Inc. | 2.3 | 2.49 | 5/96<br>5/95 | 0.71<br>0.63 | 12.7% | 5980.0<br>5816.8 | 2.8% | 214.6<br>197.5 | 3.6%<br>3.4% | 8.7% | 2.34<br>2.06 | 13.6% | 16.5 | 42.5 | 96 | 20.4 | 17.1 | 13.8 |
| 1.52 | CPC Intl | 2.3 | 3.74 | 3/96<br>3/95 | 0.82<br>0.73 | 12.3% | 2409.5<br>1955.0 | 23.2% | 204.8<br>192.0 | 8.5%<br>9.8% | 6.7% | 3.52<br>2.35 | 49.8% | 17.5 | 67.0 | 106 | 18.9 | 16.5 | 14.2 |
| 0.36 | Disney (Walt) Co. | 0.6 | 2.99 | 3/96<br>3/95 | -0.04<br>0.60 | -106.7% | 4543.0<br>2951.0 | 53.9% | -49.0<br>484.0 | -1.1%<br>16.4% | -110.1% | 1.99<br>2.42 | -17.8% | 25.1 | 57.4 | 101 | 28.9 | 24.8 | 20.7 |
| 0.32 | Gap, Inc. | 1.0 | 1.41 | 4/96<br>4/95 | 0.28<br>0.18 | 55.6% | 1113.2<br>848.7 | 31.2% | 134.8<br>82.8 | 12.1%<br>9.8% | 62.8% | 1.34<br>1.06 | 26.4% | 20.2 | 31.1 | 97 | 26.9 | 20.8 | 14.7 |
| 0.28 | McDonalds Corp | 0.6 | 2.22 | 6/96<br>6/95 | 0.59<br>0.52 | 13.5% | 2670.0<br>2467.6 | 8.2% | 452.1<br>435.1 | 16.9%<br>17.6% | 3.9% | 2.08<br>1.82 | 14.3% | 19.4 | 45.4 | 113 | 20.0 | 17.1 | 14.3 |
| 1.36 | Merck & Co. | 2.1 | 3.02 | 6/96<br>6/95 | 0.80<br>0.69 | 15.9% | 4910.0<br>4135.7 | 18.7% | 1268<br>1115 | 25.8%<br>27.0% | 13.8% | 2.90<br>2.53 | 14.6% | 19.9 | 64.6 | 101 | 24.7 | 19.7 | 14.8 |
| 0.60 | Modine Manufactrng | 2.3 | 2.49 | 6/96<br>6/95 | 0.54<br>0.52 | 3.8% | 248.5<br>239.2 | 3.9% | 23.7<br>30.3 | 9.5%<br>12.7% | -21.8% | 2.04<br>2.27 | -10.1% | 11.7 | 26.5 | 90 | 15.8 | 12.9 | 10.1 |

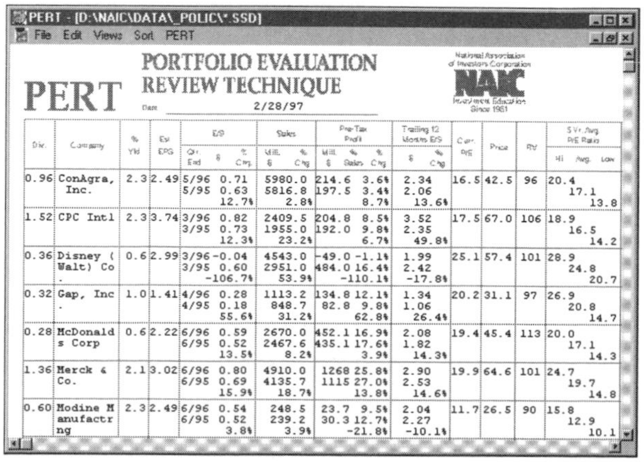

**Figure 16.1**
NAIC's Portfolio Evaluation Review Technique

# INVEST REGULARLY

While the power of compounding works magic over time, in order to meet your financial goals you'll need to invest regularly in the market. Whether you plan to invest on a set monthly schedule or not, it's important to make a commitment to add to your portfolio holdings throughout the year.

An important advantage of investment clubs is the discipline they impose on members to invest each month. Even if it's just $20 per month, you can build a portfolio worth thousands of dollars in a few years.

Some investors rely on a technique called *dollar cost averaging* to invest in a particular security on a regular basis. If you invest a set dollar amount each month in a certain stock, the number of shares you acquire with each purchase increases as the share price decreases. That means that you end up buying more shares when the stock is selling at a bargain price and only buy a few shares when the stock is "expensive." The end result is that you can benefit from the price fluctuation of your holdings.

Here's an example. Investor A buys 120 shares of stock at $10 a share on January 1st. The stock's price rises and falls during the year, but he holds on to his investment. At the end of the year, the share price has increased 15 percent, to $11.50 a share, and the investor's original holding is worth $1,380.

Investor B, on the other hand, decides to invest $1,200 during the year. Rather than invest it all in one lump sum, however, she decides to invest $100 each month in purchasing the same stock, no matter what the share price may be at the time. Table 16.1 demonstrates what happens.

Within three months of her first purchase, the share price falls nearly 14 percent. The investor

**the swami speaks**

Here's a simple navigational aid from the Swami. When you hold your mouse cursor over a link on a Web page, whether a graphic or a text link, the cursor changes from an arrow to a hand. In the status bar at the bottom of your browser, you'll see the location of the link. This can give you an idea of where you'll be headed once you click, either on the same site or to another server altogether. You must have the status bar displayed in order to see the link. Also, Internet Explorer has a *friendly URL* option that doesn't display the entire URL but a shortened version; this must be disabled if you want to see the entire URL.

sticks to her plan, and slowly the share price increases to end the year up 15 percent, at $11.50.

However, due to the price fluctuation along the way, Investor B was able to lower her average share cost and purchase more shares. Her portfolio was worth $1,429.36 at the end of the year, 3.6 percent more than Investor A's.

In this example, the low price for the year was 25 percent below the high price. However, the typical stock on the New York Stock Exchange sees its stock price change 50 percent in an average year. While dollar cost averaging isn't as effective in a steadily growing market, it's important to realize that an investor doesn't need a huge sum to get started investing.

Dividend reinvestment plans often have automatic investing plans that allow an investor to have funds withdrawn from a bank account and used to purchase shares in the DRIP account each month.

**Table 16.1**

Over time, dollar cost averaging can allow an investor to purchase more shares at a lower average price than a single lump sum investment.

| Invested Monthly ($) | Share Price | Shares Purchased | Total Shares | Total Value ($) |
|---|---|---|---|---|
| 100.00 | 10.00 | 10.00 | 10.00 | 100.00 |
| 100.00 | 9.50 | 10.53 | 20.53 | 195.00 |
| 100.00 | 9.125 | 10.96 | 31.49 | 287.30 |
| 100.00 | 8.625 | 11.59 | 43.08 | 371.56 |
| 100.00 | 8.875 | 11.27 | 54.35 | 482.33 |
| 100.00 | 9.125 | 10.96 | 65.31 | 595.92 |
| 100.00 | 9.00 | 11.11 | 76.42 | 687.75 |
| 100.00 | 9.375 | 10.67 | 87.08 | 816.41 |
| 100.00 | 10.00 | 10.00 | 97.08 | 970.84 |
| 100.00 | 10.50 | 9.52 | 106.61 | 1,119.38 |
| 100.00 | 11.125 | 8.99 | 115.60 | 1,286.01 |
| 100.00 | 11.50 | 8.70 | 124.29 | 1,429.36 |

# AIM TO DOUBLE YOUR MONEY EVERY FIVE YEARS

If you can outpace the market by just a bit and generate an average annual return of 14.87 percent on your portfolio over time, you can double your investment every five years. Usually, this figure is rounded to 15 percent for convenience.

While you should aim for an average 15 percent annual total return on the securities in your portfolio, that doesn't mean every stock you own must provide a 15 percent return. You may decide to invest in a blue chip stock and accept a slightly lower rate of return in order to add quality and safety to your portfolio. To balance that decision, you might purchase a faster growing stock with the potential to exceed your goals.

# EXPECT TO BE RIGHT 80 PERCENT OF THE TIME

NAIC's Thomas E. O'Hara and Kenneth S. Janke, Sr. describe a portfolio management theory, the Rule of Five, in their book, *Starting and Running a Profitable Investment Club.* Put simply, the Rule of Five states that, in the long term, one of every five stocks you purchase will greatly exceed your expectations; three will perform just about as well as you projected; and one stock will turn in a lousy performance.

Put another way, if you are a studious and careful investor, you will probably be right 80 percent of the time.

The problem, though, is that you'll be wrong 20 percent of the time. Chances are that the outperformer in your portfolio will more than make up for the laggard, but you need to acknowledge that you will make mistakes along the way. Expect to be

**Up** Don't be too discouraged if your portfolio's return doesn't seem to meet your goals, especially if you're just starting out. In time, you will get better at picking stocks and managing your portfolio. You'll also become better equipped to recognize opportunities as they arise, taking advantage of bargains in the market. Experience will bring greater success, so make sure you have a long-term time frame for your investment education as well as for your portfolio!

**Down** Different data sources, such as *Value Line*, MarketGuide, Standard & Poor's, and Dow Jones & Company, all use slightly different industry sectors. Diversification is more of an art than a science, so don't get hung up when one source lists a company in Communications Services and another categorizes the same company as part of the Technology group. As long as your portfolio is exposed to stocks in a variety of different businesses, your diversification plan should remain unchanged.

wrong with one in every five stock purchases you make, and be prepared to deal with the disappointments. Chapter 17 will offer some advice on dealing with the underperformers in your portfolio.

## DIVERSIFY BY INDUSTRY

Diversification reduces risk. If you invest in a single stock, your return depends solely on that security. If the stock does well, your portfolio will prosper. If that security flops, your return will be severely affected. Putting all your eggs in one basket, so to speak, increases your risk to intolerable levels. Likewise, if you invest solely in technology stocks, your portfolio would suffer in the event of a major downturn that affected all companies in that industry. MarketGuide provides a directory of companies arranged by market sector to help you diversify (see Figure 16.2).

The answer is to build a portfolio that includes stocks from many different industries. This will help minimize the impact of problems that affect a particular sector of the market or economy. For example, NAIC Personal Record Keeper allows users to

generate a report of the industry diversification of a portfolio (see Figure 16.3).

One of the problems of successful stock picking is that one stock could appreciate so quickly that it becomes an overwhelming part of you portfolio. Diversification is a lot like shooting at a moving target—you achieve what you see to be the optimal mix of industries and your next purchase has the potential to upset the balance completely.

You should hold stocks from at least six separate industries, though there are no hard and fast rules

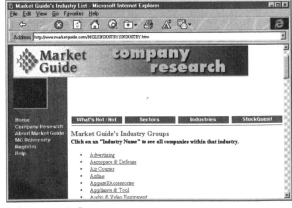

**Figure 16.2**
MarketGuide provides a directory of companies arranged by market sector.

| INDUSTRY | SYMBOL | COST BASIS | MARKET VALUE | % OF STOCKS | UNREALIZED G/L | % G/L |
|---|---|---|---|---|---|---|
| **CONSUMER GOODS, CYCLICAL** | | | | | | |
| 2 | OLS | 38.76 | 37.50 | 6.69 | -1.26 | -3.2 |
| 1 | RBD | 26.13 | 24.63 | 4.39 | -1.51 | -5.7 |
| | | 64.89 | 62.13 | 11.08 | -2.77 | -4.2 |
| **CONSUMER GOODS, NON-CYCLICAL** | | | | | | |
| 1 | HCCC | 45.13 | 41.63 | 7.42 | -3.51 | -7.7 |
| | | 45.13 | 41.63 | 7.42 | -3.51 | -7.7 |
| **FINANCIAL** | | | | | | |
| 1 | WRE | 16.00 | 17.75 | 3.17 | 1.75 | 10.9 |
| | | 16.00 | 17.75 | 3.17 | 1.75 | 10.9 |
| **INDUSTRIAL** | | | | | | |
| 1 | NDSN | 55.00 | 61.25 | 10.92 | 6.25 | 11.3 |
| 1 | TRN | 29.88 | 32.63 | 5.82 | 2.75 | 9.1 |
| | | 84.88 | 93.88 | 16.74 | 9.00 | 10.6 |

STOCK INDUSTRY DIVERSIFICATION

Abbreviated report.
Select Print/File for full report.

[ Print / File ]  [ Cancel ]  [ Help ]

Date range:
All dates

**Figure 16.3**
NAIC Personal Record Keeper lets you create a report on a portfolio's diversification.

about the percentage of companies that should come from each industry group. It's reasonable to try to hold fairly even amounts of each industry group.

# DIVERSIFY BY COMPANY SIZE

Another way to diversify your portfolio is by company size. In Chapter 13, you learned about the life cycle of successful businesses and how companies see their growth rates change as they get larger.

In your portfolio, you want to include small companies that are growing rapidly, mid-sized companies that are growing moderately, and large companies that are growing slowly but surely. This strategy decreases risk by not concentrating your holdings in riskier small-cap stocks and increases returns by owning more than stalwart blue chip companies.

NAIC recommends a good mix for your portfolio: 25 percent of your holdings should be small companies, 50 percent should be mid-sized companies, and 25 percent should be large companies. For example,

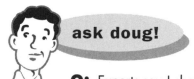

**ask doug!**

**Q:** Experts say I should diversify my portfolio with international stocks. Is that a good idea?

**A:** It's not that it's such a bad idea, but there are some important prerequisites to investing internationally. First you need to understand the impact of currency risks, political risks, and economic risks on investing in securities in a country other than the U.S. Then you should understand a foreign country's securities laws (or lack thereof), speak the language, and have access to a ready source of news and data about the company, its industry, and its competitors. If you can do all that, your next step should be to get a job as an analyst with a mutual fund company.

For most investors, investing in stocks from other countries is probably not a good idea, for all of the reasons outlined above. This is one time that a good mutual fund may be your best option. You can also look for U.S. companies who derive significant revenues from overseas markets. Both these options give you the chance to participate in global expansion while minimizing your risk.

NAIC Personal Record Keeper allows users to generate a report of the diversification of a portfolio by the size of the companies owned (see Figure 16.4).

Use a company's revenues, not its market capitalization, to determine its size. Market cap (share price times number of outstanding shares) is a representation of other investors' opinions of what a stock might be worth, and other investors are often wrong. By measuring a company by its revenues,

```
□ Size.txt - WordPad                                    _□×
File Edit View Insert Format Help

                              COMMON STOCKS DIVERSIFICATION REPORT
                                    DIVERSIFICATION BY SIZE
=====================================================================
                                        MARKET    % OF     % OF
SIZE        ISSUE              COST      VALUE     SIZE     STOCKS

SMALL
    1       Novellus Systems   52.63    89.25     72.63    15.92
    1       Washington REIT    16.00    17.75     14.45     3.17
    1       Woodhead Industries 12.88   15.88     12.92     2.83
                              -------   ------    ------   ------
                               81.51   122.88    100.00    21.91

MEDIUM
    1       Century Telephone  29.13    30.63     12.21     5.46
    1       HealthCare COMPARE 45.13    41.63     16.59     7.42
    1       Linear Technology  34.13    47.25     18.83     8.43
    1       Nordson Corp.      55.00    61.25     24.41    10.92
    2       Olsten Corporation 38.76    37.50     14.95     6.69
    1       Trinity Industries 29.88    32.63     13.00     5.82
                              -------   ------    ------   ------
                              232.03   250.88    100.00    44.74

LARGE
    1       Cisco Systems      19.50    64.88     34.69    11.57
    1       Microsoft Corp     41.25    97.50     52.14    17.39
    1       Rubbermaid         26.13    24.63     13.17     4.39
```

**Figure 16.4**

NAIC Personal Record Keeper diversification report by size of the companies owned

Some investors wonder about the recommendation to invest solely in a portfolio of common stocks and whether other assets should be included. The reason that diversified portfolio of common stocks works so well for long-term investors is that studies show that since 1950 there has been no ten-year period in which stock investors would have seen a negative return. Annual returns fluctuate widely, but those who hold on reap the long-term benefit from the long-term upward trend of the market.

you eliminate the subjectivity inherent in the market cap calculation. Most investors consider a mid-sized stock to have between $500 million in sales and $5 billion. (Since it seldom hurts to state the obvious, small companies would have revenues of less than $500 million, and large companies would have more than $5 billion in revenues.)

# DON'T OWN TOO MANY STOCKS

Owning too many stocks can be detrimental to your portfolio. You shouldn't own more stocks than you can comfortably and reasonably follow. You need to be able to keep up to date on the news that affects each company in your portfolio, and you need to keep accurate records of each transaction. That requires time and effort.

You need a minimum of six stocks to diversify your portfolio reasonably well. Most investors can manage a portfolio of 12 to 15 companies without too much difficulty. Even if you can manage more than 15 stocks, your portfolio may suffer by being spread out too thinly. The more stocks you own, the greater the chance that your total return will drift towards the market averages. Since your objective is to beat the market, don't let your returns be hampered by an overly diverse portfolio.

If you have discovered a stock with plenty of potential and you think it's a good buy, consider replacing one of your holdings with the new security. By continuously challenging your existing holdings and replacing when you have found a better investment, you can upgrade the quality and increase the return of your portfolio.

NAIC's Challenge Tree (see Figure 16.5) is a form that can help you compare an existing holding to a new stock. The Challenge Tree is based on your subjective interpretation of the potential of both stocks, rather than numerical analysis.

Never let your portfolio become stagnant. Weed out the losers and replace them with fresh stocks with a better upside potential.

| | DISNEY (WALT) COMPANY | PEPSICO INC |
|---|---|---|
| Current Price | $55.00 | $29.25 |
| Estimated 5 Yr High | $106.78 | $50.32 |
| Estimated 5 Yr Low | $45.00 | $15.76 |
| Gain to 5 Yr High | 94.1% | 72.0% |
| Loss to 5 Yr Low | 18.2% | 46.1% |
| 5 Year Up/Down Ratio | 5.18 | 1.56 |
| Buy Below Price | $65.59 | $27.28 |
| Sell Above Price | $86.19 | $38.80 |
| S&P Financial rating | A | A+ |
| VL Timeliness | 3 | 3 |
| 6 to 18 Month Upside Action | | |
| Challenge Tree Date | 2/26/97 | 2/26/97 |
| Earnings Advancing | yes | yes |
| Business Cycle Upswing | no | no |
| Industry Outlook | good | good |
| Up/Down Outlook | ok | good |
| Price Appreciation Pot | poor | good |
| Technical Base Forming | perhaps | no |

**Figure 16.5**
The NAIC Challenge Tree helps identify the best replacement for an existing holding.

*the*
**swami speaks**

If you encounter a site with frames that are sized so that it's nearly impossible to read pages on the site, try re-sizing the frames yourself. The Swami says that Web developers have the option of making frames user-adjustable, so if your mouse cursor changes to a double-headed arrow as you move over a frame border, you can click and drag that border to a new position. This will allow you to create a larger area for reading pages on the site.

## GLOSSARY

DIVERSIFICATION—The holding of securities from different asset classes or industry groups in an effort to reduce risks.

INDUSTRY GROUP—A subcategory of a sector. For example, software developers are an industry group within the technology sector.

LARGE COMPANY—A company with over $5 billion in annual revenues.

MID-SIZED COMPANY—A company with more than $500 million and less than $5 billion in annual revenues.

SECTOR—A broad classification of companies according to their primary operations. Examples are industrial, consumer, technology, utilities, and energy.

SMALL COMPANY—A company with less than $500 million in annual revenues.

# Chapter 17

# Tracking Your Investments

"All you need is to look over the earnings forecasts publicly made a year ago to see how much care you need to give to those being made now for next year."

—Gerald Koeb

**Buy, sell, or hold?** That's the question investors regularly ask about their holdings. In order to figure out the answer, investors have to keep track of developments that affect the companies in their portfolios. Managing a portfolio of common stock, even with a long-term perspective, requires regular maintenance.

After analyzing the impact of a particular piece of information, investors need to know how to determine which of three actions is required: to buy more shares, to sell shares, or to hold on to what you already own.

## THE DAILY NEWS

Investors have traditionally relied on daily newspapers or television broadcasts to get the news that affects their portfolios. The problem with these methods of distribution is that they require you to find and retrieve the news yourself. If you're traveling or happen to miss a story buried in the back of the business section, you'll never know what happened that sent your stock plummeting.

Fortunately, the Internet provides several services that can help with this problem. Customized news can be delivered directly to your computer so you can get the scoop on news that affects your portfolio quickly and conveniently.

Closing Bell, from Mercury Mail (http://www.merc.com), is a popular e-mail service that delivers customized quotes and news to users. Because it uses e-mail, you never have to worry about missing a day's worth of quotes or news—each daily edition will still be delivered to your Internet mailbox. The service is free, supported by the unobtrusive ads that accompany most mailings and appear on their Web site.

Closing Bell (see Figure 17.1) offers a variety of choices to suit each user, so you can customize the service to fit your needs. You can elect to receive any

or all of their selections: the "Morning Call," which is sent shortly after the market opens, or a "Midday Update" with major news and market highlights in the afternoon. "News Alerts" are delivered throughout the day with major news about any of your stocks. The "Early Closing Bell" includes unofficial closing prices of stocks and market indices, and the "Full Closing Bell" is delivered later; it carries official prices of stocks, mutual funds, and market indices as well as news briefs and final market summary. The "Weekender" is a Saturday price report that includes your stocks' 52-week high and low prices and trailing 52-week Price/Earnings Ratios.

Closing Bell has a few more specialized reports, too. The "Internet Daily" is a summary of each day's business news related to companies in the Internet and online sector. Their "Currencies Report" follows 52 foreign currencies vs. the U.S. dollar. Three separate commodities reports follow grains, precious metals, or oil.

You can receive your customized Closing Bell portfolio in either of two ways. The standard report format includes symbol, security name, closing price, price change, and trading volume. The expanded report format replaces the security name

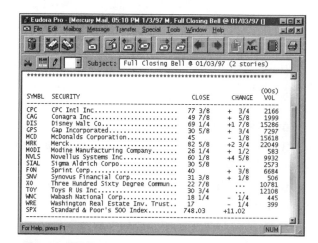

**Figure 17.1**
Daily quotes via e-mail from Closing Bell

As you track your existing holdings with one of the many portfolio tracking services online, consider setting up a watch list portfolio. Use this portfolio to follow stocks you've recently studied. If a temporary problem develops and the company's price drops, you'll know about it soon enough to review the facts and consider a purchase.

with percentage price change and daily high and low prices. You also can receive your stock price data in a file that can be imported into NAIC Personal Record Keeper, Quicken, or another program to manage your portfolio.

## NEWS SUMMARIES

Even more important than getting the quotes that Closing Bell provides are the news summaries that accompany the price information. These single paragraph briefs fill you in on the market-making news of the day. Many also have links to the full text of the news stories on Mercury Mail's Web site.

The PointCast Network (http://www.point-cast.com) is another service that delivers customizable news and other information directly to your computer over the Internet. PointCast uses a separate program that acts as a receiver for "Web broadcasts" on several "channels."

PointCast (see Figure 17.2) delivers content via a variety of channels that users can choose to include or exclude from their own Webcasts. Among the channels available are the *Cable News Network, The New York Times, The Los Angeles Times, Boston Globe, Miami Herald, Tampa Tribune, Chicago Tribune*, and *Seattle Times*.

### the swami speaks

The Swami would be pleased to interject a few comments about Point-Cast Network. Shortly after PointCast's introduction and fast ascendancy as one of the super-cool new developments on the World Wide Web, the computer technicians at some companies began to see the traffic on their Internet servers increase severely, over-taxing their resources. They soon discovered just how popular PointCast was with their employees. A large number of users, all updating their personal news simultaneously, can put an enormous strain on a company's Internet servers. PointCast later released a corporate version of their software that helps distribute the load. Small business owners may want to watch out for employees over-using the program, and even individual users should not request updates from the network too frequently.

Users can receive industry news, sports, weather, and lifestyle news, in addition to tracking their own stock holdings and receiving regularly updated quotes, news stories, and charts. A stock ticker scrolls across the screen with delayed quotes. Old news stories are retained for a period, so you never have to worry about missing an important development. The frequency of updates can be adjusted to suit each user's personal preference. PointCast is free, supported by innovative animated advertisements in the corner of the screen.

Yahoo!'s free quotes and portfolio service (http://quote.yahoo.com) allows users to set up several different portfolios of stocks and funds. A click takes

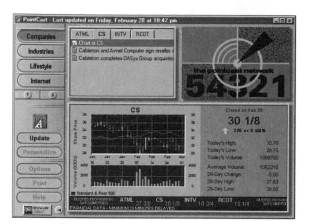

**Figure 17.2**
PointCast Network

turbulence. It could be that quarterly earnings came in a bit shy of analysts' estimates, or that the company announced it was writing off the costs of a failed venture.

As an independent investor, you need to understand how external and internal factors affect the stocks you own. You also need to be able to recognize danger signs as soon as possible. When you read important news about the stocks that you hold, here are some of the questions you should ask:

- Is there any indication this might be a problem that could affect long-term profitability?

- Is this a temporary setback likely to be resolved soon?

- Does the news offer good reason to purchase additional shares?

- Does a drop in the price of shares represent a buying opportunity for a long-term investor?

- Is there a change in management that could negatively affect the company's future? A business's leadership is key, and if a senior member of the company leaves unexpectedly, the company may have difficulty in its transition to new leadership.

you from the portfolio screen to a list of recent news stories for a particular stock. Articles are archived from the past several months, so if you miss a story in the daily news, you can still catch the scoop here.

Another personalized news service is available on the Web from NewsPage (http://www.newspage.com) from Individual, Inc. Users can set up a Personal NewsPage, as in Figure 17.3, for free on the site and receive unlimited access to headlines, briefs, and full-text stories from a collection of Basic sources. Additional subscription packages are available for access to Premium sources or Pay-Per-View resources. E-mail delivery is another option.

One drawback of the NewsPage service is that it is based on pre-defined topics you select, which include many, but not all, publicly traded corporations. Stories are usually available for a week or two, and you can search for other stories not in your Personal NewsPage.

## INTERPRETING THE NEWS

What do you do when bad news happens to good stocks? As you follow the stocks in your portfolio, undoubtedly some of them will encounter occasional

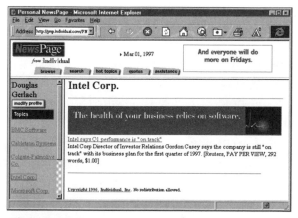

**Figure 17.3**
Personal NewsPage

The market as a whole often over-reacts to bad news. There are lots of investors, both individuals and institutions, who believe you should sell a stock at the first sign of trouble. The individual who stands his ground and understands the difference between mountains and molehills can profit by a dip in a stock's market price that results from the market's general hysteria.

 Do not become too emotionally attached to your investments. You may be proud of your great stock picking ability, but if a company has run out of steam you have to be able to objectively assess its future potential. If you are tied to the stock for reasons other than its likelihood to generate your required return in the future, you're shortchanging your portfolio.

- Is the news unrelated to a company's fundamentals? An analyst may reduce a recommendation to "outperform" from "buy" only because of an increase in price. It's not necessarily a signal that you should consider selling.

It's a good idea to use a company's quarterly earnings announcement as a trigger to update your study of its stock. Get a copy of the company's 10-Q filing with the Securities and Exchange Commission and evaluate the company's performance to see that its revenues and earnings are on track with your expectations.

# TEN REASONS TO SELL A STOCK

Knowing when to sell is almost as important as knowing when to buy. If you adhere to a long-term, buy-and-hold strategy, you will seldom be faced with worrying about selling stocks from your portfolio. However, there are some situations where it may be appropriate to consider selling a particular stock:

1   You need cash. It doesn't make sense to run up debt on your credit card and pay 18 percent or more in interest when you have securities you could sell to raise cash. Likewise, if you require funds for tuition, medical bills, or other cash needs, you should not hesitate to sell securities from your portfolio.

2   You have found an investment that will provide a greater total return. Managing a portfolio requires constant effort, so if you find an investment with a greater potential return, you should consider replacing a current holding. However, beware of the effects of taxes and commissions to ensure that your new stock is actually likely to provide a greater return.

3   You want to upgrade your portfolio. An opportunity may arise for you to replace a company you own with a better-managed company in the same industry. You should always challenge your current holdings with an eye towards improving your portfolio's overall quality as well as return.

4   You need to re-balance your portfolio. Ironically, the success of one or two of your stock picks can wreak havoc with the balance of your portfolio. A stock that has skyrocketed since your purchase can become a disproportionately large part of your overall holdings. This puts the return of your overall portfolio at the mercy of this stock's performance. Remember that diversity increases return while decreasing risk. Besides

Don't second guess your decisions to sell. Short of a crystal ball, there's no way of predicting how a stock or market will perform. It is possible to learn from your mistakes, but make sure to do your own diligent study before you make a sell decision. If you've processed all the available information at the time and determine that a sale of the security is appropriate, don't look back.

the impact that a single large holding can have on your return, a portfolio should be diversified by company size and industry sector. If your portfolio has too many large-cap stocks, or too many technology stocks, you may need to sell one of those holdings to achieve greater balance.

5   The stock is overvalued. Consider the stock's Relative Value, the comparison of its current P/E Ratio compared to its past five-year average. If the stock is currently valued at more than 150 percent of its average P/E Ratio, the stock should be considered a candidate for selling.

6   There is a change in management—for the worse. When a corporation's founder and long-time visionary retires, the succeeding management team may not have the skills and experience needed to maintain the company's presence in the market. Companies usually plan very carefully for the succession of management. If they don't, and a key member of their leadership departs, the company may flounder.

7   The company's fundamentals are deteriorating. If profit margins are declining or new competition appears on the scene or other factors conspire to reduce the company's sales and earnings, the company may be a candidate for selling. This can be a very tough call. By the time

it's clear that a company is experiencing problems that will affect its long-term profitability, and not just having temporary setbacks, the stock may have declined substantially.

8   The company's debt has increased substantially. Debt is not a bad thing. Too much debt can be a problem. If a company is borrowing for specific purposes, such as making acquisitions, that may be a good use of debt. If funds are being borrowed for other purposes and the economy slows, keeping up with the costs of a large debt load will likely stifle earnings.

9   The company is dependent on too few products or customers. Some companies become dependent on a single product or have a single customer who accounts for half or more of sales. If the company loses this customer or has problems with their sole product, their business will be severely affected.

10   You need to take a tax loss. A capital loss from the sale of securities can be used on your tax return to offset capital gains, and an additional $3,000 can be deducted from ordinary income. If you have capital gains, you may wish to sell one of the losers in your portfolio to generate an offsetting capital loss. Beware of the wash sale rule that says you can't buy back the same security for 30 days if you've sold it for a tax loss.

# TEN REASONS NOT TO SELL A STOCK

Just as there are some reasons that you should consider selling one of your holdings, there are some reasons why you should not sell a stock.

1   The stock has reached a pre-set price goal. In the first place, you probably shouldn't set price

goals for your stocks. Why not? Simply look at a long-term price chart of a quality growth stock such as Microsoft or Coca-Cola (see Figure 17.4) and you'll see one thing in common: a stock price that has continued to increase over time. Well-run companies can support the growth of their sales, earnings, and stock price for many years. Investors could have purchased stock at any time during the ascendancy of the stock price and still made a profit.

Setting a limit order to sell at any point along the way would have eliminated the chance of participating in any of the stock's future gains. (From Interactive Quote, http://www.iqc.com.)

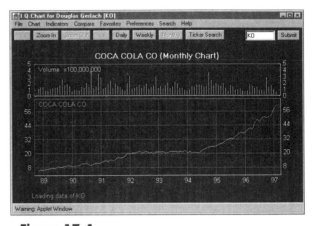

**Figure 17.4**
This chart of Coca-Cola's price over eight years shows a clear upward trend.

**ask doug!**

**Q:** What does the term *Cost of Switching* mean?

**A:** STB Stock Analyst from STB Investors Software (available from NAIC, http://www.better-investing.org) is a full-featured comprehensive fundamental analysis program. Following NAIC's precepts, Stock Analyst uses the Stock Selection Guide to study long-term growth stocks and find the best candidates for purchase.

One of the unique features of the program is a function called Cost of Switching. First, you input the value and total gain of an existing investment, its expected future rate of return, estimated capital gains taxes, and estimated commission expense. Next, enter the share price, projected rate of return, and brokerage commission of a new stock. The program calculates the number of years required before the new investment surpasses the return the original holding would have generated

had you held that stock. A graph provides a visual representation of the calculation.

It's important to realize that a replacement investment must provide a significantly higher return after taxes and fees than the current holding in order to be a more profitable holding. It's even more important that your analysis be correct. Since you must make two correct decisions (that the current holding will not perform to expectations and that the new stock will), there is twice the risk of being wrong.

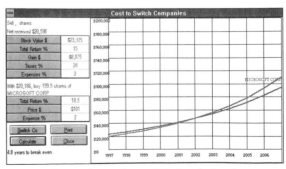

Cost of Switching, from STB Stock Analyst

**2** You want to lock-in a profit. If you sell a stock simply to preserve a profit you have made, you may end up selling all the winners in your portfolio and leaving the dogs.

**3** The stock price has declined. If you've done your research in the first place and have selected quality companies for your portfolio, this may be a chance to buy more shares. Never sell on the basis of price alone. Take the time to study the reasons behind the loss, and remember that the market is not a rational place.

**4** An analyst has downgraded the stock. The stock analysts who write research reports for brokerage firms and institutions may not share your long-term goals. Analysts often focus on the short term, so temporary problems can be overemphasized in their analysis. Also, by the time the research report reaches you, several hundred of the firm's brokers around the country have called their clients and dumped the stock, depressing the stock's price even further.

**5** The price hasn't moved. Stock prices tend to move in bursts rather than slow and steady upward climbs. You may need to hold a stock for a long time before its price increases significantly. Just keep your eye on the long-term horizon. Undertake a new analysis of the stock and determine if the company's fundamentals are still sound.

**6** The company has reported bad news. This calls for your own research and review of the company's situation, not an immediate sale of the company's stock. Find out if the bad news is likely to present a temporary setback to the company, or if the news represents some larger fundamental problems.

**7** The market is crashing. The likelihood of a major correction happening to the stock market is

 The prices of many stocks seem to be driven by how well the company can meet the consensus earnings estimates made by analysts who follow those companies. Companies who meet their estimates are rewarded, and companies who fall short are punished. Occasionally, companies who still turn in exceptional performances see their stock prices fall because the Street was hoping for an *earnings surprise*—results a few cents above the consensus estimates. These estimates drive much of the market, yet they can be hazardous to your short-term return. Be sure to keep your long-term perspective in focus.

100 percent. The only problem is that no one knows for sure when that might occur. You should be prepared for an abrupt 10 to 30 percent decline in the stock market to happen once every five to ten years. That's how the market has acted in the past 100 years. The market has recovered from every single crash or correction, and though it may take time for the market to reverse action, converting your paper losses to real losses isn't going to help. You should sit tight on your stock portfolio and wait for the inevitable upswing. No doubt, when the correction does come, you may lose some sleep thinking of your portfolio falling through the floor. History is on your side, so don't sell in a panic.

**8** Insiders are selling. Insiders such as corporate officers, directors, and employees often own shares in their own companies. There are investors who follow insider activity in order to determine if the people who ought to know best about a company's prospects are buying or selling. It's important to remember there are many reasons for insiders to sell parts of their holdings—to fund a child's education, to buy a new home, or to diversify their own personal portfolio. There is only one reason insiders buy, though–they believe that it will be a profitable decision. If there is a pattern of rampant insider selling coupled with other indicators that a company may be undergoing difficulties, a sale might be considered.

9    Out of sympathy for the problems of another stock in the same industry. Often, stocks in the same industry group move in tandem, and if one company has trouble, its peers may also be negatively affected. Unless there is a clear indication that a particular circumstance may have a sector-wide impact, don't sell.

10   You are panicking. Needless to say, if you can't think clearly enough to understand what is really happening to cause one of your stocks to fall drastically in price, then you shouldn't take any action until you do understand the situation. By

**the swami speaks**

The Swami suggests that you avoid rush hour traffic on the Internet whenever possible. Log on during off-peak hours and you'll meet with less congestion as you jump from site to site. Just remember that what may be off-peak hours where you live could be prime time in another part of the country or halfway around the world.

the time individuals can react to breaking market news, it's probably too late—the pros have already beaten you to the punch.

Remember, every time you buy a stock, someone else is selling (and vice versa). One of you is likely to be right!

## GLOSSARY

BAIL OUT—To sell a security at a loss because of expected future price declines. Often, the investor probably should *load up on* (buy more of) the stock, instead of selling.

CORRECTION—A sharp drop in the price of a security or the value of a market following a significant upward trend, and not attributable to any particular fundamental factors.

CRASH—A major decline in the securities market.

EARNINGS ANNOUNCEMENT—A company's statement of income earned in the prior quarter.

EARNINGS SURPRISE—Quarterly earnings that are greater than what analysts expected for a company. Earnings that are below the consensus estimates constitute a *negative surprise*.

INSIDER TRADING—Purchases and sales of a company's stock by employees, directors, or others close to the company. Insider transactions are regulated by the SEC.

ORDER IMBALANCE—A surplus of either buy or sell orders that makes it impossible to fill any of them. Imbalances often happen after unexpected news is announced and may trigger a trading halt.

TAX LOSS—The capital loss incurred in the sale of a security and applied to an investor's tax return against capital gains and, in some circumstances, ordinary income.

TRADING HALT—The temporary suspension of trading in a security by an exchange to give all of the members of the financial community time to hear news that is expected to affect that security's price.

# Chapter 18

# Portfolio Recordkeeping

> "Between eighteen and twenty, life is like an exchange where one buys stocks, not with money, but with actions. Most men buy nothing."
>
> —**André Malraux**

**You can't forget** the details that accompany your forays into the markets. While updating the stock prices in your portfolio can be fun, other tasks like preparing tax reports or reconciling accounts are not quite so exciting. Fortunately, there is some online and computerized help available.

# KEEPING GOOD RECORDS

Keeping records of all the transactions in your portfolio is very important, not only to the IRS, but to your heirs if something should happen to you. Good record keeping will also make your life a bit easier if you have to sell some of your holdings.

You could record all of your investment transactions on ledger paper with a pen or pencil, as in olden times, but today's personal finance software can make the task pretty painless. Coupled with resources on the Web, the task of portfolio record keeping can be quick and easy.

To start, you'll need some software. Personal finance programs such as Quicken, Managing Your Money, and Microsoft Money '97 are very popular with investors. All can track investment accounts, along with bank accounts and other asset classes. Being full-featured programs, they all handle a lot of different functions, but since they are not specifically designed for portfolio management, they may not provide the best tools for the job of tracking your portfolio. For instance, these programs won't allow you to generate reports of your stock portfolio sorted by industry group or company sizes, two important measures of diversification. Some have trouble with the concept that it is possible to own a fraction of a share of stock, even though thousands and thousands of investors do just that in dividend reinvestment programs.

There are some portfolio record keeping programs that have been built with the investor in mind. One of these, NAIC Personal Record Keeper, has many of the same features professionals need to manage clients' portfolios. But no matter what solution works best for you, here are some basic tips for keeping track of your portfolio.

1   File every document. That includes all account statements, confirmations, year-end reports, receipts, and other documents you receive in conjunction with your accounts. You should set up a filing system to keep track of all paperwork associated with all of your investment accounts. You'll need to be able to verify the purchase prices of securities when you sell them.

2   Be complete. You need to enter every transaction into your accounting system. All income and expenses should be recorded—no item is too small or insignificant.

3   Be accurate. Software can only be as accurate as you are, so enter transactions carefully. Reconcile your accounts on a regular basis, to make sure that your bookkeeping, and that of your broker or mutual fund company, is correct.

4   Don't be obsessive about updating your portfolio's share prices. Some investors waste too much time updating their portfolio quotes several times a day. For most individuals who are investing for the long haul, you can get by updating your quotes on a weekly or monthly basis.

5   Don't confuse record keeping with portfolio management. While record keeping software can be an important tool to help you record your holdings, you must constantly manage a portfolio of stocks, weeding out the losers and finding replacement stocks, determining if a price drop is a good time to purchase more shares, and making sure that the portfolio is adequately diversified.

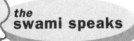

**the swami speaks**

Even the Swami's hand and wrist are prone to pain from too much pointing and clicking. That new ergonomic mouse helped a bit, but the Swami still uses some keyboard shortcuts to navigate through Web pages, giving his mouse hand some much needed rest. In Internet Explorer, use the Tab key to move from link to link (you'll see a faint outline around the link currently in focus) and press Enter to click on the link. In both Explorer and Navigator, you can press the Alt and the Left Arrow or Right Arrow key to take you back (Alt+Left Arrow) or forward (Alt+Right Arrow) one page. F5 is the Refresh key in Explorer while Control+R works in Navigator. Control+O will bring up the Open URL dialog box in either program.

## PORTFOLIO RECORD KEEPING

On the Web, the PAWWS Financial Network (http://www.pawws.com) offers a cost-basis tax-lot portfolio accounting service for subscribers and clients of affiliated online brokers. Starting at $9.95 a month, the service tracks all of your portfolio transactions and generates year-end tax reports. Much more than a portfolio tracker, this service is a full-featured online software application. Subscribers can get access to other analysis, research, quotes, and news in conjunction with their portfolios.

The National Association of Investors Corp. (NAIC) Personal Record Keeper is a Windows program developed by QUANT IX Software, a company founded by a Wisconsin money management firm. QUANT IX was born out of frustration with the software portfolio managers that were then available.

Since none fit the company's needs, they decided to build their own program. The NAIC has endorsed the program and now sells it to its membership and others (http://www.better-investing.org).

Personal Record Keeper is easy to use, but the program doesn't feature a lot of bells and whistles. The focus is on providing information.

The process of setting up the program is fairly simple:

1   Create a portfolio. You can create a single portfolio that corresponds to actual accounts (such as E*Trade brokerage or Vanguard Funds). Or create multiple portfolios using your own customized criteria (for instance, retirement account and non-retirement account). Consider what would work best for you.

2   Add assets. An asset is a stock, mutual fund, investment club, bond, cash, or other investment vehicle. Before you enter a purchase, you need to enter some details about the security, such as its name, ticker symbol, and what type of asset it is (see Figure 18.1).

3   Enter transactions. Now you can buy and sell the assets in a portfolio. Personal Record Keeper

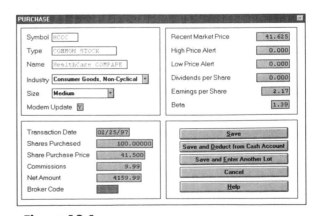

**Figure 18.1**
NAIC Personal Record Keeper transaction entry screen

provides straightforward transaction entry screens. You can set alert prices to help you keep tabs on your holdings (see Figure 18.2).

**4** Create reports. Once you've entered some transactions, you can generate reports. Personal Record Keeper's real strength is in its reports—call them professional-strength reports. The program can generate annualized performance reports, as well as reports of time-weighted performance returns using linked rates of return, a procedure that generates a more accurate return calculation.

To maintain your portfolio, Personal Record Keeper can import quotes from several online sources, including Closing Bell from Mercury Mail.

## DOWNLOADING AND IMPORTING QUOTES

A popular use of the World Wide Web is to get quotes to update a portfolio. Some programs, such as Quicken, can automatically get free quotes from the Internet at any time and update the prices in your portfolios. Other software programs allow us-

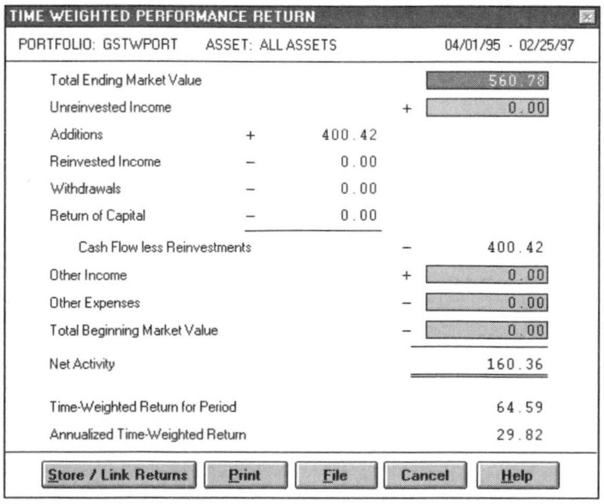

**Figure 18.2**
NAIC Personal Record Keeper performance report

ers to import securities quotes contained in text files. In addition, there are special quotes retrieval and conversion programs that can grab stock and fund quotes online and save them to files in a variety of formats (see Chapter 2). You could then import those quotes into your software or spreadsheet.

When you start dealing with quotes files, you'll have to learn some strange new acronyms and abbreviations. You may come across the term *ASCII text file*. ASCII is pronounced ask-key, and it stands for American Standard Code for Information Interchange. ASCII is the standard character set and text format used in DOS, and ASCII text files are often referred to as *plain text* files. ASCII files can be read on every kind of computer and in every word processing program. Many database programs offer the capability to convert data to and from ASCII files.

A quote to be imported contains at least three different fields: Date, Ticker Symbol, and Price. Other fields could be added, such as Daily High, Daily Low, or Volume. In order to separate these fields, a special character called a *delimiter* is used, commonly a comma or a tab character, with each quote on a different line. Data files that use commas to delimit the fields are called Comma Separated Value (CSV) files.

Occasionally, fields in ASCII files are surrounded by quotation marks. Most programs can interpret files with or without those characters. The list below shows some of the variations of CSV quotes files that are commonly used, with varying fields (ticker, date, high price, low price, closing price, and volume). The next time you open an ASCII file that looks like this, you ought to be able to figure out what it means:

- "XYZ","50.25","01/10/97"

- XYZ,50.25,01/10/97

- "XYZ","52.75","49.75","50.25","2132400","01/10/1997"

- XYZ,52.75,49.75,50.25,2132400,01/10/1997

On the Web, Yahoo! Quotes (http://quote.yahoo.com) provides a free portfolio tracking feature that enables you to download your portfolio's quotes in spreadsheet format. This is actually a CSV file, and it can be imported into many personal finance programs to update their quotes.

Closing Bell, from Mercury Mail (http://www.merc.com), delivers customized quotes and news to users via e-mail. The service gives users the option of receiving stock price data in either Quicken (see Figure 18.3) or Lotus/Excel format, as either an attached file or an appended file. Some e-mail programs support attachments, where files sent to you arrive intact on your computer.

Other e-mail software, and particularly the software used by some commercial online services, can't handle attached files. For these users, Closing Bell provides an appended format, where the data is sent at the bottom of the body of the e-mail message. To use the data in an appended message, simply select all the data with your mouse, copy it, and paste into a text editor (such as Windows Notepad). Save the text file to your hard drive in order to create a data file that can be imported into your financial software.

Personal Stock Monitor, a shareware program for Windows developed by Anatoly Ivasyuk (http://www.clark.net/pub/aivasyuk/psm), can receive quotes from any number of free quote servers on the Internet. Besides providing price updates at any schedule you set, the program can export data (see Figure 18.4) in a number of formats that you can use in other programs.

# TAX CONSIDERATIONS

Hopefully, your investments will prove to be profitable. Of course, where there are profits, the Internal Revenue Service is ready to participate in the sharing of your wealth. In addition to the tax liabilities you incur as part of your investments, you also have the chance to deduct some investment-related expenses from your tax return.

As with any tax-related issue, there's no replacement for discussing these matters with your tax preparer or accountant. Each individual's situation is different, and the advice of a qualified professional is very important in interpreting the tax code for your particular circumstances. There may have been changes in the tax code, as well.

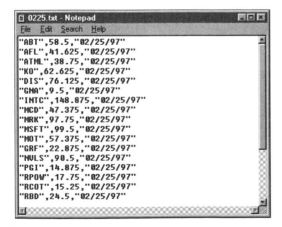

**Figure 18.3**
Closing Bell attached file in Quicken format

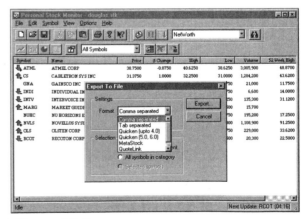

**Figure 18.4**
Personal Stock Monitor

*the*
**swami speaks**

The Swami wants you to remember that you can and should add many of the sites in this book to your browser's Favorites list. When you add a site to your list of Favorites in Internet Explorer, you have the option of naming the page as it will appear in your Favorites list. Some Web pages have titles that make sense in the scheme of their site, but standing alone amidst all your bookmarks, they may not make sense. In Navigator, you can only change the name of a bookmark after it's been added to the list, by selecting Go to Bookmarks from the Bookmarks menu, highlighting the item, and selecting Properties from the Item menu.

Once you begin investing, you should be prepared to give up the thought of filing your taxes on Form 1040EZ. If you receive capital gains distributions or dividends, or have a capital loss or gain, then you must use Form 1040 or Form 1040A.

## CHECKLIST OF ALLOWABLE INVESTMENT EXPENSES

In Publication 17, the IRS says, "You can deduct investment fees, custodial fees, trust administration fees, and other expenses you paid for managing your investments that produce taxable income."

These expenses that you incur in managing your investments are deductible as miscellaneous itemized deductions on Schedule A of Form 1040, subject to the 2 percent adjusted gross income (AGI) floor. That means you can only claim the amount of all your miscellaneous expenses that are greater than

2 percent of your AGI. In order to deduct these expenses, you must file an itemized return.

The following are some of the more common expenses that are generally allowable:

- Safety deposit box rental
- Subscriptions to investment services, publications, and newsletters (including books like this one)
- Computer software for investing
- Fees paid to set up or administer an IRA, if paid separately from a regular IRA contribution
- Accounting fees for keeping records of investment income
- Salary of a bookkeeper, secretary, or other employee hired to keep track of your investment income
- Investment management fees, except when related to tax-exempt securities
- Travel expenses of trips away from home to look after your investments or confer with an accountant or other investment adviser about producing income
- Legal expenses related to investment activities

The following are expressly non-deductible investing expenses:

- Trips to investigate a potential rental property
- Costs of attending a convention, seminar, or other meeting that deals with investment
- Costs of attending an annual stockholders' meeting
- Brokerage commissions (these increase an investor's basis and decrease their gain)
- Home office expenses, unless investing constitutes a business

The IRS has ruled that the costs of transportation and other expenses you incur in attending shareholders' meetings are not deductible expenses. It doesn't matter if you are a shareholder or if the meeting provides information that may be helpful in making further investments. You can forget about buying stock in that Hawaiian utility in order to take a yearly expense-deductible vacation.

## INVESTMENT INCOME

There are several kinds of income that can be generated by investment activity. Whenever you sell property, you create a taxable event, whether a gain or loss. If you receive dividends, interest, or capital gains distributions, you have a taxable event. Each must be accounted for in different ways.

If you own stock and receive $10 or more in dividends, you should receive a Form 1099-DIV from your broker or dividend reinvestment plan account. Some companies send this form regardless of the amount, so if you receive less than $10 in a particular account, you may not receive Form 1099-DIV. However, it is still your obligation to report all taxable dividend income, even if you do not receive this form. You don't have to file Form 1099-DIV statements with your return, so just keep them with your tax records. Also, you can't file on Form 1040EZ if you have any dividend income.

If you sell stock, a bond, or mutual fund, you will likely have either a loss or gain on the sale. In order to determine the amount of your sale or loss, you need to know the tax basis of those securities, which is not necessarily the same thing as their original purchase price. To determine the basis of a stock or other security, you must add costs, such as commissions and recording or transfer fees to the purchase

price. If a stock had a stock split, your basis is adjusted along with the number of shares.

If you received a security as a gift, then it's a bit more complicated to determine your basis. If the fair market value of the security at the time of the gift exceeds or equals the donor's adjusted basis, then your basis is the donor's adjusted basis plus any gift taxes the donor paid. If the donor's basis is below the market value when the gift is made, your basis for gain is the donor's adjusted basis, but your basis for loss is the fair market value. You don't have to worry about any taxes, though, until you sell the security.

For the definitive word on how the IRS handles investment income and expenses, get a copy of their Publication 550, *Investment Income and Expenses* (see Figure 18.5). This publication will tell you which forms and schedules you need and how to record various types of income and expenses. You can get a copy from the IRS Web site at http://www.irs.ustreas.gov.

Things get more complicated if you have bought varying quantities of the same security at different times. If you sell the entire lot at once, determining

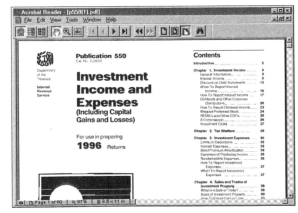

**Figure 18.5**
IRS Publication 550, *Investment Income and Expenses*

your tax basis is as easy as adding up the purchase prices and commissions of all shares.

If you only sell part of your holdings, then you must follow certain procedures in order to identify which securities have been sold. If you don't, then your basis is computed on the first-in first-out (FIFO) method. The first securities you bought are the first sold.

You can control your tax liability somewhat by choosing to sell the least appreciated securities in your holdings, as long as you can identify which shares you are selling. If you are selling shares for which you hold certificates, it's a fairly simple matter to demonstrate that those shares were bought on a certain date for a certain price.

If you are selling shares in street name by a broker, you must do the following at the time of the sale in order to identify the particular lot or lots you wish to sell:

1   Tell the broker which particular shares are to be sold, and

2   Receive a written confirmation of this from the broker.

You can't make this determination after the sale has been completed.

If you sell shares from your dividend reinvestment plan, you can choose which shares to sell as long as you keep a record of which lots were sold.

## CAPITAL GAINS AND LOSSES

When you sell a stock, you either show a profit or a loss. These are known as capital gains and capital losses and are subject to some special rules.

Capital gains are subject to ordinary income tax rates; however, the highest rate that may be applied to these gains is 28 percent. Periodically, you will hear talk in Washington of cutting the capital gains tax, and this 28 percent figure is the rate that is being discussed.

Want to avoid all this nonsense about taxes and investments? Simply never sell anything! While that seems like advice of a slightly shallow nature, there is actually a lot of truth in it. If you invest for the long term (as you should if you invest in common stocks), then one of your best strategies may be to hold on to your stocks until you pass away, never selling any of those securities. At your death, the cost basis of the stocks in your portfolio is *stepped up* to the fair market value at the time of your passing (or six months later, to allow for valuations to be made on less liquid assets). Your heirs are liable for estate taxes, but the capital gains disappear! Consult your financial planner or attorney for how to include this in your estate planning.

Capital losses are deductible on your tax return from your capital gains. If your losses exceed sales, then you can deduct the remainder up to $3,000 of other income on Form 1040. Any losses above $3,000 can be carried forward and used in future tax years.

Both capital gains and losses are reported on Schedule D. If you sell a stock from a brokerage account, you should receive Form 1099-B, or an equivalent statement, from your broker.

It's easy to calculate the tax basis of mutual fund shares that you sell. Even if you acquired shares at different times and for different prices, your basis when you sell any part of those shares is simply your average basis. You must have left the shares in your account, which shouldn't be a problem. If you prefer, you can use the FIFO or specific-lot method of determining the basis of shares sold, but the average basis method may be much easier if you have reinvested distributions and dividends in the account and made other purchases.

You'll often hear investors selling a stock so they can take a tax loss. While it's appropriate to consider the tax ramifications of any security sale or purchase, some investors become blinded by the thought of tax savings they can generate by selling stocks and deducting the capital loss. However, there are relatively modest limitations to the amount of losses that can be deducted from capital gains and other income, so the tax savings are unlikely to amount to much. Remember: you'll never get rich selling at a loss.

Taxes on capital gains are a compelling reason for investors to adhere to a buy-and-hold philosophy. Constantly buying and selling stocks can be great for your broker and accountant, but it's unlikely to fatten your portfolio.

Consider this example: You purchase 1,000 shares of stock at $10 per share, paying a $35 commission to your broker:

- 1,000 shares @ $10/share = $10,000

- $10,000 + $35 commission = $10,035 (your cost basis)

Now, let's say that after a few years, the share price increases from $10 to $15 a share and you decide to sell, locking in a healthy 50 percent profit:

- $15,000 market value of stock - $35 commission = $14,965 proceeds from sale

Using your proceeds from the sale, $14,965, you determine your capital gains:

- $14,965 proceeds—$10,035 cost basis = $4,930 capital gains

At the capital gains tax rate of 28 percent, you now owe the IRS a total of $1,380 in capital gains taxes:

- $4,930 capital gains—$1,380 capital gains tax = $3,550 net profit

**ask doug!**

**Q:** Aren't there ways of getting around the capital gains tax?

A: Yes. The first is by dying, which most of us don't find a viable alternative. The cost basis of appreciated securities left to your heirs is stepped up at your death to fair market value at that time (see related sidebar). The other option is to make a gift of appreciated securities to your favorite charity. Most charities can accept gifts of stock instead of cash; when you give stock that you've held for longer than a year, you receive credit for the fair market value of the stock on the date of the gift. But your basis in the stock is also stepped up to the fair market value, eliminating any capital gains liability. Contact your favorite charitable organization for information on how they accept gifts of securities. Most prefer to have shares wired to their account and will provide instructions upon request. Also, the gift is not considered complete until the securities are delivered to the charity, so take that under consideration at the end of the year.

From the $10,000 you started out with, you now have a profit of $3,550, for a return of 35.5 percent. What happened to your fat 50 percent profit? It's been eaten up by taxes and commissions. What's more, in order to get back to the $15,000 you had before you sold, your $13,550 has to grow by 10.7 percent. The first gains shown by your replacement stock are really just getting you back to where you were before you sold. If your original investment is still growing, your new stock might never catch up to your former holding.

# GLOSSARY

BASIS—Also tax basis, cost basis, or adjusted basis. The adjusted acquisition cost of an asset.

CAPITAL GAIN—The increase in value in an investment.

CAPITAL LOSS—The decrease in value of an investment.

DEDUCTION—An expense that reduces a person's tax liability.

ESTATE TAX—An inheritance tax.

GIFT TAX—A tax on gifts made to another person. There is a $10,000 annual exclusion per gift recipient from this tax.

PORTFOLIO—A group of investments.

TAX AVOIDANCE—The legal reduction of tax liability.

TAX EVASION—The criminal action of intentionally avoiding payment of taxes.

TAX SHELTER—An investment vehicle designed to generate large current deductions that can be used to offset other income.

TAXABLE INCOME—Income subject to taxes.

# Chapter 19
# Fraud, Scams, and Just Plain Bad Advice

*"The company of just and righteous men is better than wealth and a rich estate."*

**—Euripides**

**There's always been** a shadowy side to the securities industry. There's hardly an investor who hasn't heard a cautionary tale about boiler room operations, penny stock manipulators, or Ponzi schemes. All too often, a person's greed gets in the way of common sense, and he or she falls prey to the machinations of someone who's no more than a common crook.

The U.S. SEC has taken action against a number of fraudulent investment opportunities that were pushed on investors over the Internet. These included promises of a "whopping" 20 percent return on a stake in an eel farm; a "guaranteed" return of 15 percent to help manufacture coconut chips in Latin America for U.S. supermarkets; and investments in portable nuclear reactors, Internet gambling, telephone lotteries, and ostrich farms. Another offering was a "prime bank security" that promised to double investors' money in just four months.

The problem with all of these ventures is that none of them actually exist. These and other similar pyramid schemes, chain letters, and make-money-fast opportunities populate every corner of the Internet. Unfortunately, these are usually lose-money-fast ventures for the investors who actually buy into them.

# CYBER FRAUD

The Internet, unfortunately, provides another tool for con artists and other unscrupulous types to put their imaginations to work coming with new variations on an old theme. But the Net is really just following in the path of a long line of technology that has been put to work for nefarious purposes. You may be familiar with some of the other technological advancements that have been used to bilk unknowing investors out of portions of their nest eggs: de-

Most states require that companies who are raising money from citizens in their states first register with their state securities agencies. You can contact your state regulator for more information. There are lists of state securities agencies available on the Web from the SEC, the American Association of Individual Investors, and the National Association of Securities Dealers Regulation, Inc.

vices such as the telephone, fax machine, photocopier (first the black and white variety, then the color version), laser printer, scanner, personal computer, typewriter, and letterpress, just to name a few. The Internet is nothing more than a new variation on a theme. A Ponzi scheme is a Ponzi scheme whether it happens in a small town or via e-mail.

Even if you're the type who would never invest in an ostrich ranch or eel farm, there are other pitfalls online. Another danger comes from the anonymous nature of much of the Internet. On a mailing list or in a chat room, it's often impossible to know if the person who's always got a great idea to share is directly profiting from the dissemination of that information. Who is really behind those hot tips that are abundantly spread around via the Internet's misc.invest newsgroups or via e-mailed alerts?

The SEC has a phrase for many of these ploys, which usually tout thinly traded securities: the "Pump and Dump." Often the person promoting the stock stands to gain by dumping shares after the stock's price is pumped up by gullible investors.

As the Internet grows, so grows the potential for abuse. With millions of people now using the Internet, a message posted to a newsgroup or a Web site hawking an investment opportunity can reach an enormous audience in a very short time.

Companies raising less than $1 million from public sources are not required to register with the SEC. They must, however, file a Form D with the Commission, which includes just the names of the owners and promoters of the offering. The SEC will provide you with a copy of any Form D that has been filed with them upon request.

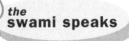

the **swami speaks**

Both the Swami and Internet etiquette dictate that you sign your messages with your real name if you are participating in an online discussion about investing. Going strictly by a handle such as FastTrader or Bob120978 won't encourage other users to trust your judgment. Users can't tell if a message has been posted anonymously because the sender has something to hide or because they don't know any better. Depending on your e-mail software, you can adjust the From field to reflect your name, or use a pre-set signature line that includes your name and any other information. If you're concerned about privacy, you can use your first initial and last name.

That's not to say that there aren't lots and lots of real communities online filled with honest investors. Many of the mailing lists and discussion boards described in Chapter 6 are places where a real sense of camaraderie and community can be found online. Often, these groups are self-policing. If someone new swaggers into town, giving everyone within earshot a dose of fast talk and hot tips, suspicions will be raised immediately and probably voiced by a member of the group. It's not that different from the off-line world. You wouldn't give the spare set of your housekeys to your new neighbors until you got to know them a bit first.

Likewise, you wouldn't bet the house on a hot stock tip you hear from a stranger in line at the grocery or hardware store, until you did your own research. Stock tips you hear online should always be validated by your own research. If you subscribe to a mailing list or are a regular participant in a discussion forum, in time you'll learn whose opinions you can respect, but you should still always do your own study before you buy.

### SEC's Office of Investor Education and Assistance
http://www.sec.gov/invkhome.htm

The mission of this department of the U.S. SEC is to provide investors with the information they need to

invest wisely and avoid securities fraud. The site includes several articles and instructions for filing a complaint with the Commission's Enforcement Complaint Center (you can even file a complaint online).

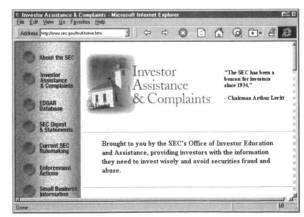

Another tactic to look out for is one employed by *stock touts*. There are many firms that specialize in providing public relations services for small, emerging public companies. Often, their job is to tout a stock to increase awareness of that security in the investing community. This often consists of publishing "research reports," which provide data and commentary about the company's potential. Sometimes these reports take the form of a full-color magazine or well-designed Web site.

There's nothing wrong with the fact that the company paid for these reports to be distributed. It can be very difficult for a small company to attract the attention of the investing community. On the other hand, it's a fairly safe bet the company would not pay for a negative report to be sent out to thousands of investors or presented on the World Wide Web. It's important that you know the source of any research and whether it's an independent source or potentially biased. Be sure to check the fine print for the details.

# INVESTIGATE INVESTMENTS

While the SEC, the Federal Trade Commission, the National Association of Securities Dealers, and other consumer organizations are addressing the problems of cyber-fraud, the ultimate responsibility remains with individuals to investigate before they invest.

Borrowing the essence of an advertising tag line used by New York clothing discounter Sy Sims, "An educated investor is the best investor." Your first line of defense against being taken for a ride on the information superhighway is to be an alert, patient, and knowledgeable investor.

Here are some basic principles to keep in mind as you use the Internet for your investing research:

1   Do your homework. While this advice is sound for any investment, it goes doubly for stocks or other opportunities that are promoted online. A con man's worst nightmare is an educated customer. Conduct an online search of Web sites

If you have been the victim of fraud, report the incident immediately. It can be humiliating to realize that you've been taken in by a scam, but hucksters count on your reluctance to come forward so that they can continue to prey on others. If you act quickly, you'll be doing a great service for many potential victims. The SEC Division of Enforcement and the National Fraud Information Center both allow individuals to file complaints on their Web sites.

and newsgroups using the major Internet search engines to find references to the investment or promoter. Use reputable sources of information for your investment research. Find out as much as you can about the company, its products, its owners, and its other investors.

2   Get it in writing. Request that written materials such as a prospectus, annual report, offering circular, and financial statements be mailed to you. If these materials are available on the Web, make a note of the URL and date for future reference.

3   Don't be in a hurry. Striving for a nice, quick profit is often a shortcut to disaster. Remember that make-money-fast schemes usually do, but for the promoter, not for the individual participants. There's nothing wrong with making money slow in quality investments in stocks, bonds, and mutual funds.

4   Beware of any investment that is "guaranteed" or promises an outrageously high return. Investing provides few guarantees, though individuals can certainly balance risk and reward to profit nicely over the long term. A proposal to double your money in a short period of time should also be considered suspect.

**5** Consider why a person is promoting an investment. Does he or she have any inside involvement with the opportunity? If the individual is engaging in the actual sale of securities, is the person registered with your state's securities agency or the SEC? Have any complaints been made against this person with these agencies?

### National Fraud Information Center
### http://www.fraud.org

The National Fraud Information Center is a project of the National Consumers League, in cooperation with the National Association Of Attorneys General, the Federal Trade Commission, and Project Phonebusters, Canada. The site focuses on Internet and telemarketing fraud, but addresses all types of consumer fraud. The Center can provide help if you've been the victim of fraud and offers helpful information on protecting yourself and your personal financial information.

If an opportunity sounds unusual and you still wish to investigate, check with your state securities regulator or the SEC. Ask if they have received any complaints about the company, its managers, or the promoter. Find out where the firm is incorporated and call that state's secretary of state. Ask if the company is incorporated and has a current annual report on file.

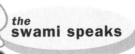

**the swami speaks**

The Swami speaks again on protocol and etiquette on the Internet. If you are discussing a stock or security in which you have a financial stake, you should also always reveal your interest. Even if you own just a small number of shares, you should make a public statement in the course of the discussion that you're a shareholder.

And don't forget the most important rule: If it sounds too good to be true, it probably is.

If you believe you've been a victim of fraud, online or off, your first step should be to contact an attorney. You should also contact your local attorney general, your state Securities agency, the SEC, the National Association of Securities Dealers and/or the National Fraud Information Center. However, many of these organizations cannot act to recover any moneys you have lost, and that's why you may need an attorney. Regulatory agencies may take regulatory action against the perpetrators of fraud but generally do not get involved in disputes between two parties.

## PROBLEMS WITH BROKERS

Both brokerage firms and individual brokers must be registered with the SEC to do business with the public. States also require that firms involved in the sale and purchase of securities register with them. Those in the brokerage business must also abide by federal and state securities laws and SEC regulations.

There are certain standards to which all brokers must adhere. They must execute trades promptly and attempt to get the best price possible. They must provide confirmations of trades with complete

It's a good idea to always keep a log of all telephone conversations with your broker, not just when trouble is abrew. Note the date, exact time, and subject of the call in a special notebook, date book, or calendar/contact software. Brokerage firms routinely record all telephone calls. If there's a problem or misunderstanding, you need to be able to tell them where to look on the tape for a particular conversation. Otherwise, they may not be able to find the discussion in question.

information about the sale or purchase. Full-service brokers must have enough knowledge of your goals and knowledge to avoid recommending an inappropriate investment. They must also not engage in activities such as churning, which is excessively trading in a client's account solely to generate commissions.

In order to become a licensed securities professional, individuals must pass a series of examinations to demonstrate their knowledge of the industry. They cannot have a criminal felony conviction on their record and must submit fingerprints to the FBI for a criminal records check.

If you do have a problem with a broker or firm, here are some things you should do:

- Speak to the branch or department manager right away. Send your complaint in writing right away to confirm your problem. Ask for a response in writing.

- Most firms have a compliance officer who is responsible for making sure that all employees conduct themselves accordingly. Speak to this officer if necessary.

- Keep written notes of all conversations, whether in person or on the telephone, recording the time

**ask doug!**

**Q:** What is arbitration?

**A:** Arbitration is a method of resolving a dispute between two parties outside the legal court system. An impartial third person, the arbitrator, serves as a sort of judge, hearing both sides of the dispute and then making a final binding ruling. Arbitration is usually an inexpensive and prompt method of reaching a settlement, at least compared to the legal system. Arbitration has long been used in the securities industry to settle differences between brokers and their clients; in fact, most account agreements stipulate that disputes be settled in this manner. If you need to take a dispute into arbitration, by all means consult an attorney first.

and date of each discussion. If any promises were made, make a note of the exact terms and time frame agreed upon. Record the names and titles of all individuals with whom you spoke.

After a reasonable amount of time, if you cannot reach a resolution to your satisfaction, then you can take your case to higher authorities. You can file a complaint with NASD Regulation, the regulatory arm of the National Association of Securities Dealers. On NASD Regulation's Web site (http://www.nasdr.com), you can find complete information about the process of filing a customer complaint and even an online complaint form, as well as other alternatives for remuneration. As a last recourse, you should consult an attorney knowledgeable in securities law and begin arbitration proceedings.

### NASD Regulation, Inc.
**http://www.nasdr.com**

NASD Regulation, Inc. is an independent subsidiary of the National Association of Securities Dealers, Inc., and is charged with regulating the securities industry. The site includes details of the process of arbitration, as well as information on filing a complaint against a broker or requesting a copy of a broker's disciplinary record. Recent enforcement actions undertaken by the organization against individuals and firms are published on the site, as well.

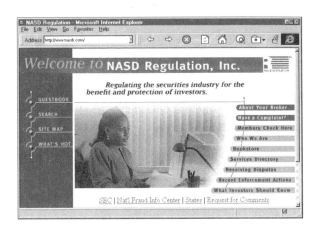

## GLOSSARY

AFTERMARKET—Trading activity in a security immediately after its initial offering to the public.

ARBITRATION—A method of settling disputes between two or more parties by an impartial person, an arbitrator, who is knowledgeable about issues in the controversy.

BLUE-SKY LAWS—State laws that require issuers of securities to register with the state before offering those securities for sale to its residents.

MEDIATION—An informal, voluntary process in which a mediator helps negotiate a mutually acceptable resolution between disputing parties. If mediation cannot help reach a conclusion, the matter can be taken to arbitration.

NASD—The National Association of Securities Dealers, the self-regulatory organization of the securities industry, responsible for developing regulations, disciplining members, licensing brokers, and operating securities markets.

REGISTERED REPRESENTATIVE—An employee of an NASD member firm who gives advice and receives commissions on sales of securities.

SECURITIES INVESTOR PROTECTION CORPORATION (SIPC)—The nonprofit corporation that insures investors against the failure of a financial firm, similar to the Federal Deposit Insurance Corp. in the banking industry. The insurance protects against financial failure of the brokerage house, but not investment losses.

UNAUTHORIZED TRADING—The purchase, sale, or trade of securities in an investor's account without the investor's authorization.

# Appendix A

# Tips for Using Lycos to Search the Web

**To search the Lycos catalog,** just enter one or more words (better known as a "search query") in the text entry box on the Lycos home page or search results page. Next, press the Enter key (or click the Go Get It button). Lycos will display the results. If you need to customize or refine your search, however, Lycos provides an easy way for you to "fine-tune" your search.

The Customize Your Search form is a tool that Lycos provides to make searching its index easy for you to do. It's especially helpful if you need to do any of the following:

- Make your search wider or narrower

- Have the search match ALL words in a query rather than ANY single word (which is the default setting)

- Search for special variations of a given term (for example, to search for several possible spellings of a word AND some other word)

Most of the time you won't need to use this search form at all if you only want to perform "wide" searches of the Web. However, Lycos gives you other Search options, which you can change if you want to search for different types of information, such as pictures, sounds, and sites that have been categorized by subject.

You can also "refine" your search by making it more narrow or wide. You can have the search match ALL words in your query rather than the default ANY word. You can also search for a number of terms which are DIFFERENT from the number you entered (for example, to search for several possible spellings of a word AND some other word).

The search form gives you two ways to control your search: *Search Options* and *Display Options*. You'll notice that both Search Options and Display Options are pull-down menus. Simply click the down-arrow in each of these pull-down menus and look at the selections that are available.

# USING SEARCH OPTIONS TO SET TERMS TO MATCH (BOOLEAN)

You might wonder why you can't do Boolean searches on Lycos. You might also want to know what exactly a Boolean search is. Boolean searches are those queries that let you search the Web for very specific combinations of words. For example, you might want to see all instances of peanut and butter together, but only where they appear without jelly.

Although you can't perform true Boolean searches on Lycos, you can come very close by using the Search Options features. Just keep these simple guidelines in mind:

- AND searches are possible by selecting the match all terms (AND) option and then entering whatever words you want in the search box. In the above example, you'd simply enter peanut butter.

- NOT searches are a bit trickier. You may currently prepend (that is, begin) a term with a hyphen to make it a negative indicator, like this: -jelly. This will only reduce the score for sites containing the word jelly, not remove them entirely. The good news is that the first set of results you get will most likely give you what you want: peanut butter without jelly.

By default, Lycos will find all documents matching any word you type in your query (except for certain words like "a" and "the" which are generally not meaningful in a search). If you type "jeep cherokee" as your query, Lycos will find all documents containing either "jeep" OR "cherokee." This is the match any term (OR) Search Option, and is what you get when you type a query into the form on the home page, or if you select the match any term (OR) option on the Customize Your Search form.

Sometimes you might want to find only documents which match ALL the words in your query. This is the match all terms (AND) option. Try it on the form and then see what Lycos returns for "jeep cherokee" when you use the "OR" option and when you use the "AND" option.

# SYMBOLS YOU CAN'T USE IN YOUR SEARCHES

You can't use + in search terms. A common instance of this is the term C++, which gets stripped down to c. Unfortunately, this leaves a single letter which, being shorter than three characters, is ignored. This behavior can be annoying, but Lycos is in the process of choosing the best solution to solve it (and related problems) without affecting the speed and performance of conducting searches. For now we suggest you search for related terms: Instead of C++, for instance, you might try programming languages. Hopefully, Lycos will fix this soon.

You also cannot search for numbers. The current version of Lycos strips out all numbers at the beginning of words. This causes problems if you search for 3DO, 4AD Records, or any other letter-number combination.

The problem is that numbers are a whole different breed of cat from letters. Lycos is trying to teach its retrieval engine to determine for itself which sequences of letters are words and which are not; once they do, you'll be able to make these searches.

## SYMBOLS YOU CAN USE IN YOUR SEARCHES

At the present time, you can use the following symbols in your search queries:

- (-) As we mentioned earlier, you can use the - symbol to help narrow down your search. For example, to search for bank, but without river turning up in the search, you would type bank -river in your search query. This is similar to the NOT Boolean search term.

- (.) Use a period at the end of the keyword to limit it with no expansions. Bank. will bring up only results with the keyword "bank" and ignore expansions like "bankers" and "banking."

- ($) Put this symbol after the keyword to make the search engine expand it. The search term "gard$" will bring up results like "garden" and "gardenias." This feature is great if you don't know how to spell a word, or if you aren't sure what you're looking for.

## LIMITING YOUR SEARCH TO A SPECIFIED NUMBER OF TERMS

You might also be wondering why you need "match 2 terms," "match 3 terms," and so on. These options give you more flexibility in your search. Suppose you wanted to find references to Sarajevo and Yugoslavia. But you're not sure whether Sarajevo is spelled "Sarajevo" or "Sarayevo." So you enter your query "Sarajevo Sarayevo Yugoslavia." To get the best results, you can use the Search Options.

You can't use match all terms (AND) because that would give you only documents which contain both spellings of "Sarajevo" AND Yugoslavia, and there probably aren't any of those. You could use match any terms (OR), because that would return all documents that contain any of these three terms, but you would also get lots of documents you don't want in the list.

Here's what you do: Enter "Sarajevo Sarayevo Yugoslavia" as your query, and choose match 2 terms. This selection will match at least two terms in each document. Since it's quite unlikely Sarajevo will be spelled two different ways in the same document, the results returned will have references to BOTH one of the two spellings of Sarajevo AND Yugoslavia.

## USING THE SEARCH OPTIONS TO SET THE SELECTIVITY OF THE SEARCH

You can change the Search Options to adjust the selectivity of the Lycos search engine. When set to "loose match," you will get more documents, but they will tend to be less relevant to the query you've made. Often, particularly when you are beginning a search and wish to cast the widest possible net, this is exactly what you want.

If you want the Lycos search engine to be more selective, change the Search Option from loose match to "strong match." Lycos will return only documents which have a very high relevance to your query. If you are on a slow dial-up connection, setting the selectivity to "strong match" can save you time by reducing the number of irrelevant hits downloaded to you.

You should try out the effect of changing various selectivity settings on the form. Try some searches with various selectivity settings to get a feel for how it affects your results.

## SETTING THE DISPLAY OF THE RESULTS PAGE SIZE

Lycos always gives you all the results or "hits" matching your query, even if there are hundreds or thousands of documents. If the number of hits is large, however, Lycos does not display them all at once, so you don't need to wait a long time for the whole page to come to you. By default, Lycos displays 10 hits on each results page. Once you've looked at those 10, you click on the "Next 10 hits" link at the bottom of the page to get the next 10 hits, and so on until all the hits are displayed.

To change the default from 10 hits displayed on each page, you can set the number in the Display Options pull-down menu. Simply choose another value from 10-40 results per page.

## SETTING THE AMOUNT OF RESULTS DETAIL YOU WANT DISPLAYED

You can also control the amount of information you want Lycos to display about each result. There are three levels of detail you can choose from:

- Standard (the default)

- Detailed (all information displayed)

- Summary (the minimum amount of information is displayed)

## INTERPRETING THE RESULTS OF A SEARCH

The percentage numbers are simply Lycos's way of showing you how close it thinks each site will match what you're looking for, based on the words you asked Lycos to search for.

When the Lycos search engine compares each page to your query, it gives higher scores to pages that contain the words as you typed them in. It also looks for pages that mention these words early on, rather than far down in some sub-section of the site. The page with the combination most like the words you typed in is ranked at the top and assigned the number 1.000. Other sites are ranked below and assigned numbers based on how much or how little they resemble your search terms.

This means that if you asked for Hungarian goulash, then a site titled The Hungarian Goulash Recipe Page will end up above sites that mention Carpathian goulash, salad, and Hungarian bread or some less precise combination.

The percentages are in no way a rating of how good Lycos thinks any page is. They're simply a tool to help you narrow down your choices.

# Appendix B

# Using the CD-ROM

**The CD-ROM** that's packaged with this book includes software for you to use. The software will not only allow you to explore the Internet and search the Web, but will also allow you to view a fully hyperlinked HTML version of the printed book, also contained on the CD-ROM. Before you can use the software, you will need to install it on the hard drive of your computer. This is a simple procedure that will take only a few minutes.

## WHAT'S ON THE CD-ROM?

The CD-ROM includes the following software and other items that can be installed on your computer:

- Microsoft Internet Explorer Web browser for PCs and Macs

- Earthlink Internet connection software for PCs and Macs

- A fully hyperlinked HTML version of the book for PCs and Macs, which you can view using your Web browser

## VIEWING THE HYPERLINKED HTML VERSION OF THE BOOK

The CD-ROM contains the fully hyperlinked text of the book, including thousands of Web sites and Internet addresses, including live links to Lycos, the search engine. Although you can use the CD and view the HTML book version without a live Internet connection, every section of the CD allows you to select an Internet address and instantly connect to the actual site. To connect directly to these Web sites, however, you'll need an Internet connection.

## USING THE CD-ROM

To view the hyperlinked version of the book, you will need to use a Web browser. Simply follow the steps below.

## Running Most Web Browsers (Including Netscape Navigator)

1 Place the CD-ROM in your CD-ROM drive.

2 Launch your Web browser.

3 Choose Open File from the File menu.

4 Select your CD-ROM drive. For PC users, this is usually drive D. Mac users, double-click on the CD-ROM icon.

5 Double-click on the file named Welcome.htm.

## Running Microsoft Internet Explorer

1 Place the CD-ROM in your CD-ROM drive.

2 Launch Internet Explorer.

3 Choose Open from the File menu.

4 Click the Browse button.

5 Select your CD-ROM drive. For PC users, this is usually drive D. Mac users, double-click on the CD-ROM icon.

6 Double-click on the file named Welcome.htm.

7 Click on OK.

## INSTALLING WEB BROWSER SOFTWARE

We have included Microsoft's Internet Explorer on this CD in case you do not have a Web browser currently installed on your computer. The steps for installing Internet Explorer are described below.

## Required PC System

- 486 Processor (Pentium Processor preferred)
- Windows OS (3.x, 95, or NT)
- 8MB of RAM (16MB preferred)
- 8MB free space on your hard drive (15MB preferred)
- 2x CD-ROM drive (4x recommended)

## Macintosh System Requirements

- Apple Macintosh or Power Macintosh (or clone) running System 7.0.1 or later
- Apple Open Transport or Mac TCP and Thread Manager
- 8MB of RAM (16MB preferred)
- 8MB of free space on your hard drive (16MB preferred)
- 2x CD-ROM drive (4x preferred)

## For All Systems

If you want to connect to the Web, a modem is required (14.4bps or faster is recommended for optimum performance).

## INSTALLING INTERNET EXPLORER

## Internet Explorer Version 3.01 for Windows 95

You must be using Microsoft Windows 95 to run Microsoft Internet Explorer 3.01. Locate the Win95 folder in the MS_IE directory on the CD. Create a temporary directory on your computer. Copy the

MSIE301M.EXE file from the Win95 folder on the CD and paste it in the temporary folder on your hard drive.

Double-click on the file. Follow the instructions that appear on your screen to complete the installation.

## Internet Explorer Version 2.1 for Windows 3.1

You must be using Microsoft Windows 3.1 to run Microsoft Internet Explorer 2.1. Locate the Win3.1 folder in the MS_IE directory on the CD. Create a temporary directory on your computer. Copy the DIMINI21.EXE file from the Win3.1 folder on the CD and paste it in the temporary folder on your hard disk.

Double-click on the file. Follow the instructions that appear on your screen to complete the installation.

## Internet Explorer Version 2.0 for the Macintosh

Double-click the Internet Explorer installer icon, located in the MSIE directory, to install. Follow the prompts that appear on your screen to complete the installation.

**Note:** Eudora Light is an Internet Mail client application that is included in Microsoft Internet Explorer 2.0 for the Macintosh. Documentation for Eudora Light is not included. To download the Eudora Light Manual separately, visit the Microsoft Internet Explorer Web site at: http://www.microsoft.com/ie/iedl.htm#mac.

## INSTALLING EARTHLINK INTERNET CONNECTION SOFTWARE (FOR MACS AND PCS)

To install Earthlink as your Internet service provider, follow these steps:

1   Double-click Setup.exe for the PC (installer icon for the Macintosh).

2   Follow the on-screen instructions.

# Credits

Screen shots of the sites listed below used with permission.

Active Investment Research site.

AlphaChart site.

American Association of Individual Investors site. Source: American Association of Individual Investors™, 625 N. Michigan Ave., Chicago, Ill. 60611; (800) 428-2244; www.aaii.org.

Anderson Investor's Software, Inc. site.

Applied Derivatives Trading site.

Atlantic Broadcasting System site.

Australian Financial Services Directory.

Australian Stock Exchange site.

Australia's Personal Investment Magazine site.

Bank Rate Monitor site. Copyright © 1997: Bank Rate Monitor Inc.™, N. Palm Beach, FL 33408

Bonds Online site.

Bruce Babcock's Reality Based Trading Company site.

The Calvert Group site.

Campbell Harvey's Hypertextual Finance Glossary site.

The Capital PC User Group Investment Special Interest Group site. Courtesy of InvestSIG, a special interest group of the Capital PC User Group.

Carlson On-Line Services site.

Chicago Board Options Exchange site. Provided as a courtesy by the Chicago Board Options Exchange, Inc.

Closed-End Funds Discussion Forum.

Closing Bell site.

CNNfn site.

Consumer Information Center site.

CPAdvisor site.

Data Broadcasting Corporation site.

Datek Online site.

Deloitte & Touche PeerScape site.

Dogs of the Dow site.

Federal Reserve Bank of New York site.

First Virtual site. First Virtual, VirtualTAG, and VirtualPIN are marks of First Virtual Holdings Incorporated.

FundAlarm site.

FX Week Web site.

Gamelan Official Directory for Java (Business & Financial Applets) site.

Great Pacific Trading Company site.

GreatStocks Project site.

Holt Stock Report site.

HST site.

The Insurance News Network site.

interactive investor site.

Investorade site

IQ Chart site.

Israel's Business Arena—by Globes site.

Lebenthal Home Page site.

MarketGuide site.

Market Timing in a Spreadsheet site.

Money Magazine Bulletin Board. Copyright © 1996 Time Inc. New Media. All rights reserved. Reproduction in whole or in part without permission is prohibited. Pathfinder is a registered trademark of Time Inc. New Media.

Money Minds site.

MoneyWorld—The UK's Personal Finance Website.

The Mutual Funds FAQ site.

*Mutual Funds Magazine* Online site.

NetStock Direct site.

NETworth: the Internet Investor Network site.

NewsPage site.

Nuveen Research Web site.

Olsen & Associates site.

Palm's Portal site.

Persfin Digest site.

Personal Stock Monitor screen.

The Pitbull Investor site.

Public Register's Annual Report Service site.

Qualisteam Banking and Finance site.

Quote Ticker Bar screen.

*Research:* Magazine site.

Robertson, Stephens & company site.

Roger Engemann & Associates's Online Investment Advisor site.

Savoy Discount Brokerage site.

SEC EDGAR site.

SecureTax site.

Securities and Exchange Commission site.

Securities and Exchange Commission EDGAR site.

Skate site.

The SmallCap Investor site.

The Stock Club site.

Strong Funds On-Line site.

The Tax Prophet site.

Tef@, The Electronic Filing Agency site.

Trader Gizmos site.

Traders' Library site.

Understanding and Controlling Your Finances site.

The Value Point Analysis Financial Forum.

The Vanguard Group site.

WallSt.com site

Wall Street Directory site.

Wall Street Simulator screen.

WhoWhere? EDGAR site.

Worth Online site.

Yahoo! On the Money site.

# Index of Site Names

## B

# Index